53-61   Hist

144

271

MODERN
TRANSPORTATION
ECONOMICS

MODERN TRANSPORTATION ECONOMICS

HUGH S. NORTON

Professor of Transportation
University of Tennessee

CHARLES E. MERRILL BOOKS, INC.
COLUMBUS, OHIO

Library of Congress Catalog Card Number: 63-22544

First Printing ....November, 1963

Second Printing ....April, 1965

Printed in the United States of America

*To My Mother
and to the Memory of My Father*

Preface

For some years, books in the field of transportation economics have, with few exceptions, followed a traditional pattern of devoting a substantial share of the text material to an intensive discussion of the historical and regulatory aspects of the industry. Likewise, considerable space is devoted to a description of the institutional aspects of the modes. This book does not depart from that time tested pattern in essence, but does contain what the author fondly hopes are some fundamental modifications of that basic framework. A significant share of the text is devoted to the macro-economic and micro-economic aspects of the industry. Further, the economic analysis is not isolated in a portion of the book, but an effort has been made to interlace it into all areas of the text and especially to focus the application of regulatory controls against the background of the economic character of the industry and the structure of the modern economy.

Since the end of the Second World War, the study of economics has centered increasingly around the aggregative aspects of the economy. Although transportation cannot be studied and understood in isolation, there are many stimulating and significant problems in micro-economic analysis in the industry, and the author has attempted to put these into the proper perspective.

Far reaching changes are afoot in the teaching of business and economics and writers in the field of transportation can, like all authors, ignore these signs only at their peril. The text is not intended to be an exhaustive reference book, but a stimulating framework within which interested and capable students can explore the economic relationships of the industry, guided by a competent instructor.

The emphasis throughout is on the economic aspects of the industry, and the various modes are given balanced treatment. The historical development of the modes is treated briefly, since for most readers this material largely duplicates that previously studied. Thus the assumption is made that the typical person will have knowledge of introductory economics and that he will have acquired at some stage a modest acquaintance with the historical development of the American economy.

While the book is designed for use in the typical class, every effort has been made to enhance its usefulness for those who wish to pursue independent study of the transportation field. Adequate selected references have been included in each chapter.

Part I is designed to give the reader an overall view of the transportation industry as it now exists. At the conclusion of his study of Part I, the reader should have an understanding of the aggregate transportation plant and the relationship between the modes. In addition, the role of transportation as an economic function is studied and examined as a part of the social and political framework.

Part II examines the micro-economic relationships of the industry. The production, demand for, and pricing of transportation service is analyzed.

Part III is concerned with the social, economic, and political basis of regulation, emphasis being placed on the American scene. Some acquaintance with political and economic history will be helpful; and here, as elsewhere, the instructor would have ample opportunity to expand upon the text material if he so desires, depending upon the intended level and purpose.

Part IV is devoted to the description and analysis of the implementation of the present system of regulation. The purpose of this section is to acquaint the reader with the existing framework of regulation and to present an intensive study of the more serious practical problems incidental to the implementation of the regulatory controls in the modern economy.

Part V, the final part of the text, is intended to consider the broad aspects of policy problems. The reader, having viewed these in Parts III and IV, should be in the position to speculate intelligently on their likely solution and to appreciate the relationship between transportation and the other areas of the national economy.

Hugh S. Norton
Knoxville, Tennessee .

Table of Contents

Part III

THE BASIS AND FRAMEWORK
OF PUBLIC CONTROL

Chapter

Part IV

APPLICATION OF PUBLIC CONTROLS

Part V

PROBLEMS AND PROSPECTS

PART I

The Industry and the Modes:

An Aggregate View of the Means and Purposes of Transport

"Railways and canals are virtually a diminution of the cost of production of all those things sent to market by them; and literally so of all those, the appliances and aids, for producing which they serve to transmit."

JOHN STUART MILL
Principles of Political Economy

CHAPTER I

Transportation, An Economic, Social and Political Function

Transportation is an economic function; that is to say, it serves along with other productive functions in the production of goods and services in the economy.

Production has been defined as the creation of utility, i.e., the quality of usefulness. Transportation creates the utility of place, and to a lesser degree, that of time. It is readily apparent that goods may have little or no usefulness in one location at one time but may have great utility in another place at another time. For example, lumber may be of relatively little value in Oregon where it is in great supply; yet, it may be extremely useful and valuable at a building site in Indiana at the time building is underway. The creation of place utility can be seen in various relationships. Some goods are so common as to be present in almost every area, and little or nothing would be gained by transporting them. Other goods may be so unique and so valuable that they can be profitably transported great distances.

As expressed in a recent study:

Transportation is one of the tools required by civilized man to bring order out of chaos. It reaches into every phase and facet of our existence. Viewed from every standpoint, economic, political and military, it is unquestionably the most important

3

industry in the world. You can no more operate a grocery store or a brewery than you can win a war without transportation. The more complex life becomes, the more indispensable are the things that make up our transportation systems.[1]

TRANSPORTATION AS A COST OF PRODUCTION

It has been estimated that transportation costs in the aggregate account for more than 20 per cent of the Gross National Product.[2] Naturally, this relationship varies from one good to another. For goods of low value, transportation costs may constitute a substantial part of the total. The opposite relationship may be found for goods of high value. Clearly, the relationship is influenced by the ease or difficulty of performing the transportation service. Producers strive to reduce transportation costs as they do other costs of production. By carrying on various stages of production in close proximity, by using light weight material, and by improving packing the producer attempts to reduce transport costs. The benefits of reduced transportation costs are substantial indeed as expressed by the Department of Commerce in the following statement: "Moreover, reduction of the cost of transportation in relation to other things increases flexibility in the location of industry, in the exploration of the natural resources, and in the achievement of industrial efficiency. There is in fact, a multiplier effect—for the quantity of improvement in the transport function is multiplied by the time goods reach the actual consumer."[3]

Since there are several means of transport, it is clear to the reader that the shipper of most products has considerable choice in the use of the mode. Thus, there is competition among the various firms in each mode (intramodal competition) as well as competition between the modes (intermodal competition). In the modern transport system monopoly exists only in remote geographic areas or for shippers who have unique products physically suitable for only one mode. Just as the shipper strives to reduce his transport costs, the carriers bend every effort toward increasing the range of products which they can economically carry.

[1] Report of the Subcommittee on the Armed Services of the House of Representatives, quoted in *National Transportation Policy*, Report prepared for the Committee on Interstate and Foreign Commerce, U. S. Senate, by the Special Study Group on Transportation Policies in the United States (Pursuant to S. Res. 29, 151, and 244 of the 86th Cong., January 1961).

[2] *Rationale of Federal Transportation Policy*, Washington, D.C.: U.S. Department of Commerce, April 1960, p. 2.

[3] *Ibid.*, p. 3.

Carriers, much the same as other entrepreneurs, attempt to reach and hold as much of a monopoly position in the Chamberlin sense, as they can.[4] However, they recognize that as producers operating largely under conditions of monopolistic competition their ability to monopolize is very limited and apt to be of short duration. An example of this action is the competitive struggle between rail and motor carriers. Over the years trucks have managed to gain more and more traffic which once was moved almost entirely by rail. At the same time, through improved service and reduced rates, railroads regain truck traffic in many areas. Few economists would find fault with this competitive process, which results from the normal free play of economic factors. The economic factors relating to rate making policy will be discussed in detail later in the book.

TRANSPORTATION AND THE COST OF PRODUCTION

In influencing the cost of production, transportation obviously affects the usefulness and also the relationships between the various productive factors. Land values and use are prime examples of this effect. The extension of transport lines into an area makes the land and the resources in and on that land more valuable in that it increases the ease of access and removal of the product of the land to places where it is useful or more useful.

RESOURCES, SPECIALIZATION, AND DIVISION OF LABOR

Transportation enables society to enjoy advantages of specialization, of resources, and the benefits of division of labor by making it possible for products to be brought great distances thus avoiding the necessity for local production of needs. Before adequate transportation facilities were developed, it was necessary for each geographic region either to produce what was needed or to do without those products which would have been impossible or uneconomical to produce; that is to say, that while few commodities are absolutely impossible to produce in any given area, their production would require such an expenditure of labor and materials as to make their production eco-

---

[4] As Chamberlin points out, each producer, through product or outlet differentiation has a degree of monopoly which he tries to exploit and maximize although he can never achieve monopoly in the pure sense. Edward H. Chamberlin, *The Theory of Monopolistic Competition*, Cambridge, 1948, Harvard University Press, Sixth Ed.

nomically impracticable. By moving goods and materials to other points, it becomes possible to maximize the economic advantages of specialization. Thus, our industrialized structure is built upon the supposition that centralized and specialized production and processing facilities are available. Each economic region can thus concentrate upon the goods and services for which it is best adapted either through natural occurrence or through historical development. The products and services of each of these specialized areas can then be exchanged with the products and services of other areas for mutual benefit. Consequently, transportation enhances the productive efficiency of an economy by making specialization feasible.[5]

LARGE SCALE MARKETING

As a result of the specialization discussed above, it further becomes feasible to engage in large scale production and marketing of goods. No modern large scale producer could sell his output on a local scale; for example, the plants producing tobacco products in North Carolina could probably produce in a few hours enough to satisfy the local needs for a year. Obviously, the economic rationale of this operation is that the large scale output is sold on a nation-wide or world-wide basis. Such marketing processes would be either impossible or economically inefficient without an adequate transportation system. The student has only to consider the tremendous complexity involved in producing and distributing products on a nation-wide basis to appreciate the contribution which transportation makes in this area of the economy.

EQUALIZATION OF SUPPLY

By observing and contemplating the effects of specialized production, the student will become aware of the fact that a supply problem is both created and solved by the specialization which exists. Clearly, for such commodities as occur naturally in certain areas, transportation operates to equalize the supply of these commodities throughout a broad area. It thus becomes possible for consumers to enjoy, at reasonable prices, the commodities and products which are produced at distant points.

---

[5] H. G. Moulton, *Controlling Factors in Economic Development*, Washington, D. C.: The Brookings Institution, 1949, esp. Chapter VIII.

GEOGRAPHIC FACTORS IN TRANSPORT

The basic features of our transportation system are a function of geography. The major cities of the early United States were located so as to give access for water transportation, and the coming of the railroads built upon this basic pattern. It is difficult to separate cause and effect in this area, since water facilities have generally been much enhanced and further developed by rail facilities. An excellent example of this is the New York metropolitan area where superb water facilities were enhanced at a later day by unusually good inland rail connections into the interior. Certain other East Coast cities were equal or superior to New York in water facilities but lacked the superior terrain for inland routes. The major historic problem in the United States was the general north-south direction of the major waterways, especially in the areas west of the Appalachian and Allegheny Mountains. Except for the Ohio and Tennessee, no major rivers are suitable for east-west transit.

The canal as a remedy for this situation was clearly inadequate. Rail transport must, for both economic and engineering reasons, follow the geographic paths suitable for their construction. The railroad map of the United States illustrates this factor clearly, especially in the Far West where availability of mountain passes was often the limiting factor in construction. Naturally, transportation routes are intended to connect the major points of traffic potential as determined by principal cities. However, these connections must be made over routes which are feasible and economical in nature; and, thus, they, in turn, gave rise to growth in the newly tapped areas.

Highways are less limited in location by geographic and economic factors than railroads are, and railroads less than canals or natural waterways. Thus, the highway system of the United States connects almost every hamlet and village and passes over geographic obstacles which would be impossible or impracticable for railroads or waterways. The aircraft, while it has almost no geographic limitations, is highly inhibited by economic factors.

Time has, of course, played an important role, so that, by the early 1930's when the airline network was under development, the economic factors underlying the basic airline net were already well formed. Location of natural resources naturally plays a major part in location of transport lines, especially rail. Coal and iron areas, as well as other mining sections, are almost always rail served, and the rail network is dense in the mining areas of the Northeastern United States.

The highway network has greatly reduced the influence of geography, since it has less dependence upon topographic limitations. However, while the highway net is almost universal, the interstate system of highways tends to connect only the major population centers and will thus carry the bulk of highway commerce. Commercial airlines likewise connect major cities because of economic limitations, although to a minor degree such geographic characteristics such as mountainous terrain may inhibit air traffic.

TRANSPORTATION AND THE MARKET STRUCTURE

By equalizing the supply of commodities and by making them more widely available, transportation helps to eliminate imperfections in the market structure. Aside from those ubiquitous commodities which are found in every locality, it would be possible for a producer of some commodity to extract a much higher price from a consumer because of market imperfections if transportation did not exist. Since the producer has at his disposal not only a means of transportation but several modes of transportation, one can be reasonably sure that in general, monopoly conditions due to inability to transport will be almost nonexistant. Consequently, transportation again enhances the productivity of the economy by removing or at least by diminishing certain market imperfections.

We have seen in this section that transportation as an economic function has brought about certain economic gains and acted in such a manner as to enhance the productivity of the economy. First of all, transportation creates or increases an already existing quality of usefulness; that is utility. By transporting a commodity from one location to another, its utility is much increased. At the same time by increasing the availability of goods and services, transportation enables the economy to maximize the advantages of specialized production and of division of labor. It increases the advantages of local or regional specialization by making goods from all regions available to all other regions and in doing this reduces the imperfections in the market.

TRANSPORTATION AND THE MARKETING PROCESS

In the modern economy the marketing process is subject to constant change. New products and products processed in different ways require great flexibility in marketing techniques. Such changes influence transportation in different ways. As expressed by a standard marketing textbook, "from a marketing point of view, transportation's job is to move goods from points of production and for sale to point of consumption in the quantities required, at the times needed, at a reasonable cost."[6] While a gradual process of industrial decentralization has been taking place since 1920, the emphasis upon a high degree of processing and the production of consumer products in great variety requires more precise and costly transportation.

It seems obvious that such modern marketing methods as are employed in most consumer goods industries would be impossible without efficient transportation service.

LOCATION OF MARKETING CENTERS

A marketing center must have certain attributes in order to be advantageous. Clearly, the most important of these is a central location in the marketing area, which at least for wholesaling and distribution might be very large indeed. There has, however, been an inverse influence at work in the retail area. The modern retail marketing system for consumer goods depends largely on personal transportation. The rural and suburban resident provides his own transportation, rather than depend upon the for-hire carrier and the mail order house. The for-hire carrier must engage in highly specialized transportation of semi-finished and highly processed products.

The United States consists, for marketing purposes, of a number of metropolitan areas of varying size, surrounded by suburban and rural areas dependent upon the metropolitan center as a source of supply. Except for certain extractive operations which are fixed, it is increasingly possible to carry on economic production of goods in many areas, which in past years were restricted to particular locations.

A producer concerned with marketing a good, can establish his distribution centers in almost any part of the area which he serves. Such proximity is not measured in miles, but in terms of time. On the local level, the suburban shopping center is an example. In 1900, each neighborhood had a compliment of shops, generally within walking distance of any point in the neighborhood. The modern suburban center serving households several miles distant would have been an impossibility. Likewise, on a regional scale an area was forced to depend upon a central supply center which by modern standards is

[6] Charles F. Philips and Delbert J. Duncan, *Marketing Principles and Methods*, Homewood, Illinois: Richard D. Irwin, Inc., Rev. Ed., p. 563.

only a few hours distant.[7] As transportation and marketing became more efficient, the area served by a given center increased greatly in size. Since modern transportation may serve a radius of 500 miles on an overnight basis, the seller may establish his operations on the basis of population, disposable income, or other factors, knowing that transportation service is available, although, to be sure, transportation cost will be a factor of great importance.

TRANSPORTATION AND MARKETING INSTITUTIONS

One of the most far reaching changes in marketing due to improved transportation is the ability of sellers to operate on smaller inventories and to enjoy the benefits of fresher stocks. Since the retail or wholesale seller is closer (in terms of time) to his source of supply, it is possible for him to operate on smaller inventories without danger of exhausting his supplies. He can thus enjoy a rapid turnover, and have substantially less money invested in inventory. His customers have the advantage of fresher and more varied goods from which to choose.

THE INFLUENCE OF TRANSPORTATION ON PRICE SYSTEMS

A producer selling a consumer good in a wide area for obvious reasons finds it desirable to quote a uniform price in the entire area. Thus a seller of a good which is marketed on a nation-wide basis will wish to establish a single price throughout the nation. Clearly, any substantial variations in freight rates will make this impossible or at least highly impracticable. Over the years, several methods have been employed to bring about a degree of uniformity, either in order to quote a uniform price, or to protect an already established producing center.

One of the most common methods for achieving uniformity and protecting established producers, was the basing point price system, recently declared to be illegal.[8] Under this system, the goods were sold at an identical price, consisting of the price at the basing point,

---

[7] In the East and South, the small size and large number of counties is said to have been dictated by the need to have a county seat (also in most cases a trading center) no further away than a day's drive by horse for the round trip. The many county seats are redundant in the modern framework of transportation.

[8] Federal Trade Commission v. The Cement Institute, 333 US 683, See: Clair Wilcox, *Public Policies Toward Business*, Homewood, Illinois: Richard D. Irwin Co., Rev. Ed., 1960, pp. 4 ff.

plus the freight rate from the basing point to the point of sale without regard to the actual source of the product. Thus under the famous "Pittsburgh plus" system, the price of steel delivered anywhere in the United States, was the price at mill plus the freight rate from Pittsburgh to the point of delivery. This price prevailed even though the actual steel had been produced at a point adjacent to the destination, or if it had been produced at a mill further away than Pittsburgh. Consequently, the advantage or disadvantage of distance was completely eliminated. In contrast to the basing point system is the system of F. O. B. pricing, under which the price is quoted at the point of production. The buyer then purchases the product and adds to the purchase price any costs of transportation which are applicable.

The F. O. B. pricing system puts the manufacturer in danger of losing distant markets, and is thus most useful in highly specialized industries where alternative sources of supply are likely to be unavailable.

In the years before 1900, the West and South often paid higher prices for manufactured products. Modern marketing methods and spreading industrialization have largely eliminated this practice. A manufacturer who hopes to sell at uniform prices on a nation-wide basis, must establish wide spread distribution points, or absorb some of the increased costs of transportation to distant markets.

Because the freight rate structure has been in existence for many years, it has had certain influences upon the structure of marketing institutions which are themselves factors of importance. For example, certain industrial processes may have grown up at particular points due to freight rate differentials in existence many years ago. Other varied external economies such as labor pool, capital availability, etc., have since become important, and consequently, the locality may continue to be favorable as a location although freight rates have ceased to be a factor. Also, producers who have located in a given area due to various non-transportation factors, such as labor or raw materials, may force rate adjustments upon the carriers, which enhance the locational advantages still further.

As this section has brought out, the marketing process is very much influenced by transportation rates and technology. Clearly this is an interdependent relationship; i.e., new developments in marketing force new methods in transportation and improved transportation brings about new techniques in marketing.

Since the marketing process is the distributive mechanism in the economy, any improvements in the process will transmit themselves into reduced prices or improved services for consumers.

By making goods available throughout a nation or the world, transportation helps to bring a great variety of goods to consumers, and to stabilize prices for such goods.

THE SOCIAL AND POLITICAL SIGNIFICANCE OF TRANSPORTATION

The social and political implications of transportation are immense. One often hears that we live in a shrinking world, a statement that becomes significant when one contemplates the possibility of continental and intercontinental travel. The exchange of ideas, of goods, cultural and political philosophies can only be classed as being advantageous.

From earliest times we are told of the benefits derived from the exchange of goods by different areas and cultures. Since the end of the 19th century, the world has made tremendous strides in increased living standards and in the enjoyment of unique products through increased trade, both interregional and international.

Scarcely a generation ago, it was only the wealthy who enjoyed the benefits of products from distant lands, or even from remote regions of the United States. The development of transport and related technology such as refrigeration has made such products available to all. Consequently, the real standard of living has improved substantially. Even a relatively small and isolated community will have available products from many foreign lands and, of course, the produce of all parts of the United States. Since in economic terms, transportation enables regions and nations to maximize their comparative advantages, each nation or region is able to produce goods and services in which it has a comparative, or in rare cases, an absolute advantage, and to exchange these goods for those in which it has little or no advantage. Consumers then enjoy the greatest variety of choice at a minimum of expenditure.

Both on an international and national level, transportation tends to break down provincialism and to broaden the outlook of individuals, with a resulting increase in tolerance and understanding. Transportation also improves the level of human understanding and education in a direct fashion by facilitating the movement of books, newspapers, various art forms, and indeed by the movement of people themselves.

It has often been said that America is an experiment in transportation. Unlike many European countries, America was so large and varied in its geographic and economic characteristics that provincialism could have been expected to be a factor of importance. Because of the superior transportation system which has been developed, the exchange of ideas and cultural backgrounds has been of great political and economic significance, and provincialism has been kept at a minimum.

There can be little doubt as to the great contribution which transportation has made to the political unity of the nation. A federation of sovereign states would have been impossible in practical operation without the transportation system. On many occasions sectional differences have created or threatened to create serious problems. It seems likely that such differences would have been more serious and more frequent without the unifying effects of transportation. In this connection, it is interesting to contemplate the possible influence which might have been exercised by adequate transportation in the mitigation of the economic factors incident to the Civil War.

Historians point out that the pre-war South had close social and economic ties with Europe and there is little doubt that more efficient transport and communications would have helped to demonstrate the economic unity which the United States achieved a generation later and which has provided the foundation of our political unity.

Indeed, modern transportation has almost eliminated political boundaries between states and has reduced the significance of national boundaries. The "metropolitan area" now embraces a very large area independent of political subdivisions, unified in an economic and social sense.

City planners point out that in future years, the area of the Northeastern United States from Boston to Washington, D. C. will be in effect a continuous urban area.[9] Such an area can exist only with the availability of adequate transportation facilities. In our modern metropolitan areas, county lines have long ceased to be of significance and state lines are of little economic or social consequence. Developments of this type have already taken place in Philadelphia, St. Louis, Washington, D. C., and other cities which lie on or near state lines. The implications of such developments are far reaching and may bring serious and complex problems.[10] Both Schumpeter, and Kuznets[11]

[9] *The Exploding Metropolis*, by the Editors of Fortune, New York, 1960, Anchor Press.

[10] See: C. Wright Mills, *White Collar*, New York, 1956, Oxford University Press, pp. 251 ff.

[11] Joseph A. Schumpeter, *The Theory of Economic Development*, Cambridge, 1949, Harvard University Press, (Translated by Redvers Opie), Harvard Economic Studies, Vol. XLVI.

Simon Kuznets, *Economic Change*, New York, 1953, W. W. Norton and Company, Inc.

emphasize the importance of interregional exchange of ideas and cultural milieu in the development of the economic and social system; the role played by transportation is clearly an important factor.

SOCIO-POLITICAL GOALS AND TRANSPORT ORGANIZATION

The economic and social goals of the American people have always influenced and been influenced by transportation developments and policies. Perhaps the outstanding development in this field was the close tie between public land policies in the United States and railroad construction.[12]

To a degree, our social and economic changes, especially urbanization and the creation of the megalopolis, have altered our whole concept of both intracity and intercity transportation. It is estimated that as of 1960 some 63 percent of the U. S. population now lives in 209 standard metropolitan areas.[13] When these metropolitan areas adjoin as they often do, for example on the East Coast from Washington, D. C. to Portsmouth, New Hampshire, the resulting area is a megalopolis. Thus what was at one time intercity transportation becomes essentially intracity or intrametro transportation. The growth of these areas, along with the rise in automobile ownership, has created fantastic problems.

From Alexandria, Virginia, to the north side of Baltimore is a distance of some fifty miles. This is too short a distance to fly and, for the most part, likewise not suitable to rail travel. By private automobile this distance is not great, but because of the traffic conditions and congestion, the trip is most difficult. Aside from the private auto there is no adequate intrametro transportation system. The interurban system, the backbone of urban-suburban transport in the years before 1930, has all but passed from the scene. The continued building of highways and parking facilities requiring vast amounts of land otherwise useful for more productive uses is clearly a short run solution.

While the economic problems incident to transportation to be dealt with in this book are essentially those relating to long distance,

---

[12] Fred A. Shannon, *America's Economic Growth*, New York, 1940, The Macmillan Company, pp. 360 ff.

[13] "Standard Metropolitan Areas," Office of Statistical Standards, Bureau of the Budget, 1959. A standard metropolitan area is composed of a city of at least 200,000 population surrounded by an area related commercially. Forty-seven of these areas were added in the years 1950-1959, and of those added all but five were contiguous to existing metros.

the concepts of these problems are rapidly changing. A trip of sixty miles between Alexandria and Baltimore is clearly a much different transport problem than a sixty mile trip between Evanston and Granger, Wyoming.[14]

The future (in fact, present) requirements for transporting to and within these areas are much different than our present concepts. Automobile, subway, interurban, air, rail and perhaps other modes must be used in a coordinated fashion to serve these projected needs. Unlike other industries, the transportation industry has a unique ability to interchange and coordinate its various components and to use them to the best advantage.

Past experience would seem to demonstrate the folly of allowing excessive dependence to fall upon one mode. In the early and mid 1930's many of our cities allowed their interurban systems to pass out of existence since the automobile was being used in such large numbers. In terms of efficient mass transportation, this proved to be short sighted indeed.

Although drastic means are being used to accommodate the automobile to the city and suburban areas, the impartial observer would be forced to admit that the battle is not only enormously expensive, but may well be impossible to win unless even more unorthodox methods are used.[15]

Public policy and private enterprise working in unison were influential beyond measure in the realm of economic development.[16] All factors considered, it might be said that the public policy of land grants to railroads, along with the railroad's own policy of colonization and development of lands provided the greatest incentive to the development of the western areas from 1860 until 1920. After 1920 the same process continued as the automobile began to perform the function which had been carried on by the railroad. The combined influence of the railroad and the motor vehicle on the economic and social life would be difficult to overestimate.

In the international sphere, nations can and do use transport lines as instruments of offense and defense, or as means of political influence. Troxel points out the historic importance of merchant ship

---

[14] An interesting sidelight on these problems is faced by retail and wholesale firms which perform "local" delivery. Local delivery round trip may be several hundred miles.

[15] The Exploding Metropolis, *op. cit.*, pp. 43 ff.

[16] P. W. Gates, *The Illinois Central Railroad and Its Colonization Work,* Cambridge, 1934, Harvard University Press; also, Louis M. Hacker, *The Triumph of American Capitalism,* New York, 1940, Columbia University Press.

and rail lines as means of penetrating into new areas of hoped-for influence.[17]

In the modern era, the instrument of prestige and policy is the "flag" air carrier. The more aggressive nations embark upon a deliberate policy of transportation development based upon a goal of military efficiency. Clearly, planned transportation development can be used to forward various national goals, including aggression, economic or military.[18]

Let us hope that the beneficial ends of transportation development will outweigh those of military or political aggression in the future development of air transportation and that transportation, like other social and economic forces, can be directed toward constructive ends.

SUMMARY

As the chapter has brought out, the transportation function has widespread effects in the economic and socio-political areas. These effects are both salutory and troublesome. As a social and economic institution, transportation does not work with precision; and, in particular, since the industry is intertwined at every point with public policy, social and political factors are frequently of equal importance to the economic factors. In the following chapters, the institutions which provide the service will be examined.

---

[17] Emory Troxel, *Economics of Transport*, New York, 1955, Rinehart and Company, Inc., p. 32.

[18] James H. Blackman, "Transport Development and Locomotive Technology in the Soviet Union," in *Essays in Economics*, No. 3 (Columbia: Bureau of Business and Economic Research, University of South Carolina, 1957). For a more comprehensive treatment, see Barbara Ward, *The Rich Nations and the Poor Nations* (New York: W. W. Norton & Co., Inc., 1962), esp. Ch. IV.

Selected References for Further Study

The general area with which the preceding chapter is concerned is so broad that no attempt can be made to select even a representative sample of the literature related to it. Almost every line of human endeavor relating to man's attempts to modify his surroundings has certain transportation aspects.

Certain historical works stress the influence of technological progress more than others, e.g., Hacker, Louis M., *The Triumph of American Capitalism*, New York, 1947, Columbia University Press; and the classic: Mumford, Lewis, *Technics and Civilization*, 1934, Harcourt Brace and Company. The role of transport in American development is well portrayed in Turner, Frederick J., *The Frontier in American History*. For a broader interpretation, see: Cole, G. D. H., *Introduction to Economic History 1750-1850*, London, Macmillan and Company, Ltd., 1952. Factors in economic development are well presented in Moulton, H. G., *Controlling Factors in Economic Development*, Washington, D. C., The Brookings Institution, 1949. Also, Slichter, Sumner, *The American Economy — Its Problems and Prospects*, New York, A. A. Knopf and Company, 1948; and Brozen, Yale, *Implications of Technological Change*, Chicago, Social Science Research Council, 1950.

CHAPTER II

Railroads, Motor Carriers and Air Carriers

THE RAILROAD SYSTEM

The transportation service of the United States is performed by various modes; viz., railroads, motor carriers, water carriers, airlines and pipelines. Each of these modes has certain characteristics, advantages, and disadvantages. Shippers or travelers may use them either independently or in cooperation with one another. While the various means of transportation are in competition with each other, they also cooperate and one can speak in a general sense of a "transportation system." Historically, the modes have in the United States been under separate ownership and management. In addition, they have been developed at different periods and are in varying stages of development, economically and technologically. The transportation industry is a complex system of railroads, motor carriers, water carriers, air carriers, and pipelines, having essentially one common characteristic: the production of transportation service.

Transportation enterprises perform a service which, since it is quoted in standard units can be measured and compared. These units are the ton-mile; i.e., one ton carried one mile, and the passenger mile, one passenger carried one mile.[1]

---

[1] The ton-mile has several major shortcomings as will be shown later. However, at this stage it is a handy measurement unit.

Carriers transport goods and people in varying quantities and through the use of several technological methods. In general, the various carriers serve a particular geographic area, but technology of the mode is influential upon the service area covered. For example, airlines by their nature may serve more geographically diverse points than railroads or motor carriers. In the same fashion the technology of the mode often influences the type of goods carried. Except for pipelines, the various modes carry a wide range of products and in fact are limited more by economic considerations than by technological problems; i.e., it would be technically possible to transport coal by air although it would be economic nonsense, except in some special case.

In this and the following chapter, the various modes will be examined, and their economic and technological characteristics will be discussed briefly. Also, brief mention will be made of their historical development. The object of Chapters 2 and 3 is to acquaint the reader with the over-all character of, and relationships between, the various modes. Later chapters will examine their economic characteristics in more detail.

The Rail Share of the Total Transport Service

The railroad system is the dominant mode in the transportation industry from the standpoint of gross ton-mile service performed, having performed in recent years about 45.6 per cent of the total ton-mile service. Table 2-1 shows the relative shares of ton-mile service performed since 1930, indicating that the rail share has declined substantially since that date due chiefly to inroads by the competing forms of for-hire transportation. It can be seen that, while the railroad industry has declined in importance relative to the other modes, it still plays an extremely important part in the total transportation effort and in the economy.[2]

The relative size of the firms in the various modes is well illustrated by the Fortune *Survey* of business firms. Among the fifty largest transport firms (ranked by operating revenue) are twenty-nine railroads. Only five motor carriers are on this list, the largest (Greyhound Corporation) being in thirteenth place. Ten air carriers are listed in the top fifty, four of which are among the top ten. No inland waterway carriers or pipelines are listed.

---

[2] *Fortune*, August, 1963.

TABLE 2-1

RAILROAD, GROSS TON-MILES, INTERCITY

SERVICE, AS PERCENTAGE OF TOTAL SELECTED YEARS

Year	Gross Ton-Miles Intercity Freight (Millions)	Percentage of Total
1930	389,648	74.3
1940	379,201	61.3
1943	734,829	71.3
1944	746,912	68.6
1945	690,809	67.3
1950	596,940	56.2
1956	655,891	48.2
1957	626,222	46.3
1958	557,000	45.6
1959	582,497	45.0
1960	578,000	43.8
1961	531,000	43.0
1962	590,000	43.9

Source: Interstate Commerce Commission, Annual Reports for the years indicated, and Bureau of Railway Economics, A.A.R.

Before 1930, the railroad represented the most practicable and in
many instances the only mode of intercity transportation. Since 1930,
the railroad has been subject to increasing competition from other
modes. Although ton-miles have increased in absolute terms, it is
likely that the railroad has failed to keep pace with the growing
economy in preserving its share of the transportation market. As a
rough measure of the potential transportation market, the Gross
National Product provides a fairly reliable guide. From 1940 to
1950, the Gross National Product increased almost 70 per cent in
constant dollar terms, while revenue ton-mile service performed by
Class I railroads increased approximately 63 per cent in the same
period. From 1950 to 1960 Gross National Product increased approximately 51 per cent in constant dollar terms, while rail ton-mile service
performed actually declined slightly less than 10 per cent. The Korean
War was in large part responsible for increased rail activity in 1950;
however, the railroads did not in net terms maintain their participation
in the formation of the Gross National Product. While competition
from other modes was the primary factor, certain other factors such as
changes in industrial organization were in part responsible.[3]

[3] Basic data taken from Interstate Commerce Commission *Annual Reports*
and the *President's Economic Reports* for the years indicated. Calculations by the
author.

The Structure of the Industry

The railroad industry in the United States is a privately owned and operated industry representing an investment of more than $30 billion, employing more than three quarters of a million workers, and ranking as one of the most important industries in the economy. The industry is dominated by the large "trunk line" systems. Most of these large carriers are designated by the Interstate Commerce Commission as Class I railroads; i.e., those having gross operating revenues of $3 million or more per year. While the number of these railroads changes from time to time, there were approximately 100 such companies by 1962. Although the Class I railroads make up only about one-sixth of the total, they constitute by any measure the most important portion of the industry in terms of earnings, investment and transportation service, performing more than 99 per cent of the total rail service.

By any measure the railroad industry is a highly significant portion of our economic system, having in 1959 an investment of some $27.5 billion and operating revenues of $9.8 billion ($8.5 billion from freight and $651 million from passenger carriage). The industry employed more than 800 thousand persons.

Although there is considerable variation within the Class I railroads as to size, even the smaller of these railroads represent substantial investment as compared with other transportation enterprises. Since by its nature the railroad must provide a right of way, including structures such as bridge and tunnels, as well as land, the capital needed for even a relatively small railroad is of considerable size. Consequently most railroads are privately owned corporations with ownership broadly held.

In addition to the Class I railroads, there are smaller roads, short lines and switching and terminal companies often owned or controlled and operated by the major systems. Many of the smaller railroads are regional carriers, or lines feeding traffic into the larger systems. Also, there are a number of industrial railroads serving as adjuncts to industrial enterprises, devoting their efforts primarily to the carriage of one product and serving one firm.

The switching and terminal roads are entirely concerned with transferring cars from one railroad to another, or from industrial plants into the rail network. Quite commonly the switching and terminal roads are owned and operated jointly by the railroads serving a specific area. Some idea of the range in size can be conceived from a comparison, such as the following; the largest railroad in the United States in terms of miles operated is the Atcheson, Topeka and Santa Fe, with

13,073 miles of line. Many of the smaller lines engaged in industrial switching and terminal work have only a mile or less of line, although they are often organized as independent railroad companies. One important feature of the railroad industry is the high degree of cooperation among the firms within the industry. That is, while there are more than 700 separate railroad companies, the shipper has at his disposal what amounts to a single system.

For many years railroads have enjoyed the advantages of a common rail gauge and a universal coupler, which with unrestricted car interchange makes it possible for a shipment to move over many lines without loading or unloading. Thus, while there is no single rail line spanning the continent, the cooperation between lines overcomes this disadvantage; and a shipper can obtain service to any part of the country, as well as a large part of North America, although he deals only with the railroad on which the shipment has originated.

Origin and Development

The railroad industry had its origin in the 1830's, and its development can be best understood by dividing the years of its development into several periods.

The Beginnings, 1830-1850. While the use of steam driven vehicles appears early in American history, it is generally agreed that the first commercial railroads of any significance were the Baltimore and Ohio Railroad chartered in 1827 and the South Carolina Railroad, chartered in 1828.[4]

These lines were rapidly supplemented, and by 1850 the New England area and the Middle Atlantic area had a well-developed rail network. The South and Midwest were served by a few local lines, most of them isolated from interregional connections, and nothing approaching a rail "system" was yet in existence. It is evident that at this date, the railroad was thought of as being a very limited carrier,

---

[4] Robert S. Henry, *This Fascinating Railroad Business* (Indianapolis: Bobbs-Merrill Company, 1942), pp. 24 ff.

The source cited above and many others provide a thorough discussion of the history of transportation development in the United States. For a more comprehensive discussion of the historical and technological development of the railroad industry, the student is referred to the standard economic history works; e.g., Harold U. Faulkner, *American Economic History* (6th ed; New York: Harper & Row, 1949), as well as the numerous histories of various railroads and geographic regions. An excellent presentation is found in August C. Bolino, *The Development of the American Economy* (Columbus: Charles E. Merrill Books, Inc., 1961), especially Chapter 7.

regional in nature and frequently supplemental to the canal. One of the limiting factors was the primitive technology of the period. Once begun, however, the railroads made rapid strides in technology and by 1850, the basic elements of the steam engine, the roadbed and the operating technique had been formulated.

The Formative Years, 1850-1880. It is not surprising that the Civil War and its aftermath had an explosive effect upon railroad growth. The war itself brought about a serious need for more rail facilities, but in addition, had a most important influence upon standardization and uniformity of practice. Throughout the military zones, the railroads began to operate as a system. In the post-war period, the lessons learned under military necessity were applied. The 1870's represented an erratic but impressive period of growth in the rail industry.

By 1880 the eastern half of the United States was served by a solid network of railroads. The nation had been spanned by rail in 1869 (Union Pacific-Central Pacific) with much public support and encouragement, and a second transcontinental route had been constructed by 1880 (Santa Fe). While the Panic of 1873 had brought serious financial troubles, the railroad industry continued to expand, especially in the Far West, with more than 70,000 miles being built in the decade of the 80's.[5]

Much of the construction during the period was stimulated by the grants of public lands made for that purpose. While considerable debate still goes on among the various modes regarding the justice and efficiency of this program, it is evident that the land grants were an important element in the construction of certain railroads; viz., the Illinois Central, Northern Pacific, Texas and Pacific, and other mid-western and southern roads, as well as the first transcontinental route, the Union Pacific-Central Pacific. In all, 158,293,000 acres were granted to aid the construction of 21,500 miles of railroads.[6] There can be little doubt that much of this mileage would not have been built so soon without the land grants. Since there is no method of determining how much mileage would have been built without grants, or how valuable the land would have been without rail service, it seems futile to speculate on the money value of subsidy resulting from the land grant policy. In any event, until 1876 the grantee railroads were obliged to render certain services to the federal government at no charge, and after that date, at reduced charges, until the

---

[5] Faulkner, *op. cit.*, p. 486 ff., also, James Marshall, *Sante Fe, The Railroad that Built An Empire*, New York, 1945, Random House.

[6] Annual Report of the Secretary of the Interior, 1941, p. 220.

repeal of the land grant provisions in 1946. The rationale of this policy will be further considered in Chapter IX.

In addition to the land grants, an important role in railroad financial aid was played by European investors. Especially in the mid-west, European capital was instrumental in encouraging railroad construction during the 1870's and 1880's.

The hallmark of this era was improving technology. The steam locomotive had, by the late 1870's, been largely converted into a more efficient coal burning machine. Freight and passenger cars were of improved design, with passenger equipment especially becoming more luxurious and dependable. Stimulated largely by the war years, standardization was becoming a more important factor. Operating techniques, signal systems and other practices, although leaving much to be desired, were undergoing development as the industry progressed.

By 1875, the railroad had become an integral part of American life, both social and economic. It would be difficult to overestimate the impact which the railroad had upon social and economic development in the last third of the nineteenth century. Life in the small town centered about the railroad station, and doings aboard the "steam cars" was staple material for press and drama.

It was in these years also that less savory developments began which were to be troublesome in later years. Railroad management began to take full advantage of their market situation. Financial manipulation became commonplace, and rumblings of discontent began to be heard.

The Years of Maturity, 1880-1920. By 1900 the railroad system was virtually complete in a physical sense, and the forty years from 1880 to 1920 were in addition to more construction devoted essentially to improving the system, to consolidation of smaller lines and to a degree, retrenching from the over-building of previous years. Many lines had been overbuilt in the 1870's and 80's, and there was much financial manipulation and speculation.[7]

This era also witnessed the first serious moves toward an eventual accomplishment of the goal of public regulation. There is no doubt that during these years the railroads carried on many practices which arose to haunt them in later years. Two additional "transcontinental" routes were constructed after 1900 (Milwaukee and Western Pacific),

---

[7] See Matthew Josephson, *The Robber Barons* (New York: Harcourt, Brace & World, Inc., 1934).

but the net mileage actually declined after 1916 as surplus mileage was abandoned and circuitous routes were rebuilt and upgraded.

Following 1910, the emphasis was upon technical efficiency. From 1910 until 1930, rail traffic was very heavy and railroad management stressed engineering developments. More powerful locomotives, larger trains, new bridges, tunnels, and other elements of rolling stock and physical plant constituted the hallmark of this era.

Although the railroads were relatively free from serious intense economic problems during these years, many difficulties were in the process of development. These problems which later gave rise to public regulation concerned the relationship between the railroads and the shipping and investing public. After the rail rate cases in 1910, much discussion centered around "the railroad problem."[8]

The "golden age of railroading" brought with it serious problems for the future. The years, 1900-1920, were years of monopoly. Railroad management could and did concentrate on the internal problems of the industry. Intercity land transportation and the railroad were essentially the same. It is not unnatural that rail management came to feel that competition was a dead issue and to assume that marketing was not a problem of serious importance. These attitudes found no difficulty in becoming ingrained in an industry which was, even at that time, almost a century old. Thus, although the railroads reached new levels of technological efficiency in these years, their ability to deal with problems, which were developing beyond the horizon, was very limited indeed. Rail mileage, equipment units and other physical measures reached the highest levels in history at this time. This age was soon to come to an end.

The Troubled Years, 1920-1940. Following 1920 new problems beset the railroad industry, with the rise of competitive forms of intercity transport and the downturn in economic activity after 1930. The railroads with large capital invested in fixed plant were especially vulnerable to economic fluctuations and to the competition created by the highway carriers. By 1940 some of the strongest roads had been forced into bankruptcy. On the eve of World War II, the railroads had somewhat recovered from the depression years, although many long-range problems remained to be solved. A major difficulty was the failure of the railroads to understand the fact that their

---

[8] As an example, see William Larrabee, *The Railroad Question, A Historical and Practical Treatise on Railroads and Remedies for Their Abuses* (Chicago: The Schulte Publishing Company), 1893.

troubles were not due entirely to the economic conditions prevailing but also the structural changes taking place in the industry and the economy. Both rail management and the regulatory agencies failed to appreciate the magnitude of these problems for some years. As the private automobile, the truck and the airplane made inroads upon the rail traffic, it became clear that railroads would never again move the overwhelming share of intercity passenger and freight traffic which had characterized them during earlier years. The Second World War brought relief in the financial area, but it also brought new operating problems to hitherto unknown magnitude.

The Modern Railroad, 1940-1960. By 1945 the Second World War had ended and the railroad industry faced the problem of maintaining its share of the increasing traffic of the post-war years. While competitive means of transport were more active than ever, the railroads faced the future with some confidence born of new technology. In the decade of the 1950's the steam locomotive gave way to the diesel, and other mechanical innovations found a place in the industry.

More important, the postwar years have witnessed an increasing willingness to accept the need for changing attitudes on the part of railroad management. Railroads have been more aggressive in pricing and in marketing their services than they have been in the past. Unfortunately, some of the managerial and technological innovations which marked these years came too late for effective result.

A serious problem in the years since 1945 has been to alter the widely-held public image, which casts the railroads in the role of a hidebound and tradition-encrusted industry. Especially in the passenger area, the efforts of the railroads have been of little avail. It seems fair to say that much of the burden is in the form of antiquated regulation largely beyond the reach of management talent, and much will be said of this matter in later chapters.

Thus, the modern railroad finds itself in the somewhat peculiar position of being an old industry faced with new problems. There is also the somewhat paradoxical situation that the industry, essential to the economic welfare of the nation, faces serious financial problems. The implications of these problems will be further explored in later chapters.

Problems and Prospects. As the railroads enter a new decade, the industry faces new problems and prospects. Perhaps foremost is the yet unsettled problem of intercarrier relationships. Railroads still move the greater share of intercity freight; but, passenger transportation is rapidly moving to other forms; and indeed the entire feasibility of rail passenger transportation has been called into question.[9] Many problems remain unsolved in the area of regulation and public policy and the labor relations sector.[10]

As the 1960's began, the railroads were actively engaged in a program of merger and consolidation which promises to be a solution to many of their problems. A number of important consolidations have taken place since 1950, and others are in process.

Likewise, great promise is shown by increased use of trailer or flat car service and by a more aggressive rate policy undertaken by the railroads.

Organization and Capital Structure

As has been noted, the railroad industry is characterized by large and complex organizations. A large railroad presents a unique management problem, since it is by nature far flung and highly specialized. Thus, the traditional form of organization has resulted in the delegation of substantial authority to operating officials situated at various geographic points, and the requirement that these officials comply with general policy emanating from the officers at headquarters. On large railroads these geographic districts are often consolidated into regions, and in recent years there has been an increasing trend toward more highly centralized control by the highest executive officers. Whatever system is used, the management of a railroad presents many complex problems.

As noted elsewhere, the financial needs of the railroad made the corporate form of organization necessary. Railroads have historically relied on the sale of bonds and other senior securities as a means of acquiring capital, rather than the sale of common stock.

Because railroad earnings are seriously limited by rate regulation, and since they require such substantial amounts of capital, with slow turnover, the investor has been much more attracted to bonds as an investment instrument rather than common stock. Consequently, the railroads have found themselves working under the burden of substantial fixed debt, upon which interest payments must be paid.

This in turn has given rise to some fundamental financial characteristics. In the event of default, it is impracticable for investors to

---

[9] In June 1958, Examiner Howard Hosmer predicted that rail passenger service will end by 1970 if it continues to decline at its present rate. *ICC Docket No. 31954,* September 18, 1958.

[10] As an example, see *Eastern Railroad Problems, The Serious Situation and Its Causes,* Jersey City, Eastern Railroad Presidents Conference, 1961.

exercise their claims upon carrier property in any direct fashion. Thus, the most common procedure is for the creditors to accept a somewhat reduced obligation and to force a reorganization upon the carrier. As a result, the carrier emerges from its difficulties as a new corporation in a legal sense, having acquired all of the physical assets (land and plant structures) of the old company. Consequently, a railroad seldom goes out of business in a literal sense, unless its reason for existence is no longer valid; i.e., it has no real economic service to perform.[11]

The financial arrangements relative to equipment are of a different nature. The bulk of railroad equipment is acquired by means of a financial instrument known as the equipment trust.[12] The equipment trust is in many respects similar to a conditional sales contract by means of which durable consumer goods are sold. There are, however, major legal and financial differences, chief of which is the time period involved. Trust certificates are most often purchased by banks, insurance companies, and other institutional investors and they generally mature in ten or twenty years' time. Until such time as the certificate is paid in full, the title to equipment is retained by the lender, although the borrower uses it without restriction. The importance of this instrument can be seen by the fact that the Association of American Railroads estimates that only about one-fifth of the diesel locomotives now in use were purchased by using cash.

In view of the fact that the lender has a claim on a salable piece of equipment, it is common for the lender to acquire equipment trust certificates without hesitation even though the carrier may be in financial difficulties otherwise. Also, the acquisition of new equipment may be the correct policy directed toward restoring the financial welfare of the carrier. In common with other public utility enterprises, railroads face a very low capital turnover and a relatively low rate of return on invested capital. The implications of this situation will be further examined in a later section.

In recent years, earnings of railroad companies have made the financial requirements of equipment trust financing rather burdensome.

---

[11] The process of financial adjustment is much facilitated by the passage of legislation in the 1930's, notably, sec. 77-B of the bankruptcy act which greatly simplifies the problems involved. For a thorough discussion of this problem, see D. Phillip Locklin, *Economics of Transportation* (5th ed.; Chicago: Richard D. Irwin, 1961) Ch. 25. Also, the classic historical account is found in Stuart Daggett, *Railroad Reorganization*, 1908 (New York: Harper & Row, Publishers).

[12] For an authoritative treatment of the legal and financial details of the equipment trust, see Arthur S. Dewing, *Financial Policy of Corporations* (5th ed.; New York: Ronald Press Company, 1953), pp. 201 ff.

Other instruments such as conditional sales contract, purchase and lease of equipment have been attracting widespread attention.[13] These methods, less rigid and often less costly than the equipment trust, will doubtlessly be more widely used in the future. Any means of improving methods of equipment financing will be of great interest to the industry.

Services Offered and Traffic Moved

Most railroads are true common carriers in both the legal and physical sense; i.e., they thus stand ready to transport any type of commodity which can be legally moved in commerce, as well as the provision of personal transportation. Railroads maintain various specialized types of equipment in order to accommodate shippers of particular products. However, to some carriers, certain products are of greater importance than others depending largely upon the geographic location of the carrier. Thus, railroads serving the coal-producing areas require hopper cars in large numbers. Although generalizations are difficult to make, the railroad industry as a whole does have certain traffic patterns depending upon the areas served. The map on page 30 shows that there are essentially seven so-called "transcontinental" routes;[14] viz., the Great Northern; Northern Pacific; Chicago, Milwaukee and St. Paul; Union Pacific-Southern Pacific; Burlington-Denver and Rio Grande Western; Western Pacific; Atcheson, Topeka and Santa Fe; and the alternate Southern Pacific route into Southern California.

All of these routes extend eastward to the Mississippi River points, or to Chicago, and connect with the major east-west lines. These lines are bisected by the north-south carriers, the Illinois Central; Southern; Louisville and Nashville; Atlantic Coast Line; Seaboard; and on the West Coast, the Southern Pacific lines extending north and south from San Francisco. It will be noted that the New England, Middle Atlantic and Midwest areas are intensively served with rail network, while in the Southwest and Far West, the network is less dense. Historically, the western roads were predominantly carriers of agricultural products; however, the growing industrialization of the West has substantially

---

[13] An excellent brief summary of these matters appears in Hunter Holding, "New Developments in Financing Carrier and Terminal Equipment," *Transportation Journal*, Spring 1963, Chicago, 1963, American Society of Traffic and Transportation, Inc.

[14] No single railroad spans the U.S., despite efforts to do so. In Canada both the Canadian Pacific and the Canadian National do so.

Fig. 2-1   Major U.S. Railroads—1962   *Source: Association of American Railroads*

increased the variety of the traffic, and more nearly balanced the flow of traffic.

Carriers serving certain regions carry large amounts of rather specialized traffic such as coal, petroleum products, citrus fruits, timber and other products. Most railroads, as do other carriers, attempt to make the range of products they carry as wide as possible, but some of the smaller carriers are content to become highly specialized. This is especially true if the carrier is a quasi-industrial road under the control of an industrial enterprise, and operated largely for the convenience of that company. Freight traffic accounts for the major share of revenue on most railroads and many roads devote their operations entirely to freight movement. Freight traffic shows great variation directly related to the output of goods, and car loadings have been an indicator of industrial production.[15]

Rail freight service can be generally divided into three classes: carload service, less-than-carload service, and the forwarding service provided by railroads, but available through the freight forwarding organizations. Consequently, the shipper has available to him, a full range of services, ranging from the movement of one or more car-loads in bulk to the pick up and delivery of a single package. Further refinements in service are provided by the operation of "piggy back" service, the movement of highway trailers by rail between various cities. The railroads offer a wide variety in quality of services ranging from the movement of bulk products such as coal and iron ore, to the transportation of high value merchandise requiring rapid and careful handling. The railroad can be thought of as a "department store" of transportation, while the other modes of transportation are somewhat more specialized and compete with railroads in all the service areas on an individual basis.

Although railway express in not classified as freight, it does involve the movement of goods. In general, railway express moves on passenger trains and is confined to small shipments requiring expedited service, performed by R.E.A. Express, Inc., an organization owned and operated by the major railroads.

As noted above, the pattern of passenger movement is undergoing substantial change. Passenger traffic falls roughly into two categories, long distance and commuter. Since 1920, the private automobile has taken increasing amounts of both types of traffic, while the airlines and inter-city bus companies have made inroads on long distance

---

[15] See Thor Hultgren, *American Transportation in Prosperity and Depression* (National Bureau of Economic Research [New York, 1948]).

traffic. Relatively few railroads are concerned to any degree with commuter traffic, and only one Class I road (Long Island Railroad) is predominantly a passenger carrier. Generally, railroads do not consider commuter traffic to be desirable, and some roads, particularly those in the East, are not highly competitive in regard to inter-city passenger traffic in general, although certain special trains are considered important. A number of railroads offer no passenger service, and are operated for freight only.

In the passenger service area, the range of services is somewhat more limited than is true of freight. The basic distinction is between coach and pullman, or "first class."[16] As the growth of long distance travel by air has proceeded, the need for elaborate and extensive overnight passenger travel has decreased. Except between the largest cities or on particular trains, sleeping car and dining car service has become rare. At the same time, the development of newer and more modern equipment has greatly improved the coach service and further reduced the distinction between "coach class" and "first class" rail service. Thus, though the number of "prestige" passenger trains in operation has been greatly reduced since 1920, and speed has been largely pre-empted by the airlines, the trains now operating are more luxurious and more efficiently designed than in the past. The use of diesel locomotives, streamlined, light weight equipment and innovations such as dome cars has greatly improved the service.[17]

In the late 1940's some attempt was made to recapture short run passenger traffic by the use of self-propelled rail cars, but it cannot be said that these attempts were successful. In the Far West passenger traffic plays a more important part in the operations of rail carriers, but freight traffic is still considered to be more profitable and desirable. After a century of service, the future of rail passenger service seems uncertain.

---

[16] Unlike European railways, U.S. roads have for the most part, offered a relatively uniform or "classless" passenger service. However, a passenger holding a "first class" or pullman ticket is generally entitled to use parlor or lounge car facilities which may be denied to coach class riders.

[17] Before 1930, railroads made great efforts to compete on the basis of speed and the elapsed time between cities; e.g., the time between New York and Chicago, or Chicago and Los Angeles was constantly reduced. After 1930, the airlines made rail speed less important, and "name" passenger trains emphasized luxury, convenience of schedule, and comfortable accommodations. For example, the airline schedules between Chicago and Los Angeles have reduced the elapsed time to a few hours. A recent schedule shows the Sante Fe Super Chief makes the trip in 37 and one-half hours. However, this luxurious train draws a heavy patronage.

Rail Technology Equipment and Operation

Railroads own and operate some 29,000 locomotives, all but a handful (some 800) of them diesel electric. In past years, the number of locomotives was much greater, having been more than 50,000 in 1945. The reduction in numbers has been due both to the rise in efficiency of the locomotive and to the decline in the share of ton-mile service performed. The railroads operate 1.6 million freight cars of all types, of which boxcars and hopper cars make up roughly a million. In the passenger area, they operate almost 26,000 cars. Here, we find the most dramatic decline, reflecting the rail withdrawal from the passenger carrying activities. In the late 1920's, there were, on the average, more than 52,000 passenger cars in operation. It was noted above that the freight car fleet operates on a nationwide basis, with cars being interchanged from one road to another. Also, a somewhat unique feature in the rail industry is the practice of allowing the shipper to utilize the car to unload or load and to keep the car on his premises for a specified period of time at no charge.

In effect, the railroad has an item of capital equipment which it "lends out'" to customers and to its fellow producers, a situation without parallel in industry.[18]

It is clearly important to utilize these cars to the utmost, since, even under the best of circumstances, they are apt to be unused for long periods. The demand for freight cars is seasonal, and the average car spends long periods in no productive use. Because of the cyclical demand for cars, it is necessary to have more cars on hand than may actually be in use for most of the year. It is also important to maximize the use of locomotives, and this, of course, is under the direct control of the railroad. Locomotive utilization is especially important, since diesel locomotives are expensive and relatively few of them are fully depreciated. Some shippers who need special cars or who need frequent access to cars can purchase or lease cars from builders or car companies. It has been noted that railroad operations are geared to a large scale. However, some attention must be paid to quality of operation, especially speed of transit.

In the early years of the century, it was common for carriers to operate long slow freight trains, maximizing the tonnage moved. With

---

[18] The railroads compensate each other for use of cars on a daily basis (per diem payments). Each road maintains a car tracing office whose function is to keep records on cars and to calculate what is owed to others and due to the home road for car use. Shippers are granted 48 hours of "free time" for loading and unloading. After this time, a charge is made (demurrage) which is designed to stimulate return of the cars to the railroad and discourage their use for storage.

modern equipment and under the lash of competition, it has become customary to stress speed and put less emphasis on gross tonnage. The complexity of rail plant makes these problems exceedingly difficult. Yards, terminal facilities, repair shops and other elements of physical plant become involved in rail operations and must be kept at a high standard if efficiency is to be achieved. This, in turn, requires constant attention to maintenance of all plant elements, and, while a period of under-maintenance will be acceptable, it cannot continue for any great length of time.

It was pointed out earlier that railroads are capable of great increases in output with fixed plant. It must be noted, however, that the quality of output may vary widely. As older equipment is pressed into service and as less efficient facilities are used, the quality of service declines and operating costs increase. For example, some steam locomotives are held in storage by various railroads for use in periods of high traffic. It would be highly uneconomic to use these locomotives after years of non-use. Much time and effort would be required to reactivate locomotives, facilities and other items necessary to operation. Costs would be such that, except for urgent reasons, it would be impracticable to operate these locomotives.

The Association of American Railroads

While not essentially a part of the railroad industry, the Association of American Railroads is a somewhat unique and essential organization to the industry. In part a trade association with the legislative and public relations duties of such an organization, the A.A.R. is much more. As we have seen, the railroad industry operates with a high degree of coordination and cooperation. In large part, the A.A.R. is responsible for this fact. In the words of the Association:

> Almost every phase of railroading is touched by the work of the Association of American Railroads. For example, in the one field of the movement of freight between two or more railroads, the Association, through its appropriate divisions and among other related activities, has set up and maintains the standards which make equipment available for wide interchange; directs the daily flow of freight cars, loaded and empty, from railroad to railroad, and marshals fleets of various types of cars to meet sudden or peak demands; establishes and maintains the basis on which cars away from "home" are repaired and on which such repairs are paid for; and arranges rules for the remittance to each railroad of its proper share of the revenue collected.

Most of the mechanical, engineering, and other technical research of the Association is carried on through more than 200 standing committees and permanent research staffs. A few typical examples of the numerous subjects covered are: roadbed and track maintenance, continuous-welded rail, signals, automatic train control, radio and radar, wheels and axles, couplers and draft gears, use of alloys for lightweight car equipment, freight containers, conservation of fuel and materials, fire prevention, lighting improvement, development and application of special business machines, use of microphotography, and improvement and speeding up of accounting procedures.

Much research work is done in conjunction with universities, technological institutions, industrial research laboratories and the laboratories of the companies which supply the railroads with materials and equipment. A Research Center built by the Association of American Railroads is located on the campus of the Illinois Institute of Technology in Chicago.[19]

Through its various departments, the A.A.R. promotes standardization and uniformity in design and operation of equipment and techniques.

Summary

The railroad industry, while no longer the primary means of intercity transportation, plays a dominant role in freight transportation and is a significant factor in passenger transport. The railroads represent a substantial investment and the industry ranks as one of the most important in the economy, both from the standpoint of invested capital and as an employer of labor.

The railroad industry is characterized by the fact that it requires a large capital investment and produces a relatively low rate of return. The industry has been the keystone of the national transportation system for a century; and, since 1930, it has been faced with problems of adjusting to the rise of new competitors, and the wide fluctuations in economic activity due to the depression of the 1930's and the Second World War. As the decade of the 1960's opens, the railroads face the future with confidence born of technological innovations and a century of experience in the transportation field.

---

[19] *Association of American Railroads, Its Organization and Activities* (Washington, D. C.: Association of American Railroads, 1949), pp. 2 ff.

MOTOR CARRIERS

The motor carrier industry performed more than 23 per cent of the total ton-mile transportation service in the United States in the early 1960's. The motor carrier industry is a very loosely organized group. Some motor carriers operate on a for-hire basis, others are private carriers, not-for-hire, carrying the property of the owner. These various categories will be more fully explained later in this chapter. The commercial motor carrier industry had its beginnings in the late years of the 1920's when the motor truck and the highway system became suitable for intercity transportation. By 1930, the intercity movement of goods by motor vehicle had become of moderate importance, and by 1935, it had reached a stage of maturity sufficient to require federal regulation as a part of the transport system.

The technological development of the automobile is well known. The motor truck is integral to the motor vehicle per se, since the early truck was a modified passenger car. Perhaps the concept of a truck in the modern sense, as a somewhat distinct vehicle from the automobile came to fruition during the First World War. From this time until the mid nineteen-twenties, the motor truck was widely used in local transportation. From 1925 on, technological progress both in vehicles and roads was rapid and intercity motor truck service became a reality. The industry grew very rapidly due largely to the ease of entry. Also, the truck performed many services such as store door delivery which the railroads had not been interested in up until that time.

Perhaps the most important technological advance in regard to the vehicle was the development in the late 1920's and early 1930's of the tractor semitrailer combination, (separate power unit and semitrailer); before this time the truck had been a single unit, very much limited in size. This factor coupled with the hard surface intercity road put the industry on the road to maturity.

Unlike the railroad, the typical motor carrier firm had very informal origins since the establishment of a motor carrier enterprise could be undertaken with a modest amount of capital. This fact has had a profound influence upon the organization and development of the motor carrier industry. It was possible for an individual to purchase a truck and add to his fleet with additional vehicles as his means allowed. In this way, a large organization could be built up unit by unit without any need for an immediate outlay of capital such as that necessary for railroad construction.

As a consequence, the sole proprietorship or partnership is still common in the motor carrier field. Even in those cases where the corporation is found, the stock is often closely held by a family or a few individuals. While there are some 700 railroads, there were approximately 18,000 regulated motor carrier firms in operation in 1960.[20] Many of these firms are very small, operating only two or three vehicles, and only a handful operate a thousand or more units. While railroad has a large investment in roadway and other real property, the typical motor carrier has an investment only in vehicles and a comparatively small amount of capital invested in terminals and other real property. In 1958, the average investment in operating property for Class I and II motor carriers was reported as $401,535.[21] In the same year the average Class I and II motor carrier operated 57.7 power units (tractors) and 179 semi-trailers.[22] Clearly, the typical motor carrier firm is relatively small, especially in comparison with railroads, and other transportation and public utility enterprises. Another unique. and significant factor is that truck ownership is still overwhelmingly in the hands of non-carriers. Only about ten per cent of the total trucks on the highway are for-hire vehicles, and even large trucks (40,000 lbs, gross weight) are owned and operated by a wide variety of non-carrier enterprises.[23]

Since the firm is small and often closely held, it is not surprising that the organization of the motor carrier is the typically simple line type with a flow of authority from the owner downward through the organization. However, in recent years, as motor carriers have become more widespread geographically, more sophisticated types of organization have become necessary. The managerial problem will be further considered in a later chapter.

The development of the motor carrier has been very rapid, and many of the founder figures are still active in the industry. Only in very recent years have motor carrier firms grown to large size with several companies now operating from coast to coast.

The development of the industry can logically be divided into three periods.

---

[20] Because many motor carriers are unregulated and are in many cases informal and engaged in for-hire trucking part time, no firm definition of a motor carrier "firm" or aggregate "industry" statistics are available.

[21] Source: *American Trucking Trends 1960*, American Trucking Associations, Inc. This figure includes investment in all trucks, tractors, semi-trailers, and other vehicles as well as land, buildings, furniture, tools, and shop equipment.

[22] *Ibid* p. 23.

[23] *Ibid*. p. 7. Of the almost 11 million trucks in operation, approximately 700,000 are large combination vehicles.

The Pioneer Years, 1920-1935

These years were those of experiment and exploration. The motor carrier industry was limited by technology of equipment and by the intercity highway system. In the late 1920's, progress began to be made on both these fronts, and the scope of motor carrier operations began to expand. While still premature by modern standards, the motor carrier had, by 1935, become a factor in the transportation industry.

The Industry Develops, 1935-1945

The decade, 1935-1945, began with the passage of the Motor Carrier Act in 1935 and ended with the conclusion of World War II in 1945. The first half of the decade was one of great growth and increasing stability as the industry adjusted itself to its new regulated status. The second half was marked by serious wartime shortages of fuel and other supplies and by traffic levels of new dimension.

Growth and Maturity, 1945-1960

The close of the war brought the motor carriers to the threshold of new development. Traffic levels remained high; and, with the return of normal conditions of supply, the motor carriers expanded rapidly. New equipment, improved methods of operation and control all had to be devised quickly. The industry grew within a few years from an essentially small scale local enterprise into a large and complex system. Most indicators point toward continued, though less rapid, growth for the future. As more of the founders of the present firms pass from the scene, the movement toward merger and consolidation should gain momentum, and the industry will doubtless change in character.

Capital Structure

The capital structure of the typical motor carrier reflects the limited size and relative simplicity of the enterprise. Motor carrier management has in the past preferred to obtain capital from internal sources, or from non-equity sources. In part, this program has been forced on the carriers through the early reluctance of the general public to acquire bonds or other senior securities in motor carrier enterprises, and the reluctance of the controlling interest to dilute control by the sale of common stock. A related factor is the rapid turnover of motor carrier capital which enables the firm to operate at a high level of business with modest working capital.

Consequently, the only pressing need for investment funds is for equipment acquisition. For various legal and economic reasons, the equipment trust as used by railroads is not open to motor carriers. Motor carrier equipment becomes obsolescent at a rapid rate and must be frequently replaced. The service life of a tractor (the power unit) is generally held to be five years. Although the semi-trailer has a longer life, the equipment trust of ten or twenty years' maturity is clearly not suitable. Consequently, motor carrier equipment has in the past been purchased through the use of conditional sale contracts, or personal loans. These methods impose a burden upon the carrier, and much thought is being given to the development of less costly financing methods, more suitable to the increased scale of operations to be carried on in the future. Only a few motor carrier enterprises have had recourse to the national capital markets and the industry is characterized by small modestly financed organizations.

The somewhat unique framework of the industry is illustrated by the way in which motor carrier services are offered to the public. While rail carriers attempt to provide transportation facilities for passengers, and all types of commodities within one organization, the motor carrier industry is highly specialized and segmented both as to type of service and commodity carried. These complexities are illustrated by Table 2-2. As this table indicates, the motor carrier

TABLE 2-2

TYPES OF MOTOR CARRIER CLASSIFIED BY
SERVICE OFFERED AND PRODUCTS CARRIED

Common Carriers
  Carriers of general freight
  Carriers of household goods
  Carriers of heavy machinery
  Carriers of liquid petroleum products
  Carriers of refrigerated solid products
  Carriers engaged in dump trucking
  Carriers of agricultural commodities (not exempt)
  Carriers of motor vehicles

TABLE 2-2 (Continued)

Carriers engaged in armored truck service
Carriers of building materials
Carriers of films
Carriers of forest products
Carriers of mine ores
Carriers engaged in retail delivery service
Carriers of explosives and dangerous items
Carriers of specific commodities not sub-grouped

Contract Carriers

That is, those offering their services on a contract basis and not holding themselves out to serve the general public.

Carriers Exempt from Economic Regulation

Those engaged in private carriage
Those engaged in carrying "unprocessed" agricultural products or other products and operating in a manner prescribed by the Interstate Commerce Act.

Passenger Carriers

Urban
Intercity

---

industry is made up of carriers classified as to commodity carried. Indeed, the specialized service offered is the hallmark, and one of the major competitive advantages of the motor carrier. In the motor transport field, the transportation of passengers is carried on by companies separate and distinct from the freight carriers.

Passenger carriage is generally of two types: (1) urban and (2) intercity. Urban bus transportation concerns the transportation of passengers within the metropolitan area, while intercity transportation is concerned with long distance intercity transportation. The intercity passenger carriers are generally of large size, extending over the entire nation, or at least large geographic areas. Intercity bus traffic while primarily concerned with passengers, is made up in part of mail and express, with the later "package" traffic becoming increasingly important. While intercity bus travel has increased greatly since 1940, rising from 10.2 billion intercity passenger miles to more than 21 billion miles in 1960, the increase has not been great in recent years, and in fact, a slight decline has taken place since 1946, a peak year. It seems likely that the increasing ownership of private cars, and the growth of air transportation along with gains in personal income, account for the failure of bus transportation to participate in the growth of traffic. The intercity bus industry is highly centralized with two broadly organized companies (each having many operating subsidiaries), accounting for a large share of nationwide bus transportation.

Advantages and Disadvantages

The great advantage of the motor carrier is its flexibility and accessibility to the shipper. No tracks or sidings are required, and the trucks or buses can give direct and immediate access to the transport vehicle. The reverse of this coin is, of course, the relatively small unit capacity of the vehicle relative to the power required to propel it. Because of its physical capacity and the various state weight limits, the motor truck can seldom carry more than from 20,000 to 50,000 pounds of payload, depending upon the conditions prevailing. Larger loads would thus require two or more vehicles with a corresponding increase in operating costs.

The flexibility of the truck also accounts for another substantial advantage, speed. While there is little or no difference in the absolute speed potential of surface vehicles (i.e., the miles per hour capacity of trucks and locomotives are about the same), the motor truck generally provides the shipper with superior service in regard to elapsed time (transit time), which is the ultimate measure of time for the shipper. Since the truck has no need to pass through classification yards and related facilities, it can proceed directly to the destination and especially on hauls of less than 300 to 500 miles, provide faster door-to-door service than the rail carriers. For distances in excess of 1,500 miles, e.g. coast to coast, transit times are more nearly equal with the rail having a slight advantage.

Since motor carriers are generally smaller organizations than railroads, the shipper may receive more personal attention and certain administrative matters such as claims for loss and damage often receive expedited service. Also, the fact that motor carriers are most often specialized insofar as goods carried is concerned, the shipper may find that the carrier gives special attention to his product. This factor is of great importance for special product shippers such as livestock or household goods.

Traffic Patterns

Motor carriers are so diverse in the geographic areas served and in the products they carry that no real pattern of traffic can be recognized. In general, motor carriers move relatively high value, light weight products, of a general merchandise nature. For the most part, the truck movement of bulky low value products is limited to short hauls. Since World War II, motor carriers have given more emphasis to the movement of trailer load traffic, and this traffic will no doubt continue to play an increasingly important part in the future. Also, motor carriers have altered the traffic pattern substantially by the increasing use of equipment interchange, and by extending the length of haul. Technological progress has also been influential. Growth of refrigerated traffic, bulk loading of various specialized commodities has expanded the range of cargoes moving by truck, all of which hinge upon technological advance.

Motor Carriers, Equipment and Operating Technology

The motor carrier has, in contrast to railroads, a simple operating technology, the basic element being the equipment. The tractor semi-trailer is the commonly used unit of equipment in intercity transportation. Unlike the rail equipment, motor transportation equipment is relatively unstandardized and is subject to rapid changes in design. Some twenty firms manufacture heavy trucks in the U.S., and a wide range of combinations of capacity, gear ratios, type of trailer, etc., is available. The service life of motor trucks is relatively short and is frequently reduced even further by technological innovation. These innovations do not occur as rapidly as they do in the passenger car field but much more rapidly than in the rail equipment market. Depending upon various factors such as funds available, geography, etc., the operator may elect to purchase high cost, heavy duty equipment ($25,000 for the tractor and trailer) or lighter, lower cost equipment ($12,000-$18,000) for the complete unit and replace the equipment more frequently. Single unit trucks are used for city pick-up and delivery and for small load, short intercity trips.

The key element in motor transport operations is the terminal. The terminal is the place where freight is processed, either outgoing or incoming, transferred from one vehicle or another, and where the business of the carrier is transacted. Local officials (or in the home terminal) and general officials have their offices here, and it serves as a general headquarters either for the system or for the local area.

The terminal manager is the keystone of the management structure. He is in charge not only of the terminal, but of the activities in and around that point, generally overseeing the activities of the drivers who work in and out of the terminal. Since there is no right of way between terminals, as is true of railroads, the terminal manager is the logical executive to supervise operations in his area. If, as in the case of some large carriers, there is a regional or area manager, he oversees several terminal managers who report to him.

Because of the large variety of firms of all sizes and the small size of most, there is not, in the true sense, a "typical" organization in the motor carrier industry. In almost every case, however, there is a direct flow of authority from the top down. The owner-founder, a common figure in the industry, is clearly the source of authority. Operations is the center of activity, and, except for the largest firms, there is little elaborate staff activity. Operating problems, although basically simple in concept, become complex as more and more area is added to the scope of operations. Equipment problems, labor relations, tax procedures and other difficulties form the major managerial burden.

Prospects for Growth and Development

The motor carrier industry is to all intents and purposes, still in the early stages of development. The industry, although it has enjoyed great growth, has existed on a national basis for only a few decades. Even twenty years ago, the industry was essentially local or regional in nature, and the interchange of freight was a precarious operation. Table 2-3 indicates the tremendous growth which has taken place in the industry over the last two decades. The American Trucking Associations estimate that by 1975 motor carriers will be supplying 700 billion ton-miles or 26% of the estimated 2,700 billion ton-miles of service performed by all inter-city carriers.

TABLE 2-3

ESTIMATED PERCENTAGE SHARES, INTERCITY TON-MILES,
SELECTED YEARS

Year	Rail	Motor	Inland Waterways	Air	Pipeline
1930	74.3	3.9	16.5	°	5.3
1940	61.3	10.0	19.1	°	9.6
1945	67.3	6.5	13.9	°	12.3
1950	56.2	16.3	15.4	°	12.1
1958	45.6	21.3	15.3	°	17.8
1959	45.0	22.3	15.2	°	17.5
1960	43.8	22.2	16.2	°	17.7

° Less than 1/10 of 1%.

Source: Interstate Commerce Commission, Bureau of Economics & Statistics.

The growth of population, the dispersal of industry, improved inter-city highways, and a more liberal attitude toward motor truck size and weight limits might be expected to facilitate such growth. As the study referred to above points out, the areas of the United States which are enjoying the greatest population increase, viz., the western and southwestern states, have relatively sparse rail networks. It seems likely that the motor carrier industry will experience substantial growth although some segments of the industry may be less fortunate than others. For example, it may be that private carriage by truck will become sufficiently important to alter the traditional pattern of common carrier service in the transportation industry. As is true of rail transport, many problems remain to be solved in the area of labor relations and intercarrier relations.

Perhaps the major problem facing motor carriers is their relationship to the public sector of the economy. Much thought still needs to be given to tax policies, size and weight limits and other factors which relate to the use of the highway system.

Motor Carriers and the Highway System

Basic to the future development of the motor transportation industry is the further extension and maintenance of the highway system, which as noted previously is the responsibility of the public sector of the economy.

Roughly speaking, the role of state and federal governments in road building and maintenance is of recent origin, with the first state aid coming in 1891 in New Jersey, and federal aid dating from 1916.

Prior to this time, highways were largely local in nature and were generally the responsibility of townships or counties. Such an arrangement was satisfactory for the local traffic of the day. Until the First World War, relatively little surfaced intercity highway mileage existed, and American road building, especially in rural areas, was a simple and inexpensive art. The increasing use of the automobile and later the truck made for enormous increases both in mileage and in quality of design and engineering. It must be noted however that not until the 1940's was there a real understanding of an intercity highway system. The roads built from 1920 to 1940 were high quality surfaced versions of the rural-urban roads of earlier years. It can be appreciated that the upgraded highways were far more costly than the local road system existing before 1920, and an entirely new concept of financing such expenditures was necessary. In pre-automobile days, the roads were supported essentially by local tax sources, principally proceeds from real estate taxes, and this arrangement proceeded for some years. No thought was given to taxes imposed upon highway users per se. At an early date, state and municipal governments began to issue license tags primarily for purposes of identification. It soon became clear that the tag, and after 1913, the fuel tax provided an ideal basis upon which to construct road taxes which thus began to be thought of as user fees paid directly by those who used the roads, viz., vehicle owners. City streets continued to be financed by general funds.

Following 1920, the rapid growth of automobile ownership forced substantial and far-reaching changes. Led by the state of Oregon, all states adopted the fuel tax, and most states began to gear the license tag fees to size-weight, or horsepower of the vehicle. Road building became a major state activity and has continued to be so.

In 1916, the federal government began to enter the road building area on a small scale. Although much discussion had taken place for some years, the first permanent plan of federal aid took form in the Federal Aid Road Act of 1916. This act focused attention on farm-to-market roads and $75 million was to be expended by the U. S. Department of Agriculture over a five-year period. More important was the fact that the act granted aid only to states exercising centralized control over road building, thus in effect, forcing the creation of state highway departments.

Further federal legislation of a minor nature continued until 1921 when a more significant change in emphasis took place. The Federal Highway Aid Act of 1921 further centralized control and increased the uniformity in road standards.

From 1922 to 1944, the basic elements of federal aid remained unchanged, although there were many minor modifications. The federal government continued to render aid on a matching funds basis, and to further encourage uniform standards. Much emphasis was placed upon the "economic pump priming" and relief aspects of road construction during the 1930's, and of course construction was largely suspended from 1941 to 1945, except for defense highway projects and basic maintenance.

Following the Second World War, a modern concept of highway planning and construction began to appear, as reflected in the Federal Aid Highway Act of 1944, and continued in the Act of 1956. The core of this concept was the interstate highway, viz., a highway designed to serve the needs of interstate traffic as opposed to local traffic. The interstate system as presently constituted is a system of some forty-one thousand miles connecting major population centers bypassing congested areas to expedite through-traffic. (See Figure 2-2.)

The years following the Second World War brought new and serious highway problems on two levels. First, it was clear that many new interstate highways must be built, and secondly, the existing highways were in need of repair and upgrading. Vehicles were increasing both in number and use. Unfortunately, also highway costs were rising rapidly and both federal and state governments were facing multiple demands for funds, other than highway construction. Consequently, great pressures arose to find new sources of highway revenue, and also to protect existing sources from the designs of other agencies in need of funds. As an example of how rapidly needs and costs advanced, it was estimated shortly before World War II that $4 billion was needed to improve and construct highways adequate to the needs at that time. By 1950, increasing needs and rising costs had raised the figure to more than $41 billion, and estimates for the ten-year period (1955-1964) placed costs at more than $126 billion.[24] Certainly figures of this magnitude raised serious questions as to public policy, as well as practical problems of finance. In many states, highway costs are a major part of the state budget. Aside from the magnitude of the figures themselves as part of the total public expenditure, the whole theory of highway taxes is undergoing change.

---

[24] Cited in Hudson and Constantin, *op. cit.*, pp. 73, 76.

THE NATIONAL SYSTEM OF INTERSTATE AND DEFENSE HIGHWAYS
STATUS OF IMPROVEMENT AS OF DECEMBER 31, 1962

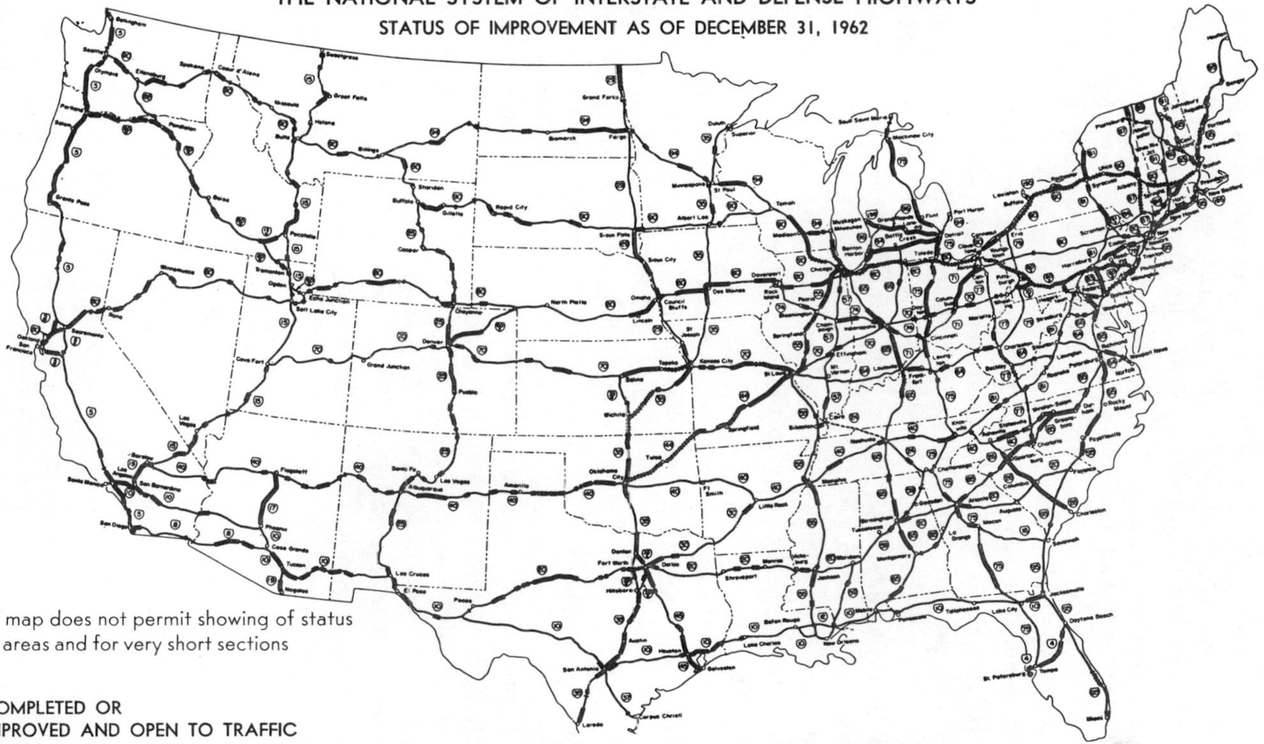

Scale of map does not permit showing of status
in urban areas and for very short sections

▬ COMPLETED OR
  IMPROVED AND OPEN TO TRAFFIC

  Completed to full or acceptable standards, or improved to standards
  adequate for present traffic; built with Interstate or other public funds.

▬▬▬ MAJOR TOLL ROADS

  Incorporated in the Interstate System.

— UNDER CONSTRUCTION

— REMAINING DESIGNATED SECTIONS

  Plan preparation and right-of-way acquisition completed or
  underway on many portions of these sections.

Fig. 2-2

Source: Bureau of Public Roads

For many years, as recounted above, highway users paid two basic types of tax, (1) registration (license fees) and (2) fuel taxes. Both these taxes had the virtues of simplicity and ease of collection.

License fees were collected annually based on weight or some related factor, and fuel taxes were collected at the time fuel was purchased. In the late 1950's, the combined revenue from these two taxes was almost $5 billion.[25] Fuel taxes ranged from 3 to 7 cents in 1956, and automobile registration fees ranged from $3 to $27. For trucks, the range was greater; a typical tractor semi-trailer (40,000 lbs. gross) could be registered for $45 in Colorado and $640 in Illinois.[26] For passenger cars, the wide diversity is not a serious problem, but for interstate trucks, the problem has serious consequences.

Numerous states imposed various and sundry fees, mostly minor and frequently applicable only to for-hire carriers, e.g., franchise or other fees.

In the early 1950's, the search for additional revenue led into new fields. State highway officials were of the opinion that fuel taxes had been increased as far as practicable and that, also, any increases in registration fees would meet substantial resistance. The result of this impasse was the adoption by several states of a third type of tax, viz., the weight-distance tax. This tax was calculated by imposing a fee based on weight multiplied by distance traveled. For example, a truck weighing 50,000 lbs. might pay 1 mill per mile. Unlike the fuel tax and registration fee, this tax was very complex and costly both to the state and the vehicle owner. Also, some doubts exist as to its ultimate worth as a producer of revenue. The trucking industry has expressed great dissatisfaction over the problem, although other highway user groups are more favorable. Another facet of the problem is that relationships between the states have become endangered through a lack of uniformity brought about by the tax.[27]

Unfortunately, the highway problem is still a long way from a

---

[25] Bureau of Public Roads.

[26] *Ibid.*

[27] A large body of literature has been created in this controversy. An excellent summary of the situation is found in *State Taxation of Interstate Trucking and the Reciprocity Problem*, 83d Congress, 2d Session (Committee Print) (Washington: Government Printing Office, 1955).

For a recent discussion of the effect of these "tax barriers" on interstate truck traffic, see J. Ayre, *Effects of State and Local Regulations on Interstate Movement of Agricultural Products*, Marketing Research Report No. 496, U. S. Department of Agriculture, July 1961.

solution. In 1956, the federal government began to impose certain taxes on highway users. Formerly, federal taxes on vehicles and their use had been part of the general tax structure. The federal use taxes are levied on tires, rubber, and upon truck use, as well as for purchase of the truck itself for heavy (27,000 lbs.) vehicles. This represents the first earmarking of federal funds from highway use. These funds are to be deposited in a trust fund for use in highway construction.

Although highway user fees are well entrenched, a good case can be made for financing highways from general funds, since the benefits of adequate highways go far beyond the actual user. On the other hand, segregating funds for highway use exclusively may bind the governing authorities into a fiscal straitjacket. Although motor carriers are not the only users of highways, they are often marked for special treatment, since they operate large vehicles and since they use the highways for business purposes. The relationship between highway carriers and the public authorities in relation to other highway users is likely to be one of the most pressing motor carrier problems for some years to come.

Functions of the American Trucking Associations, Inc.

Like the Association of American Railroads, the American Trucking Associations is engaged in both legislative and public relations activities and industry-wide standardization and cooperative activities. The A.T.A. is not so comprehensive in its work as the A.A.R., and it faces a much more difficult task because of the great diversity in the trucking industry.

However, the A.T.A. serves as a clearing house for the increasingly industry-wide problems resulting from trailer interchange, safety, labor relations and other problems common to the motor carriers. Unlike the A.A.R., the A.T.A. is a federation of the various state motor carrier organizations. Because of the impact of state taxes and other motor carrier regulations, state trucking activities are of great importance.

While the A.A.R. has as its members all the major railroads, the A.T.A., because of the diversity of membership, does not enjoy such comprehensive membership. Also, many groups within the A.T.A. do not hold wide common interests (e.g., the household goods carriers and the petroleum carriers); consequently, they often pull in opposite directions.

Summary

As we have seen in this section, the motor carrier industry has, in a short period of time, grown from a very small part of the transport system to a major factor in the industry. Although there are firms of large size in the industry, the small motor carrier still plays a dominant part in the industry.

Motor carrier firms, unlike railroads, are highly specialized, and the common carrier segment of the industry is divided into specialized groups, depending upon the commodity transported.

Future growth and development seem to be favorable, but many problems are present. Perhaps, the most pressing problem facing the industry is the close and necessary relationship with the public sector in view of the use of the highway system. Motor carrier fees and taxes have developed largely on a catch as catch can basis, and there is a clear need for further thought in these areas.

THE AIR CARRIERS

Air carriers are the newest member of the transportation industry. As might be expected, the air carrier share of the total transportation market has grown rapidly in recent years. In 1960, airlines performed 48 per cent of all passenger service performed in the economy. Although substantial growth has taken place in cargo movements, the transportation of freight by air still accounts for a very small part of the total ton-miles of service performed, being about 500 million in 1958, as compared to 551 billion for railroads in the same year.[28]

The largest and most influential segment of the airline industry is made up of the domestic trunk lines, i.e., those carriers operating over long distances between the principal cities of the United States. In 1960, there were twelve such lines. The second group of air carriers consists of the domestic local service lines. These thirteen lines operate on a regional basis, largely serving as feeders to the trunk lines and seldom serving more than a few states or cities. (See Figure 2-3.) It is obvious that the airline industry differs in several basic respects from the railroad and motor carrier industry. In the first place, the number of airline operators is extremely small. Opportunities to establish a profitable airline are geographically limited, whereas railroads, and especially motor carriers, can operate to and from innumer-

---

[28] *Air Transport Facts and Figures*, Air Transport Association, 1958.

able points. Secondly, the trunk lines portion of the industry serves widely divergent points. In fact, four of the twelve trunk carriers serve both east and west coasts, and the others serve large portions of the United States, as well as foreign points. One of these lines (Pan American) operates entirely between cities in the United States and points outside the U. S. Thirdly, the air carriers are only to a small degree involved with the movement of goods. While freight and express movement by air is increasing in importance, the airlines are still passenger oriented.

In addition to the airlines listed in the following tables, there are smaller lines serving the territorial areas, all cargo or all mail lines and helicopter lines. In all, there are fifty-six air carriers of all types based in the United States. The larger carriers fall into various categories, and the reader will notice that there is much duplication between the carriers listed in Table 2-4. Pan American is the only carrier operating solely between U. S. points and overseas points. Also, while there are six all-freight lines, most of the major U. S. trunk lines carry on freight operations in addition to passengers.

More than fifty foreign "flag" lines operate into the United States, but not within it, linking foreign countries with American cities, e.g., New York, Miami and San Francisco. None of these lines offers domestic service, but they compete with American carriers to and from foreign points throughout the world.[29]

Origin and Development

The air carrier industry had its origin in the early years of the present century and developed largely from the early operations in

TABLE 2-4

U. S. AIRLINES BY CLASS, 1962

Domestic Trunk Lines, 1962	
American	National
Braniff	Northeast
Continental	Northwest
Delta	Trans World
Eastern	United
	Western

[29] For an excellent discussion of the early years of the industry emphasizing the economic factors underlying its development, see Henry L. Smith, *Airways: A History of Commercial Aviation in the United States* (New York: Alfred A. Knopf, 1942).

TABLE 2-4 (Continued)

Domestic Local Service Lines, 1961

Allegheny	Ozark
Bonanza	Pacific
Central	Piedmont
Frontier	Southern
Lake Central	Trans Texas
Mohawk	West Coast
North Central	

Major U. S. International Air Carriers, 1961

American	Pan American
Braniff	Pan American-Grace
Delta	Trans World
Eastern	United
Northwest	Western

Source: Air Transport Association, *Air Transport Facts and Figures.*

the carriage of mail and express.[30] By 1940, the carriage of mail, which, in 1931, had accounted for 82 per cent of total income, had declined to 26 per cent and, by 1960, to less than 1 per cent for the domestic trunk lines. However, for the local service lines, mail revenue continued to be important, accounting for almost one-third of the total revenue in the latter years.[31] From the carriage of a few passengers, more or less incidental to mail transportation, the airlines have achieved a position in passenger transportation which accounts for almost half of the total revenue passenger mile service performed by common carriers.[32]

TABLE 2-5

AIRLINE SHARE OF DOMESTIC
INTERCITY PASSENGER MILES, SELECTED YEARS

Year	% of Total Airline Share
1939	2.3
1949	11.4
1955	32.9
1956	35.9
1958	43.3
1960	43.9 est.

Source: *Air Transport Facts and Figures.*

[30] Various factors, especially the over-capacity created by the jet plane, have intensified this competition and may create serious problems. See John McDonald, "Pan Am: Peril and Opportunity," *Fortune*, August 1962.

[31] *Air Transport Facts and Figures*, Air Transport Association, 1958.

[32] *Ibid.*

As Table 2-5 indicates, the growth of air passenger transportation has been rapid in the years following World War II. While air freight has been increasing in importance, it still constitutes less than one-tenth of 1 per cent of the total freight moved by all carriers.

The growth of the commercial airline industry can be divided into essentially two periods. The years 1930-1945 cover the early growth and development of the passenger carrying industry. While air mail was carried on a regular basis from 1918 on, passenger travel was of minor importance before 1930. From 1930 until World War II, progress in technology and equipment was rapid. On the eve of the war, the Douglas DC-3 had become the standard aircraft for the trunk airlines. Like the motor carriers, the pace of airline progress was somewhat dampened by the war but resumed with great vigor immediately afterward.

The years from 1945 to 1960 were devoted to what has been called the "jet age." The piston-powered aircraft gave way by progressive stages to the jet airliner and gave rise also to serious financial and operational problems. The future of the airlines seems assured, but they face severe managerial and financial tests before their growth is complete.

Type of Organization and Capital Structure

The airline industry is characterized by a large investment in equipment and facilities, despite the fact that airways and airports are largely publicly supported. The modern airliner is an expensive piece of equipment and requires an elaborate and costly array of technical personnel and instruments to keep it in safe operation. Also, through technical developments and pressures of competition, it has been necessary or desirable to alter and replace this equipment at frequent intervals. Consequently, capital requirements have been high and continue to rise, even though there is no need for right of way expenditures.

Most significant in the rising capital requirements is the cost of the planes operated by the modern airline. In 1947-48, the airlines were able to purchase the Douglas DC-6, a plane seating fifty-two, for an average price of $640,000 each. The largest commercial plane then available was the Boeing "Strato-cruiser," which cost up to $3,000,000, depending upon various factors. The jet aircraft available in 1960 range in price from $5,000,000 to $7,000,000 each, not including the investment in parts and equipment nor in crew training and orientation. While the large jet planes can carry up to one hundred fifty passengers, the increased capacity must be intensively utilized to offset the increase in equipment costs.[33]

To add to these problems, airlines face growing problems of disposing of obsolete aircraft. In past years, small lines provided a ready market for planes cast off by the trunk lines. Because of the higher carrying capacity of the large piston planes and airport limitations, the local service lines no longer provide a satisfactory market.

While airport costs, per se, are still borne chiefly by governmental organizations, carrier ground equipment and facilities necessary for adequate loading and unloading of passengers, handling of cargo, luggage and servicing or refueling become much more costly as planes and airports increase in size.

However, it must always be kept in mind that investment per passenger or per-passenger mile will become more favorable, provided the load factor (passengers per number of available seats) is kept at a high level. Jets not only carry more passengers per plane, but their speed makes many trips possible in a given period of time. Thus, investment and costs per passenger mile could be reduced greatly if load factors are favorable and more passengers can be carried per day or week with fewer planes.

Consequently, the jet may enable the airlines to become truly mass transport agencies and to reduce unit costs accordingly. Because the jet is a relatively new plane, the airlines have, as yet, comparatively little experience relative to costs of operation and economic matters in general. In the early stages of an innovation, it is most difficult to measure the net effects, although it is clear that the jet has had an impact upon the capital structure of the airlines even greater than was the case with the piston aircraft.

Until World War II, capital requirements were modest; and, in fact, many airlines were closely controlled by individuals or groups, with little dependence upon outside sources for capital. However, the increasing costs of equipment, and the expansion of the airlines after World War II, made wide distribution of ownership necessary, and the trunk lines now rely heavily on outside sources for capital.

In 1947, six of the then major airlines reported large holdings by individuals.[34] By 1960, most of these holdings had been diluted through death and public sale of securities. TWA, the last major

---

[33] Cost figures from Air Transport Association and "International Airlines, the Great Jet Gamble," *Fortune*, June 1958.

[34] Civil Aeronautics Board; company reports.

airline under personal control (Howard Hughes, through Hughes Tool Company) had submitted to substantial outside control in order to facilitate jet purchase loans.[35]

Since airline equipment is short lived with questionable resale value and the airlines own little real property or other assets, it has been necessary to rely on loans or on issues of common stock as a capital source. Unfortunately, since airline earnings are regulated by public authority, common stocks of airlines have never been held in high regard. Much of the capital for equipment has come from loans made by insurance companies and other financial institutions, as well as the manufacturers of equipment. For various reasons the equipment trust as widely used by railroads has never been popular in the airline industry.[36]

Type of Organization

Like other large enterprises, the airlines are organized as corporations and have an operating organization similar to that of rail and motor carriers. However, since airlines have developed in an era of rapid communication, they are somewhat more centralized in management than other carriers, with substantial emphasis upon staff functions.

Largely because of the emphasis on safety, the airlines have put great stress on problems related to operations, and a large number of employees devote their time to weather analysis and other efforts which need little or no attention by other carriers. The international character of airline operations does present some problems which are unique. However, there is no evidence that these matters are more burdensome than domestic managerial problems, except on a policy level.

Services Offered

While airlines concentrate their efforts on passenger transportation, movement of mail, express and freight is of importance to them. Originally, passenger service was of one type, and airlines stressed

---

[35] *Fortune*, May 1961.

[36] In addition to the short life of the equipment, the question of legal liability has caused lenders to shy away from this instrument, although lenders are willing to accept a mortgage since it does not involve ownership by the lender.

the luxury aspects of air travel and non-price factors such as meal service and personal attendance. Following World War II, the rise of competition from non-scheduled flights forced the airlines to introduce "coach" class flights stressing low cost and a minimum of services.

Advantages and Disadvantages

The outstanding advantage of air travel is speed. No other form of transportation can approach the aircraft in speed of travel over long distances. Aside from the more obvious advantages to the passenger, speed has great influence in efficient utilization of equipment. Thus, even though the capacity of the largest aircraft is very limited relative to a train or ship, it can, through rapid turn-around, carry a surprisingly large number of passengers between two points in a given time.

Clearly, the major disadvantage is the high unit cost of transportation. In addition to limited capacity, the unit of movement requires expensive protective and handling devices between and at terminals. While the capacity of the aircraft has been steadily increasing, the effects of the increase have been somewhat diminished by costs of terminal and operational facilities and the necessity for moving terminals further from urban areas. Larger planes require that airports be more remote from urban areas, thus increasing costs and time required to reach the plane from downtown points. While most of these costs are paid by the traveler or shipper and are relatively minor as a part of the total cost of movement, they must be counted as a disadvantage. A closely related problem is the fact that air travel costs are such that large volume is necessary to bear them and that the flight must be of such length as to make the operation economical. This means that large cities are heavily served by airlines while smaller points may be ignored. Airlines generally encounter serious competition at terminal points of importance, e.g., New York, Chicago, Washington, D. C., while mid-points may be served by only one line.[37] To some degree, this characteristic is also found in other modes of transport. However, railroads, and especially motor carriers, can operate on a very small scale and profitably serve a number of points in a geographically restricted area.

---

[37] The June 1960 issue of the Official Airline Guide indicates that Washington, D. C., is served by 15 airlines and Chicago by 19. Omaha, a typical midpoint city is served by 5 lines.

Traffic Patterns

Air traffic patterns, for obvious reasons, follow the route patterns outlined above. That is, the number of passengers moving between major cities is such as to allow a great number of and variety of flights. Since airlines are passenger oriented to a high degree, schedules must be arranged with the convenience of passengers in mind. Consequently, smaller points may have not only fewer flights, but these flights may have been scheduled so as to provide convenient service to the major cities. Traffic flow, thus, tends to be very uneven with heavy concentration at certain key points. Mail, express and freight tend to follow roughly the same pattern; however, data on commodity movements by air are almost non-existent. Obviously, air freight is composed almost entirely of high value products, which must be marketed with great speed. By undertaking to move a wide variety of products and by broadening the classes of passenger service offered, the airlines have expanded their market greatly in the years since World War II.

As Frederick points out, the airlines are reaching a stage of over-capacity, where they must compete as effectively as possible to maintain their market. Much improvement must be made in scheduling, passenger and baggage handling, and other areas in order to realize the true potential of air travel markets.[38]

Airline Equipment and Operation

As we have seen, airlines have the most serious equipment problems from the standpoint of obsolescence. Airline equipment, except for the brief period of the DC-3 (1936-1945), has never been in any sense standardized. To a large extent, the managerial and operating practices have had to be formulated as they occurred, and little in the way of standardized practice has been possible in the relatively short period of airline existence.

The total airline fleet is small in comparison to the units of equipment operated by other modes. In the early 1960's, there were nine more or less standard types of aircraft operated by the domestic U. S. airlines.[39] Somewhat more than 1,800 planes were operated in 1960.

---

[38] John H. Frederick, *Commercial Air Transportation* (5th ed.; Homewood, Illinois: Richard D. Irwin Company, 1961), pp. 403 ff.

[39] Douglas, Viscount, Lockheed, Gruman, Convair, Martin, Boeing, Fairchild and Curtis. Roughly 1,000 of these planes are Douglas planes, ranging from the DC-3 to the DC-8. Data from the Federal Aviation Agency, Statistics Division.

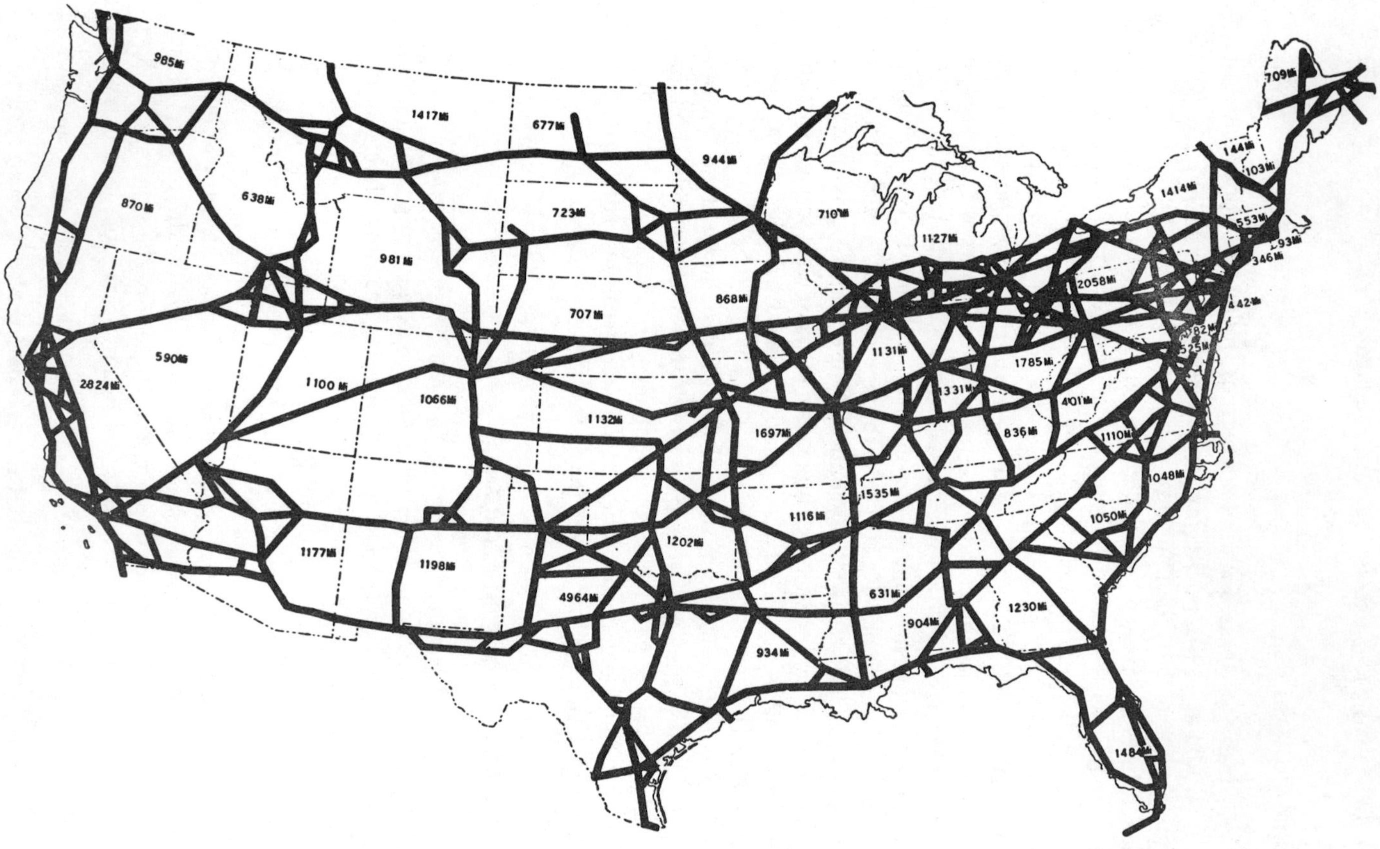

Fig. 2-3   U. S. Trunk Airlines 1960.

Source: Civil Aeronautics Board

Aircraft standardization is very important for airlines, since they must make a sizable investment in parts and supplies, in addition to the aircraft itself. The airlines have found (as have motor carriers) that standardization is hard to achieve. Not only is there the problem of rapid technological advance, there is also the complication of planes acquired by merger.[40] Also, no complete standardization can be worked out because of the varying needs. A large airline has to supply planes for non-stop flights nation-wide or transocean and also short flights of one hundred miles.

Operating problems have been severe, and, in many ways, the technical difficulties attendant to keeping aircraft in safe operation have been more complex than those of any other carrier. Although such activities as safety, weather analysis and other matters require much time and effort, airlines have kept other activities at a minimum. One unique factor in airline management has been their awareness of public relations and advertising. They spend more for this activity than any other carrier and have doubtless reaped considerable benefits from these expenditures. It is estimated that airlines spend $3.62 out of each $100 in revenue for public relations purposes in contrast to the 13.9 cents spent by railroads out of the same amount.[41]

Airways and Public Aid

The airlines have benefited greatly from public interest in air transport, both civil and military. Following World War I, military expenditures were instrumental in the development of improved aircraft; and federal, state and local funds were significant in the provision of airways and airports. It has been noted previously that the granting of airmail contracts was of material aid in financing the operations of the early airlines.

As indicated above, the major airlines have become substantially independent of airmail payments, although the feeder lines still receive substantial "public service revenue." However, it seems likely that much public aid will continue to be necessary for the provision of larger airports, and especially for air traffic control. The tremendous growth of air traffic, both civil and military, had created a serious control problem by 1950. Immense amounts of capital are necessary

---

[40] For example, United Airlines has for many years operated Douglas planes as standard. When the Capital fleet was acquired in 1960, it included a number of Viscounts.

[41] *National Transportation Policy, op. cit.,* p. 329.

to provide the complex equipment needed to assure adequate air traffic control. Since expenditures of this nature are beyond the capabilities of the airlines and, also, in view of the fact that the operation of military and private aircraft is a factor of importance, it seems likely that public funds must be used to defray the bulk of these expenditures.

Airlines pay certain user charges in the form of landing fees, rentals and related charges, but little doubt exists that these fees cover only a small portion of the total costs of the service. As is true of motor carriers and has been true of railroads in the past, there is an element of subsidy in the air carrier industry, although the extent of this subsidy is a matter of great debate.

In 1959, the Administrator of the Federal Aviation Agency estimated the total federal aid to airports since 1933 at $2,681,762,412.[42] This figure does not include sums spent by airlines on terminal equipment and facilities. Unfortunately, there seems to be general agreement that the present airway and airport system is barely adequate for safe operation in the jet age. Even before jets, increasing traffic had thrown a serious load on the airway system. Clearly, much remains to be done in the areas of traffic control and airport construction, both involving tremendous expenditures. Consequently, some further expenditure of public funds seems to be inevitable if any real progress is to be made. The problem is complicated by the fact that there are competing control systems; and, to a large degree, the whole area of airport design and traffic control is in a constant state of flux.

Indeed, the entire art of airport construction and operation is undergoing major re-evaluation. In the early years, airports were often located purely by chance and seldom by design. With large planes and more dense traffic, problems such as loading, claiming baggage and other factors, which were formerly of little circumstance, become of major importance. In the pre-jet age, airports separated by twenty miles presented no air traffic problem. When jet traffic becomes significant, the control problems are vastly multiplied. For example, in the fifty mile radius from the center of Washington, D. C., there are seven major civil and military airports and several private small fields. A jet passenger plane could fly through this circle (100 miles) in approximately ten minutes. Friendship Airport in Baltimore and Dulles Airport south of Washington are separated by roughly sixty ground miles, a distance which could be traversed by a jet in slightly more than five minutes.

---

[42] Quoted in J. H. Frederick, *op. cit.*, p. 42.

Problems in Growth and Development

As the youngest of the various means of transport, the airlines have tremendous potential growth. However, they have, in the past, been prone to overestimate their market in the immediate future. The capital requirements of buying and maintaining modern aircraft are tremendous, to say nothing of those for traffic control and airports which have largely been ignored by the airlines in the past. As airlines enter the jet age, these problems are especially pressing. Many serious problems of adjusting the short run demand for air travel to the increased capacity of this new equipment are yet far from solution. Some more adequate means of financing equipment must be worked out. It seems likely that this problem will become especially acute as the armed forces move away from manned aircraft into the missile area and, thus, put more of the developmental cost burden upon commercial aircraft users. Increasing stress also seems to be in the offing in the area of labor relations. Clearly, these problems will call for all the managerial talent the airlines can muster.

The airlines, in the relatively short period of their existence, have come to dominate the for-hire carriage of passengers. Their freight operations are still negligible but will doubtless become more significant as time passes. Airlines, like motor carriers, have to overcome problems in their relations with the public in use of facilities. Major problems have arisen in recent years with the need of more adequate financial operations due largely to the increasing costs of capital equipment. These problems are likely to be overcome as the scale of operations increases.

Selected References for Further Study

Various works are available relating to the specific modes which discuss the development, operation and other problems in more detail.

In the rail field, the following works are typical of those available. For a general discussion of the organization and operation of the industry, although somewhat dated, see Henry, Robert S., *This Fascinating Railroad Business* (New York: Bobbs-Merrill Company, 1942). Many volumes exist relating to the historical development of specific carriers or regions, as well as the standard texts in the field of economic history, e.g., Shannon, Fred A., *America's Economic Growth* (New York: Macmillan Company, 1940), and Faulkner, Harold U., *American Economic History* (6th edition; New York: Harper & Brothers, 1949).

Motor Transportation: Hudson, William J., and Constantin, James, *Motor Transportation* (New York: Ronald Press Company, 1958); Taff, Charles A., *Commercial Motor Transportation* (3d edition; Homewood, Illinois: Richard D. Irwin, Inc., 1961). For an interesting account of the historical growth of a typical motor carrier, see Broehl, Wayne G., Jr., *Trucks, Trouble and Triumph* (Englewood Cliffs, N. J.: Prentice-Hall, Inc., 1954).

Air Transportation: Frederick, John H., *Commercial Air Transportation* (5th edition; Homewood, Illinois: Richard D. Irwin, Inc., 1961). An informal and well-written history of the early development of air transportation is found in Smith, H. Ladd, *Airways* (New York: Knopf, 1942).

The periodical literature is an excellent source of current and historical material in all fields. *Modern Railroads,* Modern Railroads Publishing Company, Chicago, is an excellent source of rail information. For the more general reader, *Trains,* Kalinbach Publishing Company, Milwaukee, is directed to the lay reader. *Traffic World,* Traffic Service Corporation, Washington, D. C., is a weekly publication with thorough coverage of legislative activities and traffic management matters.

In the motor field, the publication of the American Trucking Association, *Transport Topics,* is a good source of current information.

The various publications of the associations, Association of American Railroads, American Trucking Associations, Inc., The Air Transport Association and The American Waterway Operators Association are all valuable sources of data and, of course, the viewpoints of the various modes.

Publications of the Interstate Commerce Commission, The Civil Aeronautics Board and other federal agencies are highly recommended and, especially, special studies such as the Report of the Study Group Prepared for the Committee on Interstate and Foreign Commerce, U. S. Senate (Pursuant to S. Res. 29, 151, and 244, 86th Congress), more widely known as the Doyle Report.

CHAPTER III

Water Carriers, Pipelines, and the Indirect Carriers

WATER CARRIERS

The water carriers to be described in this section are the inland waterway carriers and the carriers operating on the Great Lakes and the coastal waterways. (See Figure 3-1.) The inland water carriers moved roughly 15 per cent of the total tonnage in 1958, on a ton-mile basis, and an estimated 2.3 per cent of the total passenger miles.[1]

Origin and Development

The inland waterways represent the oldest form of transportation of all the modes now in use. The inland waterway system consists of the natural and artificial waterways, approximately 27,000 miles.[2]

---

[1] I C C Bureau transport economics and statistics.

[2] Even the "natural" waterways require a substantial degree of maintenance and modification in order to be used efficiently in commerce. Of the 27,000 miles referred to above, some 4,000 miles—New York State Barge Canal; the Mississippi, Ohio, Monongahela and Missouri Rivers; and the Illinois Waterway—are by far the most important. All of these waterways require substantial routine maintenance aside from any artificial structures, such as locks, dams, and navigational aids.

The development of the inland waterway system falls generally into two periods: the first period, the years of its original development from Colonial times to about 1860, when the Civil War, followed by the interest in railroads, largely superseded progress in waterway development; and the second period, soon after 1900 when a revival of waterway shipping took place stimulated by federal interest. This movement became especially strong after 1920 and reached its apex during the Hoover Administration.

The history of waterways is interesting, in that it represents a mode of transportation which has passed through various stages of development. From Colonial times, waterway transportation was significant and formed a large part of our national history. Both freight and passenger carriage, which reached substantial levels before the Civil War, fell to very low levels in the face of rail competition. Passenger traffic of the type which flourished on the western rivers in pre-Civil War days has never been revived, but freight traffic has enjoyed a resurgence.

Waterway traffic, due to its nature, has never enjoyed the spectacular growth common in the air and motor transportation industries.

Much of the future development of the waterways seems likely to hinge on the economic factors involved in user charges and the public policy relative to waterway improvements. These questions will be further explored in later chapters.

Inland waterways depend for their development upon public support, since few, if any, of the natural waterways can be successfully navigated by modern commercial craft without some improvement; and the magnitude of these improvements requires public aid. Aid to waterways has always occupied a somewhat privileged position in the United States, congressional efforts along these lines being largely exempt from serious attempts at reduction, since the multipurpose project has wide appeal.[3]

The present waterway system consists, for the most part, of several well-defined areas, as noted below. The degree of work which must be done, as well as the way in which operations are carried on, differs greatly among the various systems.

The Great Lakes and St. Lawrence Seaway. The Great Lakes system provides, via the St. Lawrence Seaway (opened in 1959), inland access for ocean going vessels. While the total tonnage moving on the Great Lakes is very impressive, it must be understood that

---

[3] Few, if any, of the present waterway improvements are for navigation only. Flood control, electric power, recreation, and water conservation are also important.

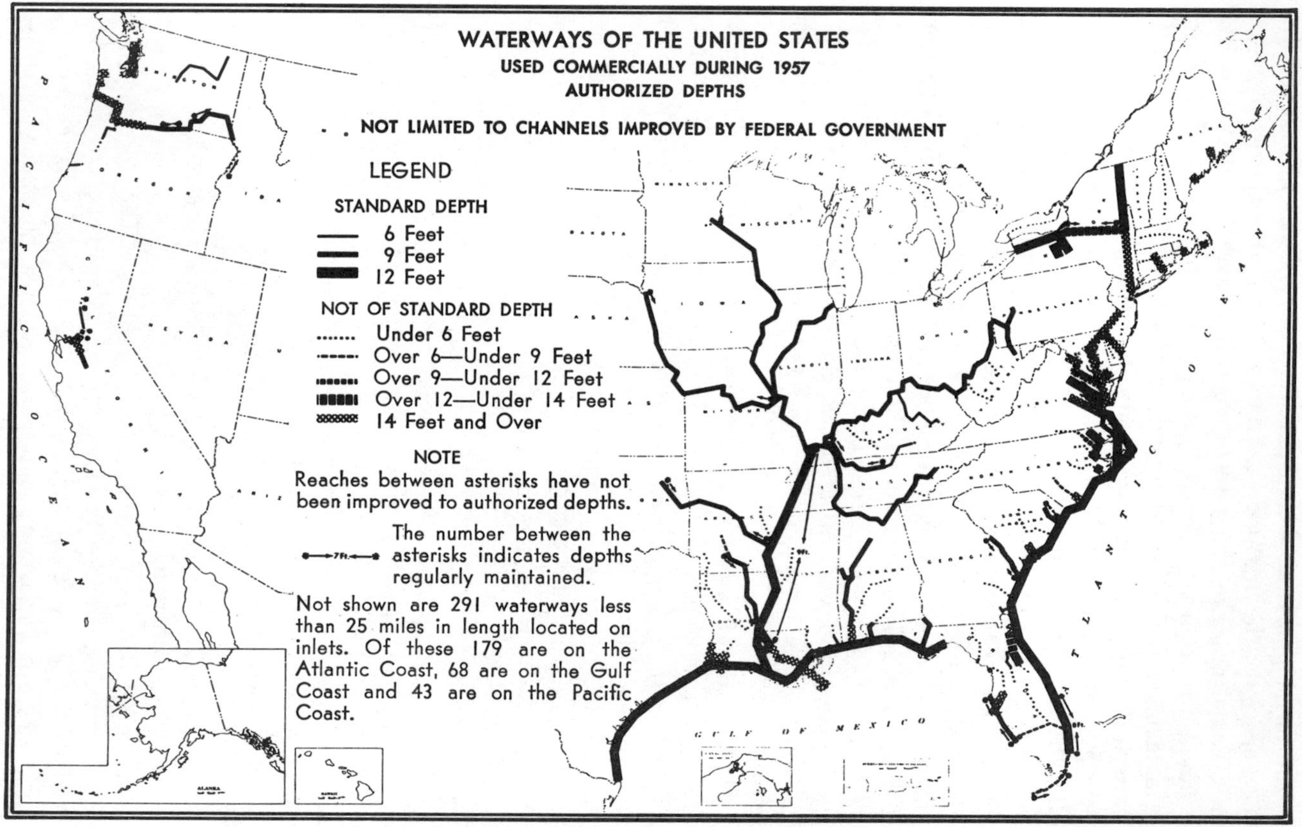
WATERWAYS OF THE UNITED STATES
USED COMMERCIALLY DURING 1957
AUTHORIZED DEPTHS
. . NOT LIMITED TO CHANNELS IMPROVED BY FEDERAL GOVERNMENT
LEGEND
STANDARD DEPTH
6 Feet
9 Feet
12 Feet
NOT OF STANDARD DEPTH
Under 6 Feet
Over 6—Under 9 Feet
Over 9—Under 12 Feet
Over 12—Under 14 Feet
14 Feet and Over
NOTE
Reaches between asterisks have not been improved to authorized depths.
The number between the asterisks indicates depths regularly maintained.
Not shown are 291 waterways less than 25 miles in length located on inlets. Of these 179 are on the Atlantic Coast, 68 are on the Gulf Coast and 43 are on the Pacific Coast.
PACIFIC OCEAN
ATLANTIC OCEAN
GULF OF MEXICO
ALASKA

Fig. 3-1 *Source: Inland Waterways Operators Association*

much of this tonnage is made up of iron ore, coal, and other bulk commodities. It is likely that the variety of products carried will increase substantially now that the St. Lawrence Seaway is in operation.[4]

Vessels used on the Great Lakes are essentially the same as those in ocean going trade, insofar as design and capacity are concerned. Very little traffic on the lakes is operated by common carriers, almost all consisting of private traffic. The Seaway has a twenty-seven foot channel, and work is underway to dredge channel and harbor depth in lake ports to this depth.[5]

Mississippi, Illinois, Ohio, and Tennessee River System. These rivers and their tributaries, which for present purposes can be considered a unit, form the heart of the inland waterway system. In combination, these rivers tap some twenty-five states in the mid-section of the United States. Traffic of this section is largely carried by barge and towboat. As on the lakes, much of this traffic consists of bulk materials of a private nature. However, there are several for-hire barge lines providing scheduled service, especially on the Mississippi and Ohio. Variety of traffic is greater on the inland waterways than on the Great Lakes, although steel, iron, coal, and petroleum still account for the bulk of traffic. Traffic patterns on the river systems are very uneven. For example, traffic on the Ohio and Monongahela Rivers, while very large in tonnage, often moves relatively short distances. Iron ore, steel shapes, etc., may move from one plant to another only a short distance away, often by private or contract carrier. (See Table 3-2.)

Domestic Deep Sea and Coastal Waterways. Domestic deep sea traffic moves from U. S. ports to other U. S. ports by ocean and inland bays such as the Chesapeake Bay-Delaware ship canal. The intercoastal protected waterways are useful principally for small craft and, except in isolated cases, are of much less commercial importance. The intercoastal waterway system still requires substantial work in order to be entirely useful for large craft. Further, since this waterway makes use of lagoons, inlets, bays, and coastal rivers, it, like the river system, will require continuous maintenance in order to remain navigable.

On the Pacific coast, the Columbia River in Washington and Oregon and the Sacramento River in California are the only inland

---

[4] See, for example, *Potential Effects of St. Lawrence Seaway on Costs of Transporting Grain*, M.R.R. No. 319, Marketing Research Division, U. S. Department of Agriculture (Washington: Government Printing Office, April 1959).

[5] *Waterways of the United States* (New York: National Association of River and Harbor Contractors, 1961).

waterways of importance to commercial shipping. The Pacific coast, unlike the Atlantic and Gulf coasts, does not lend itself to coastal water development.

Type of Organization

Water carriers bear some resemblance to highway carriers, in that they operate their own equipment on the publicly provided right of way. Also, a large amount of the traffic moving on waterways is carried by private and contract carriers. Since the acquisition of barges, tugs and other types of water equipment requires a large investment, the industry is organized most frequently on a corporate basis, although there are a number of small scale operators.

Table 3-1 shows the amounts and types of equipment used by the estimated 1,700 operators in 1959.

TABLE 3-1

EQUIPMENT IN USE ON INLAND WATERWAYS, 1959

Towing vessels	4,139
Dry cargo barges and scows	13,902
Tank barges	2,387
Total vessels	20,428

Source: Inland Waterways Operators Association.

Since 1940, much progress has been made in equipment technology. The all-steel diesel towboat has replaced the steam boat, and much progress has been made in standardized barges. A modern 6,000 horsepower towboat can handle a tow of twenty barges with ease at 6-8 miles per hour, depending upon river conditions. Various electronic and power devices have greatly improved steering and navigation efficiency. These technological improvements have also had an influence upon the ability of firms to enter the industry and compete with success with existing firms. A modern diesel towboat costs several million dollars, depending upon size and accommodations. A firm hoping to compete in trade on the Ohio River, for example, would require several towboats and a number of barges. A contract carrier often utilizes barges belonging to the shipper and may also use loading and unloading equipment docks and other necessary items provided by the shipper. In any event, the ease of entry which has always marked the waterway industry is very likely not as great as it has been in the past.

Type of Service Offered and Traffic Patterns

In view of the fact that traffic which can move economically by water is limited, both by type and location, the range of products which makes up water traffic is fairly narrow. Because the greatest disadvantage of water transport is lack of speed, only those products in which rapid movement is unimportant can move in any volume by water. As shown by Table 3-2, petroleum, ore, sand, gravel, steel products, chemicals, and other heavy products moving in bulk make up the predominant share of waterway traffic.

Some general merchandise traffic does move on scheduled service, especially on the Ohio and Mississippi, but, in terms of tonnage, this service is relatively unimportant. The great significance of a few products in water traffic has made private carriage very significant. Steel companies, refineries, and others who can use water service to advantage find it feasible to acquire equipment for their own use. This is especially true of shippers who require some specialized facility to move liquid loads, such as chemicals, or other material in bulk. The degree of private carriage intensifies the nature of water traffic to be somewhat unbalanced. Few water carriers, especially those moving bulk materials, can enjoy return traffic; thus, the economies must be great enough to offset this disadvantage.

TABLE 3-2

COMPOSITION OF INLAND WATER TRAFFIC

Commodity	Tonnage	Per Cent
Petroleum and petroleum products	134,215,943	32.5
Bituminous coal and lignite	86,776,396	22.5
Sand, gravel, crushed rock	52,014,333	13.3
Sea shells, unmanufactured	22,203,976	5.1
Grain and grain products	7,762,227	2.0
Iron and steel	7,566,204	1.9
Chemicals and chemical products	7,645,230	1.9
Total	318,184,309	91.2

Source: Inland Waterways Operators Association.

The claim is made that much of the traffic now moving is not competitive with rail traffic but is peculiar to barges, in that it moves from one river point to another in very large quantity.[6]

---

[6] See *Hearings, Problems of the Railroads,* U. S. Senate, Subcommittee on Surface Transportation, Committee on Interstate and Foreign Commerce, 1958, pp. 1270 ff.

Advantages and Disadvantages

The great advantage of water carriage is the large unit capacity of the vehicle. A 6,000 horsepower towboat can move 20 barges or several train loads of cargo (20,000 tons). The tremendous carrying capacity makes the ton-mile cost of transportation extremely low, about four mills per ton-mile. The outstanding disadvantage is clearly the time required for water movement. Shipments from New Orleans to Pittsburgh, up stream, often require twenty-one days and eleven days for the return trip down stream. For certain bulk products, this presents no serious problem, but most general merchandise cannot be shipped under such conditions. Perhaps the most serious disadvantage for shippers, in general, is the locational factor. Unless the shipper is located on or near a waterway, the destination is on or near a waterway, the use of water transport is either impossible or very costly. While public policy encourages the joint use of waterways and other modes of transport, trans-shipping from one form to another increases costs substantially. This is especially true on inland waterways where transfer facilities are technically very costly and difficult to construct due to the extreme rise and fall of water.

In view of these facts, many persons contend that water transportation is useful for only a small group of shippers and question the use of public funds for waterway development. Waterway advocates counter this by the contention that even the threat of water transport keeps freight rates on other modes lower than they would otherwise be and, thus, benefits all shippers. The argument is further complicated by the fact that many, if not most, publicly aided waterways are multi-purpose in nature, having been built to enhance flood control or to provide power and recreational areas, as well as to promote navigation. Since no universally accepted method exists of separating these purposes and assigning costs and benefits, the problem is likely to remain unsolved.

The Corps of Engineers estimates that on one waterway, the Ohio River system, accumulated navigational benefits from 1929 to 1960 amounted to more than $1,400 billion, while accumulated costs were slightly more than $300 million. In addition, cumulative benefits of flood control and related work amounted to $900 million. Clearly, some of these benefits, such as the prevention of a flood, may be nil for years and incalculable at a time of emergency.[7]

---

[7] *Economic Justification of Water Resource Projects*, Corps of Engineers, U. S. Army, Ohio River Division, 1961 (mimeographed).

A substantial controversy exists as to the justice of user charges imposed on waterway users. For obvious reasons, the railroads favor user charges, while water carriers and river shippers favor the present system of free use of public waterways. It seems likely that, in view of the long history of free waterways as well as the burden of calculation, the present system will continue. Waterway proponents point out that even a small user charge would disturb the presently existing competitive relationships, since the shipper must enjoy a very low rate to compensate for loss of time.[8]

Equipment Technology and Operations

The basic item in waterway operation is the modern diesel tow boat. In contrast to other modes, the inland waterway operator moves his cargo almost continuously during the trip. The tow boat (except those for local use) is complete with living and eating facilities for the crew, and the crew members rotate on duty so that the vessel is underway at all times except for stops to pick up or drop cargo. By their nature, waterway operations are slow. A large tow is, under the best conditions, unwieldy and requires much time to pick up and drop barges, pass through locks and other necessary maneuvers.

Barges are of various types, open, closed, tank, and various special purpose for chemicals and other such products moved in bulk.

Terminals are fairly simple, and, in most cases, the terminal facilities are those of the shipper. Except for merchandise traffic which is of little importance, bulk traffic such as coal, petroleum, sulphur, etc., can be picked up and delivered to the facilities of the shipper.

Summary

Inland waterway transportation, although very low in cost, has the serious disadvantage of being limited to relatively few locations and to a small range of products. It is also dependent upon large expenditure of public funds for the provision of and maintenance of facilities.

----

[8] Statement of William J. Hull, Chairman of the Legislative Committee Ohio Valley Improvement Association, A.W.O. Seminar, Louisville, Kentucky, June 23, 1961.

Historically, no user charge has been imposed for direct use of locks or other facilities incident to navigation, although from time to time this question arises and is still far from final solution.

PIPELINES

Pipelines are a unique mode of transportation, in that the right of way and the vehicle are the same unit and that the movement is entirely in one direction. Pipelines are also the most highly specialized of all carriers, being almost entirely limited to fluid or gaseous commodities.

TABLE 3-3

U. S. PIPELINE MILEAGE, 1955

Type of Line	Mileage
All Lines	188,540
Gathering Lines (Crude)	73,526
Trunk Lines, Total	115,014
Crude	78,594
Product	36,420

Source: American Petroleum Institute, *Petroleum Facts and Figures.*

Although pipelines have been used for centuries,[9] they were first used in their modern form in the United States in the Pennsylvania oil fields in the era just prior to the Civil War.[10] These lines were used as gathering facilities, and no attempt was made to transport oil over long distances. The pipelines transferred oil from the field into tank cars at nearby points.

As technology improved, it became feasible to transport oil and other products over long distances and over various types of terrain.[11] Today, pipelines carrying all types of petroleum products and other liquid cargoes form a nationwide network. In 1958, the United States had 201,800 miles of pipelines serving forty-six states.[12] (See Figure 3.2.)

---

[9] *Facts about Oil* (New York: American Petroleum Institute, 1960), p. 10.

[10] Alvin Harlow, *The Rise of the Moguls,* Mainstream of America Series (New York: Harper & Row, Publishers, 1956).

[11] By 1879, a 110-mile line had been completed across the Allegheny Mountains in Pennsylvania. (Oil Facts, *op. cit.*)

[12] *Ibid.,* p. 11.

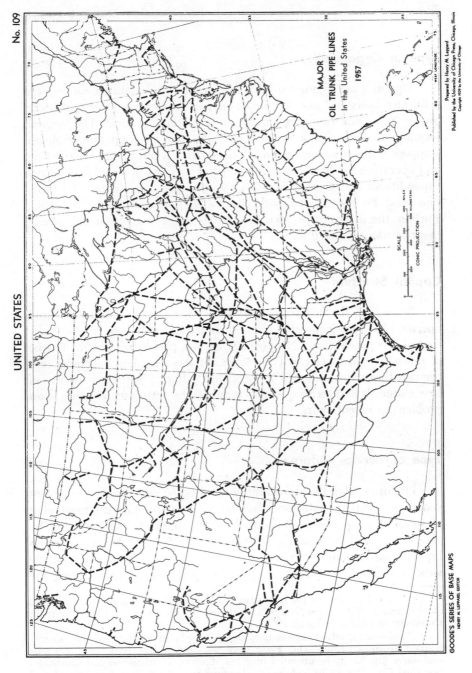

UNITED STATES

MAJOR
OIL TRUNK PIPE LINES
In the United States
1957

Prepared by Henry M. Leppard
Published by the University of Chicago Press, Chicago, Illinois
Copyright 1939 by the University of Chicago

SCALE

CONIC PROJECTION

GOODE'S SERIES OF BASE MAPS
HENRY M. LEPPARD, EDITOR

Fig. 3-2
Pipeline Map, U.S.

Type of Organization

Pipelines are organized both as common and contract carriers on a for-hire basis and also as private carriers. However, most privately owned pipelines function legally as common carriers. The capital required to construct a pipeline is such that a group of petroleum shippers will often engage in a cooperative venture in constructing and operating the line. Since the construction of a line involves heavy expenditures and since it is so highly specialized in its use, the pipeline must be constructed with the traffic potential firmly available. Further, the line must be used to capacity so as to amortize the investment as soon as possible.[13]

Capital Structure

In view of the fact that pipelines are most frequently owned and operated by petroleum producers, their capital structure is essentially that of the parent firm. No peculiar capital problems exist, as is true of railroads and other carriers, except for the speculative element and the fact that depreciation is inclined to be high. However, the use of new materials and techniques has reduced the seriousness of this latter problem in recent years.

Type of Service Offered

Pipelines offer the most limited service of all carriers. In recent years, some experimental work has been carried on with the movement of solids such as coal.[14] Nevertheless, the bulk of traffic moving by pipelines is and will, no doubt, continue to be petroleum and other liquid or gaseous products. In past years, it was customary to separate various batches of cargo by a "plug" of water to prevent mixing the

---

[13] For a discussion of the importance of the amortization problem, as well as other economic factors, see George S. Wolbert, Jr., *American Pipelines* (Norman: University of Oklahoma Press, 1952).

[14] Pulverized, mixed with water, and pumped. At destination, the "slurry" is dried by special equipment. Plans were disclosed in late 1961 for a 350 mile coal-slurry pipeline to be operated by Texas Eastern Transmission and Consolidation Coal Co. This 20-30 inch line is designed to move 5-10 million tons of coal per year. *Hearings* before the Committee on Commerce on S. 3044, *Coal Slurry Pipeline,* 87th Cong., 2d Sess., April 18, May 1-4 and 21, 1962 (Washington: Government Printing Office, 1962).

different products. However, modern technological progress has made this unnecessary, and relatively little mixing takes place. Likewise, great strides have been made in manufacture and treatment of metals to make pipelines more durable and resistant to corrosion, thus reducing the maintenance problem.

The pipelines currently in operation carry all types of gas and fluid commodities, including finished petroleum products. However, the distribution of gasoline is so widespread that most of it continues to move in tank cars and by truck. As Table 3-4 indicates, the cost per ton-mile of transporting petroleum products by pipeline is very low. It must be kept in mind, however, that the economics of pipeline transportation require substantial volume. Most pipeline transportation firms have minimum tender requirements, ranging from 10,000 to 100,000 barrels. Thus, the shipper must tender the minimum before his shipment will be accepted. The Interstate Commerce Commission has, in the past, established certain regulations on tender.[15]

Advantages and Disadvantages

Low cost of bulk service is the primary advantage of the pipelines. Table 3-4 illustrates the very substantial advantage which pipeline service has over the other forms of land transportation. Transporta-

TABLE 3-4

ESTIMATED PER TON-MILE COSTS OF PETROLEUM TRANSPORT

Mode	Cost Per Ton-Mile	
Rail tank car	8.3	mills
Motor tank truck	1.5-5	cents
Pipeline	0.6-3.2	mills

Source: Interstate Commerce Commission, Bureau of Transport Economics and Statistics.

tion of petroleum by ocean vessel compares favorably in cost with pipelines, being 0.7-1.2 mills per mile. However, the shipment must move over highly circuitous routes compared to pipelines.

In addition to the low cost, the pipeline is almost totally unaffected by weather, which may create problems for other modes of transportation. With pipelines, no problem of returning empty vehicle units exists, nor is it necessary to control the distribution of vehicles as is

---

[15] Brundred Bros. vs. Prairie Pipe Line Co., 68 I C C 458 (1922).

true of other modes. The most serious disadvantage relates to the highly specialized nature of the pipeline. That is to say, the pipeline is very specialized both as to product carried and as to points served and also as to direction of movement. Consequently, great care must be exercised both as to the long run quantity of cargo available and the destination, as well as technical considerations such as the diameter of the pipeline and pumping capacity. The investment must be amortized; and, while there is some flexibility, the movement and reuse of any substantial section of the pipeline is almost economically impossible.

Growth and Development

While pipelines will doubtless grow and develop further in the future, it seems clear that their development is somewhat circumscribed by the technical considerations relevant to commodity movement. As noted above, the pipeline has been used to move some nonliquid commodities, but, obviously, even this practice is quite limited. Costs of preparing the commodities and of reconstituting them after shipment must be added to the cost of shipment, and this, in effect, eliminates one of the major advantages of pipeline transportation, namely, the fact that no packing or other preparation is required.

Substantial progress has been made in recent years in the technology of pipeline operation, especially in control of remote stations and in traffic control through the use of electronic devices. The pipeline industry has become perhaps the most automated of the transportation system.

THE INDIRECT CARRIERS

Indirect carriers are those organizations which aid and assist other forms of transportation and, in general, do not themselves perform any line haul or intercity transportation. The freight forwarders perform such a service.[16] Their task is to gather less than carload shipments and to consolidate them into carload lots destined to various points. At the terminal point the process is reversed, and the various shipments are broken down and distributed to the consignees. The

[16] Some authorities would question the status of forwarders as separate carriers, but, for purposes of this chapter, they will be so classified.

forwarder operates by charging the shipper a rate somewhat higher than the carload rate but lower than the less-than-carload rate. The forwarder then proceeds to ship the cargo in carload lots, often at all commodity rates, using the intercity facilities of common carrier agencies of transportation. The forwarder issues a bill of lading to the customer and is, thus, legally both shipper and carrier at the same time.

In general, the forwarder limits his service to larger cities to which substantial traffic flows can be expected. Obviously, it would not be practicable for the forwarder to try to consolidate shipments to small cities. The forwarder must deal with the time element; because the shipper will tolerate a small delay in return for lower rates, but, clearly the forwarder must minimize the time during which he holds a shipment for consolidation and movement to destination. He is competing with the less-than-carload or truckload facilities of the carriers themselves, as well as with the postal system and R.E.A. Express.

Forwarders offer a wide variety of services, including piggy-back, consolidation of overseas shipments, and other shipping services. Obviously, forwarder traffic consists almost entirely of merchandise traffic which is moving to and from urban centers. The services which the forwarders perform must be financed on a relatively small margin between carload and less-than-carload rates. This margin must bear the cost of pick-up and delivery and the cost of administrative services involved, as well as the profit.

On the other hand, there is a continuous growth of merchandise traffic and a dispersal of population centers, which should work to the advantage of the forwarder agencies. Because of the specialized nature of the business, the industry consists of a relatively small number of firms. Although almost one hundred firms are in the field, there are less than a half dozen major firms engaged in the business on a nationwide basis, of which three perform well over half of the business.[17] In addition to the for-hire forwarders, there are many cooperative associations, especially in the agricultural and food processing industries, engaged in forwarding operations. These cooperative forwarders do not hold themselves out to the public as forwarders, dealing only with the members of the group.

The role of the indirect carriers is rather precarious, since they

---

[17] The big three—Acme Fast Freight, Universal Carloading and Distributing Company, and National Carloading Corporation—perform 58 per cent of the total service (Interstate Commerce Commission).

operate only as an adjunct to the intercity carriers. They are thus highly competitive with both rail and motor carriers, and their use of various innovations, e.g., piggy-back service, has been helpful.[18] Motor carriers have viewed these developments with considerable alarm and allege that forwarders are engaging in volume transportation which may have an unfortunate effect upon motor traffic. The outcome of this situation will have to be seen. Certainly, there is no doubt that rail-forwarder service via piggy-back is a formidable competitive weapon, and motor carriers are protesting this situation with great vigor.[19]

Forwarder traffic tends to be concentrated on the high value commodities, since the spread in carload and less-than-carload rates must be sufficient to bear the costs and provide a margin of profit.

Although railroads originally viewed the operations of forwarders with alarm and attempted to halt forwarder traffic entirely, they have since become very desirous of such traffic and compete for it.[20]

Freight forwarders deal, for the most part, with railroads. However, they also utilize the facilities of air and motor carriers.

In addition to the freight forwarders operating independently, there is some justification for classifying the R.E.A. Express operation discussed above as a forwarder organization, since some of its activities compete directly with the independent forwarders. Forwarder operations in conjunction with motor carriers are limited by the fact that motor carrier service has always been very similar to forwarder service in all respects.

Piggy-back Service

The transportation of semi-trailers by rail is an old concept which has recently enjoyed a resurgence. Horse-drawn wagons were shipped on flat cars before the Civil War, and, in the mid-1920's, piggy-back was widely used. For reasons which are not clear, the movement did not take hold in general and was then revived in the mid-1950's. The

---

[18] Walter Guzzardi, "Freight Goes Forward with Forgash," *Fortune*, 66:132, July 1962.

[19] *Transport Topics*, February 12, 1962, p. 1.

[20] In Interstate Commerce Commission vs. Delaware, Lackawanna and Western Railroad Co., 220 U. S. 235 (1911), the railroads contended unsuccessfully that the forwarder did not own the shipment and was not entitled to shipper status. The courts held that the forwarder was a shipper in his relationship with the railroad.

service has numerous advantages and, in fact, gives to the shipper many of the advantages of both rail and motor carriage.

Piggy-back service is performed under varying circumstances, depending upon which shippers are involved and which carrier is in control. There are five plans under which piggybacking can be carried on, as follows:

Plan 1. The railroad moves the loaded trailers owned or controlled by a common carrier trucking company. The shipments move on a carrier bill of lading under regular motor carrier tariffs. The trucking company pays the railroad on a "division" basis or a flat charge per trailer.

Plan 2. The railroad furnishes all equipment and services, including pick-up and delivery, at railroad rates.

Plan 3. The railroad moves two loaded trailers owned or leased by a shipper or freight forwarder. The flatcar loading and unloading is done by the railroad, while the cartage to and from the piggy-back ramp is the responsibility of the shipper or forwarder. Rates are based on a flat charge, in other words, a stated amount in dollars and cents per car.

Plan 4. The railroad performs linehaul rail service with a flatcar and trailer or trailers furnished by the private shipper or freight forwarder who may own or lease the equipment. The railroad makes a charge for movement of the flatcar and trailer or trailers, loaded or empty.

Plan 5. Railroads and motor carriers perform joint through service at joint rates. The railroad furnishes the flatcar and the motor carrier furnishes the trailer.

These five basic types of piggy-back plans offered by the railroads are presented in detail in Table 3-5, showing the following: (1) the originator of the shipment, (2) the participant who furnishes the equipment and performs the transfer services, (3) the participant who performs pick-up and delivery service, and (4) the rate basis used in computing charges for the piggy-back service.

In late 1961, almost seventy railroads were offering some type, often all types, of piggy-back service.[21] Motor carriers have been very willing participants in piggy-back, although, as noted above, they are alarmed as to the role of freight forwarders in the trailer movement

---

[21] *Hearing* before Surface Transportation Subcommittee, Committee on Interstate and Foreign Commerce, U. S. Senate, on Trailer on Flatcar Service Known Popularly as TOFC or Piggyback Service and Its Effects on the Transportation Pattern of Wyoming and Contiguous Areas, April 10, 1961, *Piggyback Transportation* (Washington: Government Printing Office, 1962), p. 8.

TABLE 3-5

PIGGY-BACK PLANS 1-5

Plan	Originator	Supplies Equipment and Transfer	Delivers and Picks Up	Basis, Rate
1	Motor Carrier	Motor Carrier, motor carrier grounds; rail carrier furnishes flatcars	Motor Carrier	Motor Carrier Rates; blanket divisional basis for all freight in the vehicle (not on individual articles)
2	Rail Carrier	Rail Carrier	Rail Carrier	Railroad Commodity rates
3	Shipper or Forwarder	Shipper or forwarder furnishes trailer (owned or leased), furnishes flatcars, and rail carrier grounds and trailers	Shipper or Forwarder	Flat rate; 60 per cent rail applies
4	Shipper or Forwarder	Shipper or forwarder furnishes flatcar and trailer	Shipper or Forwarder	Flat rate; 60 per cent rule applies
5	Motor Carrier	Motor Carrier	Motor Carrier	Rail carrier tariff for joint motor-rail rates

Source: Senate Committee on Interstate and Foreign Commerce, *National Transportation Policy*, Preliminary Report prepared by the Special Study Group on Transportation Policies in the United States, 87th Congr., 1st sess., January 3, 1961 (Washington: Government Printing Office, 1961), p. 674.

of full loads. One of the major advantages to the motor carrier has been the rapid movement of trailers over rail through congested highway areas and the freedom from highway weight limits. Unfortunately, this has raised certain issues with the Teamsters union which sees a reduction of employment for over-the-road drivers. Despite this sort of opposition, the movement seems to be growing in a satisfactory fashion.

One of the most important aspects of piggy-back is the fact that it represents an approach to integration of transport facilities. Piggy-back service will not eliminate the rail or motor problems, but it will go far toward reducing them and is a step in the right direction.

Other Indirect Services

The Pullman service is not, strictly speaking, an indirect service, in view of the fact that since 1946 the service has been operated by the railroad companies. Prior to this time, the Pullman Company operated its equipment (sleeping cars, lounge cars and private rental cars) under contract to the various railroads. Following anti-trust action, the Pullman Company elected to retain its manufacturing activities and to sell its operating division to the railroads.

THE COMMON CARRIER CONCEPT

In both common law and practice, the concept of the common carrier is deeply imbedded. It is necessary for us to reconsider these concepts in order to appreciate the role of the common carrier and its more modern variations. The common carrier holds himself out to transport within the limits of his capability for all who wish to avail themselves of his services. His services are offered to the public on a non-discriminatory basis and are a matter of common knowledge. Anyone who wishes to avail himself of these services may do so on the basis on which they are generally offered. Schedules, rates and charges are posted or published. An excellent example of the common carrier is the railroad passenger train. A train operating between two points may leave point A, for example, at 9:00 a.m. Those who must leave at an earlier or later hour must avail themselves of other means. Likewise, this train may operate only a limited type of equipment; if a traveler wishes more elaborate equipment, he must make other arrangements. It can be seen that the common carrier serves the general public. It does not cater to the needs of the shipper or traveler who has special problems or needs. The common carrier has particular responsibilities. The carrier must serve the "convenience and necessity" of the public. These requirements cannot be outlined on a detailed basis, except on an *ad hoc* basis. Schedules, for example, must be "reasonable." A train might be operated once per day, or twice weekly, depending upon the circumstances. Likewise, in the matter of equipment, the carrier must own and operate a "reasonable" amount and types of equipment. Consequently, in this area, as well as others, the customer may find that only his general needs can be accommodated. Perhaps the most significant duty of the common carrier is to hold himself out for service at all times. Operating on a schedule from a known base, the common carrier is available at all times. This is a heavy responsibility, since the carrier must maintain a certain capacity, even though it may not be used at all times. By the same token, the shipper may not find that service is always available to him of the type and quantity which he would prefer. Consequently, it sometimes becomes desirable for the shipper to provide his own transport service.

Before the development of the motor carrier, intercity transportation by private carrier was not practicable because of the limited technological ability of the horsedrawn vehicle and the economic limitations of water transportation. Ocean transportation was often provided on a contract basis, and local transportation was likewise provided on a contract basis long before the motor vehicle was brought into use.

Other Types of Carriage

Carriage other than common is of two types, contract and private. Contract carriage is provided by a carrier on specific contractual terms to one or more customers.[22] The shipper, thus, has service which is suited to his needs. He pays fees as arranged in the contract. Standards of service and related matters are likewise matters of contractual agreement. The contract carrier, unlike the common carrier, enjoys the benefits of being able to forecast his traffic. No railroads provide contract carriage, but it is widespread among motor and inland waterway carriers.

---

[22] Both contract and private carriers by water and motor present various legal problems which are considered elsewhere in this book.

Private carriage, in essence, is the carriage of products by the owner. For example, if a manufacturer of furniture wishes to transport finished products to market or raw materials into his plant, he is free to do so. While relatively few business enterprises could undertake the scale of investment necessary for private rail carriage, private motor carriage is within the reach of many businesses. The present development of private carriage had to await the motor vehicle and its present technology. Private carriage provides the shipper with the ultimate in service, since he, of course, controls all of the operations and welds them into his overall activities. The disadvantage is clearly that a major investment must be made and complex management problems must be faced. While certain illegal and quasi-legal aspects of private carriage have influenced the economic aspects of the situation, the ultimate decision is one of service compared to cost. In this area, as in others, the businessman may make irrational decisions and management errors. The legal and economic relationship between for-hire and private carriage has not yet been formulated, and many problems remain to be solved. Clearly, the common carrier has a vital role to play in the economy, but, at the same time, those who wish to acquire transportation service by contract or to provide such service through their own organization must be free to do so.

In the preceding two chapters, the roles of the various modes were discussed. It will be necessary for the student to keep in mind the changing relationship between common carriage and its variations in evaluating the role of each.

Services and Obligations of Carriers

In this and the preceding chapter, we examined the operating and economic characteristics of the various types of carriers. Let us now summarize the services which they offer and the obligations of the various carriers. The service obligations of the various types are fundamentally the same, although there are notable differences. As we have seen elsewhere in the text, the duty of the common carrier is to serve without discrimination. However, the carrier can refuse to render certain types of service.

In general, a carrier can refuse to accept articles which are improperly packed or those tendered at an improper time or place. The carrier may also refuse to transport articles of extraordinary value such as jewelry, objects of art or securities. The carrier may also refuse to accept articles for which it has no facilities, e.g., livestock. Once accepted for shipment, however, the goods are in the carrier's hands and must be transported under the legal obligations prevailing.

The Bill of Lading

The contract between shipper and carrier is known as the bill of lading and in this country is a standard document. Thus, when a shipper uses the services of a common carrier, he ships under the terms of the contract generally known to him and does not need an individual contract. When he utilizes the services of a contract carrier, the parties execute an individual contract (usually covering a long period of time, but not always).

The liability of the carrier is greater than that of an ordinary bailee. An ordinary bailee, such as a warehouse or repair shop, is liable for damage or loss of goods if the damage arises from his negligence. The carrier is liable for any loss or damage to goods in his possession, whether or not the damage or loss results from his negligence. In common law, the carrier was viewed as one who performed his service largely outside the view of the customer and thus made collusion difficult to detect. This concept has descended into modern law in the form of carrier liability. The bill of lading also serves as a receipt (to show that goods were turned over to the carrier) and as an evidence of title, so that they may be claimed by the consignee who has received the bill of lading. Both the rail bill of lading and the motor bill are standard and fundamentally the same, although differing somewhat in format. The liability of the carrier, though great, is not unlimited. There are five exceptions or conditions under which the carrier escapes liability. The conditions are these: (1) an act of God, (2) an act of the public enemy, (3) an act or default of the shipper, (4) an act of public authority, and (5) an inherent defect or nature of the goods. An "act of God" refers to some extraordinary and unavoidable event, such as flood, lightning, or tornado, and does not include bad weather conditions which the carrier might reasonably expect to experience in the route over which it operates. "Acts of the public enemy" refer to acts of organized armed forces and not mobs, riots, and strikes. "Act or default of the shipper" covers any neglect of the shipper to mark accurately or to pack or load the goods according to accepted standards and regulations. "Act of public authority" applies to attachment for debt or other seizure by legal process or in conformity with regulations. "Inherent defect or nature of the goods" includes disease of plants or animals and damage to merchandise occurring before shipment.

It can be seen from the above descriptions that, except for default of the shipper or inherent defect, these exceptions are rare. In few cases is there a serious question, and the carrier pays the vast majority of claims without legal action being necessary. Railroads are self insurers and pay claims out of their resources. Motor carriers more often cover these claims by liability insurance (on a deductible basis). Because of special hazards and their international character, somewhat different liability applies to ocean and air carriers. These are rather technical matters and are beyond the scope of this book. Carrier liability is an old and well-settled matter, and only rarely does a serious issue arise. It is often felt that legislation has tended to lag behind the technological advance of the carriers' vehicles and operating procedures.

Services Offered

Bulk freight service: This refers to the carriage in bulk of such materials as iron ore, petroleum, coal, timber, and other predominantly raw materials. All carriers, with the exception of air carriers, participate in bulk freight movement. Since bulk freight needs little handling and no packing, it is moved at low cost and, for the most part, at low rates in carloads, truckloads or barge loads. Bulk freight moves essentially from point of production to point of use or processing and is thus apt to be highly concentrated in areas. Coal hauling roads, such as the Norfolk and Western, will carry tremendous quantities of coal, often in solid train loads.

Bulk freight is apt to be highly seasonal in nature and is also very sensitive to economic fluctuation. When steel output falls, for example, iron ore and coal traffic both decline substantially. Most railroads, especially coal and ore carriers, depend heavily on bulk traffic, and lake and river carriers are almost entirely dependent upon bulk service. Under modern conditions, the bulk carrier is, to all intents and purposes, a conveyor line. Certain railroads offer service by the "unitized" train, which is essentially a train permanently made up, shuttling back and forth between origin and destination.

Expedited service in volume: By the use of scheduled or "time" freight trains, the rail carriers offer what is essentially bulk service for carload lots on a rapid service basis. These cargoes are not, strictly speaking, "bulk," because they may be and often are packed in carload lots. These trains operate on fast schedules, often "blocked" in trainloads of livestock, automobiles or other heavy freight. Since many carloads are often consigned to one destination, the handling, switching and other time-consuming operations are kept at a minimum. Railroads often name these services and advertise them widely such as the New York Central Pacemaker or the Baltimore and Ohio Sentinel Service.

Motor carriers participate heavily in this service through truck-load shipments. One coast-to-coast motor carrier offers service from New York to Los Angeles in nine days (vs. eleven days for less than truckload freight in general). Motor carriers cannot, of course, move merchandise in such volume movements as the railroad.

Merchandise freight and express: All carriers, except water and pipelines, participate in this service. The cargo here consists of packaged freight of all sizes and generally of rather high value. The merchandise service is lucrative, but also highly competitive, and requires many costly services such as pick-up and delivery services to support it. In recent years, forwarders have moved into this service in depth, using a highly-integrated service. Merchandise service by air, although growing, is still confined to high value products. Merchandise service has also been a fertile field for private carriers.

Express service: Rail (REA, Inc.), motor carriers, airlines and bus companies all participate in express service, the transport of small package, high value merchandise. It can be seen that these services are not distinctly separated, but blend together. The distinction between merchandise freight and "express service" may be fairly small, depending upon the circumstances. Many carriers do not actively promote carriage of less than carload or less than truckload freight because of the costs involved. Table 3-6 indicates the carrier participation in these services.

TABLE 3-6

CARRIER PARTICIPATION IN SERVICES

Bulk Freight	Expedited Volume	Merchandise	Express
Rail	Rail	Rail	Rail
Motor	Motor	Motor	Motor
Water	....	....	....
Pipeline	....	....	....
....	....	Air	Air
....	Forwarders	Forwarders	Forwarders

As Table 3-6 shows, pipelines offer only one type of service, as do water carriers; air service is highly restricted, while rail and motor carriers offer service "across the board."

Passenger and mail: As we have seen, rail, motor and air carriers dominate the for-hire passenger services, with slight participation by water carriers. We have noted earlier that the airlines play the major role, and the once great importance of the railroads is rapidly being diminished. From the carrier standpoint, passenger traffic presents many problems (this will be further discussed in Chapter XXII) due to the need for feeding, sleeping and otherwise caring for human cargo. Further, passenger traffic is highly seasonal and subject to weather and other unpredictable factors. Airlines and motor buses are devoted principally to passenger carriage; while railroads, with few exceptions, are dominated by freight movement, and many railroads do not participate at all in passenger traffic. Passenger carriers also carry mail, and for airlines, in particular, this has always been an important source of revenue, as we have seen.

Railroads, since the early 1930's except for the immediate war years, have suffered from the "passenger deficit," ranging from $600 to $700 million per year and made up from other revenue sources. The major cause of the deficit is the low load factor for rail passenger trains, coupled with the high unit cost of providing service. As we have seen, some substantial doubts exist as to the practicability of continuing rail passenger service.[23] The efficiency and profitability of these services vary greatly, depending upon the topography and economic structure of the route, size of carrier, quality of management, and other factors which will be discussed more fully later. In summary, the service structure of the carriers can be presented as follows:

Rail:

Bulk freight
Merchandise and expedited freight
Express
Mail
Passengers

---

[23] A standard passenger train, with a crew of five, must operate with load factors above the 25 to 26 per cent figure typical of recent years to avoid out-of-pocket loss. This does not take into account the expense of related services such as station expense (partly allocated to other services) or such expensive loss items as dining cars. Some technical controversy exists over the calculation of this deficit, but this is essentially an accounting problem.

Motor:

> Bulk freight (often short distance)
> Merchandise and expedited freight
> Express

Motor Bus:

> Passengers
> Mail
> Express

Air:

> Passengers
> Mail
> Express
> Merchandise freight

Water:

> Bulk freight (small amount of passenger
> and merchandise freight traffic)

Freight Forwarder:

> Merchandise freight
> Express

Pipeline:

> Bulk freight

As can be seen, the railroad operates the greatest variety of service. Motor freight carriers and bus lines in combination offer the same service, while the other carriers offer a narrower range of services.

Summary

The indirect carriers and the pipelines are somewhat unique, since their function is highly specialized. Both these carriers perform a necessary, although small, function in aggregate terms. The indirect carriers are also unique in that they operate almost entirely in cooperation with other carriers and perform few services on an independent basis.

Pipelines may be on the threshold of a broadening of their services through the movement of prepared solid products, although the extent of this service is yet to be seen.

Selected References for Further Study

The literature relating to water and other carriers is much less extensive than that relating to the other modes. Valuable and informative material is found in the pamphlets and similar items produced by the carriers and their trade associations. Some survey type textbooks do exist in the ocean carriage field, e.g., McDowell, Carl E., and Gibbs, Helen M., *Ocean Transportation* (New York: McGraw-Hill Book Co., 1954).

The Inland Waterways Operators Association is a valuable source of data on the inland waterways. See *Waterways of the United States,* Locher, Harry O., ed. (New York: National Association of River and Harbor Contractors, 1961).

One of the most valuable sources of current economic data in the area of inland waterway transportation is the testimony of the *Hearings, Problems of the Railroads,* Vol. 2, Committee on Interstate and Foreign Commerce, U. S. Senate (Washington: Government Printing Office, 1958).

Material relating to canals in detail, as well as other modes, is found in Taylor, George R., *The Transportation Revolution.*

The pipeline industry is comprehensively treated in Wolbert, George, *American Pipelines: Economic Status and Legal Implications* (Norman: University of Oklahoma Press, 1952). See also Johnson, Arthur M., *The Development of American Petroleum Piplines* (Ithaca, N. Y.: Cornell University Press, 1956); and Cookenboo, L., Jr., *Crude Oil Pipelines and Competition in the Oil Industry* (Cambridge: Harvard University Press, 1955).

CHAPTER IV

Transportation Labor

Essentially the problems relating to labor are the same for the transportation industry as they are in other industries in the economy. However, some distinctions do appear. Collective bargaining is and has been widespread for many years, and most transportation workers are subject to special legislation which defines the allowable area and means of bargaining. Roughly two million workers are engaged directly in some aspect of the transportation industry.[1] While it is clearly difficult to make generalizations for such a large number of heterogeneous workers, these workers have historically enjoyed generally higher pay and status than industrial workers in general. This has been especially true of operating employees.

As in other industries, recent years have brought technological advances which have reduced the number of workers needed to produce a given level of output, a tendency especially noticeable in rail and pipeline transportation. The high degree of union organization and a degree of legislative protection have aided the workers in their efforts at resisting the effects of changing technology, although

---

[1] Rail and for-hire motor transportation each employs about 800,000 workers; approximately 150,000 work for airlines; and some 50,000 are employed in other modes. Source: *Association of American Railroads, American Trucking Associations, American Association of Waterways Operation, and Air Transport Association.*

the long range decline in employment is clearly apparent, especially in the railroad industry.

Mergers and consolidations throughout the transport industry can be expected to hasten this trend. Although legislative protection is given to those workers who are currently employed, the number of workers necessary for future operation is greatly reduced by these factors. Despite the influence of automation, there is still a unique need for workers somewhat more skillful and resourceful than is the case for industry in general. One must keep in mind that operating employees are not by the nature of their jobs under constant supervision similar to factory or office workers. An engineer, conductor or truck driver is responsible for an expensive item of equipment, and he must be able to operate it at times when he is completely outside the control or immediate supervision of superiors. Consequently, it seems likely that a somewhat independent minded and able person is necessary to perform many tasks in the transportation industry.

RAILROAD LABOR

An average of slightly less than 700,000 workers were employed in the railroad industry in 1961.[2] In general, rail employees enjoy relatively high compensation and security. Unionism is strong in the industry, and it has been entrenched for a number of years. Railroad labor is, for the most part, highly specialized; seniority is of substantial importance in the industry; and, consequently, it requires a long period of time for a worker to become established in a permanent job. The important position of railroad workers in the economy is evidenced by the passage in 1926 of the Railway Labor Act, which has provided the rail worker with a degree of status long denied to other workers.[3]

Railroad unions rank with the oldest labor organizations, beginning with a "protective association" of locomotive engineers in 1855. The Brotherhood of Locomotive Engineers was established in 1863 and is the oldest of the railroad unions now in existence.[4] The

---

[2] The number of workers has declined substantially in recent years, having been 1,326,000 in 1948. This decline is due largely to labor-saving innovations and to substantial reduction in services, especially in the passenger train area. Source: *A Review of Railway Operations in 1960*, Washington, D. C., 1961, Association of American Railroads, and Supplement, October 1961, Railroad Employment by States, and 46th Statistical Summary, AAR, August 1962.

[3] Railway Labor Act of 1926, 44 United States Statutes 577 (1926): 48 U. S. Statutes 926 (1934).

various shop craft unions, such as machinists, boilermakers, etc., are affiliated with the Railway-Employees Department of the AFL-CIO, as are the operating unions. The comprehensiveness of rail unionism and the length of time which it has been established in the industry have given rise to certain rigidities in the working agreements. Railroad management claims that many such rules are antiquated and cause undue stress in labor relationships. The unions, on the other hand, point out that such rules are necessary to protect their interests. The outcome of this argument will have great influence upon the future of the industry and, to some extent, upon industry in general.

The issues here center around union and job security. A strong union or group of unions, faced with an aggregate decline in job opportunities and having a measure of legislative protection, will adopt a mode of operation appropriate to the situation. Thus, emphasis is upon rigidly interpreted work rules which draw tight lines between jobs and workers who are allowed to hold such jobs. Also, the unions have shown great reluctance to permit changes in work procedures, shifts in personnel or downgrading of jobs. All of these actions interfere to a greater or lesser degree with management prerogatives, and management often refers to all such arrangements as "make work" or "featherbedding." Unions defend such practices on classic grounds of insuring safety, welfare of workers and other claims. These conflicts between workers and management are typical when a strong union in an old and declining industry attempts to preserve itself.[5] Clearly, there are potent arguments on both sides of this question; and, since the area of collective bargaining in the railroad industry is circumscribed by legislation, these questions may be ultimately determined by public policy.

In summary, the rail workers have achieved a substantial degree of unionization and have materially improved their income and working conditions, despite the fact that their industry has been declining in employment opportunities for some years. In part, because of tradition and also because of legislation which will be discussed elsewhere in the text, labor relations in the rail industry have, in recent decades, been carried out largely by peaceful means. Labor disputes resulting in strikes are rare in the rail industry.[6] A substantial amount of administrative machinery exists for the purpose of settling disputes,

---

[4] Harry A. Millis and Royal E. Montgomery, *Organized Labor* (New York: McGraw-Hill Book Company, 1945), pp. 56 ff.

[5] See Selig Perlman, *A Theory of the Labor Movement* (New York: The Macmillan Company, 1928).

and rail unions have historically been conservative in their viewpoints. The fact that rail unions have not hesitated to use their political power has cast much doubt upon the efficacy of the Act.[7]

MOTOR CARRIER LABOR

Unlike the railroad labor referred to above, motor carrier workers are almost all members of one union, the International Brotherhood of Teamsters, Chauffeurs, Warehousemen, and Helpers. The Teamsters is one of the largest unions in the country and is widely known as an aggressive and growing union. The Teamsters is an "industrial" type union in that it has organized all workers in the motor carrier industry regardless of trade or skill. Drivers of delivery trucks, private trucks of all kinds, and many related workers are found within their ranks. As a result, the Teamsters are in a very powerful bargaining position. Virtually all of the regulated motor freight lines in the United States have signed contracts with the union.[8]

While the Teamsters have been widely criticized for some of their tactics, there is no doubt that they have enjoyed great success in raising the economic status and improving the working conditions of the workers in the motor carrier industry. The "aristocrats" of the motor carrier industry are the "over the road" drivers who generally enjoy a high income relative to their training and background. Drivers of local pick-up and delivery trucks are somewhat less well off as regards pay and status. Other employees such as dock workers and clerical employees enjoy income and status on a level generally comparable to that of their counterparts in other industries.

Unlike railroad and airline employees, motor carrier workers do not have unique legal status. The relationships between union,

----

[6] No complete nationwide strike of rail workers has taken place since 1922, although various groups and various individual railroads have been involved. Historical precedent would indicate that a nationwide rail strike would be almost impossible to carry out without governmental intervention, even though all the legal technicalities had been observed; see: S. T. Williamson and Herbert Harris, *Trends in Collective Bargaining* (New York: The Twentieth Century Fund, 1945).

[7] H. R. Northrup, "The Railway Labor Act and Railway Disputes in Wartime," *American Economic Review*, June 1946, pp. 324-43.

[8] The Teamsters claim almost two million members, and many of their members are employed outside the for-hire trucking industry by private carriers, cab companies, etc. In theory, the union claims jurisdiction over everyone who operates a vehicle for commercial purposes.

workers, and employers are governed by the Labor Management Relations Act of 1947 (Taft-Hartley Act).

The Teamsters Union carries on active and militant collective bargaining on an area wide basis. Under this arrangement, the union and various groups of company representatives write a "master" or uniform contract applicable to all of the operators in that category in a given geographical area, taking into account local conditions. Under the circumstances, i.e., a large number of employers, this system makes for uniformity and simplifies the bargaining process, although it may force certain employers into an unsatisfactory situation.

In many ways the Teamsters present an interesting contrast to the rail employees. Rail unions, especially the operating brotherhoods, have been (at least since 1920) strongholds of the Samuel Gompers type of pragmatic unionism.[9] On the contrary, the Teamsters Union, while nothing if not pragmatic, has been much more aggressive and has faced the task of welding together a very heterogeneous group of workers into a unit. Teamster members have less common ground than is true of rail workers, and the emphasis of the union has been toward increased participation in the profits of the industry with less orientation toward security. The Teamsters have demonstrated a political skill equal in effectiveness, if not in subtlety, to that of the rail unions. Perhaps as the motor carrier industry ages, the goals and objectives of the Teamsters will change.

AIR CARRIER LABOR

Air carrier labor is somewhat unique in that it contains one group whose skill and bargaining power have put them into a highly favorable bargaining position; viz., the pilots. The airline pilot and his union, the Airline Pilots Association, have long dominated the airline labor situation.

Except for the mechanical employees, no other union group has any substantial amount of bargaining power. Part of the pilots' prestige has derived from the emphasis the airlines have been forced to put on airline safety. Fear of accident has always been a factor in the demand for air travel, and airlines are reluctant to take any action which can be construed as having an adverse influence on safety.

---

[9] Some interesting views of this matter are found in Frank Tannenbaum, *A Philosophy of Labor* (New York: Alfred A. Knopf, 1952); also, Charles F. Lindblom, *Unions and Capitalism* (New Haven: Yale University Press, 1949); and, more recently, Sanford Cohen, *Labor in the United States* (Columbus: Charles E. Merrill Books, Inc., 1960), pp. 658 ff.

The airlines have benefited from the fact that they are a relatively new and glamorous industry. They have thus been able to secure the services of a number of better than average non-operating employees at salaries somewhat lower than those paid by other carriers. With the exception of the pilots and the mechanical employees, unionism is not widespread among airline workers. Again with the exceptions noted above, airline employees are younger and turnover is higher than among other transportation employees, especially rail workers. No doubt, as the industry grows older this situation will change, and there seems to be some evidence that such change is now taking place.

COMPARATIVE STATUS OF TRANSPORTATION WORKERS AND OTHERS IN THE LABOR FORCE

Skills and training: With few exceptions, workers in the transportation field do not require a high degree of formal training to perform their jobs. Most of the skills required can be acquired by experience and informal trade type training. It would seem that mature judgment, experience, and ability to deal with emergency situations are more important than technical skills per se. That is to say, the operation of most vehicles is essentially a manual skill which might be mastered by an individual of average intelligence. Beyond the mere technical operation, however, the need for judgment is clear; and the value of a mature and experienced pilot, locomotive engineer, or truck driver cannot be denied. These factors, in addition to the strength of unionism, doubtless account for the comparatively high earnings in the field, as shown in Table 4-1.

TABLE 4-1

COMPARATIVE AVERAGE ANNUAL EARNINGS,
TRANSPORTATION WORKERS AND OTHER SELECTED GROUPS

Workers	Annual Earnings (1960)
Transportation:	
Rail	6,228
Motor	5,957
Air	6,868
General	5,928
Manufacturing, general	5,372
Automobile workers	6,558
Service workers, general	3,587

Source: U. S. Department of Commerce

In view of the declining opportunities for transportation workers, due to automation and other factors discussed above, the long range forecast for employment in the industry does not appear to be optimistic. Although railroad workers have been most strongly influenced in the immediate past, technological changes in the air and motor industry will have similar effects, unless overall growth in the industry is sufficiently strong to overcome the adverse influences.

Most transportation workers have long since passed the stage of "wages and hours" unionism and have concentrated for many years on fringe benefits of various types, such as the work rules discussed above and others such as pension plans and vacations. As is true of other industries where unionism has existed for many years, the question arises as to what future goals might be achieved. The question is especially interesting as it relates to the airline pilots whose earnings are frequently greater than those of executives of the airline industry and whose hours are limited by federal law.

In recent years, some interest has been expressed in the formation of a mass union embracing all transport workers. Aside from the likely political resistance such a move would have to overcome, there seems to be little likelihood that such heterogeneous groups as make up the various transportation unions could successfully merge their varied interests.

THE LEGISLATIVE FRAMEWORK

As has been noted, rail and airline workers enjoy unique legal status in the area of labor relations. The legislation surrounding this area is quite extensive and deserves some attention, since it represents an attempt to deal with a difficult problem.

Early Legislation

As early as 1888, after considerable and often violent unrest in the railroad industry, Congress saw fit to give attention to the serious problem of interference with work stoppages in the railroad industry. The Arbitration Act of 1888 provided for voluntary arbitration of disputes but failed to provide any procedure and is generally considered to have been a complete failure. The second attempt, the Erdman Act of 1898, proved to be little more effective.

This legislation was limited to the settlement of disputes involving employees connected with the operation of trains, but it did inaugurate procedures for mediation and arbitration. The administration of the law was the responsibility of the Chairman of the Interstate Commerce Commission and the Commissioner of Labor. If interested parties could not settle a dispute by negotiation, either party could invite the government officials to settle the issue by mediation or conciliation. If this failed, it was the duty of the officials to try to get the disputants to arbitrate. If they agreed, each side was to select an arbitrator, and these two were to select a third member who would be the neutral chairman. The award of the board was final and binding, and was to remain in effect for a minimum period of one year. The weak spot in this legislation was the pressure on the one neutral arbitrator. In 1913, the Congress tried to solve the problem once again by passing the Newlands Act.

This legislation recognized the need for continuity of personnel and machinery to deal with railroad labor disputes. It established a Commissioner of Mediation and Conciliation who was to serve full time and for a period of seven years. He was to be assisted by two other government officials appointed by the President, the three forming a Board of Mediation and Conciliation. This board could act upon its own without waiting for an invitation. If the disputants agreed to arbitration, the Board of Arbitration could consist of three members or six. It was required to reach a verdict in thirty days, but its decisions were not binding on the parties. If a dispute was settled by mediation or arbitration, either party could call upon the Board of Mediation to interpret the meaning or define the application of the terms of settlement.

This act was a considerable improvement and operated with some success until the pressure for the eight hour day became an issue shortly before World War I. The result of the union demands for an eight hour day was the Adamson Act of 1916, which provided for an eight hour work day for employees operating trains. The act was severely attacked by the railroads but eventually became standard during the period of federal ownership. The Act of 1920 attempted to cover (among other things) rail labor relations but was not successful, giving rise to the Act of 1926.

The Railway Labor Act of 1926

The Railway Labor Act of 1926, which replaced all previous legislation designed to deal with labor disputes, incorporated all of the measures that had been included in previous laws, except for the noncompulsory wage determination of the Act of 1920. Its coverage was also extended to all railroad employees. In thus relying on collective bargaining, with conferences and conciliation or mediation as the primary methods of settling disputes, it represented the accumulated experience of the previous attempts at a solution to the problem of maintaining an atmosphere of collective bargaining while still assuring service. The heart of the act lies in the Adjustment and Mediation Boards.

The National Railroad Adjustment Board

The act provided that bipartisan adjustment boards were to be set up by agreement between the carriers and the unions to handle disputes arising out of grievances. Difficulties were encountered in establishing these, however. This led to the creation of the National Railroad Adjustment Board by the legislation of 1934. This agency was given exclusive jurisdiction over disputes arising out of grievances, or out of interpretation of agreements concerning rates of pay, rules, or working conditions. The Board is composed of 36 members, 18 selected by the carriers and 18 by the unions. For operational purposes the Board is organized into four divisions, each of which has jurisdiction over a particular class of employees. If a division fails to reach a decision in a case, a neutral referee is to be selected to break the deadlock. The decisions of the adjustment boards are final and binding on both parties. If a carrier fails to comply, labor can file civil suit against it, but no corresponding remedy is afforded the carrier.

National Board of Mediation

The Act of 1926 provided machinery for dealing with disputes that could not be settled by collective bargaining. The government could step in to try to resolve the issues through mediation, arbitration, and emergency boards. A National Board of Mediation, consisting of three members appointed by the President with the advice and consent of the Senate, was created by the Act of 1934. The term of office of the members is three years. This Board has jurisdiction over disputes involving rates of pay or changes in rules and working conditions where the parties to the dispute have been unable to effect a settlement. Either party may invoke the services of the Board, or the latter may act on its own motion in the case of an emergency. The function of the Board is to endeavor to bring about settlement through mediation. It does not decide the issues. It also has the duty, in the event of a split between members as to representation, to investigate and, if necessary, hold a representation election.

In the event that the National Mediation Board is unable to bring about a settlement, it must attempt to effect an arbitration, which, if done, results in a binding award.

Emergency Boards

If a dispute is not settled by any of the methods described, and if the National Mediation Board has reason to believe that the dispute threatens to interrupt interstate commerce to a degree sufficient to deprive any section of the country of essential transportation service, the Board must notify the President, who may then create an emergency board to investigate the dispute and report its findings to him. The Emergency Board's conclusions are not enforceable, but many of these boards have been created and have proved of great value in bringing about an amicable settlement of disputes, although the long range results are sometimes questionable.

LABOR MANAGEMENT POLICIES

Carrier management in general, and especially rail management, has not been inclined to take the initiative in dealing with unions. Large manufacturing enterprises have generally made more progress in labor relations than has been true of carriers. Several reasons for this situation are likely. In the railroad industry, in particular, the complex and rigid work rules, growing out of concessions to labor combined with unique operating problems, have been a significant factor limiting management policy. Also, since rail labor relations have, for some years, been conducted on an industry-wide basis, there has been little scope for an individual company to pursue an imaginative independent policy. It seems likely also that public policy, chiefly the Railway Labor Act of 1926, made collective bargaining more or less a formality for both parties. That is, management and labor both were aware of the fact that a strike (the ultimate weapon) was almost an impossibility for practical purposes. Thus, the whole process of collective bargaining was carried on in a rather closely defined area. Only recently has rail management begun an aggressive campaign against the more important of the work rules.

Motor carrier management, being under the jurisdiction of the Labor Management Relations Act of 1947 (Taft-Hartley), is somewhat less restricted legally. However, as noted above, the Teamster bargaining tactics have made unilateral action very difficult for motor carrier firms.

Airline management has been forced to temper a strong policy toward the Airline Pilots Association, realizing that the public should not be made uneasy about the skill and general professional qualities of the pilot. The workers in the airline industry are also subject to the Railway Labor Act. This Act, once thought of as a model act in the control of essential industries, has not proved to be entirely successful. As Reynolds puts it, the Act has satisfied the objective of maintaining continuity of operation in the railroads, but most of the major problems have worn down by attrition.[10]

The Act, as amended, provides for the settlement of two types of disputes, those arising under an existing contract and those arising from attempts to arrive at a contract. The former are adjusted by the National Railroad Adjustment Board, composed of eighteen members representing labor and eighteen representing management. The Board is subdivided so as to deal with various types of disputes, e.g., train operation, maintenance, etc. If the question at issue cannot be solved by the Board, an impartial referee is selected, either by the Adjustment Board itself or, if they cannot agree, by the second board, the National Mediation Board. A decision by the referee is binding. Disputes over the contract per se are the province of the National Mediation Board from the beginning. If mediation cannot solve the dispute, the Board urges arbitration via special panels appointed for the purpose. If the parties agree to this procedure, the award is binding subject to judicial review. If this procedure is not successful and a serious work stoppage seems likely, the President may appoint an emergency board to make recommendations. If after sixty days a settlement has not been reached, a strike would be legal.[11] As this brief account makes clear, the machinery of the Act is complex and time consuming. At a minimum, several months may elapse before

---

[10] Lloyd G. Reynolds, *Labor Economics and Labor Relations* (3d ed.; New York: Prentice-Hall, Inc., 1954), pp. 290 ff.

[11] Even a "legal" strike is not likely, since public and congressional opinion would be aroused, and the parties seek to avoid this unpleasant situation. However, various loopholes have been found, e.g., an "epidemic" of illness among a group of workers may bring about desired ends without a strike.

any action might be taken. Unfortunately, also, some disputes are carried all the way to the President hoping for a political settlement more favorable than an economic determination. Under these circumstances the preliminary provisions are merely matters of formality.

It seems likely that labor matters will continue to be one of the most important matters facing carrier management. This will be especially true as competition becomes more intense.

In 1960, the President appointed a Railroad Commission consisting of five carrier, five employee and five public representatives to investigate the railway labor problem and make recommendations. The Commission met and made its final report in early 1962, covering the following areas: wages, rules and working conditions, and social security for the operating employees of the railroads of the entire country. The traditional procedures for emergency boards were not followed because it was felt the issues were unusually broad and complex. Every appropriate method to understand the practices of the industry and the issues involved was employed. Separate recommendations for action were made for each of the topics dealt with. The report concluded (1) that the rules governing the manning of engines and trains need to be revised to permit the elimination of unnecessary jobs and at the same time to safeguard the interests of the individual employees adversely affected, (2) that the entire complex and intricate system of compensation needs to be overhauled, and (3) that the procedures for the administration of rules and the disposition of grievances need to be revised.[12]

The conclusion, which was not surprising, was that a thorough-going revision needs to be made in the entire body of labor-management relations in the rail industry. Both rail and union members disagreed with either all or part of the report, although the public members signed unanimously. The Commission hoped that the solution to the problems could be found in the framework of collective bargaining. This is certainly a desirable goal, although events since 1926 would not hold out much hope for its achievement.

The continuing federal interest in this problem is indicated by the statement in the President's message on transportation presented to the Congress in 1962. Speaking of labor problems, the President said:

(A) *Labor Relations*
 Technological advance in transportation must be explored and developed if we are to meet growing requirements for the movement

---

[12] *Report of the President's Railroad Commission*, Washington, D. C., February 1962 (mimeographed).

of people and goods. New equipment often requires new skills, sometimes displaces labor, and often requires retraining or relocation of
manpower. An overall reduction in manpower requirements in transportation is not inevitable, however; and the new Manpower Development and Training Act will help those transportation workers in need
of new jobs or new skills.

For the long-range benefit of labor, management, and the public,
collective bargaining in the transportation industry must promote
efficiency as well as solve problems of labor-management relations.
Problems of job assignments, work rules, and other employment
policies must be dealt with in a manner that will both encourage
increased productivity and recognize the job equities which are
affected by technological change. The Government also has an obligation to develop policies and provide assistance to labor and management consistent with the above objectives.[13]

Carrier Labor Problems

The carriers face serious problems in the labor area which, as
indicated, are somewhat obscured by the apparent lack of strife in
the industry. As we have seen, the industry and the workers have,
under the provisions of legal and political policies, largely avoided
the frequent strikes which have marked bargaining in other industries.
This era may be nearing its end.

In the rail industry, in particular, management has begun to
move toward a more aggressive position as regards work rules and
related matters. It seems likely that, in past years, the carriers and
outside arbitration boards have operated largely on the assumption
that the demand for transportation service was largely inelastic and
wage increases could be recouped through rate increases. The fallacy
of this assumption must be increasingly apparent as private carriage
makes continued inroads on the industry and as traffic shifts from one
mode to another.

The decline in openings for rail workers has been rapid and substantial since 1950. Workers and their unions cannot ignore these
developments. Unfortunately, these factors, in turn, cause workers
to stress the job security to be found in the status quo and thus force
the industry into rigid patterns. Even in the airline industry where
expansion has been rapid, recent years have witnessed a bitter dispute
over job classification between pilots and flight engineers.

---

[13] *Message from the President of the United States* relative to the transportation system of our nation, April 5, 1962, 87th Cong., House Document No. 384.

Equally dangerous is the increasing dependence upon outside aid or pressure for a settlement. There is widespread belief that in the rail field neither party has, at least in past years, been willing to exert much effort in the early stages of bargaining, knowing that the ultimate decision would be made by others or at least strongly influenced by them. In the motor industry, the most serious problem has been the unequal distribution of bargaining power. The Teamsters Union, with its size and strategic power, has had most motor carrier companies at a severe disadvantage. Motor carriers must overcome some of their internal differences and present a more united front.

SUMMARY

The workers in the transportation industry are somewhat unique in several ways. Both airline and rail employees enjoy a particular legal status under the coverage of the Railway Labor Act of 1926.

Transportation workers, in general, enjoy relatively high status and are well paid in relation to other workers of comparable background. However, since the end of World War II, transportation employment, especially in the rail industry, has declined due to various factors, including automation.

Unionism came early to the transportation industry and is a very significant factor. Transport workers have long since become concerned with "fringe items," having passed beyond the wages and hours stage of collective bargaining.

Selected References for Further Study

An excellent study of labor relations in the Teamsters Union is found in DeArmond, Fred, *Managers vs. Teamsters* (Springfield, Missouri: Mycroft Press, 1959). The various standard texts in the area of labor economics discuss the fundamentals of labor matters as they apply to the carrier industry, as well as to others. In particular, thorough treatment is given to the historical aspects of rail unions, since these organizations figured prominantly in the early history of unions. See, for example, Millis, Harry H., and Montgomery, Royal E., *The Economics of Labor,* Vol. III, *Organized Labor* (New York: McGraw-Hill Book Co., 1945); and, for a more contemporary treatment, see Cohen, Sanford, *Labor in the United States* (Columbus: Charles E. Merrill Books, Inc., 1960). Historical accounts of various episodes, such as the American Railway Union strike and the Pullman strike, appear in various standard and particular histories—in particular, Dulles, Foster R., *Labor in America* (New York: Thomas Y. Crowell Co., 1949), which contains excellent material on the Pullman strike. An even more detailed account is found in Lindsey, Altmont J., *The Pullman Strike* (Chicago: University of Chicago Press, 1942).

PART II

The Economics of the Industry, Cost-Output Relationships, and Pricing

CHAPTER V

The Cost of Producing Transport Services, The Demand for Service and Pricing

OUTPUT UNITS, MEANINGS, AND DEFINITIONS

Transportation service, like other services, must be produced in measurable units. From the technological standpoint, units of transport are measured in terms of weight or units carried relative to distance, hence the ton-mile, i.e., a ton carried one mile, and the passenger-mile, viz., a passenger carried one mile.

The ton-mile and the passenger-mile are the standard output units of the industry. They can also be varied in such a manner as to reflect output opearting efficiencies from the technical standpoint, such as the ton-mile per train-hour or the ton-miles per day produced by a given plant.

It must be emphasized that the ton-mile is a physical measurement and not a measure of profit or economic efficiency. For example, a carrier might perform many ton-miles of service in a given period and yet make a poor financial showing, if the product carried was heavy and of low value relative to weight or was unduly expensive to transport realtive to the rates established. Many writers have made the point that the output of the transportation industry is heterogeneous in nature, a fact which makes any universal definition of output units highly theoretical.[1] More recent authors have been inclined to steer clear of this problem by making appropriate but often unrealistic assumptions. As Wilson points out in his stimulating monograph, "If one examines some of the principal textbooks in the field of transportation, he will note that the various diagrams that purport to show cost and demand relationships for transportation enterprises do not label the abscissa."[2]

Troxel, whose textbook maintains a generally high level of theory, divides the output units into various classes but still fails to come to grips with the problem.[3]

It seems clear that the ton-mile, while by no means a homogeneous unit, is the only practicable unit of output measurement.

Just as the ton-mile gives no indication as to the value of the commodity being carried, it is also meaningless as to the quality of the service being performed, e.g., time consumed, nor does it indicate whether the carrier is moving many tons a few miles or a few tons for a long distance. Clearly, ton-mile or passenger-mile figures must be interpreted with reference to the specific service being performed.

The ton-mile is heterogeneous on both sides of the market, both the demand side as well as the output or cost side, and is related to the specific situation existing in any given case.[4] As Wilson points out, it is not surprising that Locklin and others were forced to label the abscissa in vague terms.[5]

COSTS OF PRODUCTION

Every productive function entails costs. It is common for economists to analyze the costs of production by classifying them into two categories, viz., fixed and variable. The fixed costs are those which are not related to output in a direct fashion, they remain independent of output throughout a given range of output changes. Variable costs,

---

[1] The problem was discussed at length in the well-known Pigou-Taussig controversy early in this century. See A. C. Pigou, *op. cit.*, especially Chapter XVIII, and F. W. Taussig, "Railway Rates and Joint Costs Once More," *Quarterly Journal of Economics*, XLVIII (August 1934).

[2] George W. Wilson, *Essays on Some Unsettled Questions in the Economics of Transportation*, Bloomington, Foundation for Economic and Business Studies, Indiana University, 1963, p. 14.

[3] Troxel, *op. cit.*, pp. 94, 95.

[4] See A. M. Milne, *The Economics of Inland Transport* (London: Putnam & Sons, Ltd.), 1955, pp. 118, 119.

[5] Wilson, *op. cit.*, p. 17.

on the other hand, relate directly to output in a manner determined by the technical output relationships.[6] For a motor carrier, for example, fuel used in trucks would be a variable cost since it is directly related to output. Maintenance of the general office building, on the other hand, has no relationship to output, except in a most indirect and tenuous fashion, and, being independent, would be classified as a fixed cost.

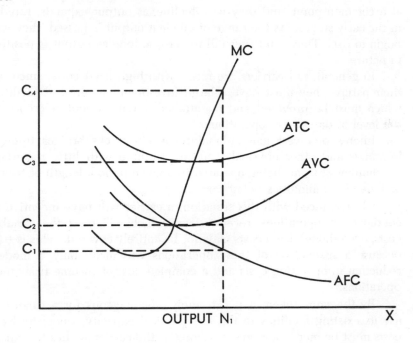

Fig. 5-1

Typical cost curves—transportation firm.

The commonly accepted method of illustrating these costs as related to each other is, as the reader will recall, shown in Figure 5-1. Where ATC = average total costs, i.e., total costs divided by output, MC = marginal cost, the cost of producing each successive unit of output; AFC = average fixed costs, and AVC = average variable

[6] See George J. Stigler, *The Theory of Price* (New York: The Macmillan Co., 1949), pp. 327 ff. In the area of measuring costs in the transportation industry, the student is referred to a most interesting and illuminating technique described in an article by John R. Meyer and Gerald Kraft, "The Evaluation of Statistical Costing Techniques as Applied in the Transportation Industry," *American Economic Review*, Vol. LI, No. 2, May 1961.

costs. Thus, at any output, N_1 costs are measured, C_1, C_2, C_3 . . . C_n. The slopes and location of the variant cost curves will be a function of the technological relationships prevailing or the "state of the arts." For our purpose, only the portions of the curves intersected by the line N are relevant, since they depict the costs at that particular output with a given array of plant. Several things can be said about these curves without regard to technology. They must begin on the Y axis at a common point, and they will decline, as output expands, rapidly in the early stages. As the range of efficient output is passed, they will begin to rise. They can never fall to zero, so long as output is positive in nature.

In general, rail carriers are faced with high fixed costs, since, by their nature, they must have a large investment in physical facilities which must be provided and maintained, often without reference to the level of day-to-day operations.

Interest on investment and maintenance of tracks, bridges, tunnels, buildings and other physical facilities continue with little regard to the number of trains being operated in a given period, length of trains, or type of commodities being carried.

Clearly, faced with this situation, a carrier will have incentive to continue any operations, revenue from which will meet the variable costs, even though fixed costs may not be entirely covered. This is true because a suspension of these operations will mean only a modest reduction in operating costs and a complete loss of income from such operations.

By the same token, it is extremely advantageous for a carrier to use its existing facilities to the full physical capacity, since the fixed costs must be met in any event so long as the carrier wishes to remain in business. As an example, suppose a rail carrier is operating at a level of 100,000 ton-miles per week with a given plant and bringing in a revenue of $50,000 at a total cost of $20,000, of which $15,000 is fixed cost. Assume that a substantial increase in ton-miles is achieved, although of such a magnitude that the same physical plant can be used. Consequently, only the variable costs, e.g., fuel, labor, etc., will increase. If revenue now rises to $70,000, costs might increase by a much more modest figure, say by $5,000, making a total of $25,000. (If the increase in traffic was so large as to require additional plant and if it was expected to be of a long run nature, fixed costs would, however, be increased.)

Let us now assume that the opposite is true, viz., that the level of business declines in the same proportion. Revenue now falls from $50,000 per week to $20,000 per week. Variable costs also decline, say, to $4,000, since the new level of traffic requires less fuel, fewer workers, and other items. Unless the decline was expected to be of long duration, the fixed plant would remain intact and fixed costs would not fall. Under this assumption, the new revenue of $20,000 per week would be just enough to cover variable costs with a small profit.

Several references have been made to the long run vs. the short run. The long run is a period of time sufficient to enable the producer to make basic changes in the plant. A widely used text in economic theory[7] refers to this as a process of transferring capital easily or when capital is mobile. Interestingly enough, the author uses a railroad example to illustrate this point. Since plant changes are involved, it is easy to see that the period of time necessary to make capital changes is a function of the technology involved. If, for example, a railroad enjoyed such an increase in traffic as to require a second track between two points and two years were required to construct this line, the long run would be two years. In contrast, a motor carrier might double its fleet in several weeks' time, in which case the long run would involve much less time. Thus, no specific time period is common to each situation but relates to the specific factors involved.

By all means, the carrier will not embark upon long run changes (either additions or deletions), unless the future course of events is reasonably clear.

In practice, many costs classifiable as variable will contain a substantial element of rigidity, enhanced in recent years by institutional factors such as union regulations (see Chapter IV) and legal requirements of various kinds.

As Dean points out, the behavior of cost depends upon various factors, including the rigidity of the relevant proportions of factors making up the productive process.[8] A very substantial amount of literature exists which would indicate the increasing rigidity of costs in modern industrial processes.[9]

Indeed, in the transportation industry, subject as it is to regulation of various types, the degree of cost flexibility necessary for managerial decisions may be seriously inhibited. Even in the more informal branches of the industry, where historically costs have been generally flexible and fixed costs almost entirely absent, institutional rigidities have crept in.[10]

---

[7] Kenneth E. Boulding, *Economic Analysis* (New York: Harper & Row, Publishers, Inc., 1941).

[8] See Joel Dean, *Managerial Economics* (Englewood Cliffs, N. J.: Prentice-Hall, Inc., 1951), pp. 275 ff.

[9] An excellent example: G. C. Means, *Industrial Prices and Their Relative Inflexibility*, Sen. Doc. 13, 74th Congress, 1st Session, Washington, 1933.

[10] Hugh S. Norton, "The Itinerant Trucker, A Problem in Business Growth," *Land Economics*, Vol. XXXIV, No. 2, May 1958.

VARIATIONS IN SCALE, ITS INFLUENCE ON COSTS

In view of the fact that fixed costs must be faced continuously once they are incurred, it follows that the scale of operations must be undertaken with this fact in mind. A large plant which involves substantial costs is feasible and indeed necessary if the output is likely to be large and sustained.[11] However, it is only partially within the power of the entrepreneur to control the scale of plant. A railroad, for example, must be built more or less complete at one time and may be capable of handling many more trains per day than the traffic originally available would call for. Likewise, a given locomotive might be capable of hauling fifty loaded cars, although it may often be unnecessary to do so. Thus, though the management will avoid any undue extensions in the scale of enterprise, it is impossible to prevent some miscalculation because of technological design limitations or failure to read the future correctly. A clear example of this problem occurs in the airline industry in the ratio of aircraft size to seating capacity. An airliner which has too few seats is clearly wasteful, since the cost per hour of flying the plane must (except for mail or express) be offset by revenue from fares or other funds. A plane which has excess capacity is also wasteful, since it must fly with empty seats. Unless patronage is so light that the flight is not undertaken, costs are the same for a flight regardless of how many seats are full or empty. The "no show" problem for airlines is serious indeed. Assuming that the cost of flying a jet plane from point A to point B is $2,500 (exclusive of amortization, capital costs, etc.) and fares amount to $60 per seat between those two points, eighty full seats would produce $4,800 in revenue while forty full seats would produce $2,400 or slightly less than the cost of the plane's operation. Ground handling costs would, to be sure, be related to number of passengers, but direct aircraft operating costs remain the same. A scheduled aircraft must operate without regard to load, hence

---

[11] Some question exists about the influence of scale, and a recent work on this subject casts some doubt on the beneficial influence of size. See Kent T. Healy, *The Effects of Scale in the Railroad Industry,* Committee on Transportation, Yale University, 1961. Healy concludes that for roads of low traffic density consolidations which increase traffic density will be helpful so long as the size does not increase to the point that scale losses offset traffic density gains and, further, that where traffic density is already high, combinations beyond 10,000 employees are likely to result in diseconomies. In the motor carrier field, Roberts, analyzing vehicle mile costs, finds no evidence of scale economies in the larger firm. Merrill J. Roberts, "Some Aspects of Motor Carrier Costs: Firm Size, Efficiency, and Financial Health," *Land Economics,* Vol. XXXII, No. 3 (August, 1956), pp. 228-38.

For a classic discussion see Edward Chamberlin, *The Theory of Monopolistic Competition, op. cit.,* pp. 203 ff.

the emphasis upon high load factors and the importance of operating aircraft of a size related to potential traffic.

Frederick[12] points out further refinements in this area, e.g., careful attention must be given to space allocated to fuel, baggage and other non-revenue producing areas of the plane. Historically, a common error for most carriers has been to overestimate the potential traffic and build a system which proved to be unduly large, at least for a considerable period of time.

Fortunately, modest changes may be made from time to time in response to increasing traffic which increase capacity and may, at the same time, actually reduce the fixed costs. For example, the use of centralized traffic control by a railroad may, although it is itself expensive, eliminate many miles of duplicate trackage, along with the related costs of maintenance and taxes. Obviously, such expensive undertakings can only be considered when traffic is at a very high level and is expected to continue.

Such internal plant variations are possible only to a degree, determined by the physical organization of the enterprise and the state of technology. In the above case some unused capacity might still exist in that the plant structure may be larger than necessary insofar as physical structures are concerned. It thus may be impracticable to reduce the scale or impossible except by the elimination of some of the plant entirely. For example, in Washington, D. C., the Union Station is much too large for present patronage, but it would be very expensive to alter or rebuild it at this time. At the time of construction (1907), the size was, no doubt, proper. For many years (except for wartime), it has been much too large. On the other hand, Washington National Airport was, for a number of years, much too small, although some time had to elapse before it became feasible to build additional airport facilities.

Thus, overcapacity or undercapacity may prevail for some time before it becomes practicable to alter the situation.

Stigler points out this dilemma by using the example of rail service in his discussion relating to the indivisibility of certain services.

Suppose a single line of railroad track can handle efficiently only 200 trains per day. Should the traffic increase beyond 200 trains per day, the railroad may do one of two things. First, it may put on more sidings, run longer and heavier trains (the diesel locomotive being capable of being used in various combinations of power helps this situation a great deal), and expand loading and unloading facilities. But this situation will become more and more expensive if traffic

---

[12] *Op. cit.*, p. 23.

continues to increase, until the company will be forced to resort to the second alternative. This latter alternative is to lay another track. But then, supposing traffic stands at 300 trains per day, the two tracks are used relatively lightly; so the cost per train is high. Increases of traffic up to 400 trains per day will be accompanied by falling average costs.[13]

Certainly for a complex plant such as a railroad, the relationship between the various segments of the plant is impossible to express in precise terms of productive functions such as might be done for a chemical product. To elaborate on Stigler's example, the problem might be solved by investing in various forms of traffic control referred to above, which enhance the capacity with much smaller outlays in the form of plant and subsequent maintenance. These innovations, in effect, increase the divisibility of the plant. Often the situation occurs where one segment of plant is properly adjusted to the scale of operations only to point up maladjustments in other areas. During the "diesel revolution" in the railroad industry, some railroads found that the diesel made road operations so much more efficient that the "bottlenecks" arose in yard capacity, etc., which, in turn, had to be corrected. Airlines have often found that larger planes made problems of passenger boarding, luggage handling and related matters much more acute than they had been previously. In other words, an innovation of one type makes others necessary, and an overall adjustment of scale may be impossible to achieve except in theory.

When equipment can be divided into small units which operate independently of each other, it is possible to be more precise in scale adjustments. Consequently, a motor carrier, having little or no physical plant and having highly divisible output units, can adjust its plant to a very small scale of operations and still operate efficiently. Also, a plant structure of this type is much better adapted to precise adjustments brought about by sharp variations in the level of output due to fluctuations in demand.

To illustrate, the example used before might be varied to relate to a motor carrier. Assume that the carrier is operating at a weekly cost of $30,000, of which $25,000 is variable and $5,000 fixed. An increase in business occurs which increases revenue from $45,000 to $55,000. Since the bulk of motor carrier costs, fuel, drivers' wages, maintenance of vehicles, etc., is variable, the operating costs rise to $40,000. Likewise, when operations decline, the cost of operation declines sharply. Clearly, the motor carrier finds that total costs of

---

[13] Stigler, op. cit., p. 133.

doing business are tied very closely to the level of output; and, unlike the railroad, a substantial portion of those costs can be avoided when operations are reduced.

This problem is acute for a pipeline which must be built to a given scale since, except for pumping capacity, a pipeline eighteen inches in diameter cannot be increased to carry more traffic nor can it be adjusted to account for reduction in traffic. Consequently, as noted above, a pipeline must be designed with careful attention to the available traffic.

LENGTH OF HAUL AND TERMINAL COSTS

Obviously, an important factor in determining the type of equipment and the economic relationships prevailing will be the length of the haul necessary to complete the movement. However, certain costs, those known as terminal costs, will be independent of the length of haul. Such costs as those incurred in loading, packing, unloading, and those incident to preparation of shipping documents will be incurred without regard to length of haul. For very short hauls, the cost of preparation, or terminal costs, might exceed the actual cost of line movement. Carrier management recognizes this factor by imposing a minimum charge on shipments of a very light or small nature which are to move only a short distance and which would give rise to costs in excess of revenue calculated on a distance basis.

Terminal costs will be related to the technical nature of the product and may be altered by technological changes. For example, loading of bulk products directly into cars or trucks by gravity is much more economical than loading small units by hand, and both shippers and carriers try to reduce terminal costs whenever possible. When the terminal costs have been incurred and the actual line haul begins, costs must increase with distance, although this increase is not in direct proportion to the distance. That is to say, a haul of 500 miles does not mean that line haul costs will be twice those incurred for a haul of 250 miles. The degree of increase depends again chiefly upon the technological conditions prevailing. A carrier operating large units of carriage, such as barges, can achieve very low unit costs on a ton-mile basis, since such costs will increase very slightly as distance increases. When long hauls are to be undertaken, it is advantageous to use the largest units available within the range of extant technology.

Since a long haul acts to spread total costs over a broad area, insofar as ton-miles are concerned, a long haul will justify terminal costs which could not be justified by a short haul. Thus, elaborate loading, packing, and other high terminal costs, which would not be feasible if the haul is short, may be justified for long hauls. An extremely short haul might not be feasible at all due to the terminal costs which might exceed the line haul costs.

Consequently, some commodities which are of low value relative to bulk may not be shipped long distances at all, except under very special circumstances. For such commodities, local sources must be developed. In his well-known early work, J. H. Von Thünen derived a model showing, by the use of concentric circles surrounding a market center, the way in which production would be carried on relative to transport costs.[14] However, it may become economical to ship such commodities if the quantity moved per unit can be increased sufficiently to make the aggregate value worthwhile. For example, it may be reasonable to ship grain in truck load lots no more than 500 miles. A train load of grain may be transported 1,500 miles, while a barge load or ship load of grain may be economically shipped several thousand miles. Clearly, the technology of the various modes of transportation is one of the determinants of this economic relationship. Thus, when terminal costs and costs per mile are extremely high, such as in air transportation, it would be economic nonsense to use such a mode for short distances. Conversely, the use of a small motor truck would not be economic for anything but short distances.

While a logical allocation of resources in transportation may be made on an economic basis because of social or other goals, this allocation may not be in effect at any given time.[15]

For a number of reasons, it may be impossible or undesirable to have an economically rational allocation of transport resources in all cases, just as it is impossible in other industries. The allocative problem will be considered further in Chapter IX.

LOAD, WEIGHT AND VOLUME

It is evident that an important economic factor in the carriage of a product is the volume of the product relative to weight and value per

---

[14] "Der Isolierte Staat," published as early as 1826. Cited in Eric Roll, *A History of Economic Thought,* (3d ed., Englewood Cliffs, N. J. Prentice-Hall, Inc., 1956), p. 328.

[15] See *Competition in the Transport Industries,* John R. Meyer, Merton L. Peck, John Stenason, and Charles Zwick (Cambridge: Harvard University Press, 1959).

unit. Thus, an ideal product for a transporter to carry would be a light, dense, high value product. Unfortunately, few products available to the carrier meet this description. The economic rationale of any classification system is thus to adjust the various economic and physical characteristics, and they appear in various combinations.

Bananas, for example, are heavy and difficult to transport, but their value makes it feasible to move them long distances. On the other hand, potatoes may be less troublesome to move but are often so low in value that they will be used only locally. Certain carriers are more sensitive to this problem than others. Motor vehicles, having relatively small carrying capacity and being subject to certain statutory weight limits, are more circumscribed than rail carriers. Conversely, water carriers may be anxious to move low value, high weight products which railroads or motor carriers would avoid. Naturally enough, air carriers are the most sensitive of all transporters to this problem, and only the most valuable freight can at present bear the cost of air transportation.

Volume and density may influence transportation cost in a purely physical way; thus, sand or gravel may have great weight and low value, but, to some extent, these disadvantages may be offset by ease of loading and remote possibility of damage. To cite some specific examples, a trailer, thirty-five feet long and having a capacity of 2,000 cubic feet, could be loaded to full volume with cigarettes which weigh 24 pounds per cubic foot. Canned goods, weighing 45 pounds per cubic foot, would fill the trailer to only slightly more than half the cubic capacity. Paint would use only 48 per cent of the capacity. Cigarettes, which are valuable and easy to load, are ideal cargo for the trucker. Paint, although heavy, is also valuable and would be highly desirable. Steel castings, weighing 100 pounds per cubic foot, would be undesirable unless their value was extremely high.

The student must contemplate the technical and economic relationships in this situation. For example, an extremely light, bulky product such as ping-pong balls would require a considerably different rate approach than a heavy dense product. From the technical standpoint, it would be desirable for cubic capacity and weight capacity of the transport vehicle to be matched; i.e., if a semi-trailer can carry 20,000 lbs. and has a cubic capacity of 1,000 cubic feet, it would be ideal to carry a product which weighed 20,000 lbs. per 1,000 cubic feet. Of course, in practice, few products will be available or can be loaded so that no waste space occurs, and the average trailer or freight car represents a wide range of products of various sizes, shapes, weights, and value, with considerable waste space because of odd-shaped containers and packages. Car load or truck load freight may be likely to be more uniform and, consequently, more efficient cargo.

COMMON COSTS

Transportation service, like many other services or products, is sometimes produced under conditions of common cost; viz., in some instances the same productive units produce distinct products, and the costs cannot be traced to their origins. It can be seen that this is only partially true in most instances. Thus, if a railroad operates both freight and passenger service, some costs are common to both services and cannot be allocated except on an arbitrary basis.[16] Cost of maintaining track and structures, such as bridges and fuel stations, is not influenced by the nature of the class of service provided. A railroad may produce tremendous amounts of one type of service and little or none of the other, as it desires or as the market dictates.

This problem is closely related to that of large capacity already discussed. Assuming that a railroad already owned tracks and lineside facilities between two points and was operating freight trains, but not piggy-back service, the facilities necessary to perform such service could be installed at relatively modest cost, enabling the service to be offered. These new costs would relate directly and solely to piggy-back service and could be allocated. However, certain costs might be common to general freight and impossible to allocate. Supervision, for example, might become somewhat more burdensome, and wear on rails and bridges might increase, but, in both cases, to only an immeasurable degree. Clearly, some of these costs cannot be allocated except artificially for accounting purposes. A similar situation arises when a railroad undertakes to eliminate passenger service. Some direct costs are thus avoided, but these costs are likely to be a small part of the total costs. However, some non-cost advantages accrue, in that the carrier may free managerial time and talent to pursue what appears to be the more profitable process, viz., freight transportation. For rail carriers' costs are so intertwined that it is most arduous to determine with precision what gains can be made by reductions or additions to the "product line."

In the transportation industry, the most common distinction between products and their cost of production is that between passenger and freight service. However, there is also a somewhat less obvious distinction between the various sub-groups, such as mail, express and

---

[16] For the historical importance of such a concept in economic thought see Alfred Marshall, *Principles of Economics* (8th ed., New York: The Macmillan Co., 1948), footnote 3, p. 395.

passenger traffic which might require specialized or unique equipment.[17] Thus, many variations are present in the outputs of the industry.

Various ways and means are under constant trial in an effort to develop standard equipment which also will be as widely adaptable as possible. Conversely, carriers seek to avoid the operation of equipment which is so highly specialized as to be uneconomic. Not only does this traffic require special cars, but it also has the disadvantage of often being one-way. For this reason, shippers of certain specialized commodities may be required to provide their own freight cars or, in the case of motor carriers, to engage in private or contract carriage. At the same time, at the other end of the cycle, a carrier might be anxious to provide special equipment or service to attract traffic which it had not before carried, if such traffic would move in large quantity.

BACK-HAUL COSTS AND TRAFFIC

It is desirable for any carrier (except for pipelines) to have a balanced traffic, i.e., for the cargo available to be shipped in each direction to be approximately equal. Such a situation eliminates the uneconomic return of empty vehicles; and, since such vehicles must be returned in any event or at least sent somewhere to be loaded, the back-haul traffic helps to defray these fixed costs. Some transport lines, by their nature, will have little or no back-haul traffic and are constructed with that factor in mind. A railroad built to tap a mining area, for example, will have a large part, if not all, of its traffic in one direction only.[18] A similar problem would be faced by a highly specialized type of motor carrier, such as a tank truck operator, whose equipment makes it unlikely that back-haul traffic will be available to him. If, however, a carrier has been operating successfully without such traffic and then such traffic materializes, it is likely that it can be carried with little addition to cost. When a common carrier serves

---

[17] Interesting cases have occurred where traffic has been developed as an incentive to idle equipment, which subsequently required specialized equipment. For example, some years ago, southern railroads began transporting pulpwood, using otherwise idle flat cars. Later, this traffic became sufficiently important to require cars built especially for the purpose. As a result, costs were increased substantially, and some of the advantage of using idle equipment was lost. Many similar instances occur in the trucking industry where specialized equipment has been developed over a period of years for cargo formerly carried in regular equipment.

[18] A railroad of this type is, in effect, an elaborate conveyor belt operating in one direction only. The Quebec, North Shore and Labrador (an iron ore carrier) is an example of such an operation. Like most such roads, this one is owned by a mining company.

many large urban points, the traffic to and from these centers is likely to be fairly well balanced, and the only limitation is upon the carrier's ability to secure and handle it. However, in more remote or isolated areas, the transporter may have to put forth great effort to obtain back-haul traffic in any amount. The reader will recall the previous discussion relative to fixed costs. In the present case, the cost of returning the vehicle or vehicles to their base of operations is a fixed cost to a degree, since it is only in part related to output, and has to be met. Since any revenue which can be obtained from such a movement is highly advantageous, carriers will often establish rates on such traffic which are lower than they ordinarily would be. This is especially true of non-regulated motor carriers who may quote rates almost entirely unrelated to the actual service performed or the costs incurred, in order to stimulate back-haul traffic and because these carriers often lack the data to make sound cost decisions.

Obviously, the back-haul problem creates great instability in rate structures. Certain traffic may be "back-haul" to one carrier and, therefore, marginal in nature; but the same goods may be most important as fundamental traffic for another carrier. Consequently, it may be very difficult for a carrier to maintain a desirable level of traffic at a remunerative rate. No doubt in the aggregate, this effect balances out, but it may be a hardship on certain carriers.[19]

OUT OF POCKET COSTS

It is often assumed that the "out of pocket costs" of performing an additional unit of service will be very small indeed and that marginal cost pricing would be practicable in an economic sense even though the operating feasibility might be slight. Even in a theoretical sense, the difficulties are immense.

For example, it is often pointed out that if a train of 30 cars is ready to depart, another car added to the train would add very little to the total cost. This may or may not be so. From where must the added car be brought? If a train is ready to depart and another car is brought from the adjacent track, costs may be small indeed if the

---

[19] For example, truckers engaged in exempt agricultural commodity carriage lease out to regulated carriers to "back-haul" regulated commodities. Regulated carriers often utilize empty vehicles by carrying exempt commodities as "back-haul" traffic. Each of these groups tends to view the other as a trespasser on his area.

These operations are aided by truck transportation brokers who arrange loads. See *The Role of Truck Brokers in the Movement of Exempt Agricultural Products*, MRR No. 525, M.R.D., U. S. Department of Agriculture, 1962.

switch engine crew is on duty and the equipment is ready and waiting. However, what is the meaning of an "extra car" if the train is departing from Chicago? The "extra car" may be on an adjacent track or it may be twenty miles away. If a truck is ready to depart from the terminal in Atlanta, an extra package loaded on destined for Cincinnati would incur only minor and perhaps immeasurable costs *assuming* that the trailer is also destined to Cincinnati. If, however, the truck is going to Columbus, where the cargo will be redistributed for points north of Columbus, the cost of the Cincinnati package may be determined by fifteen miles of driving through heavy urban traffic to reach the Cincinnati terminal, plus the cost of local delivery. The pitfalls of using such vague terms are well illustrated by Wilson.[20]

Summary

The production of transportation services in common with other products and services involves costs which are divided into fixed and variable. The relationship between these costs is of great importance in the operation of the firm.

Generally, railroads are characterized by a high level of fixed costs relative to the total, while motor carriers tend toward a low level of fixed costs; however, these are relative and not absolute measures.

In large part, the high level of fixed costs in the railroad industry stems from the large scale on which the firm is constructed. The ownership of large amounts of real property and the investment necessary to acquire and operate equipment make large scale orientation necessary. Within limits, the scale of operations, or of any specific operation, may be modified as the technology changes.

While length of haul is of fundamental importance in cost calculations, it is only one of several factors. Value of the commodity carried, weight, volume and other factors are all influential. Certain costs involved in transportation are of a joint nature; i.e., they are common to the production of two or more services. Many of these costs cannot be allocated to any one type of service. Consequently, if the carrier ceases to produce one class of service, only a portion of the costs involved may be eliminated. On the other hand, only a small amount of additional cost must be incurred if certain additional services are undertaken.[21]

---

[20] George Wilson, *op. cit.*, pp. 32 ff.

[21] As an illustration of the complexity of the problems involved, see D. R. Ladd, *Cost Data for the Management of Passenger Services* (Cambridge: Harvard University Press, 1957.

Selected References for Further Study

The economics of costs, output, demand and other production relationships are well analyzed in Troxel, Emery, *Economics of Transport* (New York: Rinehart & Co., Inc., 1955) and in Bonavia, M. R., *The Economics of Transport, Cambridge Economic Handbooks* (new ed.; New York: Pittman Publishing Co., 1947).

Many studies on technical aspects of cost finding and measurement of demand appear in publications of the Interstate Commerce Commission and the Civil Aeronautics Board, e.g., ICC Statement No. 25025 Study of Railroad Motive Power 1950 (mimeographed) and ICC Statement No. 5614 *Survey of Class I Motor Carriers of Property 1939-1954*, 1956 (mimeographed).

Tremendous amounts of cost data have been published by the ICC and CAB through the years, since almost every rate hearing involves the presentation of cost data and other economic information.

A comprehensive treatment for management use is found in White, Joseph L., *Analysis of Railroad Operations* (New York: Simmons-Boardman Publishing Co., 1946) and in White, D. R., *Cost Data for Management of Railroad Passenger Services* (Cambridge: Graduate School of Business, Harvard University, 1957).

Many demand studies relative to transportation service have been made by all of the modes utilizing empirical data. A surprisingly small amount of theoretical literature exists in the pure field of transportation micro-economics.

Transportation has long been recognized as fundamental and influential in the area of macro-economic analysis; see, for example, Partington, John E., *Railroad Purchasing and the Business Cycle* (Washington, D. C.: The Brookings Institution, 1929).

The various trade associations, as well as the regulatory groups, compile and publish large quantities of data relating to the overall performance of the various modes. Doubtless, the volume of basic economic data is greater in the transportation field than in any other area.

An excellent treatment of the theory of location is found in Smithies, Arthur, "Optimum Location in Spatial Competition," *Readings in Price Theory, Vol. VI, American Economic Association* (Stigler and Boulding, eds.) (Homewood, Illinois. 1952, R. D. Irwin, Inc., 1952), p. 485.

Many of the current theoretical problems are well treated in Wilson, George W., *Some Unsettled Questions in the Economics of Transportation*, Bloomington, Foundation for Economic and Business Studies, Indiana University.

CHAPTER VI

The Demand for Transport Services

The modes of transport produce and sell transportation service, which, like other service, is an intangible item produced and consumed at the same instant. Basically, this service is of two types: (1) the transportation of persons and (2) the transportation of goods. The demand for these services hinges upon several factors, and it will be instructive to examine them separately.

THE MOVEMENT OF PEOPLE

Clearly, the demand for personal movement is a function of personal place utility. Persons may wish to travel for various personal or business reasons, and the desire to use any particular mode or type of transport will be derived from the same source. In common with the demand for many consumer products or services, the demand for passenger travel may be predicted with accuracy only to a small degree. Such factors as economic growth, disposable personal income, geographic distribution of population, and other factors will influence the demand for passenger movement. Since many irrational factors which cannot be predicted are involved, passenger travel is less predictable than the movement of freight. Carriers attempt to stimulate passenger traffic much in the same fashion as producers of other consumer services. Advertising and other means will be used to "sell" passenger travel, since, except for commuter traffic and business travel, passenger travel is not a derived demand and must be created. Great doubt exists among students of the problem relative to the degree to which passenger travel can be stimulated; or, in other words, to what degree is the demand for passenger travel elastic?[1]

For many years, carriers have experimented with lower fares, improved facilities, and other means in an effort to influence the demand for the service. Unfortunately, there are so many factors which must be accounted for that it would be almost impossible to draw firm conclusions. For example, the following factors might be influential either individually or in various combinations: (1) relative fare per mile; (2) elapsed time in transit; (3) schedule, i.e., arrival or departure at main points; (4) equipment in service; (5) services offered, such as meals, lounge or club car, credit cards, etc.; and (6) intangible factors, such as employee courtesy, personal habits, and related factors.

The importance of personal factors in transportation is apparent from the overwhelming use of the private automobile for intercity transportation and for commutation purposes. There is little doubt that a realistic appraisal of the economics of the situation would dictate the use of for-hire transportation. However, the convenience of the private automobile is well established and overcomes cost considerations.

THE MOVEMENT OF GOODS

The demand for movement of goods is largely a derived demand, i.e., goods are more useful in one place than another; and the owner is willing to pay for the creation of place utility, not for the movement of goods as such.

Macro-economic Factors

Let us first consider the aggregate demand for goods movement. One would expect, and does indeed find, that increases in gross

---

[1] For an example of techniques employed to investigate the demand characteristics of rail travel, see Interstate Commerce Commission, Statement No. 4129, *Preliminary Investigation of Factors Affecting the Demand for Rail Passenger Service,* Washington, D.C., U. S. Government Printing Office, 1941.

For Air Transport, C.A.B. Docket No. 730 et. al., 1946, Atlantic Airlines.

national product and national income will be reflected by increases in goods movement. Thus, when the level of economic activity increases, the demand for movement of goods likewise increases.

TABLE 6-1

ORIGIN, NATIONAL INCOME, SELECTED YEARS, TRANSPORTATION
AS A PERCENTAGE OF TOTAL, BILLIONS

Year	Income Source		Percentage Transportation
	All Industries	Transportation	
1929	87.4	6.6	7.55
1935	56.8	3.6	6.34
1940	81.3	4.9	6.03
1945	182.7	10.5	5.75
1950	240.6	13.3	5.53
1952	291.6	15.5	5.32
1953	305.6	15.8	5.2
1954	301.8	14.4	4.8
1955	330.2	15.8	4.8
1956	350.8	16.8	4.8
1957	366.9	17.2	4.7
1958	367.4	16.4	4.5
1959	399.6	17.6	4.4
1960	417.1	17.8	4.3

Source: *The Economic Almanac,* New York, National Industrial Conference Board, 1953-54, pp. 140 ff., and 1962, p. 117.

However, as Table 6-1 shows, the percentage of national income originating in the transportation industry has declined from 7.55 per cent in 1929 to 4.3 per cent in 1960, although the income originating from transportation services more than doubled during the period in absolute terms.

Thus, transportation as a whole did not participate in the growth of national income in these years to the same degree as other industries. Table 6-2 shows relative participation in income origin in dollar amounts for the three major modes.

TABLE 6-2

ORIGIN, NATIONAL INCOME, MAJOR TRANSPORTATION
MODES, 1929 AND 1960, MILLIONS OF DOLLARS

Year	Rail	Motor Freight	Air
1929	4,600	482	—3
1960	6,733	5,725	1,267

Source: *The Economic Almanac,* New York, National Industrial Conference
Board, 1953-54, pp. 140 ff., and 1962, pp. 289 ff.

As Table 6-2 indicates, both motor and air transport have enjoyed
substantial increases as compared to rail in the amounts of dollar
income originating in the production of transport service by those
modes, although all of the modes have increased their contribution to
national income in absolute terms.

Many factors may influence this situation. For example, changes
in technology or changes in the location of industrial activity may
alter the flow of goods or the relationship between the modes.

In some cases, these changes may have no effect upon the net
flow, since they may cause only a shift in commodity types or direction
of flow. In other instances, the total traffic may be influenced.

The student will appreciate the importance of this relationship,
when it is recalled that car loadings and truck loadings are well known
indices of business activity. The macro-economic demand for goods
transport will also be influenced by seasonal and cyclical variations of
many kinds.[2]

As Table 6-2 shows, the demand for goods movement in the
aggregate may be spread among the various modes of transport in a
very uneven fashion. One mode may increase its share either relatively
or absolutely, or both. Thus, motor and air carriers have substantially
increased their share of traffic carried, and this increase has, in part,
come out of an increasing total of goods moved by all carriers and in
part from the traffic formerly moved by other modes.

As the gross national product increases in total, the aggregate
quantity of goods to be moved increases, but not necessarily in the
same proportion. Consequently, all modes may transport more than
they did previously, but some modes may make a larger proportionate
gain than others or those in other geographic regions.

Changes in industrial organization or marketing processes may
alter the flow of goods being shipped in ways which have little or no

---

[2] Hultgren, *op. cit.*

relation to the aggregate quantity of goods produced.[3] In general, a dispersal of industry would tend to create a greater demand for transportation services, while concentration of industry would bring about a reduction in demand.

The student should be cautious in interpreting the figures relative to various shares of traffic moved by different modes.

Since rail transportation was the primary mode of intercity freight transportation before 1930 and motor carriers have made great strides since that date, it is obvious that the relative rail share of the total would have to decline. A more significant comparison relates to the relative shares of the increased traffic held by the various modes.

Micro-economic Demands for Goods Transport

The micro-economic demand factors, those relative to the movement of an individual good, are dependent upon the character of the good and its economic uses. It was previously stated that transportation creates the utility of place, viz., transferring a good from one place to another in order to make it useful or more useful. Thus, if coal is more useful in Philadelphia than at the mine in West Virginia, it is wise to transport it. Transportation acts to shift the demand curve for the product to the right, making the product more useful and enabling an owner to command a higher price.

Clearly, the owner of the product cannot pay more for transportation than the increased value of the goods indicates; e.g., if the value of coal is $6 per ton at the mine and $9 per ton in Philadelphia, the coal seller cannot pay $4 per ton for transportation to Philadelphia.

Certain products which are unique may command high rates for transportation. Fresh fruits, for example, may be transported for great distances and sold at a profit, while bricks may move only short distances and in most instances are locally manufactured.

The student can appreciate that there are hundreds of price-place relationships which will determine the economics of transporting any given commodity from or to any given production or market center. Also, it must be remembered that these price-place relationships are dynamic and not static. Some brief reflection upon the origin, modes of travel, interstate and local, and ultimate destination of any common consumer product will illustrate the problems involved. For example,

[3] See E. W. Smykay, D. J. Bowersox, and F. H. Mossman, *Physical Distribution Management* (New York: The Macmillan Co., 1961), esp. Ch. XI.

copper ore is produced in the western states of Montana, Utah, Nevada, and Arizona. The bulk ore is transported by rail or truck only very short distances since it is of relatively low value and great bulk. The copper "pigs" or blocks resulting from the smelting (reduction) process are then transported great distances, usually by rail. When the pigs have been converted into sheet, bars, wire and other basic copper items, usually in the eastern United States, they are shipped by rail or truck to plants in nearby areas. At this point, the copper is manufactured into finished industrial and consumer products and, being relatively valuable, is transported throughout the nation by various forms of transportation. Thus, from ore to electrical cable, the copper has been transported in various forms on various modes, each relative to the physical form, monetary value and destination of the product, and subject over time to the dynamic effects of economic changes of various magnitude.

Ubiquitous Products

Certain products, because they are widely available or manufactured from local materials, may almost never be transported for long distances. Such items as clay, sand, gravel, and their end products, such as bricks, are almost always locally available and, because of their relative low value, great weight and bulk, are seldom worth transporting any distance. However, it must be emphasized that it is the economic factors which are basic to this analysis.

Weight or size may be of little consequence if there is an effective demand for the goods, and heavy machinery or bulky materials such as iron ore may be transported great distances if they can command a sufficient price.

THE MARKET STRUCTURE FOR TRANSPORTATION SERVICES

The demand for transportation service is a function of market structures faced by producers in the industry. Decisions relating to price, or to enter or refrain from entering a given market, relate to the market structure which exists at any given time. Sellers of transportation service are faced with many competitors, both intermodal and intramodal. These competitive relationships differ as to degree and as to type. A given seller may find that other firms compete for traffic to and from certain points, or other firms compete in regard to certain types of traffic. Competition may be present at terminal points but non-existent at intermediate points. Consequently, a carrier may occupy the entire spectrum of market relationships, i.e., monopoly, oligopoly, duopoly, imperfect competition, and, to some extent, approaches perfect competition. For example, a carrier may exist in a medium-sized city which has two railroads, three airlines, a pipeline, and twenty-three motor carriers. Between some of these carriers, e.g., pipelines and motor carriers, there is almost no competitive relationship, since the demands for these services are insulated from each other, the total market is segmented and, indeed, some of the markets are completely separated.

The various segments of the market might be as follows:

Monopoly (a single seller). The carrier may serve a point or a plant served by no other carrier and, thus, enjoy a locational monopoly. The carrier may have equipment or legal rights to carry a particular product and, thus, have a product monopoly.

Duopoly (two sellers). The carrier may serve points or carry products which are served by another carrier and, thus, share the traffic available.

Oligopoly (several sellers). This would be a common market situation for carriers. Here again, the structure would be in terms of termini, points served and products carried. For some products, or at some points, the carriers might compete in an aggressive fashion while in other areas competition is more restrained.

Imperfect Competition (a number of sellers, each having a market share somewhat insulated from the others). This market structure probably embraces the large bulk of transportation firms and is especially characteristic of the motor carrier segment. In the classic mold each firm attempts to increase and to hold its market share by the intensive use of product and service differences which make it attractive to the buyer. In this market, a carrier may find itself in competition with several or many others carrying the same product and serving the same points. Under such circumstances, the seller must attract buyers (shippers or travelers) by innovations in product or service. Frequently, such competition is of the non-price type, in that, price is uniform or virtually so for all sellers, and buyers make a choice upon the basis of the non-price factors in the market. An excellent example of this type of competition is provided by the airline industry. Thus, four major airlines offer direct service between New York and Los Angeles. Fares for a given class of service are identical, and the carriers attract customers through non-price factors such as more modern aircraft, luxurious service, more convenient departures, food service and many other factors, most of them of an intangible or superficial nature.

Since these factors are available to all the lines, each knows that it cannot achieve a monopoly, although each can attempt to compete away a portion of his competitors' market.

Perfect Competition (an infinite number of sellers, none of which can influence the market; complete knowledge on the part of buyers and sellers; free entry to and exit from the market; and an homogeneous product). Few, if any, firms can be said to meet the classic conditions of this market situation. Perhaps the carriers of "exempt" agricultural commodities come closer to this situation than any other, but, even here, there are imperfections due to institutional factors.

It can be seen that most carriers operate in all of the above markets, some to a greater degree than others. Although generalizations are most difficult, a rough approximation of the competitive status of the industry might be shown as in Table 6-3.

While there are many variations in the total market situation, Table 6-3 does indicate in most general terms the market structure in which the various modes operate.

It will be seen in Table 6-3 that, although some modes tend toward monopoly or tend toward pure or perfect competition, none (except in certain segments) is in those categories.

The seller of transportation, thus, faces a number of demand situations, and he must follow price-output policies accordingly. The pricing policies of carriers will be considered in Chapter VII.

The existence of these various market types makes it possible for carriers to engage (within legal limits as seen later) in price discrimination. Thus, the carrier may, in the face of strong competition, reduce price to a low point and maintain price in cases where, because of monopolistic elements due to location or product type, a higher price can be maintained. Since the buyer of the service is fully aware of these forces, he, in turn, attempts to protect himself by having available multiple sources of transport services in order to increase his bargaining power and reduce the likelihood of monopolistic power being used against him.

Since the firm can locate in many places, depending upon factors such as labor and raw material availability, the limiting factor is apt to be the character of the product.

For example, a paper mill might be so located as to have rail, water and truck service available. Rolls of newsprint might leave the mill by rail or water, but the weight of such products might preclude some truck movements. A frozen foods producer might find that,

TABLE 6-3

APPROXIMATE MARKET STATUS
TRANSPORTATION MODES

Least Competitive ↑		Tends Toward Monopoly ↑
	Pipelines Termini, routes and products highly specialized, few firms, legal regulation, controlled entry.	
	Water Carriers Termini and routes fixed, products limited, and few firms. Legal regulation, controlled entry.	
	Air Carriers Termini, routes fixed, products limited, few firms, legal regulation, controlled entry.	
	Rail Carriers Termini, routes fixed, wide range of products, many firms, legal regulation, controlled entry.	
	Motor Carriers 1. Contract and specialized: Termini and routes fixed, few products regulated, many firms, controlled entry. 2. General Commodity Carriers: Termini and routes fixed, wide range of products, many firms, controlled entry. 3. "Exempt" Carriers: No fixed termini or routes, many products, very large number of carriers, no economic regulation, free entry.	
Most Competitive ↓		Tends Toward Perfect Competition ↓

although several motor lines serve his area, only one of them has the necessary equipment and experience to provide satisfactory service. To be sure, competing carriers will not allow these elements of monopoly to go by default. For example, in the early years of the frozen food industry in Florida, motor carriers had some advantage over rail carriers, since the latter took some time to produce adequate refrigerated cars, whereas motor carriers were quick to begin operation of refrigerated trailers. However, this advantage was quickly overcome and was no longer a competitive factor.

Most carriers attempt to make the range of their services as wide as possible, although there are a few who prefer to exploit in depth a segment of the market. This is especially true of motor carriers which are able to maximize their specialized equipment and technical advantages.

It must be clearly understood that competition in transportation is of a very special nature. Although there are many transportation firms in every mode serving many communities, the competition is in fact oligopolistic, or competition among the few. A common carrier, although transporting a vast range of products, is likely to be in intensive competition for only a relatively few products. He may thus gain the bulk of his revenue from a few shippers and find himself dealing with, on the selling side of the market, two or three of his fellow carriers who serve specific points. Under these circumstances competition is not similar to that which prevails in a market situation where there are both many buyers and sellers, or where there are a few sellers with multiple products. Carriers facing this situation may become so concerned about retaining their share of the vital market that they are led to take irrational competitive actions. The consequences of this competition where the actions and reactions of the few producers (and consumers) are well known to each other are obviously of the type described by Fellner in his classic treatment of the competitive situation in the oligopolistic market.[4] Each producer takes the actions of his competitor into account and no action is taken without this information being thoroughly analyzed as to the probable reaction to be expected. Competitive situations of this type are common in transportation.

These actions lead into unpredictable situations, as phrased by Triffen: "Thus oligopoly usually results in fighting and chaos, unless determinateness is inserted through extra economic influence such as the intervention of the political umpire."[5] Thus there is the classic economic argument for political regulation of such enterprises.[6]

---

[4] William J. Fellner, *Competition Among the Few,* Oligopoly and Similar Market Structures (New York: A. Knoff, reprinted 1960; A. M. Kelley, 1949). Fellner's cases or conditions of oligopoly fit the transportation industry with reasonable accuracy. See pp. 41 ff.

[5] Robert Triffin, *Monopolistic Competition and General Economic Theory* (Cambridge: Harvard University Press, 1949) p. 51.

[6] It is interesting to note that, as Triffin points out, this argument is expanded by Stackelberg to justify state control under National Socialism. H. Von Stackelberg, "Nerves Schrifttum Uber Unvollestandigen Wettbewerb," *Schmollers Jahrbuch,* LIX (1935).

Even under those circumstances where competition increases, it rarely goes beyond the stage of monopolistic competition, and from the sellers viewpoint becomes more intense. This occurs mainly through the development of technological development in the industry which as we have seen gives the shipper more alternatives. However, even in this situation these alternatives are severely limited. Because of physical and institutional limitations (location of sidings, schedules, points served, etc.) most shippers have recourse to only two or three carriers at the most, and for some products to particular points, perhaps only one.

Summary

The demand for the movement of goods is a derived demand and, thus, rests upon the demand for the good being transported. In general, when the gross national product increases, the demand for goods transportation in the aggregate increases.

However, on a micro-economic basis, the demand for transporting any specific good depends upon many factors. All such factors are, in turn, dependent upon the demand for the good per se and the uses to which it lends itself. It is, thus, possible to make reasonable predictions as to the demand for transporting goods, and such predictions are helpful in formulating rates.

For passenger transportation, on the other hand, demand predictions are less reliable, since personal transportation rests upon subjective factors. Aside from business travel, which is a derived demand, persons travel on various modes for personal reasons which have little or no economic basis.

A wide range of market situations prevails, influenced by location, technology, price and non-price factors. Each mode and each firm within the mode, thus, faces a wide range of market structures and must deal with each accordingly.

CHAPTER VII

Pricing the Service

DEMAND AND SUPPLY

The prices of all goods and services are, in the final analysis, governed by the relationship between demand for the product and the available supply. As indicated in Chapter VI, the demand for transportation service is a function of the transport users' evaluation of the benefits to be derived (utility created) from the transport process.

As an extreme example, the reader might consider the illegal, but very profitable, transportation of gold into China during the Second World War. Transporters were willing to pay extremely high rates, rates, moreover, which had no relation to costs because of the enormous speculative profits to be made. Under more normal circumstances, the buyer would be more restrained and rational. For the seller of a given good, transportation costs are one of a number of costs which must be met in order to market his goods. If the market is, in his judgment, profitable, the process of transportation is a necessary and often minor part of the production process. For most industrial or consumer products, transportation costs are a relatively small part of the total costs incurred in order to get the good into the hands of the consumer. Consequently, increases or decreases in transport costs will have little influence upon the ultimate demand for transportation.

For industrial and consumer goods, the demand for transportation is a derived demand, in that it is required in order to produce the product, not as an end per se. For personal transportation, the demand is likely to be subjective, in that the traveler may wish to travel for reasons having nothing to do with rational economic motives.

In general, the effective demand for a good (or service) is compounded of two factors: (1) subjective or objective desire for the good, and (2) the relationship between the price of the good and the available money held by the consumer or the position the price occupies in the consumer budget. Thus, the traditional example of household salt. Observation tells us that the demand for salt is highly inelastic. Without regard to the nutritional need for salt, it is further evident that the annual consumer expenditure for salt is a microscopic part of the annual food budget. Under these circumstances, a percentage increase in the salt price of even 100 per cent would remain an insignificant part of the consumer budget. One might then conclude that, if the total transportation cost was a minor part of the total costs of a product, an increase, even a large increase percentagewise, would be likely to produce only a small reaction on the part of the shipper. However, caution is necessary in this analysis. If the ultimate market is highly competitive, the buyer who hopes to sell must use every means to reduce price or to prevent it from rising due to any circumstance within his control. Also, even slight increases tend to pyramid and to be magnified as they move through the production process, causing the ultimate sales price to be inflated.

In general, the aggregate demand for transportation is fairly stable, due largely to the fact that, while changes take place, one commodity movement replaces another, and some transportation is always necessary.[1] In any given case, the producer must gauge the demand for his product in order to estimate the way in which it will be influenced by changes in transport costs (see Chapter V) and demand for the service (see Chapter VI).

The seller of transportation service will, like other sellers, attempt to set a price which will be profitable to him and, at the same time, encourage rather than discourage future traffic. In general, the basic principles of pricing will prevail. The carrier will not, except for short periods or for special purposes, establish prices lower than the direct or "out of pocket" costs of performing the service. The carrier will

---

[1] Thor Hultgren, *op. cit.*, pp. 4 ff.

give due consideration to the competition which is present or potentially present in the market and to any non-price or service advantages or disadvantages which are relevant.

In order to give due and systematic consideration to these many factors, it is necessary for the carrier to set up a classification system and then to modify and adapt the classification system to meet special circumstances. The classification system, along with the tariff, is thus an elaborate price list, made necessary because of the infinite variety of goods carried by a transportation company. The classification represents an attempt on the part of the carrier to account for the many economic factors involved and, at the same time, keep the administrative process within reasonable bounds. Even the "grouping together" process in the classification results in several thousand items. One can contemplate the confusion which would result from an attempt to weigh the economic factors relating to each item moving in commerce to and from the thousands of points served.

In pricing transportation, the following factors would have to be considered in one way or another:

1. Weight—volume ratio of the good
2. Possibility of damage to the good
3. Possible damage to other goods
4. Market value of the good
5. Distance to be shipped
6. Regularity and volume of movement
7. Competition or lack of competition from other carriers or from private carriers
8. Costs incident to performing the specific service in question

Obviously, the pricing process is one involving the exercise of judicious discrimination and weighing of factors. Clearly, some of these factors are more influential in a given case than others.

For example, manufactured tobacco products are transported at high rates relative to many other products. Manufactured tobacco products have many characteristics conducive to low cost transportation, i.e., they are dense and compact, not easily damaged, and move in great volume with regularity. However, they are of high value and are thus greatly influenced by item 4 above. Indeed, in this case, item 4 clearly overcomes several other items which, in themselves, would indicate a low rate.

Items of this nature may be carried at rates far above the actual cost of providing the service, while items of low value may move at rates lower than the actual cost of providing the service.

Table 7-1 shows that, in practice, the rate charged may be much more or less than the fully distributed costs incident to performing the service.

TABLE 7-1

SELECTED ITEMS, U. S. CLASS I RAILROADS, 1955

RATIO OF CARLOAD FREIGHT REVENUE

TO FULLY DISTRIBUTED COST

BY ICC COMMODITY CLASSES

Item	Ratio to Fully-Distributed Cost (Percentage)
Explosives	370
Bathroom Fixtures	157
Tobacco, Unmanufactured	131
Asphalt	111
Lumber	100
Oranges, Grapefruit	84
Coke	76
Animal Feed	71
Copper Ore	28

Source: *Problems of the Railroads, Hearings,* before the Sub-Committee on Interstate and Foreign Commerce, U. S. Senate, 1958, Part 2, pp. 1218 ff.

As Table 7-1 indicates, the ratio of revenue to actual costs of movement varies greatly, depending upon the product being carried.

Figure 7-1 indicates graphically the distribution of cost-rate relationships of various commodities moving by rail in 1955. It can be seen that, while a number of products are carried at rates less than fully distributed costs, a larger number of products return revenues in excess of full distributed costs. The magnitude of the spread in each case is also important to note.

Both carrier policy and public policy have long justified a practice of allowing certain products to move at rates in excess of their attributable costs, thus enabling the lower value products to be transported as a means of promoting the aggregate economic welfare.[2]

Because of the multiplicity of services and the heterogeneous character of the markets served, rail costs do not provide a satisfactory basis for full cost pricing. This is especially true for rail carriers, and

---

[2] For a classical discussion of this problem, see A. C. Pigou, *The Economics of Welfare,* (4th ed.; London: The Macmillan Co., 1946). Chapter XVIII, esp. pp. 310-317.

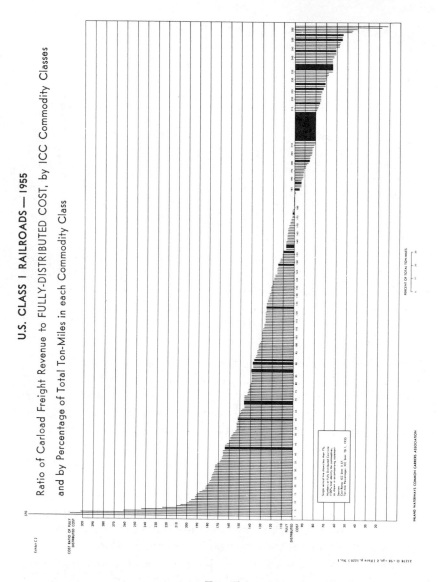

Fig. 7-1

Source: *Problems of the Railroads, Hearings,* before the Sub-Committee on
Surface Transportation of the Committee on Interstate and Foreign
Commerce, U. S. Senate, 1958, Part 2, pp. 1219 ff.

the fallacy underlying the arguments for pricing rail services on a fully distributed cost basis is well expressed in a recent statement as follows:

> Thus, the full distributed cost doctrine does not reflect valid principles of pricing, where fixed costs are significant. Application of this false criterion in the railroads' present competitive environment would bring about prices which (for much traffic) would shrink volume. If the same total constant costs were then distributed on the shrunken traffic volume, even greater fully distributed unit costs would result, and if this should cause the railroads to raise rates still higher relative to the prices of other modes of transport, then rail traffic volume would probably be still further reduced. A costing procedure which can inaugurate such a destructive cost-price spiral is not qualified to serve as a basis for pricing in the railroad business or in any other with unallocable costs and unused capacity.

> The social costs of such a pricing method could be enormous. The railroads could not function economically and quite possibly could not survive the use of this misguided basis of pricing. Under it, much traffic either would not move at all or would be moved only by modes of transportation with higher actual economic costs. The end result would be a greater total transportation cost borne by the whole economy in return for a reduced total volume of transportation service.[3]

Another frequently encountered problem unique in the transportation industry is the part played, both voluntary and otherwise, in the equalization of price. As expressed in a recent study:

> A particularly troublesome problem for common carriers arises from the practice which has grown up that it is somehow the function of transportation to equalize the competive position of widely separated producers in the marketplace. Thus, for example, railroads will attempt to equalize the transportation price of Florida and California oranges in the New York market without regard to the transportation costs involved. This practice is justified on the basis that the more distant product would not move into the market and the carrier would thus lose that volume. The discrimination in favor of the more distant product must be accomplished by transferring a portion of its proper share of constant cost and profit to some other traffic which then shifts to alternative transportation. Especially in a situation of excess capacity and/or decreasing total traffic this sets off a vicious spiral of steadily increasing rates for the remaining users of the particular mode and, if unchecked, cannot fail to drive away increasing amounts of traffic with resulting carrier demise. This feature of pricing

---

[3] William J. Baumol and others, "The Role of Cost in the Minimum Pricing of Railroad Services," *The Journal of Business of the University of Chicago*, XXXV, No. 4 (October 1962).

philosophy may have once had some validity, but it has little today in a relatively mature industrial economy faced with the problem of devising sound long-range policies for insuring greater efficiency in transportation investment and better utilization of a transportation system composed of different modes.[4]

There may have been a measure of justification for these policies in the years when rail service was in a monopoly position. This situation no longer exists and the shipper has, except in few cases, adequate protection in the market by virtue of alternatives.

While the economics of the relation between freight rates and costs of performing are clear, there is perhaps an element of public policy involved. On economic grounds, traffic should be carried by the mode most suitable to it and should not burden other traffic. If public policy, for some reason, wishes to have traffic move in some other fashion, there should be a clear policy to this effect, not based on economic grounds but on social grounds with adequate safeguards in order to prevent competitive dislocations.

NON-PRICE FACTORS

As is true with other products and services, the sale of transport service is influenced by non-price factors. The consumer of transportation service is often concerned with non-price items such as speed, damage to the shipment, courtesy of carrier employees and other matters which often cannot be measured in money terms.[5]

Further, it is obvious that the influence of these factors is relative and must be evaluated within a given frame of reference. Shippers often cite non-price or service factors as being of great importance. Superficially, it would appear that the shipper has little concern with price factors. The economist would, no doubt, question such a conclusion. What is likely is that the shipper responds on the assumption that the rates are and will remain in their present relationship. That is, non-price factors are of great importance if rates are at parity or near it. When the shipper is asked to name the reasons why he uses a given mode, and in the order of importance lists rates far down the scale, he is doubtless assuming parity. It would be interesting to ask a second question, viz., "Suppose one carrier or mode reduced rates

---

[4] National Transportation Policy, *op. cit.*, p. 386.

[5] Many such studies have been made. As an example, see *Transportation of Apples in the Appalachian Apple Belt*, 1952-53, Washington, 1954, U. S. Dept. of Agriculture, p. 19.

by 50 per cent, would you revise your evaluation?" Thus, though non-price factors are important, their significance is relative to price ratios.

If service is so poor that it amounts to no service, or negative service (loss or damage), then, clearly, it will not be attractive at any price, including a price of zero. However, if the service is "adequate," the shipper or traveler will be willing to make certain allowances to secure price advantages. It seems clear from the experience of the airlines in marketing coach class service that the consumer will willingly forego some services if price is reduced.

Obviously, the consumer has in mind what might be called a basic or minimum standard of service. If he fails to get this minimum, he, no doubt, feels that he has no service worth paying for. Beyond this point, however, his standards become elastic.[6] However, the market, especially for passenger travel, is highly segmented. That is, the importance of these services depends to a high degree upon the conditions in the specific area of the market. For example, an executive traveling on an expense account would be much less willing to sacrifice service for rate reductions than would a traveler on a strict budget paying his own expenses.

For shippers the analysis is more objective. The shipper demands a certain standard of service, and, beyond this, he is likely to be indifferent except where special circumstances enter into the situation. Shippers of perishable products or very fragile products, for example, would be much more concerned with rapid and safe transit than a shipper of coal or gravel.

Since the major portion of the transportation industry is subject to rate regulation by public authority, the industry is inhibited in its ability to price in accordance with its short run estimate of the market. Some of the effects of this regulation will be considered later in this chapter. Suffice it to say here, that carriers are not entirely free to price as they might prefer to on a purely economic basis. Every producer would prefer to set the optimum price (in his view), while every seller would prefer to pay the lowest price possible and still obtain the product. These buyer-seller attitudes thus establish a floor and ceiling, below which or above which price may not fall or rise except in special cases and generally for short periods of time.

---

[6] For example, one perhaps could devise a "hedonistic" or "Paretian" scale showing the degrees of service, such as stewardesses, meals, soft seats, inches of leg room, etc., an air passenger would give up for each $10 reduction in fare from one point to another. See the "Scale of Preference" in J. R. Hicks, *Value and Capital* (2nd ed., Oxford: Clarendon Press, 1946) p. 18.

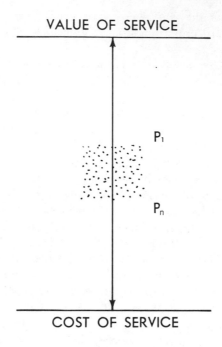

Fig. 7-2

In Figure 7-2, the actual prices charged, P_1—P_n, and tend to cluster around the middle range, few being located at the extremes. In practice, the price will fall near the extreme only if there are marked differences in bargaining power. That is, if the seller is weak (buyers market), the price will tend toward the lower end; while, if the buyer is weak (seller market), the price will tend toward the upper end. In a free market, (non-regulated), each party will exercise all possible means of securing a price which maximizes his own interest. However, suppose that public authority imposes restrictions upon the bargaining area as in Figure 7-3.

In this case, the range of price is limited by public authority to the MIN-MAX area indicated by the broken lines. Thus, even if buyer and seller wish to and are capable of forcing the price toward one of the extremes, they cannot legally do so. In the transportation industry, this situation is not unique. Public authority may establish a minimum price, a maximum price, or an exact price such as P_1 above.

As a matter of public policy or carrier policy, the price may fall below the cost of service, at least on a temporary basis. For example, a carrier may be forced to establish a rate below the actual cost of

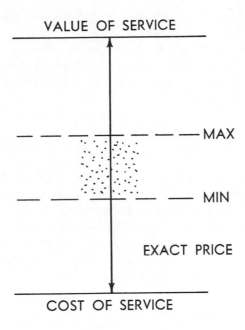

Fig. 7-3

service, in order to move the product at all or to utilize partially unused equipment, hoping perhaps that this situation will be of short duration.

There are certain elements of welfare economics involved in this arrangement, as noted above, as well as public value judgments having little to do with the fundamentals of classical price theory. For example, the public would doubtless condone higher rates on liquor and tobacco than on various other products similar in value and physical character, if such considerations were subject to broad public discussion.

As this section has brought out, the process of pricing transportation services is fundamentally the same as other goods and services. Transportation pricing is somewhat more complex because of the wide variety of goods carried. The practical result of this has been the necessity of a classification system which takes into account the many physical and economic factors relating to the goods to be transported.

Some goods are carried at prices in excess of the costs incurred, while in other instances the price charged for transportation may be less than the actual cost incurred. Non-price or service factors are of importance in the rate structure, especially for particular types of goods.

Transportation rates are unique, in that they are at least; in part, subject to public authority and are thus only to a degree established in the free market. Elements of public policy and welfare economics influence these rates substantially.

CARRIER PRICE POLICY—THEORY AND PRACTICE

Great controversy exists regarding the ability of carriers to compete with each other in the area of price. It was noted in a previous chapter that rail carriers are characterized by high fixed costs and relatively low variable costs. What are the implications of this as regards their ability to use price as an element of competition? Some light can be thrown on this factor by using marginal analysis. Referring to Figure 7-4, we note that the variable costs constitute a rela-

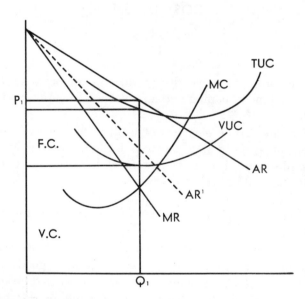

Fig. 7-4
INFLUENCE OF DECLINING REVENUE,
FIRM WITH LOW VARIABLE COSTS
AR—Average Revenue
TUC—Total Unit Costs
MR—Marginal Revenue

tively small part of the total and that, at price OP_1, the firm is enjoying a pure profit. It is also in equilibrium, since MC = MR at an output of OQ_1. Now suppose that a general reduction in rates is undertaken, tantamount to a shift of the AR curve to the left. As AR-MR shifts to the left (AR^1) (assuming no other change), the area of pure profit will be diminished and ultimately disappear. Since the AR curve slopes downward, the student will recognize that the firm represented has a degree of monopoly power.

If the AR curve shifts further to the left, as revenue declines the area of fixed costs will be encountered. It will still be feasible to continue the reduction until the area of variable costs begins to be invaded. At this point, output will no longer be practicable, since at each unit of output the variable costs exceed the sale price per unit. Rates must be increased or, depending upon the elasticity, more traffic secured.

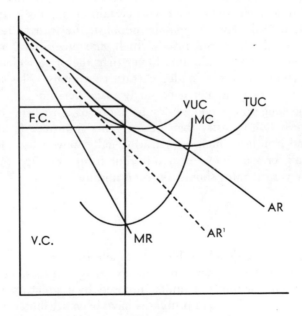

Fig. 7-5

RESULT OF DECLINING REVENUE IN FIRM WITH
HIGH VARIABLE COSTS

AR—Average Revenue
TUC—Total Unit Costs of Output
MR—Marginal Revenue

Let us now turn our attention to Figure 7-5. In this case, the variable costs are a larger part of the cost area which is typical of the motor carrier industry. If now the firm reduces price, thus, shifting the AR-MR curves to the left (AR^1), what takes place? The shifting has turned the pure profit area into loss and soon will invade the area of fixed costs. At a point much earlier in the game than in Figure 7-4, it encounters variable costs at which point the firm must cease to produce. Thus, in Case I (Figure 7-4), the rail carrier can, because of its high fixed costs, reduce rates substantially (for a given product) and remain in operation, although admittedly not a very profitable operation. In Case II (Figure 7-5), the motor carrier soon reaches a point beyond which price reduction cannot go. In addition to the cost factor involved, it must be remembered that removal from a market and possible subsequent re-entry is, in most cases, more difficult for a rail carrier with specialized facilities than for a motor carrier.

It must also be kept in mind that the analysis above refers to a specific market of the firm, and, as was noted earlier, the transport firm has a highly segmentized market with certain monopolistic areas under its discretion. Like any prudent monopolist, the transporter must be careful in establishing the price which maximizes total revenue, a price which may be considerably lower than the price which might be extracted from the buyers under certain conditions. The seller must maximize total revenue, not necessarily price per unit.

In the long run, monopoly is no more of a realistic concept in the transportation industry than in any other industry. Products such as coal and iron ore which have traditionally moved by rail may not move at all, or may move in a different form (finished products or electric power) if rates should become unduly high.

Selective Pricing

Since, as was noted earlier, they sell their services in such a segmentized market, carriers are able to engage, at least in theory, in selective pricing within the limits imposed by regulatory legislation. Some of the current railroad problems have been attributed to a failure on the part of railroad management to exploit selective pricing opportunities to the fullest extent.[7] It seems likely that one of the principal problems involved in a program of selective pricing is the amount of administrative work involved. Ideally, the rate-making officials

---

[7] See James C. Nelson, *Railroad Transportation and Public Policy,* Washington, D. C., 1959, The Brookings Institution.

would have to keep abreast of an infinite number of market situations in order to obtain the optimum price in each market. While the ideal situation is not practicable for a slow-moving organization like a major carrier, there seems to be little doubt that much more could have been done, especially by the railroads, than has been the practice.

Importance of Non-Price Competition

Because of the homogeneous character of service rendered by the carriers within any one mode and because of their cost similarities, the role of non-price competition within the modes has always been important. Intermodal competition, on the other hand, has been less marked by non-price competition, and this tendency will likely become more noticeable. The area for manipulation of non-price factors is rather narrow, even on an intermodal basis, but the possibilities are likely to be greater than has been thought in the past. Thus, more flexibility might well be introduced into transport pricing on an intermodal basis, and carriers might still carry on a brisk competition by non-price means in the intramodel area. This situation will be further discussed when rate regulation is considered.

Long Run Pricing Policy and Costs

Much favorable opinion exists toward long run pricing oriented around costs. One factor is that no firm, especially one dealing with such complex demand factors as a transport company, can measure these factors with any degree of accuracy. There is little question that from the standpoint of aggregate resource allocation such a program is sound.[8]

There are unfortunately formidable objections to a policy of closer alignment between rates and costs. The weight of past practices, the possible disturbance of long standing and favorable rate-cost relationships and other factors are firmly against cost oriented rates on any large scale. However, it must be noted that a sizable group is also in a position to gain from a policy of cost related rates. It was seen in this chapter that many products are carried at rates far in excess of fully distributed costs while others moved at rates below costs. The shippers of the former group of products would have much to gain from a reorientation of this practice.

---

[8] See Myer, Peck, Steanson, and Zwick, *op. cit.*, pp. 240 ff.

Summary

As this chapter has indicated, the pricing of transportation service is a complex exercise in the pricing process. Both cost and non-cost elements must be taken into consideration. The transport firm, like all firms, wishes to operate at a profit and will, like other firms, avail itself of such opportunities for maximizing profit as present themselves. Unlike most buyer-seller relationships, the transportation pricing process is built within a framework of regulation and must be carried on within the limits of public policy. Both buyer and seller are, thus, somewhat inhibited, and price tends to be somewhat rigid.

As a consequence, buyers and sellers tend to give substantial weight to non-price factors, such as schedule, which, in turn, further inhibit the role of price. However, there is some evidence that price is becoming more definitive as regulatory rigidities are somewhat relaxed.

CHAPTER VIII

Transportation Rates and the Pricing Process

The economic function of transportation, like any other economic function, has a cost which must be paid by the user of the service or by someone else. That is, the cost of transportation is included along with the cost of labor and materials in the total cost of the product. Somewhere (and by someone) in the production process, this cost must be paid.

Compared to other costs, the transportation cost of most products is a relatively small part of the total. This relationship depends, of course, upon the total cost of the product. Thus, the total transportation cost involved in producing an automobile may be $400 total, or 10 per cent for a $4,000 automobile. For a low value commodity, the cost of transportation may be much higher percentage-wise. Transportation cost is relatively small when compared to other factors such as direct labor and materials, as shown in Table 8-1. To be sure, these costs are influenced by the technology involved. Producers attempt to reduce transportation costs, just as they attempt to reduce other costs relevant to the goods they produce and sell.

Since the proportion of the total cost attributable to transportation differs as between products, changes in freight rates influence producers in different ways. Sellers of transportation service are well aware of the influence which freight rates have upon the output and

149

TABLE 8-1

RATIO RAILROAD FREIGHT REVENUE, SELECTED COMMODITIES
TO AVERAGE WHOLESALE PRICE AT
DESTINATION, 1956

Commodity	Percentage Freight Revenue to Value
Gravel and Sand	56.14
Bituminous Coal	41.14
Pulpwood	27.17
Iron Ore	18.56
Gasoline	11.21
Wheat	8.20
Sugar	5.86
Automobiles	4.68
Cigarettes	1.24
Airplanes and Parts	0.23

Source: Bureau of Transport Economics and Statistics, Interstate Commerce Commission, *Freight Revenue & Wholesale Value at Destination of Commodities Transported by Class I Line Haul Railways, 1956,* Washington, D. C., . . . 1958.

prices of goods of various types. Increases in freight rates influence the price of products in the same manner in which any factor cost increase influences price. That is, the influence depends upon the elasticity of demand for the good per se and upon the relative magnitude of the increase. For example, if the price of the $4,000 automobile referred to above increases by $8 due to a freight rate increase, it will, in all probability, have little or no influence upon the demand for the car and, further, can doubtless be passed on to the ultimate consumer with ease. Clearly, this is due to various factors, all of which contribute to inelasticity of demand. Perhaps, first of all, the consumer has very little concern with an increase in price of two-tenths of one per cent if he has already decided to make a purchase of $4,000. Thus, the $8 increase escapes the consumer's notice by being relatively insignicant, if he knows about it at all.

Looking at the situation from the producer's viewpoint, a somewhat different view appears. The producer, unlike the consumer, takes an aggregate view, since he looks at the total transportation bill which he must pay to market his output. Depending upon his estimate as to the ease or difficulty of passing the increase on to his customer, he will resist such an increase. Here again, an example may be helpful. If a proposed freight rate increase amounts to $50,000 per year added to

Fig. 8-1
Typical blanket rate area.

the producer's costs, he is likely to view this in the same way as any other increase, such as wages or materials. To the extent that the demand for his product is inelastic in regard to price, the producer can pass these increases along to the buyer (or shift them back to the supplier) in whole or in part. All factors mentioned above and others such as consumer knowledge, desire for the product, total price as a part of the budget, etc., will determine the degree of elasticity which prevails.

From the standpoint of the transportation agency, it is desirable to impose rate increases upon those commodities or classes of commodities for which the transport demand is inelastic. If this can be done, there is less likelihood that the traffic will be diminished or shifted to other means of transportation. The seller of transportation is, thus, in the position of all sellers, in that he must pay close attention to the elasticity of demand for his product or service.

The demand for transportation of a given good may be influenced in two ways due to an increase in rates. First, the quantity of goods tendered for shipment may decline in absolute terms. Secondly, the goods may shift to other means of transport. There is a continuous shift of traffic as industries rise and fall and as price relationships change. Traffic shifts back and forth between various modes or between carriers within a given mode, as previously discussed.

As noted earlier, however, certain carriers enjoy traffic which is, at least to a degree, almost immune to competition from other modes or other carriers. Commodities of great weight or of a specialized nature may move exclusively by rail or pipeline with little regard to the rates imposed by other carriers. The governing factor here is obviously the technological nature of the commodity.

Other traffic moves between modes based entirely upon rates, since there is no technological barrier, and the volume of this type of traffic is growing as technology changes.

A common case might be the combination of the two factors mentioned above, where a shipper located on a single rail line may have motor and air facilities available, but they are not suited to his product. Shippers in one location may lose markets to shippers in another area, so that shifts take place, even though the aggregate traffic moving remains the same.

To sum up, a shipper faced with an increase in freight rates might do any one or a combination of the following:

1. Shift his traffic to another mode, insofar as his product and location will permit.
2. Pass the increase along to the consumer to the degree that demand allows.
3. Shift the increase back to his suppliers on the same basis.
4. A combination of 2 and 3 above.
5. A combination of all above.
6. Absorb the increase into his own cost structure.
7. Reduce the output shipped or provide private carriage.

From the carrier standpoint, any of the alternative courses of action would be satisfactory, except for No. 1 and No. 7.

Following this reasoning, the carrier would be likely to avoid increasing rates in those geographic or product areas where such action is likely and concentrate on commodities which would be likely to involve alternatives 2 through 6.

By the same token, the carriers have, by their own actions, increased the shipper's advantage by broadening their own technology and capability. Such a trend has been especially noticeable in the area of rail-motor competition where the range of traffic moving by motor carrier has constantly increased over the years, generally at the expense of the rail carriers. The result is that transportation monopoly, except for the isolated case, is increasingly rare.

As we have seen, the carriers arrange the vast array of goods which they transport into various classes in order to simplify the pricing process. After a long period of experimentation, the carriers have arrived at a uniform classification. There have been a number of classifications in use over the years, but the present rail classification, Uniform Freight Classification No. 6 for Railroads, and the National Motor Freight Classification A-6 for Motor Carriers, represent a consolidation of the various systems formerly in existence.

Since as has been noted there are commodity rates and other "exception" rates, the pricing process can never become completely a matter of organized classification. The freight classification gives not a rate, but a *rating*, which must be applied to a tariff in order to obtain a "rate" or the price (usually expressed in cents per 100 pounds) for the shipment. There are some 75,000 tariffs in use, published by carriers, by rate bureaus and conferences. These tariffs are issued on both a specialized commodity basis and a geographic basis. The format, information and other data included in the tariff must be presented in accord with Interstate Commerce Commission regulations. A carrier or a large shipper will have, depending upon the circumstances, a large file of tariffs which relate to various geographic areas and to specialized commodities. As rates change, these tariffs are supplemented and superseded. Thus the task of keeping the tariff file in current order is formidable. As we will see below, the principle element in the rate is the factor of distance. A distance rate constructed solely on the basis of line haul costs per mile, plus terminal costs would be the most simple rate. However, because of various economic factors, differences in competition and regional pressures, for example, the construction of rates on a purely distance principle is seldom practicable.

TYPES OF RATES AND INFLUENCE ON PRICE

Mileage scales: To the degree that freight rates are based upon length of haul, price will obviously be increased as distance from origin to destination increases. However, rates bear only a general relationship to distance. Many factors have been incorporated into the rate structure which mitigate the influence of distance. Considerable economic pressure is brought to bear upon carriers to adjust and modify the effects of mileage influences.

While transport costs increase with distance, they do not increase in direct proportion. Consequently, a carrier is economically rational in making modifications in the rate on the basis of other factors.

Blanket or group rates: The most significant departure from the distance principle is the establishment of group or blanket rates. Under this system, the carrier imposes a uniform rate to all points within an area. Depending upon various factors, the area in which identical rates apply may be relatively small, including only a radius of 30-50 miles, or very large, embracing two or more states. In some cases, these areas have been established largely for the convenience of the carrier. For example, in Figure 8-1, a large number of small producers is blanketed into a single area rate, since each is separated from the other by only a short distance. In other cases, the blanket area has been established by pressures from shippers and from regional interests. Once a blanket area comes into existence, there is a tendency to enlarge it and to bring into it more and more producers or localities. Aside from local pressures, the carrier often has a substantial incentive to create a large area group rate, in order to more effectively compete with other modes. Thus in the Midwest and southeastern United States, blanket rates may make it much less attractive for shippers to use inland waterway transportation. Clearly, to the extent that such rates are used, distance is entirely eliminated as a factor in the rate structure within a specific area. Consequently, producers can compete within this area entirely without regard for rates, despite the fact that they are in different locations.

Tapering rates: As noted above, rates are only indirectly related to distance. This fact also acts to mitigate the handicap under which distant producers might suffer. The tapering principle is illustrated in Figure 8-2.

As shown in Figure 8-2, the rate based in distance (100 miles) is 50¢ per 100 lb., from A to B and also 50¢ from B to C. However, a thru

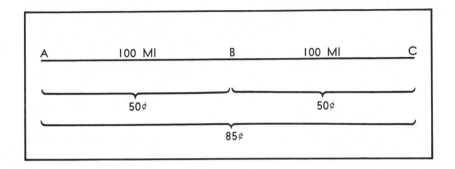

Fig. 8-2

Illustration of tapering rate.

rate from A to C is only 85¢, or 15¢ less than the two segments combined. In Figure 8-3, the same principle is illustrated in a somewhat different fashion. The line "P" traces the points which rate would follow if it increased in accord with the distance.

In Figure 8-3, the line P traces all cost-distance relationships which would prevail if costs were directly proportional to distance, (excluding terminal costs) the cost of transporting the cargo 400 miles would be exactly twice the cost of transporting 200 miles. However, this hypothetical situation does not prevail, and the actual situation is indicated by the line D which shows the rate rising as distance increases, but at a declining rate. Under these circumstances, the rate at 400 miles is only some 50 per cent greater than at 100 miles, terminal costs being constant throughout.

The major economic factor which influences the effect of distance on rates is the element of cost. In performing transportation service, certain costs are incurred without regard to the actual movement per se. These terminal costs as discussed earlier may be of great importance and account for a large portion of the total rate.

Although the line haul cost element is the most important factor, there are external factors which influence the cost-distance relationship.

Special facilities: The effect of distance is influenced by various competitive factors and practices in the industry. Important among these is the provision of various special inducements to the shipper such as the transit privilege. Under the transit privilege, the shipper is given the right to perform certain basic processes upon his product,

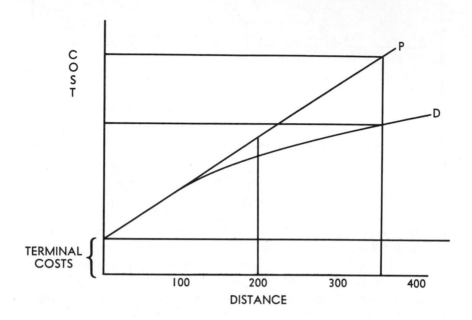

Influence of terminal costs and line haul on carrier rates.
Fig. 8-3

such as milling grain or "rough" finishing lumber. These processes can be done without a second shipment being involved.[1]

For example, rice produced along the Gulf Coast may move to a nearby point for processing, e.g., Houston. The finished rice is then shipped to a market such as Chicago; and, although this involves two actual movements, it is treated as a single movement with one bill of lading and one rate. The rate is slightly less than the combined total of the local rates (Origin to Houston and Houston to Chicago). The finished product will be less in volume than the raw product—in the case of rice, about two-thirds. By-products are sold locally, or at least are not shipped on as a part of the transit transaction.

From the carrier viewpoint, the advantage is the fact that the shipment is arranged for in its entirety and not liable to be transferred to another carrier in the finished stage. The advantage to the shipper

---

[1] The transit privilege is a highly complex operation and, as a technical traffic matter, is beyond the scope of this book. The reader seeking further information is referred to several standard works on the subject, e.g., Thurman W. Van Metre, *Industrial Traffic Management* (New York: McGraw-Hill Book Co., 1953), and Charles A. Taff, *Traffic Management, Principles, and Practices* (rev. ed.; Homewood: R. D. Irwin Co., 1959).

is that he has a fixed rate and only one transaction to undertake from raw material to finished or semi-finished product. It can be seen that a relationship must exist between the rate on the raw product and the rate on the finished produce, since, if the finished product has a completely different character, the rate differential would be too great. In the rice case above, for example, the total of the two local rates might be $1 per 100 pounds; the transit rate is $0.85 plus $0.05 transit charge or a total of $0.90. The final product in this case is finished rice, not rice cooked or processed ready for consumer sale, which would be an entirely different product.

Obviously, such a procedure is an inducement to the shipper and, in addition, may involve more circuitous shipping, thus violating the mileage principle entirely.

Also, the provision of such services within the basic rate is an inducement to the shipper to refrain from diverting his traffic and is, thus, an element of non-price competition. Since the transit privilege encourages the use of facilities which are already established, it tends to minimize distance as a factor and, thus, to protect the market interests of the more distant shipper.

Competitive rate adjustments: As noted earlier, the modes and carriers are almost continuously engaged in efforts to entice traffic away from competing carriers. While some of this effort is of a non-price nature, the most effective effort is price or rate competition. Rate increases (or reductions) may be general or selective in nature.[2]

The major incentive for a carrier to make a rate reduction (or to refrain from rate increases) is clearly the possibility of stimulating the flow of traffic or to meet aggressive action on the part of a competitor.

Thus, a shipper whose traffic is considered valuable or whose bargaining power is great may find himself in an advantageous position. Since (as will be discussed later) the transportation industry is subject to a high degree of regulation, there is the possibility of political or social pressure being brought to bear upon rate adjustments, both general and specific.[3] Since no carrier or mode of trans-

---

[2] Since the end of World War II, the general or blanket rate increase has tended to be more common for a variety of reasons. Consequently, shippers have been anxious to be exempted from a general rate increase; although, in the years of rising prices, some fortunate shippers have enjoyed rate reductions chiefly due to competitive forces within the transportation industry.

[3] The uncertain fate of the Hoch-Smith Resolution of 1925, makes it doubtful that direct legislative relief could be tendered to any industry. See *Ann Arbor Railroad Co. vs. the United States*, 281 U. S. 658 (1930). However, there is no doubt that a strong plea before the regulatory groups may be very effective in preventing or modifying a rate increase. For this reason, a large number of industries and firms maintains representation before the regulatory bodies for the purpose of preventing, or at least modifying, rate increases in their specific areas. See, for example, *Interstate Commerce Commission*, Statement on

portation seeks to lose profitable traffic, any proposed increase will be tempered by the realistic appraisal of likely traffic losses. On the other hand, certain traffic may be held in low regard, and upward rate adjustments may be looked upon as a means of discouraging such traffic. For example, certain less-than-carload or less-than-truckload traffic has been discouraged by substantial rate increases which make such traffic uneconomic to ship. Such traffic frequently must be moved by private carriage.

General relationship between prices and freight rates: As noted above, this relationship is complex and depends upon specific cases. However, certain conclusions can be drawn. It seems evident that, while freight rates are an element in prices of commodities, such costs are of little importance when compared to labor and materials costs. Also, it is likely that such costs tend to decrease in importance in the modern economy due to improved means of transport and to industrial dispersion and improved means of marketing which results in less movement among markets.

TRANSPORT PRICING AND THE TRAFFIC MANAGEMENT FUNCTION

Although not directly employed by carriers (the carrier traffic department is a rate making group), industrial traffic departments are closely allied with transport firms, and some mention might be made of this group. Industrial traffic managers purchase transportation service and arrange for incoming and outgoing products to be moved in the same manner in which a purchasing agent arranges the purchase of raw materials. Traffic management is an increasingly important industrial function. In recent years, the rise of competitive forms of transportation has made the traffic manager's task one of weighing the various alternatives, calculating costs and making decisions as to the distribution of traffic. Frequently, also, if the firm has private transportation, the traffic manager supervises this operation.

Depending upon the size and complexity of the firm, the traffic department may be large or small, and its duties and responsibilities are varied.

The routine work of the traffic department includes, in addition to arranging for transportation, checking freight bills, making claims

Behalf of the Secretary of Agriculture in re: Class Rates Nos. 30416-30660, 1954, before the Interstate Commerce Commission, for an elaborate treatment of this type of action.

for loss and damage, consulting with the carrier representatives regarding changes in rates or classification and, in general, representing the company's interests in the transportation function. By working through the various trade associations, the traffic manager can make his influence felt in the general field of his concern.

The basic tools of the traffic manager are the classification issued by the carriers and the tariff. The traffic department will maintain a current file of these publications, and, in most cases, the actual work of calculating the rate, completing the bill of lading and other paper work will be done by the traffic department in its own office.

The most important single function of the traffic department is the role it plays in the pricing process. Rates made by carriers or rate bureaus are not made in isolation. The carrier representatives will consult with industrial traffic department representatives either directly or more often through their representatives on the National Shippers Advisory Boards or other traffic associations. The shipper will thus have opportunity to present his views and to this extent "bargains" for a particular rate. Further, the traffic department will keep close watch on existing rates and bring pressure for change wherever it seems likely to be advantageous. Thus the traffic department is the representative of the shipper in all respects which concern the purchase, use prices paid, comparison of quality and other factors relating to transportation.

Summary

As this chapter has pointed out, the cost of transportation is an important, though widely varying, element in the production of goods. For the most part, the importance depends upon the elasticity of demand for the product and, hence, to the degree to which any increase can be shifted to others. From the carrier viewpoint the relevant factors are the desirability of the traffic and the ability to gauge the possible effects of rate changes. Although distance is probably the most important single factor in rate construction, it may be modified by many other factors which the carrier might wish or be forced to take into consideration.

Rate increases (or decreases) may be either general or specific, although, in recent years, the general change in rates has been more common. Freight rates, like other prices, are influenced by technological change and shifts in population and the rise or fall of industries. Shippers obviously tend to resist increases in rates and to bring about improvements in their own organizations which will tend to reduce shipping costs.

The relationship between freight rates and costs is so complex that, in any specific case, the factors may be unique, and each case must be dealt with on an individual basis.

Selected References for Further Study

The student who wishes to pursue the subject of transport rate making further will find that it is essentially an exercise in price theory in general. Elements of price behavior are, of course, described in the various elementary textbooks and more thoroughly in, e.g., Stigler, George, *Theory of Price* (New York: 1949, The Macmillan Company); Fellner, William J., *Competition Among the Few*, oligopoly and similar market structures (New York: A. M. Kelley, Reprint, 1960 (originally published in 1949 by A. A. Knopf); Williams, Ernest W., Jr., *The Regulation of Rail-Motor Rate Competition* (New York: Harper & Row, 1951); Chamberlin, Edward H., *The Theory of Monopolistic Competition* (Cambridge: Harvard University Press, 1948); Robinson, Joan, *The Economics of Imperfect Competition* (London: The Macmillan Co., 1948); Marshall, Alfred, *Principles of Economics* (8th ed., New York: The Macmillan Co., 1948) (especially Appendix H).

As in the other economic areas, vast amounts of empirical data exist in the form of studies made by individual carriers, rate associations, regulatory groups and others.

CHAPTER IX

Transportation and Resource Allocation

As an economic activity, transportation uses certain economic resources in the production of its service. Because they are limited in supply, it is in the interest of society to utilize resources in the most efficient manner. Any economic activity requires some resources, and obviously resources used in activity "A" cannot also be used to carry on activity "B," i.e., petroleum used to propel a diesel locomotive cannot be used to drive a truck or ship. As a consequence, society benefits if the resources are used most efficiently. If activity "A" is more productive than "B" and uses an equal amount of resources, then "A" should be carried on in preference to "B."

In the free capitalistic society, the principal allocating mechanism is the price system. To use the above example, if "A" is more profitable than "B" then entrepreneurs will bid away resources from "B" and use them to produce "A." If it is more profitable to produce television sets than radios, then the materials and technical knowledge available to the electronics industry will be channeled into television manufacture as opposed to radio. It will immediately become apparent to the reader that the test of "profitability" may not always be a reliable guide in terms of general welfare as society conceives it. For example, it may be much more profitable to produce opium using resources otherwise devoted to the production of vegetables. However, society has banned the unregulated production of opium in the name of public welfare, even though it is economically profitable. To this extent, the public authorities have prevented the free working of the allocative process. No doubt, the actions of society in this area would be generally accepted, although in other areas the prevention of free allocation might raise more questions. As will be pointed out below, the production of transportation service is very much influenced by public considerations in allocation.

For many reasons, there are frequent misallocations of resources. In the free economy, entrepreneurs may misjudge the future profit possibilities of various efforts. There is duplication and waste due to technical inefficiency and inadequate managerial skill, and, above all, there is confusion of goals and there are arbitrary changes in direction.

OPTIMUM ALLOCATION OF RESOURCES

What, then, is the optimum allocation of resources? It seems certain that, if optimum allocation ever occurs, it must be momentary and largely accidental. In the transportation field, the so-called National Transportation Policy—The Preamble to the Interstate Commerce Act— might be taken as a goal embodying optimum allocation of resources.

> It is hereby declared to be the national transportation policy of the Congress to provide for fair and impartial regulation of all modes of transportation subject to the provisions of the Act, so administered as to recognize and preserve the inherent advantages of each; to promote safe, adequate, economical, and efficient service and foster sound economic conditions in transportation and among the several carriers; to encourage the establishment and maintenance of reasonable charges for transportation services, without unjust discriminations, undue preferences or advantages, or unfair or destructive competitive practices; to cooperate with the several States and the duly authorized officials thereof; and to encourage fair wages and equitable working conditions; and all to the end of developing, coordinating, and preserving a national transportation system by water, highway, and rail, as well as other means, adequate to meet the needs of the commerce of the United States, of the Postal Service, and of the national defense. All of the provisions of this Act shall be administered and enforced with a view to carrying out the above declaration of policy.[1]

Certainly, no one could quarrel with the objectives, although he might well take issue with the means of achieving the goal. Likewise,

---

[1] Eighty-Second Congress, Senate Document No. 72, *The Interstate Commerce Act* (Washington: U. S. Government Printing Office), 1951, p. 1.

at any given point of time, these objectives seem rather indistinct. No truck operator would maintain that trucks should perform services which railroads could perform more efficiently, but he would be very reluctant to admit that there were many services which fall into this class! Consequently, there is a substantial amount of duplication in the provision of transport services, and some carriers are performing service which could be performed by other carriers at less cost to society.

One must, however, bear in mind that the decisions of this type are in the broadest sense to be made by society through the operation of the price system and, in the long run, will be so made.

PLANT ORGANIZATION AND SPATIAL LIMITATION

It is desirable as a means of improving resource allocation to locate productive facilities in the most advantageous manner; viz., so as to reduce total costs of production.

The transportation plant plays a large part in the economic arrangement of production. There is doubtless a high degree of cross-hauling and duplication of effort because of inefficiencies or lack of planning, either in the production of goods or in the transportation complex. A substantial amount of such inefficient production is made necessary by the physical and geographical arrangement of industry and materials and location of natural resources. Such arrangements have become entrenched over the years. For example, it would be possible and perhaps more efficient to have the center of automobile production in Kansas City instead of Detroit (and in fact Kansas City is a major assembly point). However, since over the years the industry has grown up in the Detroit area and many external economies are present, it would be difficult for a manufacturer to locate elsewhere. From the pure transportation viewpoint, it would be desirable to locate activity in the geographical center of any market; however, in practice, this can rarely, if ever, be done. Spatial location is obviously of great importance in the cost of production and distribution of goods. While present locational arrangements are not necessarily the most efficient, they are likely to continue.

RESOURCE ALLOCATION, PUBLIC AND PRIVATE, THE HISTORICAL MIXTURE

The transportation industry represents a mixture of allocative processes. Since public authority is called upon to enter most areas of the transportation industry and since private funds are also involved, resources are allocated in accord with both public and private decisions. For reasons noted above, this has been true of the transportation industry in the United States almost from the beginning of the republic.

Public grants of land, money or other encouragement has been a unique feature in the growth of the transportation industry. Basically, there is no conflict between the long run goals of either public or private allocation of resources. Simply stated, the goal is to allocate resources so as to maximize product at minimum costs. In the short run, private goals often come into conflict with public goals. For example, producers of coal, natural gas, lumber and other natural resources have frequently, in years past, operated without regard for general public welfare. To some extent at least, public authority attempts to prevent mis-allocation of resources in the transportation field by various means—principally, control over entry. Unfortunately, this presupposes the ability of the public authorities to gauge the proper allocation. That is, it is wasteful of resources to have more transportation service between given points than needed, but who can say with certainty what is needed or what will be needed? The regulatory bodies go through various procedures, taking testimony from potential shippers, competitors, etc., in an effort to gauge the need for additional service in light of the public interest.

It seems obvious that conflict arises because there is no generally accepted criteria regarding the weight given to various factors. For example, some groups consider roadside billboards as economic waste or worse. On the other hand, defenders point out the fact that consumer choice and information are enhanced by billboards. Clearly, consumer choice is important, so also is an unobstructed view of the countryside. Society must decide through legislation and through the market which one must have priority.

One can only say that any given allocative choice must be weighed in the light of social and economic values prevailing. Let us examine a given case in this light. From 1850 to 1870, railroads were encouraged to expand into the sparsely settled western areas by land grants. Much controversy has taken place over the wisdom of this policy, over the value of the lands and other matters. Such argument seems both futile and sterile. Clearly, the value of the lands to the national welfare was incalculable. By the same token, it may be that an incalculable loss would have occurred if the step had not been taken. Let us consider the conditions prevailing at the time. The United States in 1850 had about 1,400,000,000 acres of unoccupied land available.[2] This enormous area of land was both valuable and worthless. Valuable because of the great store of resources and worthless because it was inaccessible to development. It seems useless to try to evaluate this land in terms of dollars per acre. All that can be said is that in 1850 it was in the public interest to develop this land and transportation (rail) was essential to this development. Thus, the allocation of a minor part of these resources to an agency in order to enhance their total value seems to have been in the public interest, as of 1850. Such a policy in 1950 would have been both wasteful and misdirected. No evaluation can, at this date, be made as to the possibility of a better allocation.

That is, could the same goal have been accomplished with only half the land being granted, or could the land have been developed by payment of cash or government bonds or in some other fashion possibly more efficient than that chosen? In the year 2060, historians may raise similar questions regarding the allocation of a portion of resources in 1960 for the conquest of space!

Some very serious problems have arisen in recent years in regard to the large amounts of land required for highway use. In urban areas, the construction of a modern highway, with interchange systems, separated crossings and other necessary construction, requires enormous amounts of land. Further, this land is transformed, in most cases, from tax-paying land to publicly-used land, thus increasing the municipal financial problems. The question arises as to how much land can economically be devoted to highway use. Much more thought and planning need to be devoted to this problem than have been in the past.[3]

No one would maintain that the present allocation of economic resources or that having been carried out in the past is or was perfect, even in the light of known goals. However, such allocations apparently served the purpose of the time, insofar as the allocators could judge the present and peer into the future. Oscar Lewis points out that only Theodore Judah, of those concerned, had the gift of vision into the future. Others who were interested in the Pacific Railway legislation viewed the project in various ways, always limited. Hopkins and Huntington looked upon it as a shopkeeper's dream of monopoly.

---

[2] Robert S. Henry, "The Railroad Land Grant Legend in American History Texts," *Mississippi Historical Review*, Vol. XXXII, September 1945 (reprinted by Association of American Railroads).

[3] See Robert B. Mitchell, *Metropolitan Planning for Land Use and Transportation*, Office of Public Works Planning, The White House, Washington, 1959.

Stanford, no doubt, saw it as a political springboard. Only Judah could see the long range possibilities of a transcontinental railroad.[4] Clearly, Judah was a remarkable and gifted man, unhampered by selfish political, social, or economic ambitions. Few such men prevail in the realm of public policy or in the area of private business. Thus, society must needs accept with minor modifications the allocations made by whatever economic and social system they have chosen. In the United States, the mixed system of public-private allocation of resources in the transportation field has worked with a reasonable degree of success. Other nations have chosen to take a course involving either a greater or less (usually a greater) role on the part of public authority in the allocation of their transportation resources. Time can be the only judge as to which system proves to be most advantageous.

It should be noted in passing that European transportation systems, almost all of which are publicly owned or controlled, have made great strides in rebuilding and in technological progress since the end of World War II.[5]

ALLOCATION AND USER CHARGES

Many serious problems arise in the area of public policy when one considers the problem of user charges. Some modes may have an actual or alleged advantage in the use of facilities which are, in part, provided by public funds. We have seen how public lands were used to further the efforts of railway builders in the late years of the 19th century. Likewise, public funds have been used to stimulate highway, water and air transportation over the years.[6] While dollar estimates are not very reliable, the Association of American Railroads estimates that more than $459 billion has been spent by state, local, and the federal governments by 1960.[7]

Questions arise as to the justice and feasibility of assessing some user charge upon those who benefit from such facilities. While many

---

[4] Oscar Lewis, *The Big Four* (New York: Alfred A. Knopf., 1941), pp. 13 ff.

[5] Wilfred Owen, *The Transport Revolution in Europe*, Washington, 1961, The Brookings Institution.

[6] See James C. Nelson, "The Pricing of Highway, Airway and Waterway Facilities," *American Economic Review*, Vol. LII, No. 2, May 1962, pp. 426 ff.

[7] *Government Expenditures for Construction, Operation and Maintenance of Transport Facilities*, *Washington*, March 1960, Association of American Railroads (mimeographed).

would favor such charges on the basis of equitable treatment, a major barrier exists as to how such charges might be calculated. Among carriers, only water carriers oppose user charges on grounds of principle. Air carriers have generally endorsed user charges, although they, like motor carriers, are not in agreement as to the level at which such charges should be imposed.

One of the most serious complexities is the fact that the public aids given to transportation agencies have taken varied forms and have been rendered for more than a century and under many circumstances. The difficulty involved in comparing aid to railroads by land grants and aid to airlines through air mail contracts or to motor carriers through the interstate highway system, and attempting to impose equitable charges for such aid, is obvious.

Even if the aid given in the past was ignored, the problem is extremely complex. The multi-purpose and multi-user nature of most publicly aided facilities makes it almost impossible to reach any agreement as to proper charges. Clearly, most groups will resist any charges as long as possible and will attempt to minimize any charges which are made. In the past, attempts to calculate or impose charges have resulted in such a welter of claims and counter claims that the whole subject has been obscured beyond recognition.

This issue was well illustrated when suggestions are made that highway user fees be increased. An immediate reaction comes from the motor carrier industry, stating, in general, that the industry is already paying a just share of taxes and that other highway users are benefiting greatly.[8] Clearly, the development of transportation facilities is very much in the public interest, and even those who do not use such facilities directly derive a degree of benefit from them. Some means must be discovered which will enable society to measure benefit and assign costs in a more equitable fashion than is currently available. While this seems at present to be far in the future, some progress is being made, at least in measuring use of highways and other facilities.[9]

The extremely high costs of providing modern transportation facilities have placed great emphasis upon the role of technological innovation. As Owen points out, the need for such innovations is

---

[8] *Transport Topics*, Washington D. C. Editorial issue of March 13, 1961, American Trucking Associations, Inc.

[9] See, for example, the various highway tests that have been carried on since 1950 with increasing efficiency and more definite results. Although much remains to be done, progress has been made, and each succeeding test has been more efficiently conducted and more definitive than the preceding tests.

especially pressing in those nations which are underdeveloped. The availability of modern technology may also enable some of the nations now being industrialized to avoid some of the waste and duplication which the older nations now face.[10]

FUTURE DEVELOPMENT OF TRANSPORTATION FACILITIES

It has been estimated that the development of transportation has historically required an investment for equipment of some 2 per cent or more of gross national product.[11]

These funds must come, as they have in the past, from private sources, and transportation must, as do other industries, compete in the capital market with other capital users. The future need for transportation service depends clearly upon the scope of economic activity carried on. Transportation development is necessary, both qualitatively and quantitatively, since the efficiency of transport media must be improved despite the need for increased facilities. Population growth, dispersion of industry and other factors make for necessary changes in transportation plant. In the same way, the various modes of transportation, railroads, motor carriers, airlines, waterway operators and pipelines gain or lose traffic in response to shipper demands and technological changes. Historically, transportation has, for the most part, been supplied by entrepreneurs who made facilities available to shippers, or, as in recent years, a large amount of transportation service has been supplied by private means, i.e., the shipper provides his own facilities. Transportation must, like other industries, be dynamic and change is constant.

Transportation from the ox cart to the jet airliner has been characterized by technological and economic development. In the mid-twentieth century, we have seen serious problems develop in the economic framework of the transportation industry. Capital requirements, especially in the railroad industry, have not been met by public sources. The entire industry has been beset by apparent overcapacity and lack of direction.

Each separately owned segment of the industry has, as one might

[10] Wilfred Owen, "Transportation and Technology," *American Economic Review*, Vol. LII, No. 2, May 1962, pp. 405 ff.

[11] Carl T. Wedel, Vice President, Transportation Department, First National City Bank of New York, Address, "A Great Future Needs Great Transportation," quoted in *National Transportation Policy, op. cit.*, p. 50.

expect, attempted to operate on as broad a scale as possible, attempting to enhance the market position.

As stated by a recent study of national transportation policy, conflicting goals, the historic mixture of public and private allocation, have created serious problems indeed.

> Each industry component is reasonably concerned with maximizing itself with but little regard to the effect of general development by others—meanwhile social investment, both public and private, in the total system has been made without regard to overall transportation needs. Unlike most industry, the total investment in transportation facilities includes an increasingly large proportion of public funds, and it must be admitted that these funds have been expended without regard to their impact on private investments. Excessive total social investment in transport facilities has already reached serious proportions. Should this policy continue we may find that the price of failure to coordinate and control total social investment in transportation facilities with the total transportation requirements of the Nation may be more than we are willing to pay. It is indeed time to see where we are going and whether we should exercise more careful control over the public portion of social investment in transportation.[12]

In the preceding chapters, it was our task to investigate these relationships and to examine the micro- and macro-economic aspects of this vital industry. It is important to recall that we are investigating an industry owned and operated by private enterprise and supported by private capital. Our economic system is committed to private ownership of the modes, and rightly so. Almost alone among the major nations, the United States retains the private enterprise-public regulated concept in our transportation system. Though the problems stemming from this policy are legion, they are not insoluable.

IMPROVEMENTS IN ALLOCATION

It was noted above that in the U. S. dependence for allocation of resources has been placed largely in the hands of private enterprise via the price system. In transportation these decisions are to a degree modified and controlled by public policy. In order to prevent wasteful practices and especially to avoid duplication and over allocation of resources into one mode, great care must be exercised. There is little evidence that our resource allocation in transportation is noticeably

---

[12] *National Transportation Policy, op. cit.,* p. 48.

better under regulation than without it, although such a determination is clearly not easily made.

The major barrier to more efficient allocation is without doubt the lack of accurate cost data. Unless the cost of providing service by different modes is known, then it is clearly impossible to compare the efficiency of these modes. The goals of the national policy cannot be achieved and the regulatory body cannot perform its assigned functions unless costs are known. Allocation in a regulated industry is performed in several ways, chiefly through the control over entry of new firms. This is more difficult in water and motor transport where there is not such a high natural barrier of cost, due to the availability of the public right of way. Here again, unless the regulatory agency is fully aware of costs, their decisions regarding entry are apt to be on shaky ground.

Public aids and especially a lack of uniformity in aid provision hinder the proper allocation of resources. It has been noted that the question of aid rendered in the past is moot, and the policy regarding aids in the present situation will be further considered in Chapter XXIII. Although in the years before regulation, allocation was by no means free from distortion and redundancy was common, great care should be taken to see that the allocative power inherent in entry control, subsidy and other eleemnts of public policy is wisely used.

PLANT LOCATION THEORY

A major facet of resource allocation is the location of economic activity in the most economic manner. As we know, certain economic activity, notably the extractive industries, is fixed in location, but, even here, society has some leeway in location of the processing industries which relate to the extractive products. For manufacturing or distributive enterprises, considerable freedom to locate exists, and, of these, transportation is a basic factor.

Production or materials oriented industries: These industries are, for the most part, those which involve substantial weight loss in processing, such extractive industries as mining and lumbering. Other things being equal, it is desirable to process these products in close proximity to the point where raw materials are found.

Market oriented industries: In this case the product is processed close to the market. For example, goods for immediate consumption, e.g., baked goods are generally produced close to the ultimate market. It can be seen that changes in transportation alter these relationships greatly. In 1890, it was customary for each community or, in a large city, each neighborhood to have a bakery, whereas, at the present time, distribution may be made from a central point to a radius of several hundred miles.

From the standpoint of allocation of resources, it is important that the location of producing and processing industries have a rational economic basis. In an ideal production distribution system (in the transportation sense), these activities would be so located as to minimize the cost of serving consumer centers. Naturally, this ideal situation is not often attainable, and what can be hoped for in reality is to avoid unduly wasteful situations.

Much of the early work in this area was done by the German economists, who, as a group, showed special interest in this problem.[13] More recent contributions have been made by Isard, Greenhut and Hoover.[14]

All these writers, both German and modern American, stress the optimum location, focusing attention on a model system. Hoover's analysis is more sophisticated; he recognizes the weakness inherent in the assumption of linear freight costs of the early writers. Hoover emphasizes the irregular shape of market areas. Greenhut stresses the imperfection of competitive relationships. He abandons the concept of optimum location based solely on costs and stresses the importance of demand. Greenhut's analysis is the most penetrating and, in modern terms, most realistic.

An industry with large and complex plant and, in particular, one in which economies of scale are present is likely to have a central location and to supply large areas, perhaps the entire market, from a central location or a location located on the outer edge of a market area.

The classic example of this is, of course, the automobile industry. For various reasons, the area of southern Michigan, northern Ohio and Indiana became the seat of automobile manufacturing. For many years, distribution costs were merely added to the cost of manufacture, plus dealer costs, in order to determine the market costs in any given location. Economies of scale were present, and the Detroit area main-

---

[13] In addition to von Thünen, mentioned earlier, we find these: Weber, *Theory of Location of Industries*, translated by Carl J. Friedrich (Chicago: University of Chicago Press, 1928). See also Stefan Valavanis, "Losch on Location," *American Economic Review*, Vol. XLV, p. 637.

[14] Walter Isard, *Location and Space Economy* (New York: John Wiley and Sons, 1956); Melvin L. Greenhut, *Plant Location in Theory and Practice* (Chapel Hill: University of North Carolina Press, 1956); Edgar M. Hoover, *The Location of Economic Activity* (New York: McGraw-Hill Book Co., 1948).

tained itself despite the growth of markets farther and farther away. However, as distribution costs became more influential, the industry began to establish assembly plants and, in some cases, branch manufacturing plants in market centers.[15] In more specialized and higher unit cost industries, these effects are even more apparent, for example, in the manufacture of steam locomotives. In early years (1830-1870), locomotives were manufactured in many locations in small numbers, often only one or two in any one place.[16]

As these informal days passed and periodic economic downturns took their toll (many builders disappeared in the 1870's), economies of scale became obvious, and the industry became highly concentrated. Only three producers of consequence were in operation by 1920: American in Schenectady, New York; Baldwin, Philadelphia, Pennsylvania; and Lima in Lima, Ohio. These firms supplied locomotives to all U. S. railroads, and few branch plants or assembly plants were established. In this industry, requiring large scale specialized facilities and likely to be of declining costs, the locational factors were unique.

In some cases, weight is added to the product, and there is, thus, a clear advantage in location near the market. The manufacture and retail distribution of soft drinks is, for example, a local industry. Nationally marketed soft drinks are often shipped to local plants in concentrate form, mixed with sugar and water (both very heavy) and marketed in the immediate area as liquid products. In other cases, national advertising and distribution, along with rigid quality control, make this impossible. A well-known brand of beer is brewed only in one city and is marketed throughout the United States.[17] Other brewers choose to use local branch plants, and, of course, the local breweries still serve local markets, although to a much smaller degree than formerly.

In some activities, location is not a factor or is a factor of indifference. A national chain of retail stores would clearly need outlets in many locations, and, here, warehouse location would be a matter of importance in order to reduce costs of distribution. A firm selling a national newsletter service to businessmen would be indifferent to

---

[15] An interesting account of these factors is found in Allan Nevins, *Ford, The Times, The Man, The Company* (New York: Chas. Scribners, Sons), p. 501; and also in Henry Ford (with Samuel Crowther), *Today and Tomorrow* (New York: Doubleday & Co., 1926).

[16] Charles E. Fisher, "Locomotive Builders of the United States," *Railway and Locomotive Historical Society Bulletin,* No. 58, R.L.&H.S., Boston, May 1942, p. 55.

[17] In cases such as this, much must be done to reduce distribution costs, e.g., use of cans to replace bottles.

distribution costs, since the product is distributed to all parts of the nation by first class postage. Thus, such a firm would locate at the point where data were available, e.g., New York or Washington, D.C.

Non-transportation factors: There are, to be sure, many factors of a non-transportation nature and, frequently, of a non-economic nature which will influence location. One such factor may be the equal pull of locational factors. An industry using raw material "A" and raw material "B" may find it feasible to locate midway between these two items and combine the best of both situations.

Production costs may vary substantially on a geographic basis due to labor, land costs, power availability, tax advantages, availability of capital and other factors which may overcome all considerations of market and raw material location.[18] Various external economies such as surrounding industries, labor pool, market "know-how" and other factors must be weighed. Various irrational or intangible factors such as climate, personal preference of executives, and other items may have some, although probably not controlling, influence.

When these various factors are known and can be calculated, the least cost of shipping and of supplying various points, given minimum levels of inventory, etc., can be worked out by various methods of linear programming technique.[19] These methods are for the purpose of assuring efficient methods of distribution to the individual firm and do not, except indirectly, influence the distribution of resources.

While many factors influence plant location, there are, in summary, apparently four primary or fundamental factors of importance, the others being secondary or fringe items. The four primary factors are: (1) location of markets, (2) location of raw materials, (3) transfer costs, i.e., cost of moving raw materials into and finished products out of the plant, and (4) the location of competing firms.[20]

---

[18] Industry-seeking states and cities often make concessions with regard to plant sites, taxes and other matters. There is often an advantage to be gained in lack of widespread unionization and similar factors which cannot be easily classified.

[19] See, for example, Robert O. Ferguson and Lauren F. Sargent, *Linear Programming: Fundamentals and Applications* (New York: McGraw-Hill Book Co., 1958), pp. 25 ff; also, David W. Miller and Martin K. Starr, *Executive Decisions and Operations Research* (Englwood Cliffs: Prentice-Hall, Inc., 1960), pp. 290 ff.

[20] The practical aspects of plant location, as well as an interesting quantitative technique of estimating the impact of transfer costs on plant location, is found in Smykay and others, *op. cit.*, pp. 164 ff., and Chapter VIII.

Summary

This chapter has considered the role of the transportation industry in the allocation of resources. The most important factor here is that a high degree of public interest attaches to the problem, and allocation decisions are influenced by public policy in large part. Allocation has been imperfect in its working, although by and large the will of society has been considered insofar as the existing conditions would permit.

Selected References for Further Study

Much has been written about economic or transportation geography, and one of the standard works on transportation devotes considerable space to this material. See Daggett, Stuart, *Principles of Inland Transportation* (4th ed., New York: Harper & Row, 1955), Part III.

An excellent general treatment is found in Bengston, Nels A., and Van Royen, William, *Fundamentals of Economic Geography* (New York: Prentice-Hall, 1938).

More specialized and technical treatments are found in Hoover, E. M., *The Location of Economic Activity* (New York: McGraw-Hill Book Co., 1948).

The German economists, since Von Thünen, have been interested in the problem of economic activity and locality, e.g., Weber, Alfred, *Über den Standort der Industrien*, Teil, Erster, *Reine Theorie des Standorts*, Tübingen, Mohr, 1909.

See, also, Isard, Walter, "The General Theory of Location and Space Economy," *Quarterly Journal of Economics*, November 1949.

For a very recent treatment relating to urban land, see Wingo, Lowden, Jr., *Transportation and Urban Land* (Washington, D. C.: Resources for the Future Inc., 1961).

An interesting and brief review of location theories is found in Richards, Hay A., "Transportation Costs and Plant Location: A Review of Principal Theories," *Transportation Journal* (American Society of Traffic and Transportation, Inc. [Chicago], winter, 1962.

In the area of water transport, the literature is less extensive. An interesting and readable history of the river boat trade is found in Hunter, Louis C., *Steamboats on the Western Rivers*, an economic and technological history (Cambridge: Harvard, 1949).

Excellent material on the modern waterway is found in the Hearings, *Problems of the Railroads*, referred to elsewhere in this work.

There is also relatively little material in the field of pipeline transportation, most of it in the periodicals. A somewhat specialized treatment is found in Uren, Lester Charles, *Petroleum Production Economics* (New York: McGraw-Hill Book Co., 1950). For a brief treatment, see Emerson, H. N., "Salient Characteristics of Petroleum Pipeline Transportation," *Land Economics*, February 1950. A classic, although somewhat dated, is found in the T.N.E.C. *Hearings on the Petroleum Industry*, 79th Cong., 2d. Sess., 1940, Parts 14 and 15.

PART III

The Basis and Framework of Public Control

"I believe that in many cases the ideal size for the unit of control and organisation lies somewhere between the individual and the modern State. I suggest, therefore, that progress lies in the growth and the recognition of semi-autonomous bodies within the State—bodies whose criterion of action within their own field is solely the public good as they understand it, and from whose deliberations motives of private advantage are excluded, though some place it may still be necessary to leave, until the ambit of men's altruism grows wider, to the separate advantage of particular groups, classes, or faculties—bodies which in the ordinary course of affairs are mainly autonomous within their prescribed limitations, but are subject in the last resort of the sovereignty of the democracy expressed through Parliament."

JOHN MAYNARD KEYNES
"POLITICS"
ESSAYS IN PERSUASION

CHAPTER X

Development of Regulation, 1887-1920

SOCIAL AND ECONOMIC ORIGINS OF REGULATION

From early times, transportation agencies have been viewed with special concern, insofar as public control over rates and services is concerned. The law is replete with references to the responsibility of the carrier as opposed to the vendor of goods or services on a local basis.[1]

Historically, much apparently depended upon the fact that the transporter performed his services at some point physically detached from the customer, a situation which made fraud and deceit relatively easy. Also, the performance of transportation service was considered to be necessary to the furtherance of commercial enterprise and was provided as a "common calling," using private property.

Consequently, the transporter, at an early date, assumed unique responsibility as a seller of service, a situation which has descended into modern law in the form of the bill of lading conditions and related legal responsibilities, as well as the broader aspects of the buyer-seller relationship. In English common law, these public-private relationships were illustrated by the classic statement of Lord Hale

---

[1] Even in the Medieval period, the transporter had a particular relationship to the customer, and the Bill of Lading was one of the earliest documents. See James W. Thompson and Edgar N. Johnson, *An Introduction to Medieval Europe* (New York: W. W. Norton and Co., Inc., 1937).

in the treatise *De Portibus Maris* in the seventeenth century, holding that, where property is used in such a manner as to be of public consequence, it is vested with the public interest.

Early American Views

Actually, in the United States, the issue of public regulation was largely academic for some time, since the early carriers were looked upon with considerable favor and encouragement. In general, from the Colonial period until the 1870's, carriers were encouraged rather than discouraged, although certain regulation was undertaken; and, in fact, transport services were considered so vital they were often provided by the public authority. Turnpikes, canals, and later railroads were undertaken by six states at various times.

Transportation problems in early America were so formidable and the movement of goods was so costly that public aid was acceptable in this area more so than in others.

Although the federal government was somewhat limited by constitutional provisions, state governments managed to overcome this barrier by the use of private corporations under state charter. By 1820, a substantial amount of turnpike mileage had been built under this arrangement.[2]

However, as Pegrum points out, changes in technology made public ownership and operation very difficult and, at a later date, posed serious problems for regulation.[3] Clearly the state faced multiple problems in the ownership and operation of a railroad which includes both right-of-way and vehicles by necessity operated by a single operator and, on the other hand, a canal or turnpike upon which various privately owned vehicles could be operated on public or private rights of way.

Regulation by Charter

The earliest instruments of regulation in the States were charters issued by the state legislature, specifying in detail what the chartered company was empowered to do. Most of the early canal and railroad companies were subject to conditions as set forth in the charter.

---

[2] Kent T. Healy, "American Transportation Before the War Between the States," *The Growth of the American Economy*, Harold F. Williamson, Ed. (New York: Prentice-Hall, Inc., 1944), pp. 172 ff.

[3] Dudley F. Pegrum, *Public Regulation of Business, op. cit.*, pp. 510 ff.

It soon became apparent that the charter was unsatisfactory for several reasons, principally its rigidity. Once the charter had been issued, it was necessary to have legislative approval in order to amend it; and, clearly, it was impossible to foresee all the conditions which might change in the future. Also, it was impossible to cover in a charter the wide range of problems which began to require detailed consideration in such fluid enterprises as those engaged in transportation.

So long as the public attitude toward these enterprises remained favorable, there was little need for any substantial regulation. Unfortunately for the carriers, the attitude of enthusiastic promotion of railroads began to wane in the years following 1860. There were several reasons for this situation—political, social and economic.

Perhaps most important was the fact that the railroads, like other economic enterprises, were not adverse to taking advantage of their economic power. Thus, communities which had been anxious to attract the railroad and had made gifts of land or money found themselves at the mercy of a corporation which had a strong incentive to exploit such economic advantages as it could. It seems more than likely that other enterprises were engaged in the same practice, but the railroads were more noticeable because of size and because they had enjoyed such a high degree of public interest. Unlike his modern counterpart, the rural resident generally had no personal contact with large corporations aside from the railroad.

Further, many individuals had made investments in railroad securities under the impression that very substantial returns would be forthcoming. When severe competition and overbuilding, coupled with downturn in economic activity in the decade of the 1870's, dashed these hopes, there was understandable bitterness. Public disillusionment was further increased when evidence came to light that mismanagement, fraud, and sharp practices had been prevelant during this era.

Thirdly, the groups who had hoped to benefit most substantially from the railroads, viz., the farmers and residents of outlying areas, were often those who felt themselves most put upon by the monopolistic practices of the carriers. No doubt, also, the railroads provided a handy target for many of the frustrations of the farmer. Americans, especially those of the frontier, had always a distrust of "big business" controlled by "Eastern interests," and the railroads were prime examples of both of these mythical persecutors of the "little man." Perhaps typical of the polemic literature of the period is Frank Norris', *The Octopus*, which, as a fictional work, traced the hardships of a group of farmers and ranchers in California under the domination of a thinly disguised railroad, obviously the Southern Pacific.[4] In the modern social and economic setting, it is rather difficult to imagine the degree of fear and contempt with which the common man regarded the railroad "giants" in the years from 1870 to 1900.[5]

Aside from these characteristics, there were apparent varied economic factors which made the competitive self-regulatory process embodied in Adam Smith's "invisible hand" difficult or impossible to apply to the public utility enterprise, especially the railroad.

COST CHARACTERISTICS

The importance of the relationship between fixed and variable costs has been noted in an earlier chapter. The costly railroad plant was highly specialized, which frequently caused rail carriers to engage in drastic rate competition in order to reap such revenue as was possible. Under such circumstances, a non-carrier enterprise (or one with a less specialized plant) would likely have ceased to operate. For the railroad cessation of operations would have been more costly than operating at a loss for a limited time.

Excess Capacity

The cost problem referred to above was complicated by the fact that railroads frequently laid down duplicating lines in their efforts to tap lucrative areas and thus suffered from excess capacity, which further intensified the tendency to use drastic rate reductions as a weapon. The upshot was predictable, in that the weapons available to one road were also available to competitors; thus, the result was most often an exhausting economic struggle ending in a stalemate and characterized as "ruinous competition."

A further obvious result was collusion among the carriers or unjust discrimination against shippers or areas which were in a weak position. Thus, the view began to develop that railroads occupied a twilight zone between the franchised single producer in an area and

---

[4] Frank Norris, *The Octopus* (New York: Doubleday and Company, Inc., 1901), Bantam Ed., 1958.

[5] A modest amount of this feeling carried over into the period of the First World War, as exemplified by the I.W.W. However, at this time, public reaction was adverse.

the competitive industries in retail and wholesale trade upon which Adam Smith had based his classic observation. It seemed logical, therefore, to construct a framework of public policy within which regulated free enterprise could be carried on.

Unfortunately, also, the railroads were apt to ignore the rudiments of public relations, even in the crude sense of the day.[6] The predictable result was the rise of a wave of public indignation against the railroads, led largely by the rural group, the Patrons of Husbandry or the Grange. The Grange, although organized in 1867 as a social and educational organization for rural citizens, was readily adopted as a vehicle for protest and political action against the railroads. The principal strength of the Grange lay in the area of the great agricultural states of Iowa, Minnesota, Wisconsin, Illinois, and Indiana. Several of these states, at the behest of rural legislators, began to enact legislation aimed at railroad control. Naturally, these laws were resisted by the railroads and challenged in the courts. The immediate upshot was the case of *Munn vs. Illinois,* decided in 1877.[7]

JUDICIAL ISSUES

Three major issues were raised by the challenge of the granger laws: (1) the basic right to regulate, (2) the right of judicial review, and (3) the power to regulate interstate commerce. The first of these issues hinged upon the due process clause. It was held that the Fourteenth Amendment was violated by the fact that the carrier would be deprived of property by the fixing of maximum rates. The court disposed of this issue by citing the common calling of transportation.

The court held that the right of judicial review did not exist and that relief must be had from the electorate and not from the courts. This interpretation did not stand for long.

The third issue, that of the right of the state to control interstate commerce, was upheld on the grounds that facilities in question were within Illinois. Other state laws had exercised control over interstate commerce, however; but this issue was soon to be made more clear, as we shall see.

---

[6] For some charming vignettes of the practices, see the classic by Adams, "The Granger Movement," *North American Review,* Vol. 120, April 1875, reproduced in E. Jones and H. Vanderblue, *Railroads, Cases and Selections,* 1925, as well as *The Robber Barrons, op. cit.;* also, "Monopoly," in *The Big Four, op. cit.*

[7] *Munn v. Illinois,* 94 U.S. 113.

The plaintiffs had also argued that, where charters were involved, the charter constituted a contract under the famous Dartmouth College Case, which could not be disturbed.[8] However, the court held that, where the state had the power to regulate, this power superseded the charter, unless the firm was specifically exempt by the terms of the charter itself.

A final issue centered around the constitutionality of commission regulation. The court held that, while such commissions could not make laws, they could administer those made by the legislature. This final point, although not appreciated at the time, has been the foundation stone for the many quasi-judicial commissions which perform such a significant function in our governmental structure.

The Munn Case actually concerned a grain elevator, but the principle of law upheld the Illinois Railroad Act passed in 1870. The state was sustained in its efforts to impose certain regulations upon a "quasi-public" industry. The court built largely upon English common law, citing inter alia, Lord Hale in De Portibus Maris. In 1886, the situation changed drastically with the court decision in the Wabash case.[9] In this case, the court held that the states did not have the power to regulate commerce between or among the states, since that power was reserved to the Congress by the Commerce Clause of the Constitution. As a matter of fact, several states had, in effect, exercised such power since 1870 without challenge. At any rate, the decision in the Wabash Case left the course of future action up to Congress.

While the Wabash Case clearly established the superiority of the federal authority in the realm of interstate commerce, two basic issues remained in an unsatisfactory state, viz., the extent of federal power in this area and whether or not the states could act if the federal government permitted them to do so. In the so-called Minnesota Rate Case [10] the right of the states to pass laws affecting local interests was upheld in the absence of congressional action, even if these laws had an influence on interstate commerce. In the following year, in a similar but more complex case, the Supreme Court held that the power of a state to fix rates could not be exercised so as to defeat the legitimate control of the federal government over interstate rates.[11] The supremacy of the federal control was further reinforced in the Wisconsin

---

[8] *Dartmouth College* vs. *Woodward,* 4 Wheat (U.S.) 518 (1819).

[9] *Wabash, St. Louis and Pacific Railway v. Illinois,* 118 U.S. 5.

[10] *Simpson* vs. *Shepard,* 230 U.S. 352 (1913).

[11] *Houston, East-West Texas Railway Co.* vs. *United States,* 234 U.S. 342 (1914).

Passenger Fares Case in 1922 and has not fundamentally changed since that date.[12] While minor issues have arisen in the state-federal jurisdition area, no real question has existed for many years.

While federal power is supreme, it must not be thought of as exclusive, and the states have substantial powers in regulation of both rail and motor traffic. In many areas, Congress has not seen fit to act, or in some cases the Commission has apparently been of the opinion that even where clear authority exists no clear need was evident.[13] The motor vehicle and the aircraft have, because of their great mobility and their "domicility" in the individual states, presented many serious problems in this area, although the basic element of federal supremacy has remained unchanged.[14] Police power and revenue regulations promulgated by the states provide the main area of conflict in these matters.

In fact, the scene of activity had some time previously shifted to Washington and had been taken up by a cast of somewhat unwilling actors. After the usual display of fire-eating oratory in the legislative halls, the Senate, at the request of President Grant, appointed a committee under the chairmanship of Senator Windom. This committee rendered a report in 1874. The report pointed out certain abuses of railroads, such as insufficient facilities, unfair discrimination, and unreasonable charges. As a remedy, the committee recommended the construction of one or more state-owned railroads and improvement of waterways as a means of keeping commercial railroads under control. For the succeeding decade, no action was taken. Various bills were introduced without result, since, as might be expected, railroads were busily engaged in fending off any serious attempts at regulation, aided by a lack of coordination in Congress, due to divergent goals set up by the proponents.

In 1885, the Senate again addressed itself to the problem via the Collum Committee. This committee undertook an extensive investigation and reported that discrimination was the paramount problem. Various abuses were pointed out and specific cases were cited. The report, issued in January 1886, was firmly in the public mind when,

---

[12] *Railroad Commission of Wisconsin* vs. *Chicago, Burlington and Quincy Railway Co.*, 257 U.S. 563 (1922).

[13] An example of this is found in truck brokerage regulation. Part II of the Interstate Commerce Act provides for this power, but the Commission has preferred to leave this in the hands of the few states where truck brokerage is important.

[14] See, for example, *Capitol Greyhound* vs. *Brice*, 70 S. Ct. 806, 339 U.S. 542 (1950); *Bode* vs. *Barnett*, 73 S. Ct. 460, 344 U.S. 547 (1953); *Northwest Airlines* vs. *Minnesota*, 322 U.S. 292 (1944).

in October of the same year, the Wabash decision was handed down, barring the states from pursuing regulation of interstate carriers. Thus, the full impact was felt within a brief period, causing Congress to pass the act to regulate commerce which was signed by the President on February 4, 1887. The immediate struggle thus came to an end, although a long road lay ahead in the implementation of the act.

Early Attempts to Implement the Act of 1887

The practical application of a major item of legislation is never an easy task, especially so when the act breaks new ground. In essence and in purpose, the Interstate Commerce Act was a simple piece of legislation, but, in practice, it proved to be exceedingly complex. Provisions of the Act:

The act was made applicable to all common carriers by railroads engaged in interstate or foreign commerce. It did not apply to common carriers wholly by water, but it did include common carriers partly by water and partly by rail, where they were under common control or arrangement for continuous carriage or shipment.

1. Reasonable Rates: Section 1 required that all rates be just and reasonable and provided that every unjust and unreasonable charge was unlawful. This was simply a statutory enactment of the long-standing common law rule, although, prior to this enactment, there was no basis at the federal level for enforcing this rule, and, in fact, it proved to be a problem for some time to come.

2. Personal Discrimination: Section 2 prohibited personal discrimination by making it unlawful, directly or indirectly, for a carrier, by any device, to charge one person more than another for a like and contemporaneous service under substantially similar circumstances and conditions.

3. Undue Preference or Prejudice: Section 3 was a broad prohibition of undue or unreasonable preference or advantage of any form to any person, place, or kind of traffic. This was not a prohibition of preferential or differential treatment, but only a limitation to what might be considered just and reasonable, requiring each case to be decided *ad hoc*.

4. The Long-and-Short-Haul Clause: This is the well-known Section 4 of the act, which prohibited a common carrier subject to the act from charging or receiving any greater compensation in the aggregate for transportation of passengers or of like kind of property, "under substantially similar circumstances and conditions," for a shorter than

for a longer distance over the same line, in the same direction, the shorter being included within the longer distance. This was designed to prevent the frequent practice of railroads taking advantage of locational monopoly.

5. Pooling: Section 5 prohibited pooling agreements. This section is a fine example of the lack of economic understanding which prevailed. Pooling would have made efficient use of redundant facilities, but public opinion was strongly opposed.

6. Publication of Rates: Section 6 of the act stated that schedules of rates and fares were to be printed, made available for public inspection, and filed with the Commission. There was to be strict adherence to the published schedules and ten days' notice was required before rates could be advanced.

7. The Interstate Commerce Commission: To administer the law, the act established an Interstate Commerce Commission, which was to consist of five members appointed by the President with the advice and consent of the Senate for a term of six years. The Commission was to be bipartisan in composition, and no commissioner could engage in any other business, vocation, or employment while holding office. Any commissioner could be removed by the President for inefficiency, neglect of duty, or malfeasance in office. There was no limitation on reappointment. By an amendment in 1889, the Commission was ordered to report directly to Congress, thereby becoming the first of a series of independent regulatory groups.

While, at first glance, these would seem to be necessary and reasonable provisions, some reflection will make obvious the problems encountered by the Commission in implementing the Act. Although the Commission was given certain powers of inquiry, lack of uniform information and court interpretation soon began to undermine the activities of the Commission to such a degree that the Act was in danger of becoming a dead letter.

Judicial Procedures

The Commission had no power to enforce its own orders but was forced to rely upon judicial order. Until 1893, when the Compulsory Testimony Act was passed, great difficulty arose in obtaining testimony from witnesses. In addition, the courts insisted on hearing all of the evidence, including new evidence introduced by the carrier, which had often been withheld at earlier hearings. Many of the problems can be illustrated by the obstacles encountered in the area of reasonable rates.

In addition to the fact that any reliable economic data were often unavailable and that accounting procedures made rate analysis largely an empirical exercise, the carriers could and did use every means at their disposal to avoid this issue. If, for example, after much delaying litigation, a given rate was held to be unreasonable, the carrier often made a minute change in the rate, which began the entire cycle again.

Aside from these technical considerations, the courts took a generally unsympathetic attitude toward the problems of the Commission.

Things began to improve somewhat with the passage of the Elkins Act of 1903 and especially with the Hepburn Act of 1906. The Hepburn Act took account of the experiences accumulated in the almost twenty years since the passage of the Act in 1887.

Elkins Act of 1903. The passage of this act solved a serious and typical problem which had arisen under regulation. Although the original act had prohibited various types of preferential treatment, the carriers were often under severe pressure to grant such treatment to large and aggressive shippers. The Elkins Act made both parties to the agreement guilty, thus relieving some of the pressure on the carriers.

The Hepburn Act of 1906. The Hepburn Act of 1906 is often considered to be the first meaningful step toward positive and effective control of the railroads.

1. It extended the Commission's authority over related activities, bringing under regulation private car lines, sleeping car companies and terminal facilities in such detail that the Commission was able to control their activities thoroughly. To compensate for the work load, the Commission was increased to seven members.

2. An old problem was solved by requiring accounting reports and allowing the ICC to prescribe the procedures to be used.

3. The Commission's power was greatly augmented by allowing it to prescribe (upon complaint and after full hearing) maximum rates. Also, the Commission was empowered to prescribe joint and through rates, which had often been a bone of contention on the part of the carriers sharing traffic.

4. The railroads were prohibited from shipping certain commodities in which they had an interest, unless these products were to be used in their common carrier activities. This (commodities) clause was designed to protect producers of various products from rail competition and is of little significance at present.

5. Orders of the Commission were to be effective within thirty days. If a carrier failed to comply, the Commission was to request

from the court an order to comply, a procedure which greatly strengthened the procedural powers of the Commission.

Evaluation of Regulation, 1887-1906

With the passage of the Hepburn Act and its interpretation by the courts, the Interstate Commerce Commission gained considerable status and became an effective regulatory agency.

In evaluating the first two decades of regulation, a clear pattern occurs. First, it was, to a large extent, a period of trial and error for the Commission and the courts. Secondly, the legislation was during those years almost entirely restrictive in nature, reflecting the national concern with monopoly and the rise of the "trusts." It also reflected the frequently demonstrated naive faith that complex economic problems can be solved through simple legislation, despite the frequently demonstrated proof to the contrary. In short, it became obvious that restrictive regulation was neither simple to enforce nor a panacea to all economic ills.

Perhaps also by the early years of the century, the role of economic villain had been taken over by the banking and credit system, and the actions of the railroads began to be less significant in the social and economic context. At any rate, the legislation after this date was inclined to be more often directed toward specific goals and to be accompanied by adequate implementing procedures, in short, utopianism began to give way to realism.

Mann-Elkins Act of 1910

The trend discussed above was further illustrated by the passage of the Mann-Elkins Act. This act brought interstate communications facilities under the authority of the Commission and empowered the Commission to suspend proposed rail rate changes, either upon complaint or upon its own initiative. This suspension was valid for a period of 120 days, during which time the Commission was to study the proposal to determine its justification. The burden of proof was to be on the carrier.

The long-and-short-haul clause was restored to life by making it applicable to all situations except as authorized by the Commission.

Also, a move was made to expedite matters by establishing a commerce court, which proved to be ineffective and was abolished in 1913.

The Mann-Elkins Act was the last major item of transportation legislation to be passed before the First World War, although two acts relating to special problems were passed during the years between 1910 and 1920.

The Panama Canal Act of 1912

Upon completion of the Panama Canal in 1912, Congress passed legislation relating to ownership and operations of common carriers by water on the part of railroads. Without specific ICC approval, railroads were not permitted to own or operate common carriers by water.

The Valuation Act of 1913

The second minor act at this time was the Valuation Act of 1913, having as its purpose the collection of data upon which to evaluate railroad rate claims. No reliable data had existed, and the Commission was very much hampered in its work, especially after the decision in *Smyth v. Ames* in 1898 establishing the "fair return on fair value" doctrine.[15] The valuation process involved a tremendous amount of time-consuming work and was not completed until the mid-1930's, at which time the problem was more or less academic.

The hallmark of the legislation from 1887 to 1920 is the gradual and often painful educational process leading from unjustified optimism to more sophisticated realization that the goal of regulation was not to be reached with ease. The years to 1910 were especially marked by frustration. After 1910, effective progress was more rapid, although, like the valuation attempt, the ultimate goals of legislation were not always clearly visible. Although the regulators were not aware of it, their structure erected with such care was to be badly shaken by events soon to be felt. It must be kept in mind that the pioneers in this legislation were without guidance, and, in view of this, it would have been very surprising indeed if the course of regulation had gone forward without incident.

---

[15] *Smyth v. Ames,* 169 U.S. 466.

Summary

Chapters X and XI have treated, in a chronological fashion, the development of regulation over the years 1887 until the early 1960's These years can be divided, 1887-1920 and from 1920 on. In the years 1887 to 1920, the focus was upon control over monopoly motivated by fear of "trusts," as well as specific acts by the railroads. The legislation during these years was generally of an experimental nature, and the years until 1910 were almost entirely devoted to the problems of implementing the original intent of the Act. By 1920, other problems had come into focus, viz., the regulation of a mature industry, and on the horizon, though not yet visible, were the problems incident to the rise of other carriers. In the stormy years of the 1930's, the regulatory agencies were forced to consider the economic factors prevailing. World War II brought this problem to an end; and, in turn, at the conclusion of the war years, a move toward somewhat less restrictive and detailed economic regulation was evident.

Selected References for Further Study

All the standard economic history and transportation textbooks contain comprehensive accounts of regulatory development. Shannon, *America's Economic Growth,* previously cited, is especially interesting in this area.

The flavor of the era can be gained by reading such works as *The Octopus* and other contemporary literature useful in explaining the frequently irrational approach to the problem.

Oscar Lewis, in the *Big Four,* has provided a lively and readable account of the activities of the Southern Pacific group in the period to 1900.

CHAPTER XI

Evolution of Regulation, 1920-1958

The entry of the United States into World War I brought new types of problems and ultimately resulted in the temporary operation of the railroads by the federal government. Upon the return of the carriers to their owners in 1920, the occasion seemed auspicious for a re-examination of the regulatory situation and perhaps a recasting of the legislation. The upshot of this thinking was the passage of the Transportation Act of 1920, which had the above objectives, as well as the immediate short run objective of returning the carriers to private operation.

It was the misfortune of the framers of the Act of 1920 that they could not foresee the far-reaching changes on the horizon. The technological changes in the area of motor transportation and the economic dislocations of the 1930's in combination were to undermine much of the Act of 1920. In 1920, the transportation question was still the railroad question. Railroads were still the dominant carriers of intercity freight, accounting for more than 80 per cent of all ton miles carried. The Act of 1920 was written within this framework, so soon to be disturbed.[1]

---

[1] The view that all problems had been solved was widely shared in academic circles. See E. J. Rich, "The Transportation Act of 1920," *American Economic Review*, X, 1920, p. 527.

TRANSPORTATION ACT OF 1920

1. Rule of rate making: The Act of 1920 made it incumbent upon the Commission to prescribe such rates as would permit the carriers under honest, efficient and economical management to earn a fair return on the fair value of property used in transportation service.

For a two-year period, the rate of allowable return was to be 5.5 per cent, after which the Commission was free to raise the return to 6 per cent. Since some carriers might earn in excess of 5.5 per cent, there was provision for a recapture clause. Under this provision, one-half of all earnings in excess of 6 per cent was to be paid over to the ICC to be placed in a contingency fund. Needless to say, subsequent events were to render this recapture provision of little consequence.

Of more lasting importance were two other rate provisions, viz., the Commission was given permission to prescribe minimum rates in order to prevent rate wars and prevent discrimination. In addition, the Commission was granted power to prescribe the exact rate. It was also directed by the Congress to work for the preservation of water transportation as a matter of national policy.

2. Consolidation: In order to help alleviate the weak-strong road problem, thus making the rule of rate making more realistic and also as a matter of policy, encouragement was given to railroad consolidation. Various criteria were laid down as being desirable and with which proposed consolidations should conform. However, the Commission had no positive power in the matter and no important consolidations were completed, chiefly because the weak roads were not attractive to the strong roads, despite the desirability of such an alliance to the well-being of the transport system as a whole.

3. The Commission was granted control over the issuance or purchase of securities by railroads, a factor which further enhanced the ability of the Commission to control railroad affairs.

4. As a result of adverse experiences during the war, the Congress included in the Act of 1920 substantial provisions for control of available rail service, such as car supply and extensions of or abandonments of line. As a matter of practice, the Commission entrusted matters of car supply to the Association of American Railroads. Matters of line extension have been largely academic since 1920, although abandonments and reductions in service became a very live issue after 1932.

REGULATORY DEVELOPMENT AFTER 1920, THE PROBLEM OF INTER-MODAL COMPETITION

Although the economic decline in 1932 and the upheaval of World War II brought lasting change, it seems likely that the most significant factor influencing regulatory policy was the rise of motor carriers and the revival of water carriage after 1920.

As recounted, the Transportation Act of 1920 fell far short of its goal, although this was not immediately apparent. From 1920 to 1940, the intercity transportation industry passed from the status of a virtual monopoly and a prime example of the public utility type of industry to a highly competitive heterogeneous industry. The impact of these structural changes was obstructed by the cyclical adjustment which had begun in 1932. Consequently, much of the early effort was of an emergency nature, treating the symptoms arising from the depression rather than the basic change in the competitive situation. Typical of these temporary measures was the Emergency Act of 1933.

EMERGENCY TRANSPORTATION ACT OF 1933

1. The act amended the rule of rate making by repealing the relevant provisions of the Act of 1920 and substituting the following:

> In the exercise of its power to prescribe just and reasonable rates the Commission shall give due consideration, among other factors, to the effect of rates on the movement of traffic; to the need, in the public interest, of adequate and efficient railway transportation service at the lowest cost consistent with the furnishing of such service; and to the need of revenues sufficient to enable the carriers, under honest, economical and efficient managment, to provide such service.[2]

2. The recapture clause, which by 1933 had become a source of wry humor, was repealed retroactively.

3. Combinations or consolidations required the approval of the Interstate Commerce Commission.

4. A federal coordinator of transportation was appointed (Commissioner Eastman) and was directed to propose studies bearing upon various facets of the national transportation problem. The collection and analysis of these data was probably the most important tangible result of the act.

---

[2] Emergency Transportation Act of 1933.

severity of competition of these other agencies under depression conditions.[4]

Even at this date, the structural change was obvious in the area of passenger carriage. Moulton estimates that the automobile has been responsible for 70 to 80 per cent of the traffic diverted from steam railroads.[5]

By the mid-1930's, it was obvious that a substantial change had taken place in the transportation industry and that railroads were not likely to return to their pre-depression status. It was equally apparent that the motor carrier industry was becoming a factor in the transportation system, and there was a substantial degree of sentiment in favor of bringing motor carriers under federal regulation.

Although subsequent events have raised many questions as to its wisdom, the general procedure was to treat the motor carrier industry in much the same manner as the railroads and to impose a similar pattern of regulation. After several attempts, the Motor Carrier Act of 1935 was passed, which later became Part II of the Interstate Commerce Act.

MOTOR CARRIER ACT, 1935 (PART II, INTERSTATE COMMERCE ACT)

1. The Motor Carrier Act recognized that certain concessions had to be made to the structure of the motor carrier industry, and several classes of carriers were established.

a. Common carriers (of various commodities) who were required to have certificates of convenience and necessity.

b. Contract carriers, required to have a permit.

c. Various carriers operating interstate but exempt from economic regulation, the most important being (1) private carriers and (2) those transporting only unprocessed agricultural products, (3) vehicles used in metropolitan areas, those transporting newspapers or U. S. mail, and those operated by state and municipal governments.

The distinctions between these groups was to become a matter of serious concern to the Commission in future years.

2. The Commission was given power to regulate rates in the same manner as rail rates, and rates were to be published. Contract carriers were to file minimum charges over which the ICC has control.

---

[4] *Ibid.*, p. 53.
[5] *Ibid.*, p. 89.

3. The Commission was granted control over consolidations, and they were to be "in the public interest" in order to be approved.

4. Issuance of securities was under control, although this was not a serious problem as was true of railroads, and any issue which, together with the presently outstanding securities, would total less than one million dollars was excluded.

5. A Bureau of Motor Carriers was established to administer the Act, and appropriate steps were taken for coordination with the state bodies in view of the great importance of intrastate motor carriage.

Immediately upon passage of the Act, the Commission found itself faced with a staggering work load. The Act had provided for "grandfather" rights to be issued to carriers in bona fide operation as of June 1, 1935. No clear idea had existed as to the possible number of applicants under this provision, and more than 89,000 applications were received. Since it was to the carriers' advantage to file an inflated claim and evidence of bona fide operation took several forms, the Commission had a serious problem in weighing the validity of each application. Eventually, this Herculean task was completed and some orderly pattern began to emerge from the chaos which had characterized the industry. However, because of the numbers involved and the informality of motor operations, the Commission never enjoyed the stability which marked its procedure for the railroads. Although the legal-judicial problems were not serious, the Commission faced procedural matters reminiscent of its early years. Many of these problems have yet to be completely solved, and they will be discussed at another point in the text.

In 1938, further complications arose with the passage of the Civil Aeronautics Act of 1938. This act, passed largely as a result of the unfortunate developments in the air mail situation in the early 1930's, put the air transport industry on a much more stable basis. Unfortunately, it complicated the total regulatory pattern since a new agency, the Civil Aeronautics Board, had been created to administer the Act. The problems created by the establishment of a second independent agency will be examined in the following chapter.

CIVIL AERONAUTICS ACT, 1938

1. Established a Civil Aeronautics Board to administer the Act, consisting of five members appointed by the President, with the advice of the Senate, this pattern having been borrowed from the ICC.

2. Common carriers were required to obtain certificates of convenience and necessity specifying routes and points to be served somewhat similar to those relating to highway transportation, except that the President was to have the power of final approval in certain cases.

3. As in the case of the ICC, the CAB was given power to control rates, including the right to specify the exact rate if necessary.

4. The Board was given control over mergers and consolidations.

By 1940, the various developments in the transportation industry had been analyzed, and the short run influences of the depression had been compensated for. Congress deemed it appropriate to re-evaluate the legislative situation and to make the first major changes since 1920. Unfortunately, like 1920, the situation was one which was to change rapidly in the very near future. The Act of 1940 was to take into account all of the structural changes which had taken place in the industry since 1920. Emphasis was, of course, focused upon the rise of motor carriers. Of importance also was the fact that water carriers had long existed in a twilight zone of regulation, and Congress took the opportunity to remedy the situation.

THE ACT OF 1940

1. The most ambitious and probably the most troublesome aspects of the Act of 1940 was the inclusion of a statement of national policy regarding transportation. The policy implications of this statement will be considered at length in a later chapter. Suffice it to say here that the Congress attempted to encompass in a single statement the national policy toward the various modes and their interrelationships.

2. The Act stated that rail consolidations need not conform to the ICC plan.

3. The Act established the Board of Investigation and Research, which was a temporary body assigned the task of preparing a far-reaching study of the transportation system. Special emphasis was to be placed upon the relationships between the various modes with the objective of illuminating to some degree the statement of policy. The Board existed until 1944, having been extended by the President from its original two-year life.

4. The land grant railroads were released from their obligation to carry government property and mail at reduced rates (except for military traffic which was not released until 1945).

5. With regard to water transportation, the Act recognized the similarity between water and highway transportation and provided for various classes of carriers, common, contract and private, with even broader exemption provisions than was the case in motor transportation. These exceptions consisted of:

a. Commodities in bulk, when no more than three commodities were carried in a single vessel (a tow of barges being a vessel for this purpose).

b. Liquid cargo in bulk.

c. Transportation by contract carrier when by the nature of the cargo the service is not substantially competitive with common carriers under the jurisdiction of the ICC.

d. Transportation by private carrier and certain incidental transportation.

Because of the nature of water transportation and the relatively narrow range of products carried, the exemptions mean that a very large amount of water transportation, probably the major share of such carriage, is not subject to regulation on the federal level.

For very obvious reasons, the years from 1940 to 1950 were not suitable for any major legislation in the transportation field. However, certain social and economic changes continued to become effective during these war and post-war years which shifted the focus of regulatory needs and, perhaps to a degree, raised questions about the efficiency of regulation per se.

These changes were substantially as follows:

1. The continued and accelerated growth of motor carriage, especially through advancing technology, which expanded the scope of motor carriage both in geographical and product categories.

2. The expansion of private motor carriage and the increasing use of the agricultural exemption.

3. The vastly increased use of automobiles and trucks with the consequent need for highway improvements.

4. The substantial participation of air carriers in the passenger transportation area and their entry into cargo movements.

5. Application of new technology to water carriage and the increase in private operations.

6. Industrial shifts in geographic location and technological changes which influenced the need for transportation service in various ways.

7. Wage-price increases which made the financial problems of carriers more serious.

In addition to these specific factors, there were the long-run structural changes in the economy which resulted from the war years. While in the past a major legislative review of the Act had been undertaken roughly each twenty years, special problems arose which appeared to make immediate action desirable. In 1956-57, the railroads, which had fared well during World War II and the Korean War, began to falter badly. Early in 1958, the Committee on Interstate and Foreign Commerce appointed a subcommittee on surface transportation under the chairmanship of Senator Smathers. The Committee began hearings which lasted for several months, and the published record of which runs to more than two thousand pages.[6] While the hearings provided a forum for all the modes and testimony was heard from many hundreds of individuals representing government, academia, and industry, as well as the modes themselves, the theme of the hearings was related to diagnosis of rail problems as the title indicates. Acting with unaccustomed speed, the Congress, as a result of these hearings, passed the Transportation Act of 1958.

Making no pretense of being a comprehensive act, the legislation is frankly a compromise measure designed to alleviate the most serious problems in a stop-gap fashion.

THE TRANSPORTATION ACT OF 1958

1. The Interstate Commerce Commission is authorized to extend emergency loans to railroads under certain rather restrictive conditions. As of late 1961, no loans had been applied for since the railroads in general apparently felt that the conditions were too rigid.

2. The Commission was given pro forma recognition of certain powers it had previously exercised over intrastate rates.

3. Increased authority was given to the ICC vis-a-vis the states in regard to discontinuance of or changes in service of trains operating wholly or partially in intrastate service. This had long been an unnecessary burden to carriers operating unprofitable branch lines in areas where state regulatory commissions were reluctant to allow discontinuance.

4. The most important and also the most controversial item was the modification in the rule of rate making (sec. 15a) as follows:

> In a proceeding involving competition between carriers of different modes of transportation subject to this Act, the Com-

---

[6] *Problems of the Railroads, op. cit.*

mission, in determining whether a rate is lower than a reasonable minimum rate, shall consider the facts and circumstances attending the movement of the traffic by the carrier or carriers to which the rate is applicable. Rates of a carrier shall not be held up to a particular level to protect the traffic or any other mode of transportation, giving due consideration to the objectives of the national transportation policy declared in this Act.[7]

While some question remains as to how effective this amendment will be, or how long it will last without further congressional action, the Act of 1958 is reasonably responsive to the changing conditions prevailing in the transportation industry. Clearly, much remains to be done, and this will be discussed in the appropriate later chapters.

In the four decades which elapsed from 1920 to 1960, two major trends in legislation can be identified. The first of these is the pattern of a major amendment to the legislation roughly every twenty years. The Act of 1920, that of 1940, and largely the Act of 1958 were in large part attempts to overhaul the act after a period of time in which weak spots began to appear. The second notable factor is the fact that in the first two cases, 1920 and 1940, major social and economic change upset the carefully laid plans of the legislators. To a degree at least, the Civil Aeronautics Act of 1938 falls into this category, since it is doubtful if it would have been passed except for the air mail troubles some years previously. The impact of the economic decline and the technological changes were profound, and the Congress and the Commission made strong efforts to account for these factors in the legislative framework. That they met with imperfect success is hardly a matter of surprise. It would be a grave error to think of the present body of legislation as complete or to think of transport regulation as a *fait accompli*. Legislation is a continuous effort, and the transportation industry is a dynamic force. Much depends upon the manner in which the regulations are administered and the climate in which regulation is carried on. It is sometimes assumed that regulation is merely a matter of passing appropriate legislation which will be self-enforcing. In the complex area of transportation, nothing could be further from the truth.

Summary

The legislation of the period 1920-1958 represents the maturing of regulatory philosophy and its adjustment to changing circumstances.

---

[7] The Transportation Act of 1958.

The economic dislocation of the 1930's, coupled with the rise of intermodal competition, made it necessary to modify the entire concept of regulation, and this process largely continues. The years 1930-1940 stand out largely as an interruption in the orderly process of development. The Act of 1958 is, on the other hand, the natural descendant of the Acts of 1920 and 1940.

CHAPTER XII

The Administrative Agencies of Control and Their Policy Making Role

The task of administering and implementing a body of regulation is equally important as the task of formulating such a program. The authors of the Interstate Commerce Act, recognizing this problem, broke new ground in the governmental area by establishing the quasi-judicial commission, first in a long line of such groups.

In general, the role of the Interstate Commerce Commission and other such quasi-judicial bodies is to carry out the will of Congress and to administer an act, taking into account the fact that a substantial degree of flexibility is necessary. The regulatory body is thus an arm of Congress, in effect performing a task which Congress wishes to have performed but is not able to perform itself because of the detailed administration involved and because of the fluid character of the problems encountered.

The task of such a group is, by its nature, difficult to accomplish. Essentially, the Interstate Commerce Commission and other like groups are supposed to restrict themselves to administrative duties, leaving policy matters in the hands of the Congress. It seems clear, however, that, strictly interpreted, such a program is almost impossible. The Commission cannot refrain from at least a degree of policy making, especially in those areas where Congress has been slow in meeting various problems. Under any circumstances, the line between administration and policy making is dim and uncertain. In many areas of regulation, the will of Congress is by no means clear, and the regulatory group must proceed until it is given more specific direction by Congress or is pulled up by the courts.

Under these circumstances, the regulatory body must have certain characteristics in order to operate most effectively. One could list three qualities which might be considered as absolutely necessary to the effective operation of the Commission. The first of these is continuity. Under the law, the Interstate Commerce Commission is a continuous body. The membership terms being overlapping and membership drawn from both major political parties, the Commission never changes its entire personnel or political philosophy, except over a long period of time.

Secondly, the Commission must have expertise. This is to say, the Commission must have at its disposal expert talent in order to deal with the various problems which arise in the technical areas of law, economics, engineering, and accounting. Thirdly, in order to perform its task, the Commission must be impartial. The Commission is constantly forced to make decisions involving the welfare of various groups and modes of transport. Obviously, such decisions must be made on an impartial basis. It seems clear that, if all the above qualities were found in a regulatory commission, there would be little ground for complaint. It is equally obvious that such qualities are likely to be found in varying degrees at any given time. Continuity can be secured by law, but expertness and impartiality are more difficult to achieve. Thus, the independent regulatory commission is a complex organization performing a tenuous and almost immeasurable service. While the federal regulatory commission has become predominant by virtue of the concept of interstate commerce, the regulatory commission was found in the states prior to 1887. It seems likely that the underlying philosophy of such a move was the same as for most of our governmental machinery, viz., the fact that an immediate problem existed rather than the fact that such a move represented a carefully thought out philosophy of government.[1]

RELATIONSHIP TO THE LEGISLATIVE BRANCH

The independent regulatory commission is directly related to the legislative branch of the government, in that it is a creature of Con-

---

[1] Such a view is supported by Cushman. See Robert E. Cushman, *The Independent Regulatory Commissions* (New York: Oxford Press, 1941), pp. 28-29.

gress and reports directly to Congress. The Congress originates legislation and transportation policy through the Senate Committee on Interstate and Foreign Committee and through the House Committee on Interstate and Foreign Commerce. The Interstate Commerce Commission administers this legislation and policy and reports to the Congress. The Commision must look to the Congress (as do other governmental agencies) for financial support through appropriations via the Bureau of the Budget.

Since the Interstate Commerce Commission is, in effect, an arm of Congress, it is not surprising that a close relationship exists. Legislation relative to transportation matters often originates as a result of Commission experience in the field, and members of the Senate and House Commerce Committees have, over the years, maintained a close relationship with the Commission.

RELATIONSHIP BETWEEN THE COMMISSION AND THE JUDICIAL BRANCH

The primary role of the courts is to interpet the rulings of the indpendent commissions in the light of the Constitution and the existing legislation. The courts have, thus, acted to circumscribe the actions of the commission in carrying out what it believes to be the will of Congress. Likewise, the court often acts to make clear the fact that further legislation is needed in order for the commission to operate effectively or to carry out actions which Congress believes to be in the publc interest. An example will make this clear. In 1902, a series of cases came before the courts.[2] The issue at stake was the right of a shipper to route his shipment. The ultimate decision of the Supreme Court was that the existing law did not give the shipper the right to route his shipment. Congress, believing that the shipper should have such a right, proceeded through the Hepburn Act of 1906 and other legislation to provide this right. Thus, those who feel that the actions of the independent regulatory bodies have been arbitrary or based upon questionable grounds may have redress through the courts. Court decisions may affirm commission rulings or overthrow them and, in this manner, point the way to more specific or comprehensive legislation.

---

[2] *Consolidated Forwarding Co. vs. Southern Pacific Co.*, 9 I.C.C. 182 (1902); *Interstate Commerce Commission vs. Southern Pacific Co.*, 123 Fed. 597 (1903); *Interstate Commerce Commission vs. Southern Pacific Co.*, 132 Fed. 829 (1904); *Southern Pacific Co. vs. Interstate Commerce Commission*, 200 U. S. 536 (1906).

Over a period of years, the actions of a regulatory body and the way in which such actions are viewed by the courts constitute a substantial body of administrative law, and the "landmark" cases become few and far between. Legal specialists become familiar with the outlines of this body of law in the same fashion as a lawyer who specializes in real estate, trusts and estates, or other legal areas.

RELATIONSHIP BETWEEN THE INDEPENDENT COMMISSION AND THE EXECUTIVE BRANCH

One of the fundamentals of commission philosophy is independence from rapid political change and, thus, from undue control by the executive branch. However, although the regulatory bodies are largely independent, there are close ties to the executive. The President appoints members of the commission with the advice and consent of the Senate, in accordance with the law. Also, the executive branch, through the Bureau of the Budget and via the appropriations procedure in the legislative branch, finances the commission's activities. The President, as the chief executive officer of the government, has a degree of influence over commission affairs through executive order and, to a degree, by virtue of his influence as President and head of his party. The law requires that the Presidential appointments to the commission maintain a political balance. However, he may choose to appoint someone who bears the appropriate political label, but whose basic philosophy may be akin to his own. During the maximum of eight years which a president may serve, he may, as chance allows, appoint or reappoint a number of members, possibly a majority. Of the eleven members serving in 1950, none was still serving in 1960, although, in former years, turnover was considerably lower, as will be noted later. It seems likely that the influence of the President depends largely upon his personal interest in regulatory policy and his strength as an executive. There seems to be little doubt that the presidents who have served in recent years have had only routine interest in commission matters, due largely to the fact that other foreign and domestic affairs were more pressing at the time.

For example, Mr. Hoover seems to have been especially interested in the Interstate Commerce Commission as a means of aiding the distressed railroads in the early 1930's.[3] Much evidence exists that

---

[3] William S. Myers and Walter H. Newton, *The Hoover Administration, A Documented Narrative* (New York: Charles Scribners Sons, 1936).

Mr. Roosevelt took an active interest in Commission affairs until the international problems became formidable in the early 1940's.[4] In his memoirs, Mr. Truman mentions the Interstate Commerce Commission rarely, and only during his tenure as a Senator, never as President.[5]

Such evidence, as is available, would indicate that Mr. Eisenhower took only a routine notice of Commission affairs, although his administration did follow an active policy of appointing younger men to Commission posts. Unfortunately, the prestige of the Commission did not seem to be sufficient to hold many of the younger appointees who soon found places in private industry. Over the years since 1930, the President has viewed his role as "policy maker" in the transport field in various ways.

In the Transportation Act of 1940, the formal statement of congressional intent as to policy was included as the National Transportation Policy. This well known statement was intended to be a guide to the Commission and not the President. However, it seems clear that if the President approved of the policy, he would use whatever pressure he could bring upon the Commission to implement it. That is, the Commission would be the logical channel to use in a policy making sense. By 1940, the President was intensely concerned with international affairs, and high level interest in transport policy continued to focus on the coordinator's office. When World War II began, Commissioner Eastman was appointed Director of the Office of Defense Transportation, and traditional policy matters became secondary to the immediate goal of the war effort.

During Eastman's service as coordinator, there seems to be ample evidence that he was forced to take a strong line as regards the relationship of the Commission to the President; to quote Fuess,

> Mr. Roosevelt with all his virtues as a statesman, was a consummate and agile politician. Eastman on the other hand, detested political strategy and opportunism. Thus, in one very important respect the two men, although superficially friendly in their personal relations, could not find common ground. The President saw in the Interstate Commerce Commission a political instrument, which ought to acknowledge his supremacy and could serve his purpose.[6]

---

[4] Clyde Fuess, *Joseph B. Eastman, Public Servant* (New York: Columbia University Press, 1952).

[5] Harry Truman, *Memoirs*, Vol. I, *Year of Decisions* (Garden City: Doubleday & Co., 1955), pp. 149 ff.

[6] Fuess, *op. cit.*, p. 245.

Eastman, to be sure, took a strict view of commission independence, and Eastman and the President were frequently at odds.[7] On various occasions, the President appointed study groups and committees which appeared to overlap or usurp commission duties, especially on the policy level.[8] However, Mr. Roosevelt continued to reappoint Commissioner Eastman (apparently without too much enthusiasm), since he recognized his standing in the industry and with the Congress. Although the decision in the Humphrey's Case[9] clearly established the independence of commissioners as to removal from office by the President except for cause, President Roosevelt did not hesitate to use various means of influencing policy. Roosevelt made frequent references to the often proposed Federal Department of Transportation, i.e., a cabinet post under the control of the executive branch.[10] On the other hand, it might be noted that Mr. Roosevelt was strongly opposed for a time to the Civil Aeronautics Act because of his belief that the provisions of the legislation should be administered by the Interstate Commerce Commission. He changed his mind in 1937 and signed the Civil Aeronautics Act of 1938, establishing the Civil Aeronautics Board.[11]

The Civil Aeronautics Act [12] gave the President some ultimate responsibility for policy matters, but only in an indirect manner. The President has the final authority on international route awards. Perhaps because aviation was a young industry up until World War II, it was quite common for advisory and exploratory groups to be appointed to consider industry problems. Many of these problems are technical in nature or are of an international character. For some years, since the formation of the President's Aircraft (Morrow) Board in 1925 and the appointment of an Assistant Secretary of Commerce for Aviation in 1926, the formation of air transport policy had been on a rather tenuous basis. Perhaps the ill-advised actions of Mr. Roosevelt in the air mail crisis in 1934 made him and his successors rather cautious regarding air policy.[13] At any rate, the Civil Aeronautics Board,

---

[7] *Ibid.*, pp. 247 ff.

[8] For example, the so-called "Brownlow" committee in 1936 made recommendations which would have removed any administrative functions from the commissions.

[9] *Humphreys Executor v United States*, 295 U. S. 602, 624 (1935).

[10] This proposal has been made at intervals for many years. For a good summary, see David I. Mackie, "The Necessity for a Federal Department of Transportation," Vol. 8, No. 1, *Journal of Public Law*, Emory University Law School, Atlanta, 1959.

[11] H. Ladd Smith, *op. cit.*, p. 303.

[12] 59 Sta. 977 (1938).

[13] Smith, *op. cit.*, pp. 214 ff.

while it has perhaps never had the prestige of the Interstate Commerce Commission, seems to have a rather free policy hand. The Office of the Undersecretary of Commerce for Aviation, which was largely promotional in nature, was superseded by the Act of 1938, which provided for the appointment of an administrator. Smith points out that the idea of an administrator was adopted in order that the President's power would not be too great in view of the Humphrey's Case decision previously cited.[14]

Of the Presidents serving in recent years, Mr. Hoover and Mr. Roosevelt faced serious economic problems, of which transportation constituted an important element. The Truman administration was generally free of such problems. Eisenhower's last years did bring some transportation difficulties, although they were much milder than those prevailing from 1932 to 1937. In addition, Mr. Roosevelt, of course, faced the problem of adjusting the transportation industry, as well as the rest of the economy, to a war footing. All four presidents, Mr. Roosevelt in particular, showed a tendency to bypass the Commission in times of crises and to establish an "outside" group for policy formulation to utilize a special committee of administration personnel to make recommendations. Mr. Roosevelt seems to be the only one of the four who apparently toyed seriously with the idea of an executive department of transportation or who, in any way, attempted to influence policy in an overt fashion. It is interesting to speculate what might have taken place if Commissioner Eastman had not been of strong character.

It seems likely that any president would be apt to turn for policy to special groups for many reasons. In the first place, the President would doubtless want very much to avoid any appearance of attempting to influence the Commission unduly in policy matters. Obviously, also, the President would be likely to have rapport with members of his own official family or with former associates. In contrast, the Commission consists of a group, many or most of whom owe him no loyalty and who, by and large, lack the "glamour" of a group especially chosen by the President. Especially if the President has in mind some policy recommendations which the Commission is likely to view with alarm, he may make an effort to bypass them entirely. It seems likely that the President could exercise little control over the Commission in any event. Some writers mention the President's budgetary control as a possible means of influence.[15] Since Congress has the ultimate

---

[14] *Ibid.*, p. 305.
[15] Locklin, *op. cit.*, p. 298.

authority in appropriation, it seems highly dubious that the President could exercise any substantial degree of control, either positive or negative, over the Commission in this way. Neither can he, except over a long period of time, exercise any significant degree of influence through appointments; although, of course, careful consideration of appointments is in every way advantageous.

The inescapable conclusion seems to be that the only practicable way in which the President can mold Commission policy is to bring the pressure of industry or public opinion to bear. If this is true, the cooperation of an outside group representing a broad element of the economy is a useful device.

Assuming that such a group has the respect of the Commission, a program of this type avoids the risk of direct presidential or industry intervention in Commission affairs and also has the advantage of being able to make policy proposals which would not be proper if made by an official regulatory agency. If such proposals are highly controversial, the outside group can send up trial balloons, and the regulatory group escapes any onus.

If, in the near future, a Federal Transportation Department is created, which seems unlikely, the situation would be considerably changed. The President would then have a definite cabinet level channel solely concerned with transport matters. Many students of the problem feel that one of the weaknesses of this proposal is indeed that the President would have too much of a policy making role and the role of Congress and the Commission would be reduced.[16]

It seems clear, at any rate, that, under present circumstances, the President's increasing use of groups within the executive branch and, in particular, the availability of the Office of the Undersecretary for Transportation has somewhat reduced the reputation for transport expertise of the Interstate Commerce Commission. It will be of great interest to students of transportation affairs to observe whether the apparent trend toward centralization of policy functions continues.

One indication of the complexity involved here is a reply from a member of the executive staff to a direct question by the author.

How would you conceive your function as policy maker in this area (transportation) vis-a-vis the appropriate committees in the Senate and the House of Representatives?[17]

This question involves an analysis of the operation of the office of

---

[16] Mackie, *op. cit.*

[17] Letter from the author to the Honorable John F. Kennedy, February 7, 1962.

the President which is beyond the scope of a short reply. Certainly the executive department has a leadership responsibility, but there are many problems which require legislative resolution.[18]

Outside the executive branch, the groups within the federal establishment directly concerned with transportation policy, in particular the implementation, are the regulatory agencies, the Interstate Commerce Commission and the Civil Aeronautics Board.

THE ICC AND CAB AS POLICY MAKING GROUPS

In the section on presidential policy, it was pointed out that the President may, in general, have little close relationship with commissions, since they are a continuous body. Both by law and by nature, the commissions are independent bodies and would not normally be closely identified with the President or his policies.[19] The President would, in the usual case, present his policy program for transportation (if he has one) through the Office of the Undersecretary of Commerce for transportation. It must be kept in mind that many policies not normally thought of as transportation oriented will influence the industry. Tax matters, for example, often have great influence in the transport area.

No doubt, the commission looks to the Congress for much policy making, although, as noted earlier, a line between policy formulation and policy execution is not easily drawn. Commissioners and administrators frequently consult with members of the Interstate and Foreign Commerce Committees on matters of proposed legislation. There is no doubt that the commissions, especially the ICC could make a much more meaningful contribution in this area, if they were inclined to do more creative research. Morgan points out in his stimulating article on research in the Interstate Commerce Commission the need for increased efforts along this line.[20]

Looking at the years 1930-1960, one very substantial advantage accruing to the commissions is their direct contact with the industry. Neither the President nor the Congress has a field staff, nor do they deal directly with the industry. Both the Interstate Commerce Commission and the Civil Aeronautics Board have direct contact with

---

[18] Letter to the author from Myer Feldman, Deputy Special Counsel to the President, February 26, 1962.

[19] *Ibid.*, It will be remembered that Eastman was by no means a supporter of the Roosevelt "New Deal."

[20] Charles S. Morgan, "The Function of Research in a Regulatory Agency," *I C C Practitioners' Journal*, Vol. XXIV, No. 8, May 1957.

the industry, both formal and informal. While this sometimes is disadvantageous, in that they may become advocates of the industry, it does enable them to be fully aware of the industry problems and prospects. They can then transmit recommendations up to the Congress for suggested legislation. Also, the Interstate Commerce Commission maintains a formal liaison with the state commissions and presumably keeps well abreast of developments in this field. It seems likely that the flow of information is adequate, and, indeed, one of the commission's major tasks is to sift these data and analyze them in a meaningful fashion.

The Interstate Commerce Commission has had another great advantage over the years, by virtue of its high degree of continuity. In the years 1930-1960, a total of thirty-seven men served on the Commission. Of these men, four (Lee, Aitcheson, Mahaffee, and Splawn) served twenty years or more (during the thirty years), while a total of fourteen men served ten or more years. (See Table 12-1.)

TABLE 12-1

LENGTH OF SERVICE, ICC COMMISSIONERS
1930-1960

20 or more	Years		Less than 5
	10-19	5-9	
Mahaffee	McManamy	Farrell	Lewis
Lee	Meyer	Tate	Woodlock
Aitcheson*	Eastman	Caskie	Brainerd
Splawn	Porter	Cross	Barnard
	Miller	Arpaia	Knudson
	Rogers	Freas	Elliott
	Aldredge	Tuggle	Clarke
	Patterson	Winchell	Murphy
	Johnson	Hutchison	Minor
	Mitchell		Walrath
			McPherson
			Goff
			Webb
			Herring

* Aitcheson served 35 years longer than any other member.
Source: Compiled from *ICC Annual Reports*, 1930-1960.

From 1940 to 1950, the Commission was very stable, with only four additions during the decade. After 1950, the personnel of the Commission changed rapidly, with a total of sixteen members being appointed during these years. The senior man serving in 1960 was Mr. Arpaia with a total of eight years' service. In 1950, by contrast, four members had more than fifteen years' service.

After 1950, several men (Cross, Knudson, Elliott, Clarke and Minor) served less than a full term. Before this date (during the period under discussion), only two men (Caskie and Barnard) had served less than a full term. Mr. Minor, who served only a little more than a year, holds the record for short service. Of the thirty-seven men who served, five are outstanding commissioners, viz., Meyer, Eastman, Woodlock, Aitcheson, and Splawn. Excluding Woodlock, since he clearly belongs in an earlier era, the remaining four are all those of long service. There seems to be no clear reason for the increase in turnover after 1950 as contrasted with the previous period.

Looking at the CAB, the situation is somewhat different. In the CAB, length of service has been the exception. One member, Mr. Ryan, served for sixteen years; Lee served fourteen years; and Branch served twelve years; the rest served for less than ten years. (See Table 12-2.)

TABLE 12-2

LENGTH OF SERVICE, CAB MEMBERS
1939-1960

20 or more	10-19	Years	5-9	Less than 5
None	Branch*		Warner	Noble**
	Ryan*		Pogue	Hinkley*
	Lee		Adams	Mason*
			Gurney	Hester
			Denny	Baker
			Rizley	Landis
				Young
				O'Connel
				Jones
				Rentzell
				Myrop
				Durfee
				Minetti
				Hector
				Gillilland
				Boyd

**Original chairman.
*Original members.
Source: *CAB Annual Reports,* 1939-1960.

Of the total twenty-five men who have served, eighteen served less than the term prescribed by law. Turnover was much greater on the part of CAB members than was true of the ICC members. Most of the alumni of the CAB, as was true of the ICC, left to return to private business or go into retirement. None went into high public office. Mr. Rentzell became Undersecretary of Commerce for transportation. Their backgrounds were diverse. The first chairman, Mr. Noble, was a candy manufacturer. Lawyers or lawyer-public servants like Mr. Landis were frequent choices. Mr. Baker is an academician, and one former U. S. Senator, Mr. Gurney, was appointed after he left office. It seems likely that none of the members has achieved the eminence that Eastman or Aitcheson did on the ICC although this may be merely a matter of time. Generally speaking, the Board probably has a more active role than the ICC in the public mind and is more frequently in the news. Since the Board has only five members, there is probably more opportunity for individual expression than is true of the Commission. Likewise, the Commission is more hidebound by tradition. The Board has, undoubtedly, presented a more "lively" atmosphere, in part because of its relatively recent organization and the fact that it probably presents more of a challenge than was true of the more routine affairs of the ICC.[21]

There can be no doubt that the major task of the future is to choose men to fill these regulatory posts who combine the virtues of creativeness and stability. The benefits of long tenure and stability should not be gained at the expense of sacrificing initiative and imagination.

ORGANIZATION OF THE INTERSTATE COMMERCE COMMISSION

The internal organization of the Interstate Commerce Commission is complex, due to the wide range of its duties. The formal statement of Commission responsibility is found in the statement issued by the Special Subcommittee on Legislative Oversight:

> The Commission has been vested with authority to regulate various types of surface transportation in interstate and foreign

---

[21] The two members with the longest service, Branch and Ryan, were on the original Board in 1939. The other members of the pioneer group served only short terms. The chairman, Mr. Noble, served only a year, leaving to become Assistant Secretary of Commerce.

commerce. The scope of this authority is briefly as follows: (1) to issue certificates of public convenience and necessity for the construction, extension and abandonment of lines of railroads; certificates of public convenience and necessity for the establishment or extension of motor common carrier and water common carrier operations; the issuance of permits for the institution and extension of motor contract carrier operations, water contract carrier operations, and freight forwarder operations; (2) to require that rates and practices of all common carriers, including freight forwarders, subject to the act be just, reasonable, and non-discriminatory, and that such rates be published, filed with the Commission and observed; and to require that motor contract carriers and water contract carriers establish and observe just and reasonable minimum rates; (3) to regulate railroads and motor carriers, including private carriers by motor vehicles, with respect to safety of operations, standards of equipment, and hours of service of personnel whose activities affect safety of operations; (4) to require personal injury, death, and property damage insurance of motor carriers and freight forwarders for the protection of the public and cargo insurance for the protection of shippers; (5) to pass upon the unification, mergers, and common control of two or more railroads, motor carriers, water carriers, express companies or sleeping car companies, and to approve or disapprove the pooling or division of traffic, service or earnings by two or more such carriers; (6) to regulate the issuance of securities by railroads and motor carriers, the financial reorganization of railroads, and the guarantee of loans to railroads; (7) to prescribe regulations governing the packaging, marking and handling of explosives and other dangerous articles which are binding upon all carriers subject to the Interstate Commerce Act and shippers, and which regulations as to marking and packing are adopted by the Coast Guard for application to water carriers; and (8) to investigate alleged violations, prosecute in court and assist the Department of Justice in prosecuting civil and criminal proceedings arising under all parts of the act and related acts such as the Elkins Act, the Clayton Antitrust Act, and the Transportation of Explosives Act. In addition to the above, the Commission has various other duties such as the prescribing of time zones under the Standard Time Act, determining reasonableness of parcel post increased rates, prescribing charges by railroads for the transportation of mail, investigations under the Medals of Honor Act, and others.[22]

---

[22] *Independent Regulatory Commissions: Comparative Operating Data, etc.*, prepared for Special Subcommittee on Legislative Oversight of Committee on Interstate and Foreign Commerce, Subcommittee Print, 86th Congress, 2d session (Washington, D. C.: U. S. Government Printing Office, December, 1960), pp. 114-15.

The Commission employs approximately 2400 persons and operates on a budget of more than $19 million.[23]

A major problem of internal organization has faced the Commission throughout its life, viz., how to deal with the constantly shifting workload. The chairman is the executive head of the Commission, assisted by the vice chairman and a managing director who bears the main responsibility for "housekeeping" with the Commission. Work is organized through three main divisions, to which various Commissioners are assigned, and three bureaus which process cases for all divisions. As will be noted, the Commission type of organization has many problems which have not yielded to organizational improvements.

ORGANIZATION OF THE CIVIL AERONAUTICS BOARD AND THE FEDERAL AVIATION AGENCY

The federal agencies concerned with regulation of air transportation are of more recent origin than the Interstate Commerce Commission and, since they relate only to air transport, have a narrower jurisdiction.

The Civil Aeronautics Board

The Board is concerned with the economic regulation of air transportation, such as issuance of certificates, regulation of fares and related matters. The basic philosophy of the Board is similar to that of the ICC in that it is an independent regulatory agency.

However, the Civil Aeronautics Board does have one substantial difference in its goals and objectives, viz., a mandate to act as a promotional agency, in that the Civil Aeronautics Act directs the Board to encourage air transportation. Thus, the Board has a much broader duty than the Interstate Commerce Commission. This provision for encouragement has caused considerable controversy in the regulatory area. Although the duties of the CAB are not so extensive in terms of mode as those of the ICC, it has been very active since it was established early in the history of air transport development, overseeing the active interest in the years since 1938.[24] As might be

---

[23] Interstate Commerce Commission *75th Annual Report*, June, 1961 (Washington, D. C.: U. S. Government Printing Office).

[24] For a well written and comprehensive account of the developments leading to the passage of the Civil Aeronautics Act of 1938, see Smith, *op. cit.*, esp. Chapters XV-XXIV.

expected, the CAB has been under great pressure, since the air transport industry has grown rapidly. Especially in the area of certification of routes, the CAB has been severely criticized on grounds of being unduly slow in procedural matters.

The CAB has faced an especially persistent problem in the area of certification and granting of routes, because the maximum number of profitable routes available to potential airline operators is much more limited than is true in the other modes. One could argue, for example, that by 1950 all of the profitable routes were adequately served, and there was no room for additional operators until further economic growth and change had taken place. On the other hand, the Board would not be permitted by congressional and public opinion to "close up shop." Thus, the Board undoubtedly certified certain carriers and routes which were not economically justified.[25] Under the circumstances, it is likely that no course of Board action would have been satisfactory to all interested parties. Unfortunately, also, the CAB has not managed to remain so free from political influence as has generally been true of the ICC.

To a large extent, the problems confronting the CAB are basically the same as those facing the ICC and other such groups and are essentially the problems inherent in the commission type of organization. By the same token, the virtues of both groups are essentially the same. At the time the Civil Aeronautics Act was passed, considerable thought was given to the idea of assigning the duties of air regulation to the ICC, as noted above. This idea was not acceptable to most members of Congress and was ultimately removed from considertion.[26] Looking back from the vantage point of twenty years, it might well be that the best procedure would have been to consolidate these agencies. This problem will receive further consideration in a later chapter.

---

[25] Other means, such as "non-scheduled" and "supplementary" carriers were also used to admit carriers without granting certified status on a permanent basis. Unfortunately, many of these solutions proved to be very short lived and they arose with new vigor to harrass the Board at later dates.

[26] Smith, *op. cit.*, pp. 302, 303. Senator Pat McCarran of Nevada and Representative Lea of California were the principal authors of the Act. President Roosevelt was in favor of using the ICC. McCarran and Lea favored a separate organization, as did other influential members of Congress. Roosevelt was finally convinced, interestingly enough, by his son, James, who was serving as his secretary, an interesting item in view of the previous discussion in regard to policy making.

The Federal Aviation Agency

The function of the Federal Aviation Agency is to oversee the technical aspects of air regulation, such as qualification of pilots and worthiness of air craft. The FAA also operates the airway system and controls civilian air traffic. The agency is headed up by an administrator who is appointed by the President. Since the responsibility of the FAA is technical, the scope of its problems is somewhat narrower but no less complex than those of the CAB.

PROBLEMS OF THE COMMISSIONS

Some political scientists have advanced the theory that the regulatory commissions attract very able men during their early history when service on such commissions offers great challenge. After the commission work becomes routine, the distinction of serving becomes much less attractive. This may be true, although, in the case of the ICC, neither Commissioners Eastman nor Aitchison, both distinguished, fit the case.

For men intent upon moving up the political ladder, the commissions do not hold a great deal of attraction. Relatively little opportunity exists for attracting public attention in any way; and, as a regulatory body, the group may engender more ill will than good. Under these circumstances, capable young men may view the Commission only as a brief stopping place; and superannuated politicians may look upon commission appointment as a desirable place to spend the declining years of public life.

Although any exact measurement is impossible, it seems likely that the Interstate Commerce Commission has achieved a considerable degree of prestige as an impartial organization. Very few instances of questionable conduct on the part of commissioners have taken place, although, in recent years, some questions of conflict of interest have occurred; and, given the dimensions of the task, the Commission has, on the whole, performed efficiently.

While complaints have multiplied in recent years, most of the adverse comment centers around procedural matters rather than the honesty or integrity of the Commission. Also, while some questions arise about the basic philosophy of regulation, the Commission must work within the framework available to it.

One obvious problem in the commission relationship to other groups is the fact that it is, by nature, unwieldy and slow-moving as compared to an agency having a more clear-cut administrative policy and a single administrator, as is true of most agencies in the executive branch of the government. Although the ICC is specifically designed as a quasi-judicial organization, it does have administrative duties which must be carried out with reasonable dispatch. This dual role often causes conflict with other governmental organizations and the public. In efforts to meet these problems, the Commission has, over the years, adopted various organization plans.[27] The Commission's work has been complicated by the fact that it has faced a constantly growing work load, due both to the growth of the transportation industry and the increasing areas of responsibility brought about through new legislation. The routine work load, among other things, has prevented the ICC from performing much needed basic research.[28]

Criticism has been directed toward the Commission on grounds that it is unduly slow in performing its duties in regard to issuance of certificates and related matters which require relatively prompt attention. In addition to the basic problems due to its nature, the Interstate Commerce Commission has the problems common to any governmental agencies, viz., an increasing work load combined with budgetary problems. The Commission, as a regulatory agency, does not enjoy such a high degree of congressional favor as the "help type" agencies, such as the Department of Agriculture, and, consequently, must overcome greater opposition in securing adequate funds.

POLICY MAKING ROLE OF THE CONGRESS

The Congress exercises its influence over transportation policy via the respective Senate and House committees dealing with the subject, viz., the Senate Committee on Interstate and Foreign Commerce and the House Committee on Interstate and Foreign Commerce. Assignment to these committees is like all committee assignments, a

---

[27] All such plans focus on the ageless problem of freeing the commissioners from routine duties in order to concentrate on "policy matters." Although the Commission has had a degree of success in these efforts, there is clearly no final and rigid solution.

[28] Morgan, *op. cit.*, pp. 816 ff. It seems likely that if more research could be done, much routine work might be eliminated through more adequately defined goals and more sense of direction. Morgan points out that the Commission often is forced to operate on a "crash basis," because it lacks the data to make recommendations. Such data could have been collected at a more leisurely pace if personnel were available.

matter of party affiliation and length of service. The Senate Committee on Commerce does not have the status of the Foreign Relations Committee nor the power of the Appropriations Committee. It might be described as a sound committee, to which a senator of medium seniority might aspire. As with most committees, the chairman often becomes closely identified with legislation in the field, and various committee members become well known as legislative experts on certain phases of transportation. If one were to choose among the various policy making units the single most influential body, it would probably be the congressional committees involved. While associations or administrators or commissioners may wish to see legislation enacted and may suggest certain measures, the ultimate power to originate such legislation lies in these two groups. Through the medium of hearings, contact with legislative representatives of the various organizations, and other means, the committee members are in an excellent and unique position to observe the conditions which exist in the industry. While members of the committees may not be any more immune to pressure of various types than any other members of Congress, they at least have the advantage of a host of well informed witnesses as well as a vast amount of data. Perhaps the best measure of the influence of Congress in the policy area is the effort, time, and money which is expended by the trade associations in attempting to put their views before the Congress. These pragmatic observers know full well the importance of congressional opinion and spare no effort in attempting to mold it.

Hearings probably constitute the most important vehicle for bringing matters to the attention of the committee. While one cannot discount the value of personal contact, the hearing is the "official ear" of the legislative branch. A major legislative undertaking involves the appearance of several hundred witnesses and many thousands of pages of testimony and exhibits. Even though some of this material is overlapping and to a substantial degree apt to be a collection of platitudes, much of it will be worthwhile. These hearings constitute a relatively painless method of education, especially for the newer members of the committee who may not be familiar with the problems involved.[29] When the committee approves an item, the entire legis-

---

[29] The contrast between those who have had the benefit of "education" in hearings and those who have not is well illustrated by the exchange on the floor of the House between Congressman Wadsworth and other members of the House in regard to the Motor Carrier Act of 1935 while it was under consideration. *The Agricultural Exemption in Interstate Trucking.* See *M.R.R. Report 188,* U. S. Department of Agriculture, 1956, pp. 42 ff.

lative body is apt to view this as a stamp of approval by the "expert" group and, thus, smooth the path for the bill.

TABLE 12-3

CHAIRMEN, SENATE-HOUSE COMMITTEES,
INTERSTATE AND FOREIGN COMMERCE
1930-1960
(71ST THRU 86TH CONGRESS)

Congress	Senate	House
71st	Johnson (Calif.)	Parker
72nd	Johnson (Calif.)	Rayburn
73rd	Dill	Rayburn
74th	....	Rayburn
75th	Wheeler	Lea
76th	Wheeler	Lea
77th	Wheeler	Lea
78th	Wheeler	Lea
79th	Wheeler	Lea
80th	White	Wolverton
81st	Johnson (Colo.)	Crosser
82nd	Johnson (Colo.)	Crosser
83rd	Tobey	Wolverton
84th	Magnuson	Priest
85th	Magnuson	Harris
86th	Magnuson	Harris

Source: *Congressional Directory,* 71st thru 86th Congress.

As shown in Tables 12-3, the Senate and House committees concerned with interstate and foreign commerce were under the chairmanship of Senator Wheeler of Montana and Representative Lea of California for a period covering five congressional sessions. It is not surprising that a substantial amount of legislation enacted during the years roughly 1930-1935 bears the imprint of these men. Both Wheeler and Lea were instrumental in the promulgation of transportation legislation.

No other team of chairmen had in recent years the advantage of a lengthy term of service. Johnson of California, who was elected to public office largely on the basis of his efforts to drive the Southern Pacific out of California politics, was nearing the end of his active political life by 1930. Senator Johnson of Colorado served two terms as chairman before the Republican victories in the 80th Congress.

Senators Dill, White, and Tobey all served through only one session. In the House there was less continuity, with more tendency toward short terms. Aside from Mr. Lea, Representative Rayburn served three terms, Mr. Crosser served two, and Wolverton served two split terms. Representatives Parker and Priest served one term each. Thus, although seven man are concerned in each case, the House chairmen were more apt to change.

There is no doubt that long and continuous service is a major element in effective legislation. Dill, White, Tobey, Parker and Priest all fall in the one term category and have the further disadvantage of having to work, in several cases (White-Wolverton, Tobey-Wolverton, Dill-Rayburn, and Magnuson-Priest), with an opposite number who was serving a first term. In one case, Johnson (California), a Republican, was faced with a Democratic opposite number, Rayburn.

In the discussion relating to the President, it was noted that the prevailing conditions make a substantial difference. This is true here. Wheeler and Lea served not only a long time but during the 1930's, the "New Deal" era when legislation was pouring forth in substantial amounts. Likewise, Johnson of California had, to some degree, acquired a reputation as a crusader against railroads before he came to the Senate.

Other Senators, such as McCarran of Nevada, co-author of the Civil Aeronautics Act of 1938 (with Mr. Lea), acquired a special interest, often through service on another committee.[30] Aside from the committees on interstate and foreign commerce, other Senate and House committees concern themselves with legislation which influences transportation policy. Committees on rivers and harbors, finance, ways and means, education and labor, public works, and others are influential in the transportation area.

In addition to the hearing as an educational device, the Congress often undertakes to conduct special studies such as the Doyle report referred to elsewhere in this study. Reports of this type usually conducted by an especially appointed expert staff are frequently used to supplement the information at the disposal of the members. Since a study of this type requires a substantial period of time to complete, it would put a severe strain on the regular committee staff, which is generally very small and geared essentially to doing routine work. For more limited studies, the Legislative Reference Section of the Library of Congress exists, and it is common practice for the Congress

---

[30] McCarran became interested through his service on the Black Committee investigating the air mail situation. He and Representative Lea sponsored the Act of 1938.

to borrow staff assistants from various federal agencies. All factors considered, the Congress is in an excellent and well informed position to evaluate the industry and to make transportation policy. Given the limits of political reality within which the Congress must work, the Congress has been responsive to the needs of the industry. Some notable exceptions can be listed, for example, the agricultural exemption; however, the practical problems in this instance are immense.

The Congress must guide and coordinate transportation policy in such a way that it becomes meshed with all the other policies relative to the politico-economic situation prevailing at any given time.

Although the President can make his wishes known and present an overall plan, it remains for the Congress to put the policy into practice by the enactment of appropriate legislation.

TRANSPORT POLICY AND THE COURTS

Throughout our socio-economic system, the judiciary determines the permissible area of action. In the field of transportation, the whole body of public regulation has developed within the framework of judicial guidance. From the cases of *Munn v. Illinois* in 1877 and the *Wabash Case* in 1886 which laid the foundation for the regulation of transportation in the United States, the courts have been instrumental down to the present day. Judicial policy determination in the area of transportation concerns itself essentially with two questions: (a) Does the law enacted by the Congress conform to the Constitution, and (b) do the administrative decisions of the regulatory commissions conform to the intent of Congress as expressed in the law?

Almost from the earliest days of the republic, it was recognized that the constitutional limitation of federal regulation of business must be subject to liberal interpretation.[31] This liberality was necessary in view of the fact that the Constitution is a document given to generalizations. Consequently, specific situations, which arise out of changing conditions, make it necessary to determine in many cases the broad "intent" of the Congress in enacting a specific piece of legislation.

Within the specific area of transport regulation, the need for interpretation became more intense when the Interstate Commerce

---

[31] See statement of Justice Story in Martin V. Hunter's Leasse, I Wheat. (U. S.) 304 (1816) quoted in Ronald A. Anderson, *Government and Business*, Cincinnati, Southwestern Publishing Co., 1960.

Commission was established. The idea of a quasi-judicial commission to carry out the intent of Congress on a broad scale was an innovation which did not meet with universal understanding or acceptance. The years from 1887 until 1910 were devoted almost exclusively to the process of judicial establishment of the allowable area of procedure to be granted to the Interstate Commerce Commission.

For example, from 1887 until 1897, a series of cases revolved around the authority of the Commission in the area of rates.[32] Court interpretations of the act and especially the limitations imposed by the courts, in turn, gave rise to new legislation to carry out the intent of Congress and to allow for the fact that the intent was changing over time.

It might be said that all the amendments to the Act up to 1920 were in response to judicial interpretations of the commission's efforts to express the will of Congress. That is to say, the amendments up through the Valuation Act of 1913 were essentially those necessary to implement the original act. After 1920, new ground was cultivated and Parts II, III, and IV of the Act represented completely de novo extensions of commission power and, in their turn, brought many more cases, even though the basic outlines of commission authority had been established. The long and tortuous history of the "Agricultural Exemption" in Part II of the Act (Sec. 203 (b) 6) is an excellent example of the manner in which the courts force active policy to conform to the interpretation of the Act or its parts.[33] This section has been given several interpretations over the years, and at least sixteen cases have the status of "landmark" cases over the years since 1940.[34] In 1958, Congress amended the section, and the need for interpretative litigation has been somewhat diminished since that date, although broad questions of theory still remain. When the intent of Congress has been clearly demonstrated and the commission adheres to that intent, a policy line becomes established. However, the perimeter of this area is constantly changing, since the Congress, the

---

[32] Eg. "Social Circle Case," *C.N.O.T.P. Railway Co. v. ICC*, 162 U. S. 184, 196, and others.

[33] *Op. cit.*, Marketing Research Report No. 188.

[34] The First Monark Case, 1940, 26 M.C.C. 615; the Second Monark Case, 1944, 44 M.C.C. 15; Harwood Case 47 M.C.C. 597; The Dunn Case, 1948, 166 F 2nd 116; The Love Case, 1948 (5 cir. 1949), 172 F 2nd 224; The Third Monark Case, 1949, 49 M.C.C. 693; The Weldon Case, 1950, *Weldon v. ICC* (6 cir. 1951) F 2nd 367; Service Trucking Co. Case, 1950 (3 cir. 1951), 186 F 2nd 400; Determinations Case, M.C.C. 968, 52 M.C.C. 511; Fourth Monark Case, 52 M.C.C. 576; Yeary Transfer Case, 1952 (6 cir. 1953), 202 F 2nd 151; Florida Gladiolus Case, 1952, 106 F Supp. 525; Kroblin Case, 1953 (8 cir. 1954), 212 F 2nd 555. Certiorari Denied (348 US 836) Oct. 14, 1954.

From a distance of three decades, it seems fairly clear that there was a tendency to overestimate the immediate impact of the depression; however, a brief review of the statistics of the time makes clear the ease with which such an error might be made.

TABLE 11-1

CHANGE IN THE PRODUCTIVE ACTIVITY OF VARIOUS INDUSTRIES, 1928-32
(AS PERCENTAGES OF 1928 FIGURES)

Item	1929	1930	1931	1932
Railroads:				
Car Loadings	102.1	98.5	72.1	54.7
Revenue Net T-M's	103.2	88.5	71.4	53.3
Passenger Miles	98.4	84.8	69.3	53.0
Steel (ingot prod.)	108.1	78.0	49.6	26.2
Autos and Trucks				
(no. produced)	121.7	77.0	53.6	29.8
Gasoline	116.6	116.9	116.2	100.5
Building Contracts	81.8	52.7	37.8	16.0

Source: Adapted from Moulton Associates, *The American Transportation Problem, Washington,* 1933, The Brookings Institution, p. 50.

As Table 11-1 indicates, although the years 1929-1932 was disastrous to rail transportation, certain other industries were, in terms of output, even worse off, giving rise to the hope that if the emergency could be endured, the pre-1929 status could be resumed. As Moulton and his associates writing in 1932 say:

> How much of the decline from 1928 to 1931 in the aggregate tonnage originated is attributable to the fall in the general industrial activity during this period is a question of considerable importance from the standpoint of possible remedial action, but one which cannot be answered with precision. One would expect in a severe depression to find a decline in railway traffic roughly proportional to the general decline of productive activity, and this what we do find, as table ...... shows.[3]

Moulton adds:

> Clearly the decline in railway traffic since 1929 reflects in part a decrease in the total amount of transportation work being done, in part a diversion to other agencies which would have taken place even under prosperity conditions, and in part the increased

---

[3] Moulton *et al.,* op. cit., p. 51.

commissions, and the courts must take cognizance of changing situations. None of these groups operates in a vacuum.

Although the courts determine the limits of jurisdiction of the regulatory commissions, they cannot be said to set policy in the full sense of the word. The courts are passive, not active. The industry or the regulatory commissions must undertake to pursue a given end; the courts may then approve or deny this action and the limitations are established.

Except in rare instances, the procedure for judicial interpretation of Commission rulings is as follows: (1) U. S. District Court, (2) U. S. Circuit Court of Appeals, (3) U. S. Supreme Court. The Supreme Court, in most instances, accepts cases only on a writ of certiorari and accepts such writs only if an element of national interest or constitutional question is involved. Relatively few cases resulting from commission rulings go beyond the Court of Appeals.

For example, in the 73rd Annual Report of the Commission, it is reported that fifty-three cases in total were instituted during the year, three of which were U. S. Supreme Court cases. Of the twenty more important cases, the commission was upheld in eighteen rulings and reversed in two.[35]

OTHER FEDERAL AGENCIES RELATED TO TRANSPORTATION REGULATION OF PROMOTION

The Federal Maritime Board. The Federal Maritime Board is essentially a promotional agency in that it concerns itself with the welfare of U. S. overseas and domestic deep sea shipping. In so doing, it carries out the following functions.

1. Applies the provisions relating to construction-differential and operating-differential subsidies.

2. When necessary, supplements private ship construction and operation, subsidized and nonsubsidized, by construction and operation of vessels.

3. Administers sale of war-built tonnage as provided by the Merchant Ship Sales Act of 1946.

4. Provides for the establishment of the National Defense Reserve Fleet.

5. Performs services and functions in support of the merchant marine operation as a whole, including the training of personnel and the acquisition of vessels by purchase or charter.

---

[35] *ICC 73rd Annual Report.*

6. Charters vessels owned by the government.

7. Conducts investigations in regard to the condition of the merchant marine and makes suggestions for improvement.

For the most part, these functions are outside the scope of this book, since they are concerned with ocean shipping. However, there is a degree of overlap and duplication.

Although the Interstate Commerce Commission, the Civil Aeronautics Board, the Federal Aviation Agency, and the Federal Maritime Board are the agencies principally concerned with transport regulation, other federal groups are involved in one way or another with the field—most of them in the executive branch.

Department of Commerce:
    Undersecretary of Commerce for Transportation
    Bureau of Public Roads
    Maritime Administration (Federal Maritime Board)
Department of State:
    Office of Transportation and Communication
Treasury Department:
    Coast Guard
Defense Department:
    Panama Canal
    Corps of Engineers
    Military Traffic Management Authority
    Military Sea Traffic Service
    Military Air Traffic Service
Post Office Department
St. Lawrence Seaway Corporation
Federal Civil Defense Administration:
    Transportation Office
Department of Agriculture
Office of Defense Management
National Advisory Committee for Aeronautics
Air Coordinating Committee
Department of the Interior
    The Alaska Railroad and certain powers of pipeline rights
    of ways.

There are, thus, at least twenty agencies or parts of agencies, in addition to the Interstate Commerce Commission, the Civil Aeronautics Board, and the Federal Aviation Agency, dealing with transportation matters on the federal level. In some cases, the agency deals only indirectly with transportation, as is the case with the Department of Agriculture; but, in others, there is a strong regulatory tie, as is true in the case of the Coast Guard. In other cases, the federal government is actually engaged in transportation, as is true of the Military Sea and Air Traffic services and the Alaska Railroad. Clearly, the role of the federal government in the transportation area is a complex one indeed. It might be noted that none of the above functions takes into account the substantial influence of the federal agencies as buyers of transportation service.

This factor gives rise to a particular problem, in that certain federal agencies, such as the General Services Administration, Defense Department and Department of Agriculture, are very large buyers of transportation service in the course of their operations and, as such, have an interest in rate proceedings in their own right. Also, some agencies, such as the Department of Agriculture, often intervene in rate proceedings on behalf of the agriculture community in general. The implications of this dual role are somewhat disquieting.

To illustrate the scope of the problem, let us consider a regulated carrier operating on the inland waters. Such a carrier would be obligated to the various federal regulatory agencies as follows:

Corps of Engineers: Provision of waterways and facilities

Interstate Commerce Commission: Regulation of rates and services

U. S. Coast Guard: Regulations concerning navigation and other technical matters

These direct responsibilities would be supplemented by irregular requests for information from the various other agencies such as the Office of the Undersecretary for Transportation. In addition, no mention is made of non-transportation regulatory relationships, such as those relating to communication and labor matters.

It seems beyond all doubt that the functions of the various regulatory agencies need to be reconsidered from time to time and the various overlapping areas given special consideration.

Unfortunately, no federal agency is likely to look with favor upon the loss of its jurisdiction over any area. Further, valid reasons may exist in favor of some duplication. For example, the Department of Agriculture has frequently made worthwhile studies, which, although they relate essentially to transportation of agricultural products, have had broad and useful application.

An important agency in the area of transportation policy making exists in the form of the Office of the Undersecretary for Transportation. As a rather recently created agency and one devoted entirely to transport matters, this office merits detailed consideration.

The Office of the Undersecretary for Transportation was established in 1950.[36] The Office of the Undersecretary acts in several

---

[36] U. S. Code, Title V Sec. 1337-15, 1952 Ed.

capacities to administer transportation matters. The Department of Commerce has been responsible for promotion and development of foreign and domestic commerce, encouragement of shipping facilities, and of course, to serve business in general. In addition to these promotional matters, the various agencies within the Department concerned with transport matters report to the Secretary via the Undersecretary for Transportation.[37] These agencies are: The Bureau of Public Roads, Coast and Geodetic Survey, Defense Air Transportation Adminstration, Great Lakes Pilotage Administration, Maritime Administration, St. Lawrence Seaway Development Corporation, and the Weather Bureau. The Undersecretary is a member of the Board of Directors of the Panama Canal Company and serves as Chairman of the Advisory Board, Inland Waterways Corporation. The Undersecretary, thus, has both policy and operational responsibilities. Since the office was established, six men served in the decade ending in 1960, two under President Truman, and four under President Eisenhower.

It is problematical as to how valuable these appointees were as policy makers. Those who occupied the position for less than a year (half of them) could hardly have been in office long enough to become well oriented. During his years in office, Mr. Eisenhower had frequent recourse to the Secretary of Commerce (and presumably to the Office of the Undersecretary) for advice and special studies, as indicated above. Certainly, if the Undersecretary was so minded, he would be in an excellent position to influence the President on matters of transportation policy and should have much better access to the President than the members (or any one member) of the Interstate Commerce Commission.

The President also has substantial leverage in other areas of the executive branch. The State, Defense, Agriculture, and other Departments have significant policy functions which the President might influence, if he was so inclined. Thus, the President has a number of outlets for policy in the transportation field, of which the Office of the Undersecretary for Transportation is probably the most adequate.

There seems to be little doubt that the existence of these agencies somewhat undermines the prestige of the Interstate Commerce Commission as an authoritative body in the field and, to some extent, the Congress as well. The Commission is under a special handicap when the executive branch has so many other bodies to turn to for advice and counsel. Not the least serious result of this situation is that the President, assuming that the policy making role of the ICC is of

---

[37] *Ibid.*

minimal importance, is likely to give only passing attention to appointments to that body. Further, those agencies of the executive branch dealing with transportation matters, and not being judicial in nature, can take a much freer policy line.

ROLE OF THE INDUSTRY ASSOCIATIONS

An informal, but nonetheless important, role in the shaping of transportation policy is played by the various trade and industry organizations. These organizations are of various types: (1) essentially trade associations which take a very partisan view, e.g., the Association of American Railroads, American Trucking Associations, and the Air Transport Association of America; (2) the non-partisan groups such as the Transportation Association of America; and (3) the "professional" groups such as the American Society of Traffic and Transportation.

These groups pursue varied policies, highly partisan in the case of the AAR and ATA and more detached in the case of the professional associations.

The effectiveness of these bodies in the realm of policy is difficult to gauge. The trade associations spend considerable time and money in lobbying on both state and federal levels and on publicity of a favorable nature for the industry. Members of Congress are contacted by legislative representatives of these organizations, and those in the industry are encouraged to write and call their representatives.

A member of Congress may make decisions to support any given bill on many grounds. A very important function of the legistative representative is to "educate" the member. For example, the Reed-Bulwinkle Act of 1948 was vetoed by Mr. Truman and, at first glance, might appear to be a flagrant example of special interest legisation. However, a member of Congress, informed of the general rate making practices prevailing, would probably have supported it. Personal contact and friendship are important in this area. The volume of reading matter received by the average senator or representative is vast indeed. Certainly most legislators cannot be expected to be well informed on technical aspects of transportation policy, and information gleaned from opposing advocates may be useful. In the course of a congressional session, a large number of bills may come before the Congress, and a member cannot be expected to know about each. In one recent session, a total of sixty-one bills having to do with transportation were introduced into the Congress.

The effectiveness of these groups may be diminished by the fact that the official position of the group may reflect only imperfectly the views of the members. A highly diverse group, such as the American Trucking Associations, for example, has a serious problem in attempting to coordinate the views of all its segmented membership. The logical outcome of this situation is the proliferation of splinter groups (which has to some extent taken place), each promoting its own ideas and thus diminishing the overall impact. We find the following groups and sub-groups:

Rail:
>   Association of American Railroads
>   American Short Line Railroad Association

Motor:
>   American Trucking Associations, Inc. (various conferences, e.g., Regular Route Common Carriers)
>   National Highway Users Conference
>   National Association of Motor Bus Operators
>   National Agricultural Transportation League
>   Private Truck Council of America
>   Perishable Commodities Carriers Association

Air:
>   Air Transport Association of America
>   International Air Transport Association
>   Independent Air Lines Association
>   Association of Local and Territorial Airlines

Water:
>   American Waterways Operators Association
>   Inland Waterways Common Carrier Association

All of the above groups are directly concerned with policy as carriers; no mention is made of groups such as the U. S. Chamber of Commerce, National Coal Association or the National Grange which are not directly involved in the transportation industry but which do take a position on most every transport issue in their role as major shippers. It can be seen that in the motor and air fields especially, specialized groups have grown up to pursue particular legislative ends. Homogeneity is probably greatest in the rail industry, but, even here, a diversity of interests exists between the large and small organizations.

In the motor field, especially, the various groups may work in harmony on a particular matter, oppose each other on another, or may be indifferent on a third. One could predict, for example, that a bill to repeal the agricultural exemption would find favor in the AAR and be bitterly opposed by the NATL and the PCCA. The ATA would probably remain neutral, although some of its component groups, such as the common carriers, might favor it. The air and water groups would probably be unconcerned.

Each group would appear at hearings, write letters, contact members of Congress, and in other ways attempt to influence policy. The sheer volume of material tends to diminish the effectiveness of the advocates. In the hearings entitled *Problems of the Railroads*[38] and the Doyle Report,[39] for example, the various carrier representatives appeared armed with elaborate and extensive charts, tables, and statistical analyses in support of the official viewpoint of their organizations.[40] All these groups make frequent use of advertising in trade journals and other media and circularize college professors, legislators, and others with a flood of pamphlets, reprints, news releases, and like material. How much of this material is read and analyzed except by rival organizations (and textbook writers) is problematical.

This is not the place to comment on the tactics of lobbying as a profession, but one can note, in passing, that the carriers rank among the leaders in terms of manpower and funds employed in lobby activities.[41]

The bi-partisan (or non-partisan) groups, such as the Transportation Association of America, have the advantage of being independent of any given mode; but it cannot be said that these groups are (as yet) influential as policy makers, although they may become so in the future.

The question may well be asked, if the trade association groups are relatively ineffectual, what is the rationale of their continued support? It seems clear that no one group could eliminate its spokesmen so long as others remained. Dependent as they are on legislative favor, the carriers cannot relinquish any possible advantage and must match each other, dollar for dollar or man for man, in order to prevent undue advantage on the part of others. Thus, the absolute effectiveness of the lobby staff might be less important than the relative standing

---

[38] *Problems of the Railroads, op. cit.*

[39] National Transportation Policy, Report of the Committee on Commerce, U. S. Senate by its Special Study Group on the Transportation Policies of the United States (pursuant to S. Res. 29, 151 and 244 of the 86th Congress).

[40] In the railroad hearings, rail witnesses testified for five days, testimony and exhibits covered 743 pages, much of it largely repetitious in nature. Water carrier testimony covered 176 pages, with elaborate data on costs, maps, charts, and other visual material.

[41] Such activities must be reported annually to the clerk of the House of Representatives.

of the staff in the industry as a whole. From the standpoint of public welfare, it is no doubt fortunate that this "balance of power" exists.[42]

When transportation matters are being considered, representatives of the non-partisan and "professional" transportation groups are frequently asked to testify. Closely related to these associations is the testimony of academic economists, writers on the subject, and other presumably disinterested persons who appear either by invitation or at their own request. Since these persons do not represent a group but appear in their own behalf or as *amicus curiae,* they may command respect not accorded to the affiliated witnesses. To some degree, however, their weight may be somewhat diminished if they are regarded as too much 'ivory tower" or theoretical in their views, and if as is frequently the case, are paid witnesses.

Frequently, hearings which are well organized produce documents which themselves become influential in the field as a symposium of views. For example, in the field of monetary policy, the hearings held in 1952 on management of the public debt have become a useful document for students in the area.[43]

"PUBLIC OPINION"

Since "public opinion" is largely a meaningless term, little can be said regarding the role of public opinion in transportation policy.

To the extent that public opinion is distinct from the opinion of the industry, it seems likely that it is of no real significance. Outside the trade journals, the space allocated to such matters in the Press is very small indeed. The various modes may "plant" an article which presents a specific viewpoint, or a popular magazine may print both sides of a public debate such as the rail-truck dispute over highway user charges. Unfortunately, the factors involved are often so technical that the general public is unable to judge the case on its merits. For example, the controversies over the "grey area" and over interpretation of the Transportation Act of 1958 are complex enough even for students of transportation, to say nothing of members of the general public.

Complexity does not mean that the public will not have opinions nor that this opinion will not have some effect. Foreign policy and

---

[42] This suggests the possible relevance of J. K. Galbraith's theory of countervailing power as a form of control. See *American Capitalism* (Boston: Houghton Mifflin Co., 1952).

[43] *Monetary Policy and the Management of the Public Debt,* Doc. #123 (2 Vols.) 82d Congress, 2d session, 1952.

farm policy are both complex, but public opinion (often uninformed) is of importance as any member of Congress is well aware.

An emotional issue, such as highway use by trucks which affects the average citizen, will obviously be much more easily aroused than an issue between two modes.

Summary

The pristine prose of the national policy statement is a poor bulwark against the competitive forces prevailing in the industry. Clearly, also, the policy is never static or final, but rather dynamic. Policy must be such as to fit changing circumstances in economics and technology. We could no more have a rigid policy in the field of transportation than in the field of foreign affairs. The formal policy statement must be subject to interpretation by the men who are in policy making positions, guided by the circumstances of the time.

The various groups and agencies discussed here have had great or little roles to play in policy formulation, depending upon the historical and personal circumstances.

Clearly, the various groups engaged in policy formulation cannot be considered in isolation. The President, Congress, the courts, the various associations, segments of the industry, and "public opinion," as well as the regulatory agencies per se, all have a voice in policy; and none of these groups can be separated from the others in tracing the development of policy. Thus, transportation policy, like monetary policy or farm policy on the national level, is the result of many conflicting viewpoints; and it must be hammered out in the politico-economic framework of the time.

Selected References for Further Study

An outstanding and readable study of the workings of the Commission focused on an individual is found in Fuess, Clyde M., and *Eastman, Joseph B., Servant of the People*. New York: Columbia University Press, 1952.

The frustrations of applying principles of economics to public problems are well described by Nourse, Edwin G. *Economics in the Public Service*. New York: Harcourt, Brace and Co., 1953.

The most comprehensive treatment of the Commission and its development is found in Sharfman, I. L., *The Interstate Commerce Commission*. New York, The Commonwealth Fund, 1931, 1935, 1936, 1937. 4 Vols.

Eastman's "A Twelve Point Primer on the Subject of Administrative Tribunals," which appears in Fuess cited above, also appears in Wilson, G. Lloyd, (ed.), *Selected Papers and Addresses of Joseph B. Eastman*. New York: Simmons-Boardman, 1948, pp. 375-77.

For a detailed treatment of the role of the executive, see Norton, Hugh S., "The President and Transportation Policy, 1930-1960," *Journal of the Interstate Commerce Practitioners Association*, March 1962.

PART IV

Application of Public Controls

It is generally supposed that the increasing complexity of the social order requires an increasing direction from officials. My own view is, rather, that as affairs become more intricate, more extended in time and space, more involved and interrelated, overhead direction by the officials of the state has to become simpler, less intensive, less direct, more general.

WALTER LIPPMAN
The Good Society

CHAPTER XIII

Regulation of Railroads

Railroads were the first of the modes to bear regulation and are the most comprehensively regulated of all the modes. The regulatory structure, as it now exists, covers essentially ~~five~~ four areas, namely: (1) economic relationships between railroads and the public; (2) the competitive relationship between the railroads and other carriers, i.e., inter- and intramodal competition; (3) regulations concerning the financial affairs of railroads, issuance of securities, etc.; and (4) regulations concerning service and the technical aspects of equipment and plant, in order to assure public safety and standards of service.

To some extent, these areas overlap and duplicate each other, and it is widely held that the introduction of regulation in one area makes it necessary to extend regulation into other areas, in order to effectively implement the original regulation. To a degree then, regulation is subject to something which might be termed "Parkinson's Law of Regulation," in that one item of regulation makes other items necessary. For example, regulation over rates made it necessary to consider the impact upon the financial welfare of the carrier measurement which, in turn, made it necessary to specify accounting procedures and require uniform reports. Similar situations have occurred frequently in the history of business-government relations. All of the areas referred to above are the responsibility of the Interstate Commerce Commission on the federal level.

While the regulation applicable to railroads has been adopted in chronological fashion since 1887, as pointed out in Chapters X and XI, it may be more easily grasped if it is discussed at this point on a topical basis, using the areas noted above as an outline of the present regulatory structure. The body of material relative to railroad regulation represents more than seventy years of experimentation and legislative evolution. Further, the years from 1887 to 1920 were devoted almost entirely to the development of rail regulation per se. In considering the areas referred to above, Area 1, economic relationships between railroads and the public includes the following elements: control of entry into the field, control over rates charged, and control over discriminatory practices.

ENTRY CONTROL (I.C. Act, Sec. 1)

The matter of entry control is not nearly so significant for rail carriers as for other carriers, since, by its nature, entry into the rail field is financially difficult; and, secondly, by 1920, when the Commission was granted power to regulate construction of new rail lines, the railroad net was physically complete except for minor modifications. Railroads must secure specific permission from the Interstate Commerce Commission in order to extend, build or abandon lines. Since 1920, the mileage abandoned has been substantially greater than the mileage constructed.[1] It seems obvious that entry control has been a relatively unimportant factor in the railroad industry.

CONTROL OVER RATES (I.C. Act, Secs. 1, 15, 15a, 19a, 22)

Control over rates is, however, another matter. In this area, the body of regulation is very substantial indeed. It was pointed out in Chapter X that rate regulation occupied a very prominent niche in the history of regulatory development, "reasonable" rates having been required in the original act in 1887. It is likely that the Commission has, over the years, spent more time and effort in this area than on any other phase of regulation. Rate questions take two basic forms: those involving specific rates on specific movements of commodities

---

[1] Rail line mileage reached its apex in 1916, with 254,037 miles in operation; by 1960, the figure had declined to slightly over 200,000. As an example, in 1942, twenty-two miles were constructed and some 2,800 miles were abandoned. *Statistics of Railways of the United States* (Interstate Commerce Commission).

or rates in general. That is, a carrier may wish to increase or reduce a given rate; or, as is more likely in recent years, the carrier, or carriers, may wish to make a general rate increase covering all, or most all, commodities which it carries. At any given time, the Commission may have under consideration proposals to increase or reduce various rates and proposals to alter the general level of rates. It must also be kept in mind that, of the thousands of rates in effect at any given time, only a relative handful have been specifically considered by the Commission. Prior to 1920, rate regulation was fundamentally designed to prevent monopoly practices on the part of the railroads. After 1920, more emphasis was put upon the factor of overall carrier stability and upon sound economic relationships in the industry and the economy as a whole.[2]

In considering a rate, the Commission must take into account many factors. It was noted in Chapter VII on pricing carrier services that the rate will ultimately fall within the boundaries of cost of service and value of service. Thus, the Commission has considerable leeway within these boundaries. In practice, when a carrier makes a rate proposal, i.e., publishes a rate as prescribed by law, and the proposal in challenged, the Commission may suspend the rate in order to undertake an investigation to determine the reasonableness of the matter in question. Such an investigation may take a considerable time. Factors considered might include some or all of the following:

1. Economic condition of the carriers proposing the rate change.
2. Economic condition of the shippers concerned, or of the aggregate economy.
3. Conditions prevailing in the competing carriers.
4. Any unique effects which the rate change may have on any industry or geographic area.

In regard to the economic condition of the carriers proposing the change, it seems abundantly clear that the Commission's exercise of judgment in this area will supplement or supersede the judgment of management. For example, in the first *Fifteen Per Cent Case*, previously cited, the carriers requested an increase in rates of 15 per cent in 1931 as a means of combatting the depression. The request was denied, Commissioner Eastman saying in part,

> It is no part of our duty to interfere with management in the fixing of rates when the question is only one of what is wise or unwise in

---

[2] As some authorities point out, after 1920 and the economic downturn, it was necessary to either relax regulation or to modify the direction. See Dearing and Owen, *op. cit.*

the exercise of sound business judgment. The difficulty here is that I am left by the record in great doubt as to whether the proposal to increase all rates 15 per cent is an exercise of the sound business judgment of the managements.[3]

Thus, in this case as in others, the carriers were not denied an increase because they were making "excessive" profits, but because in the judgment of the Commission this proposal was unwise under the prevailing circumstances.

This is rate regulation in the broadest sense, in which the Commission is concerned not with a specific rate, but with the whole rate structure.

Although at the time of the *Fifteen Per Cent Case,* the railroads were anything but profitable and needed additional income, the Commission took the broader view of the influence which such an increase would have, even citing the fact that adverse public opinion might hinder helpful legislation then under consideration.[4] It cannot be denied that the Commission is acting more or less as a "super board of directors" for the industry in a case such as this, right though they may have been.

ROLE OF THE RATE OF RETURN IN THE REGULATORY PROCESS

It became obvious at an early date that some device must be adopted for the purpose of measuring the welfare of the rail carriers if regulation of rates (or the rate level) was to be carried out fairly and efficiently. In 1898, the United States Supreme Court made an effort to draw a line between confiscatory rates and those which avoided confiscation. In the landmark case of *Smyth v. Ames,* the rule of "fair return on value" was established.[5] The burden of this concept was that property held out for public use, and thus subject to public regulation, was entitled to a fair return relative to its worth. Although it seems that the *Smyth v. Ames* rule was intended to be a protection against unduly low rates imposed by legislative or administrative action, it actually developed into a genuine standard for rates. Certainly, much depends upon the breadth of interpretation which is given to the word "fair." If fair is equated to reasonable, then the Smyth-Ames rule would be an adequate rule of rate making and not

---

[3] Concurring opinion of Commissioner Eastman in Fifteen Per Cent Case, 1937-38, 261, ICC 41, 152.

[4] Fifteen Per Cent Case, 1931, 178 ICC, 539, 575.

[5] Smyth v. Ames, 169 U. S., 966, 1898.

merely a minimum standard. As many writers on the subject point out, there is an element of danger in this procedure, since a commission may fix rates which avoid confiscation but which are hardly "fair" or "reasonable" when compared with earnings in other industries, and which will not provide leeway for capital accumulation.[6]

However, it cannot be said that such a problem has existed in practice. Without question, the most significant problem was that of implementation. In 1913, Congress, after much prodding from the Commission, passed the Valuation Act, directing the Commission to prepare a plan to evaluate railroad property. No specific direction was given the Commission, and, in fact, the specific authorization to use the valuation data in rate making was not to make its appearance until the Act of 1920, in the famous "rule of rate making" embodied in Section 15a.

Although, in theory, the principal of valuation seemed to be a path leading straight to "fair value," in practice, it proved to be a boulder strewn and hazardous route.

Two conflicting methods of procedure sprang up: (1) the theory of reproduction value and (2) the theory of original cost, less depreciation, plus any additions or betterments which had been made. The first procedure, reproduction value, would be implemented as follows: A physical inventory of property would be made. The property would then be evaluated by imposing a scale of prices (as of some given date). It can be appreciated that this procedure is extremely cumbersome and time consuming in administration. More serious, however, was the objection that the valuation might not reflect the true value of property, depending on the relative level of prices. Much railroad property was, even at that time, more than a half century old, and the cost of reproduction in most cases would be many times the original dollar cost. On the other hand, this property was often in daily use and, thus, represented great value to the carrier.[7]

The alternative proposal, original cost, presented equally serious pitfalls. The procedure here was to determine the original cost, add the cost of additions and subtract reasonable depreciation and costs of property eliminated from the rolls. While this procedure did not involve the complex physical valuation, it had the equally serious problem of depending upon records which were often inaccurate or sometimes missing entirely. Also, there was no assurance that com-

---

[6] E.g., Locklin, *op. cit.*, pp. 344 ff.

[7] For example, the Baltimore and Ohio Railroad bridge at Point of Rocks, Maryland, was built more than a century ago and is in current use. The cost of building such a bridge now would be many times the original cost.

peting carriers had purchased property under similar conditions. There were advocates for each procedure among lawyers and economists who were concerned with the situation.

Clearly, no clear cut preference for either procedure was acceptable to all parties. Although many economists favored the investment cost basis, no one was able to determine what was or was not prudent investment or expenditure made in good faith.

The Commission continued to wrestle with this problem until 1929, when the O'Fallon decision followed closely by the depression made further valuation work impracticable.[8] Up to this time, the Commission had been using a formula of its own devising, since no guidance had come either from the courts or the Congress as to what procedure to follow. This problem will be examined more thoroughly in a later chapter.

VALUATION AND THE RECAPTURE CLAUSE

The recapture clause indicated in Chapter XI had been directed toward recovering "excess" earnings. The Commission had pursued its policy of valuation as a means of implementing the recapture of earnings. The so-called formula, perhaps more aptly characterized as an outline, considered the following factors:

1. Cost of reproduction as of 1914.
2. Added investment since that date, less depreciation of 18 per cent.
3. Appreciated right of way based on value of adjacent land.
4. A stated amount of working capital.

As an example of the complexity of this task, the final report for valuation purposes of the Texas and New Orleans Railroad System[9] covers 229 pages, and the value was found to be $251,078,868.[10]

The O'Fallon decision was critical of the Commission procedure, in that it failed to give sufficient weight to present reproduction cost. This decision, along with the repeal of the recapture clause in the Emergency Transportation Act of 1933, made the whole valuation

---

[8] 279 U. S. 461 (1929). This case involving a nine mile railroad constituted a test of the ICC formula for valuation.

[9] The T.&N.O. System embraced fourteen railroad corporations, and the T.&N.O. was itself operated as an integral part of the Southern Pacific System, a major stockholder in T.&N.O.

[10] *Interstate Commission Reports,* Valuation Reports Vol. 47, August 1933-April 1938. Valuation docket #1196.

procedure highly questionable and clearly impracticable. The work of valuation continued until 1938, costing the government an estimated $50 million and the carriers more than $150 million.[11] Although the valuation procedure was not satisfactory as a guide for rate making, it did apparently settle one long standing argument. Many of the advocates of valuation had been anxious to determine the amount of over-capitalization which existed in the industry, since this question had been a bone of contention for many years. Senator LaFollette and other liberals of the period had long been of the opinion that a valuation program would show gross over-capitalization. Actually, in terms of 1914 prices, the Commission, in 1938, fixed the value of the railroads for rate making purposes at approximately $21 billion, or some $2 billion more than the value of outstanding securities at that time.

In any event, the usefulness of the valuation procedure would have been doubtful when the monopoly status of the railroads ceased to exist after 1930.

As noted earlier, the rise of other forms of transportation forced the Commission to give more consideration to the relationship between rail rates and rates of the other carriers. After 1935, when the Commission was given formal authority over motor carrier rates, this trend was especially noticeable. Of course, after the passage of the Transportation Act of 1940, the national transportation policy embodied in this act formally required the Commission to consider the entire transportation system and the effects of intermodal competition, as well as the effects or rates on the economy as a whole.

From 1930 until World War II, the Commission was much concerned with the economic welfare of all carriers, and the railroads presented a particular problem, in that they were suffering from structural changes as well as economic dislocation due to the depression. Working under the rate making rule embodied in the Act of 1920, viz., the right of the railroads to earn a fair return on fair value, the Commission found that the industry was, as a whole, unable to earn anything approaching a fair return as conceived in the law, since rates were forced down by competition. There were seven rate cases in the period between the two world wars.[12]

Of these cases, the most important were probably the *Fifteen Per Cent Cases* discussed above. Rates increased in the immediate

---

[11] Henry, *op. cit.*, p. 386.
[12] 58, ICC 220, 302 and 58, ICC 320, 489 (1920); 68, ICC 676; (1922); 113, ICC 3 (1926); 178, ICC 539 (1931); 195, ICC 5 (1933); 208, ICC 4 1935); 226, ICC 41 (1938).

aftermath of World War I in face of increasing costs, then fell sharply as the depression progressed.

In the second *Fifteen Per Cent Case*,[13] the railroads tried to gain revenue to compensate for the period of deferred maintenance of the early 1930's, by taking advantage of the generally improving business scene.

After World War II ended, the railroads, facing high traffic levels combined with rising prices, asked for and were granted a series of increases netting a cumulative increase of 107.7 per cent for the nation as a whole.

Ex parte 175, 166, and 206 combined resulted in increases in freight revenue of almost $400 million, 1957 over 1955, although less tonnage was originated.[14] From 1955 through 1960, railway net operating income declined from $1,128,000,000 to $583 million, and the rate of return fell from 4.22 per cent to 2.13 per cent.[15] As Table

TABLE 13-1

RATE OF RETURN, CLASS I RAILROADS, 1930-1960

Year	Per Cent	Year	Per Cent
1930	3.59	1947	3.44
1931	2.20	1948	4.31
1932	1.38	1949	2.88
1933	2.03	1950	4.28
1934	1.98	1951	3.76
1935	2.15	1952	4.16
1936	2.87	1953	4.19
1937	2.54	1954	3.28
1938	1.61	1955	4.22
1939	2.55	1956	3.95
1940	2.93	1957	3.36
1941	4.28	1958	2.76
1942	6.30	1959	2.72
1943	5.71	1960	2.13
1944	4.71		
1945	3.77		
1946	2.75		

Source: *Railroad Transportation: A Statistical Record, 1921-1959* (Washington: Association of American Railroads) and *A Review of Railroad Operations in 1960, op. cit.*

[13] 226, ICC 41 (1938.)
[14] ICC, *Statistics of Class I Railways*, for the years indicated.
[15] Association of American Railroads, *A Review of Railroad Operations in 1960* (Washington: 1961), p. 26.

13-1 indicates, the rate of return rose above 5.75 per cent only since the entire thirty-year span 1930-1960.

By the late 1950's, competition had again begun to influence rates, and railroads began to seek more freedom to reduce rates on a selective basis. Senate hearings were held, as recounted elsewhere, and resulted in the Transportation Act of 1958. The results of this act have not yet had full opportunity to work out, but railroad rate reductions in several areas have restored a substantial amount of traffic.[16] In essence, the Act of 1958 directs the Commission to permit rate changes without as much consideration as previously given to the effects of such changes on other modes. Other carriers claim that such a procedure is contrary to the national transportation policy in the Transportation Act of 1940. The net outcome of this conflict remains to be seen.

CONTROL OF REBATES AND DISCRIMINATION
(I.C. Act, Secs. 2, 3, 4, 10)

One of the earliest and most troublesome areas attacked by regulation was the widespread practice of favored treatment given to particular shippers. Many of these practices pointed out in Chapter X were difficult to eradicate. Rates must be on file and available to the public; those in force cannot be changed without due notice. The Commission may at any time inspect books and records of the carrier to see that the legal rates have been charged and that every reasonable effort has been made to collect the amount due.

Claims must be investigated to see that they are not being used as a subterfuge for secret rebates. In short, a shipper cannot be given any preferential treatment which is not given to all shippers who are in similar circumstances. Naturally, differences in treatment which can be justified are permissible. For example, car-load rates lower than less-than-car-load rates can be justified by cost figures and are permissible, although the small shipper may be held to be, in a sense, at a disadvantage. Neither is it possible to discriminate against a particular place. Under the famous "short haul clause" (Section 4), the carriers are prevented from charging more for a short haul than for a long haul which is performed under substantially similar circumstances. Section 4 has been amended various times and court interpretations have influenced it, but the intent was clearly to prevent

---

[16] Rate reductions, coupled with innovations in freight car design, restored to the rails much traffic, e.g., new automobiles formerly moved by truck.

a monopolistic railroad from taking undue advantage of some point which is adversely located unless other factors justify it. After a history of varied fortunes, the fourth section was amended by the Act of 1920.[17] Under these provisions a rail carrier may petition for Section 4 relief which will be granted providing certain conditions are met, viz:

1. It must be shown that the reduced rates are compelled rates, lower than reasonable rates for application via the petitioning line or route, and not within its control.

2. It must also be shown that the lower rates for the longer hauls are "reasonably compensatory."

3. The third point that must be established in order to obtain Section 4 relief is that the rates at the intermediate points are reasonable in themselves.

In general, these conditions have been adhered to in granting Section 4 relief. For the most part, relief has been granted to enable rail carriers to deal with water competition.

As in the case with various other items in the original act, the long and short haul clause has taken on a somewhat different cast with the rise of motor carrier competition on a large scale. Two unsuccessful attempts have been made to repeal the clause, and it may be that serious consideration should be given to such a move. Producers of transportation service cannot overcome disadvantages of geographic location, and they must be granted a degree of freedom in defending themselves against competition.[18]

FINANCIAL OPERATIONS OF RAILROADS (I.C. Act, Sec. 20a)

Unlike the rate regulations discussed above, the Commission's control over railroad financial affairs in a formal sense is relatively simple. It was found necessary at an early date to prescribe a system

---

[17] In 1897, the decision in the Alabama Midland case, 168 U. S. 144 (1897) nullified the 4th section for all practical purposes by holding that any form of competition made for dissimilar circumstances. From this time until 1910, when it was amended, the section was inoperative. The Mann-Elkins Act of 1910 and the Transportation Act of 1920 amended and strengthened the short haul clause and provided a degree of administrative flexibility.

[18] A reasonably compensatory rate in this instance is defined as one which will (1) cover and more than cover the extra or additional expenses incurred in handling the traffic to which it applies; (2) be no lower than necessary to meet existing competition; (3) not be so low as to threaten the extinction of legitimate competition by water carriers; and (4) not impose undue burden on other traffic or jeopardize the appropriate return on the value of carrier property generally, as contemplated in section 15a of the act.

of uniform accounts for railroads in order to facilitate regulation of rates and earnings.

The Hepburn Act of 1906 empowered the Commission to require certain periodic reports from carriers; and, in 1907, a system of uniform accounts was established and has been revised and modified from time to time.

Without going into the highly specialized accounting system in detail, it can be seen that a high degree of control is necessary in order to separate, on a uniform basis, expenditures for capital improvements and those for operating expenses and to prescribe a uniform system for depreciation accounting and related matters.[19] A valuable by-product of the uniform accounts and reports is the data which exists in the industry and can be used as a management and research tool.

It will be remembered that one of the early causes of disenchantment with railroads was the fact that many sharp practices had developed in the area of finance. Complaints were heard of "watered stock," excessive payment of dividends, inflated costs of construction, and other activities, although it does not appear that railroads were any more inclined toward these practices than was true of other businesses of the era.[20] The Collum Committee had mentioned this factor in its report in 1886; little real sentiment for federal regulation took hold until 1907, at which time the Commission recommended federal control.[21] Perhaps the activities of Messrs. Hill, Morgan, and Harriman had some effect, although there seems to have been little public clamor as a result of the famous Northern Pacific battle of that year.

In 1911, a report was made by the Hadley Committee which had investigated the problem. The Committee did not favor federal regulation, but it was critical of various practices and recommended further state action. Interestingly enough, the years from 1900 to 1914 probably represented the peak years of financial manipulation, as apart from the era of actual building and promotion. Not until 1920, however, was control granted to the Commission. Under Section 20a and its various amendments, the Commission was given broad powers of control.

Railroads must obtain Commission approval in order to issue securities, except for certain short term issues. These regulations were further revised in 1948 by the passage of Section 20b.

---

[19] A comprehensive analysis of the prescribed system can be found in Locklin, *op. cit.*, chap. XXIV.

[20] See, for example, Harlow, *op. cit.*, and Josephson, *op. cit.*

[21] 12, ICC 277, 305-6 (1907).

Since 1920, issuance of securities, other than equipment trust certificates, has been much less important than it was prior to 1920.[22] During the years since 1920, indebtedness, other than equipment certificates, has, in fact, been reduced through reorganization and retirement of debt from earnings, despite large capital expenditures.[23]

Although stock and bond issues were of little importance in the years 1930-1960, one financial matter of great importance was the factor of bankruptcy and reorganization of carriers.

For some years, the procedures in this field had been somewhat neglected by the courts, and it had become extremely cumbersome and time consuming to carry out reorganizations of large enterprises.[24] Under the equity proceedings then in use, the Commission had no real part in reorganization plans. When Section 77 of the Bankruptcy Act was passed in 1933, these procedures became much more realistic and simplified, although still highly complex. Under Section 77, a carrier could proceed voluntarily, or other interested groups could proceed to file a plan for reorganization. If this plan was acceptable, the court could appoint one or more trustees to take charge of the property until such time as the reorganization was complete.[25]

In order to be acceptable to the Commission, the plan must have several attributes: (1) the plan must be "compatible with the public interest," (2) the fixed charges must be within the earning capacity of the carrier, and (3) the plan must be fair and equitable.

Although the procedures under Section 77 have greatly expedited the bankruptcy procedures, the Commission has been subject to some degree of criticism in their interpretation of certain phrases of the plan. Especially as regards the provision relative to earnings, the Commission has followed a very conservative policy requiring carriers to scale charges down to the earnings level likely to be attained. In those reorganizations which took place in the late 1930's, the Commission was, as later events were to prove, unduly conservative. Under such a policy, the equity of some junior security holders is likely to be eliminated, since dividends on the stock which they hold were apt to be considered to be beyond the earning power to the reorganized company. The problem is further complicated by the so-called "Boyd rule."[26] Under the Boyd rule, creditors of a bankrupt corporation are

---

[22] Dewing, *op. cit.*, p. 201, states that by 1949 more than $1.5 billion was outstanding in equipment obligations.

[23] Yearbook of Railroad Information, *op. cit.*

[24] See Norman S. Buchanan, *The Economics of Corporate Enterprise* (New York: Henry Holt & Co., 1940), pp. 416 ff.

[25] In most cases the time required was often several years.

[26] Northern Pacific Railway v. Boyd, 228 U. S., 482.

taken in the order of seniority of holdings. Thus, the equity of stock-holders may be wiped out although later events prove that earnings were sufficient to have provided for them. No one can read the future, and, clearly, the Commission did not foresee the long period of high earnings which followed World War II. An amendment to the Bankruptcy Act was passed in 1948, which allows the Commission to reconsider the provisions of a plan which has been influenced by changes of an unforeseen nature.[27]

It can be seen from the above discussion that the Commission has a very comprehensive control over the financial activities of rail carriers. The Commission can regulate rates of individual commodities; it can control the rate level and, thus, the earnings of the carriers. Carriers must file uniform reports and maintain uniform accounting records under the supervision of the Commission. Mergers and consolidations, issuance of securities, and reorganization of the corporation all come under the purview of the Commission.

SERVICE AND SAFETY (I.C. Act, Secs. 1, 3, 25)

Railroads as common carriers have an obligation under common and statutory law to perform certain services. With some clear-cut exceptions such as illegal, highly valuable or dangerous articles, rail carriers must transport goods which are offered and for which they hold themselves out as carriers. Railroads, as indicated earlier, are technically capable of performing a wide range of services, although a given carrier may limit the services available. For example, since 1930, many carriers have ceased to offer passenger service. As a rule of thumb, railroads must offer "reasonable" service. Thus, a given railroad may offer service on a highly restricted basis depending upon prevailing conditions. On a branch line, service twice weekly might be entirely reasonable, although such a standard would be completely unsatisfactory on the main line of the carrier. In the final analysis, service is a function of demand, and no intelligent management will ignore demand for a profitable service.

Service includes various related matters such as car supply, terminal services, joint facilities, and other items, as well as the basic provision of transportation service per se.

Within the bounds of "reasonableness," the rail carriers have a fairly high degree of discretion as to service, schedules and equipment. In the years before 1920 when fewer alternatives were available,

---

[27] 62 Stat. 167.

travelers and shippers were much more concerned with service standards than is the case at present. Carriers can make changes in schedules, alter equipment, modify train service or reduce the scope of
service within reason. In order to eliminate service entirely, the carrier
must obtain permission from the Commission, as well as the state commission or commissions involved, a matter which may prove to be
somewhat more difficult to do. In the absence of shipper complaint,
the carrier is not likely to be restrained. In recent years especially, the
Interstate Commerce Commission has been generous in allowing reductions in service when evidence indicates that it is not remunerative
and little hope exists that it would become so.

CAR SERVICE AND SUPPLY (I.C. Act, Secs. 1, 3)

Except for periods of emergency, shippers encounter little difficulty in obtaining a sufficient number of cars to meet their needs.
Following World War I and the serious car shortage which developed
at that time, the Act of 1920 granted the Commission power to control
rail car supply. As a practical matter, the Commission has not seen
fit to exercise these powers directly but has delegated the function of
car supply to the car service division of the Association of American
Railroads. The car service division, through its headquarters and
thirteen district offices, keeps abreast of car supply and demand and
issues directives to carriers regarding supply of various types of cars.[28]

Although periodic shortages may develop, especially for certain
special types of cars, the situation which prevailed during World War
I has not been repeated. Carriers are not obligated to supply cars of
an unusual nature unless there is a reasonable demand for such cars.
Consequently, many shippers operate private cars to assure that their
needs will be satisfied. Cars must be furnished in usable condition, and
ice, heat or other necessary services must also be made available. As
has been noted earlier, cars circulate freely on the rail system, and
the shipper is assured of interchange service.

JOINT RATES AND ROUTING (I.C. Act, Sec. 3)

The carriers are required to provide facilities for interchange and
to provide reasonable routings and joint rates. Rail carriers are further

---

[28] *Association of American Railroads, Its Organization and Activities* (Washington: A.R.R., May 1959), p. 10. This organization operated successfully, even
during World War II when demand for cars reached a high point.

required to provide reasonable facilities for interchange with water carriers and also to establish joint rates with such carriers.

A shipper is assured the right to use the routing of his choice, and the carrier is obligated to inform the shipper as to the reasonable routes available.[29]

TERMINAL FACILITIES (I.C. Act, Secs. 1, 3)

Rail carriers generally provide extensive terminals and related facilities such as warehouses, elevators, lighterage (transfer of cars by barge) service, cranes, bulk loading equipment, and other facilities. No specific obligation exists to provide such elaborate equipment. However, where these facilities exist, they must be available without discriminatory treatment.

Carriers are required to provide connections and construct sidings for delivery of carload shipments to private sidings and to provide "team" (public access) tracks for loading and unloading. Switching service for these tracks must be provided on a reasonable basis. As a matter of practice, railroads often organize subsidiary switching and terminal companies, often on a joint basis, to perform these services.[30]

Since many terminal areas are served by two or more railroads, either joint ownership and operation is necessary or some reciprocal arrangement must be made. In past years, railroads frequently refused to cooperate with each other in joint use of terminals, since an exclusive terminal might be a very important competitive advantage. However, the Commission has, in various cases, established its authority in such matters, and a carrier is required to allow joint use unless such use would impede the functions of the owning carrier.[31] Throughout the nation, countless examples exist of joint use of terminals, trackage rights and many other examples of cooperation.[32] In cities where

---

[29] For many shippers the right to route is of little importance, but for others, routing is of serious concern. Railroads naturally take great pains to assure the maximum amount of traffic over their lines.

[30] For example, the Washington Terminal Co. owns and operates the Washington Union Station and terminal facilities in the Washington, D. C. area. The Washington Terminal Co. is jointly owned by the Baltimore & Ohio Railroad; The Chesapeake & Ohio Railway; Pennsylvania Railroad; Richmond, Fredericksburg & Potomac Railroad Co.; and Southern Railway.

[31] A number of cases have been decided which involve this issue, e.g., use of Northern Pacific tracks at Seattle by Great Northern, 161, I.C.C. 699 (1930).

[32] Cooperation often extends to line facilities. In one well-known case, the Southern Pacific and Western Pacific tracks run parallel to each other for some hundred miles in Nevada. The two railroads operate this segment as a double track railroad.

two or more railroads have facilities, the degree of duplication of various segments of the plant has made joint use highly desirable in order to prevent unnecessary costs.

After 1920, intramodal competition was largely replaced by cooperation as railroads faced competition from other carriers and little was to be gained by a policy of restriction in such areas where savings and convenience to shippers would result.

ABANDONMENTS AND CONSTRUCTION OF NEW LINES
(I.C. Act, Sec. 1)

As was pointed out above, little new construction was undertaken after 1920, while substantial mileage was abandoned. The great bulk of abandoned mileage since 1920 had clearly outlived its usefulness, and little question arose as to the economic effects.

After 1930, relatively few communities were dependent entirely upon rail transportation and passenger traffic, in particular, fell to very low levels.

In general, the Commission has been generous in granting permission to abandon, having approved about 94 per cent of the applications since 1920.[33] Although the Commission has been criticized in the past on this issue, it has largely lost its significance at the present time.

More question arises as to the enforced construction of lines. While abandonment of an existing line may bring some hardship to those who have become dependent upon it, the construction of new facilities raises many different issues.

Much depends upon what "facilities" are to be constructed. The construction of sidings and interchange facilities, both of which are within the power of the Commission, are in a sense extensions of facilities and involve construction. On the one occasion in which the Commission attempted to enforce a major line extension (187 miles), it was not upheld by the courts.[34] It seems clear that the decision as to whether or not to invest funds and embark upon a new venture is a far different issue from the question relating to continuance of service once it has begun or the construction of minor items of plant in order to avoid discrimination.

---

[33] Locklin, *op. cit.*, p. 612. See also Charles E. Cherrington, *The Regulation of Railroad Abandonment* (Cambridge: Harvard University Press, 1948).

[34] 288 U. S. 14, 40 (1933).

POOLING AND COMBINATIONS (I.C. Act, Secs. 1, 6, 7)

Pooling of traffic, mergers, and combinations had, of course, been the natural outcome of destructive competition. Along with discriminatory practices, pooling had been one of the principal targets of early regulation.

The Act of 1887 prohibited pooling of equipment or of potential traffic. In 1912, the Panama Canal Act demonstrated that fear of monopoly had not faded, by providing that railroads could not operate or have an interest in water carriers using the canal without Commission approval.

By 1920, the advantages of pooling and combination as means of eliminating wasteful duplication had become obvious. Much discussion relating to combinations followed the period of federal operating during World War I. The Act of 1920 allowed pooling with Commission approval, as well as lease or stock control. Further, the Commission was directed to draw up a master plan for consolidation.

RELATED SERVICES (I.C. Act, Secs. 1, 3)

As recounted in Chapter II, railroads offer many supplementary services such as the transit privilege, reconsignment and diversion, and other supplements to transportation per se. The general view of the Commission has been that these services are provided by the carriers as a shipper convenience and that they are not legally required as part of "reasonable" service. However, if such services are made available, it seems likely that they would have to be available on a non-discriminatory basis. Certainly, carriers should be free to offer various competitive inducements and innovations without the fear of regulatory interference.

SAFETY (I.C. Act. Sec. 25)

Railroads are subject to highly detailed regulations regarding safe operating practices and equipment. Equipment such as cars and especially locomotives are subject to federal inspection; and signal systems, along with operating plant items, must meet certain requirements. Hours of service for employees operating trains are strictly regulated. The Commission has encountered no policy problems in this activity, and the technical problems are beyond the scope of this book.

MISCELLANEOUS PROVISIONS

Reed-Bulwinkle Act of 1948:

In 1948, Congress passed the Reed-Bulwinkle Act, which gave formal legal sanction to railroad rate bureaus. Rate bureaus had been operated by rail and other carriers for many years, although their status, in view of the anti-trust laws, was somewhat doubtful. The Reed-Bulwinkle Act disposed of this question.

Denison Act of 1928:

This act provided for the establishment of minimum differentials between competitive all-rail and rail-water rates. Further, the Commission was empowered to compel through routes using rail-water on the inland waterways and set rate divisions.

Transportation Act of 1958:

Amended the rule of rate making as regards minimum rates, giving the Commission more freedom to de-emphasize consideration given to the effect of rate changes on the protesting carrier, as discussed above. The effects of this provision remain to be seen. The Act of 1958 also authorized the federal government to guarantee loans up to fifteen years for capital investment up to $500,000, total loans not to exceed $500 million. No loans had been made several years later, since several restrictive provisions were included. The Act of 1958 strengthened the hand of the Commission in abandonment proceedings, giving them more power over state commissions to expedite abandonments.

Section 22, Rates:

Section 22 of the Interstate Commerce Act provides for the transportation of federal government property at rates set by negotiation. In view of the volume of such traffic, these rates are very important to certain carriers, including railroads.

GENERAL EVALUATION OF RAILROAD REGULATION

It is evident from the preceding pages that railroad regulation is very comprehensive. The body of law and administrative regulation has been compiled over a period of years since 1887 and represents possibly the most comprehensive attempts to regulate an industry ever undertaken. Almost every phase of railroad operations is covered in some form. Because of the time it has been in force and the extent of this body of regulation, the railroad industry has long been well acclimated to it and operates accordingly, so much so that much of this regulation has become institutionalized. While railroad management sometimes makes substantial complaints about regulatory matters, especially in the rate area, given the extent of regulation, these complaints are relatively few. This may be due to the fact that the present generation of railroad executives came into the industry long after the pattern of regulation had been established.

Summary

As this chapter has brought out, the railroad industry is subject to a comprehensive program of federal regulation involving both economic and technical aspects of the industry. The body of regulation now in force has been accumulated, revised, and modified since 1887, when the original Part I of the present Interstate Commerce Act was passed.

Many of the aspects of regulation are now routine and raise no policy problems. Uniform accounting and reports are examples of this situation. In other cases, much regulation exists in an area which was once a lively theatre of conflict but which has since become static due to economic and social change. Control over provision of new lines and terminal facilities are examples of this type. Control over rates, and especially rates which relate to intermodal competition, however, remains a very live issue. While no clear line exists between regulatory necessity and infringement on managerial policy, there are some areas which it seems logical to leave to managerial decision. For example, the provision of facilities and continuation or discontinuance of service might be more clearly in the realm of management; and, indeed, the Commission seems to have (often under judicial directive) been moving away from a strong line in such areas.

For many years the Commission pressed for more control, and, from 1887 until 1920, its jurisdiction became sufficient for its purpose. Since World War II, the tide may be running in the opposite direction, or at least the body of regulation has become somewhat less extensive, and perhaps the complexities of implementation have become more clear.

CHAPTER XIV

Regulation of Motor Carriers

Federal regulation of motor carriers has, of necessity, taken a different form from that applying to railroads. Several obvious factors account for these differences; namely, the physical character of the motor carrier industry, the large number of firms and the small size of the typical firm, the heterogeneity of the industry, and the relatively recent date of regulation in the industry.

While there was, as one might expect, a significant element within the railroad industry favoring regulation, there were also many in the motor carrier field who actively promoted regulatory efforts. One must recall that entry into the motor carrier field was not financially burdensome. The technology of the industry made it possible for an entrepreneur of limited means to enter the industry and to build up his physical plant on a unit basis. Those who had gained a foothold were anxious to establish some claim and to prevent encroachment upon their business. Likewise, others in the transportation industry, especially those in railroad management, were anxious to prevent or at least reduce the scope of truck competition. After several attempts, the federal regulation of motor carriers began with the passage of the Motor Carrier Act of 1935, now Part II of the Interstate Commerce Act.[1]

---

[1] The Commission is vested with great and very comprehensive authority in the regulation of motor carriers (see Eastern Motor Express, Inc., v. United States, 103 F. Supp. 644, 700), except in those matters relating to intrastate use of the state highways in each state (Eicholz v. Hargus, 23 F. Supp. 587, 590).

ENTRY CONTROL (I.C. Act, Secs. 202-6)

As we have seen, physical entry into the field was simple. The foundation of any regulatory system is the means of controlling the right to do business. The Motor Carrier Act attacked this formidable problem on several fronts.

A motor carrier operating for hire in interstate commerce must (with certain exceptions) obtain a certificate for common carrier operation or a permit to engage in contract carriage.

To protect the many carriers who were in operation at the time the legislation was passed, a "grandfather clause" was included, which granted certificates to carriers in bona fide operation as of June 1, 1935. The Commission was occupied for several years in processing the claims under the grandfather clause. As one might surmise, many inflated claims were filed, since carriers were anxious to obtain the most generous operating authority allowable. It was especially important to obtain the right to serve as many geographic points as possible. In general, the Commission adopted a rather stringent policy in regard to "grandfather" claims. The key was "bona fide operation." The Commission accepted various types of evidence as indication of bona fide operations, including such items as bills of lading, statements by shippers, advertising media and other data.[2] For several years, the Commission was occupied with the task of examining "grandfather" claims and granting certificates to those whose claims proved to be valid.[3]

It was common for the Commission to reduce the claim of a carrier and to issue a certificate which was more restrictive in scope than the carrier had hoped to receive.

CONTRACT CARRIERS

Contract carriers were required to obtain a permit in order to engage in interstate transportation. Contract carriers who were in bona fide operation as of June 1, 1935, were granted permits under the "grandfather" clause. Contract carriers, as pointed out in Chapter II, are carriers who perform transportation service only for those with

---

[2] Mitchell & Robertson Common Carrier Application, 24 M.C.C., 737, 738; see also Loving v. U. S., 32 F. Supp. 464.

[3] There were more than eighty-nine thousand such claims submitted, a staggering total in view of the Commission's resources.

whom they have contracts. For some years, confusion existed as to the difference between common and contract carriers, since a contract carrier often had a large number of contracts. In 1958, the legal definition of contract carriers was amended so as to clarify the situation. The definition now reads:

> One who conducts its business other than as a common carrier under continuing contracts with one person or a limited number of persons for the furnishing of transportation services through the assignment of motor vehicles for a continuing period for the exclusive use of each person served, or for the furnishing of transportation services designed to meet the distinct need of each individual customer.[4]

CARRIERS EXEMPT FROM REGULATION (I.C. Act, Sec. 203)

The Motor Carrier Act of 1935 recognized that there were unique elements in motor transportation, viz., that there were many vehicles engaged in interstate service which were not used in for-hire carriage and, secondly, that several thousand for-hire truckers operated on such an informal basis that regulation in an economic sense would be largely meaningless and administratively almost impossible. Much discussion had centered around these problems during legislative debate on the act, and they have continued to be matters of serious controversy.[5]

In the first case, i.e., private vehicles, no serious question arose. Those vehicles operating on a not-for-hire basis were exempted from economic regulation, along with vehicles operated by governmental units, vehicles operating in cities only, school buses and various others, including those vehicles solely engaged in transporting newspapers and U. S. mail. Unfortunately, however, another group was more controversial. Many trucks were engaged in the interstate transportation of agricultural products. Most often, these firms were owner-operators, frequently itinerant in nature. Imposing economic regulation on these carriers would have been both burdensome to the Commission and of doubtful benefit to the public interest, as well as politically unpopular. Section 203 (B) 6 of the act exempted from regulation those carriers engaged in the transportation of "unprocessed agricultural products." This provision has presented a serious policy issue, as will be discussed later.

---

[4] Public Law 163, 85th Congress.
[5] *The Agricultural Exemption in Interstate Trucking: A Legislative and Judicial History,* op. cit.

Thus, entry control was effected by requiring certificates or permits for common and contract carriers and allowing the various groups of exempt carriers to operate without economic regulation. This arrangement gives a basis of regulation while acknowledging the unique nature of motor transportation as compared to railroad service.

In addition to the "grandfather" certificates, the Commission has, of course, issued many certificates over the years to carriers offering service. Various factors must be taken into account in the Commission's decision to issue or deny a certificate. The ultimate question is, of course, one of the *public interest*." Clearly, the term *"public convenience and necessity"* must be interpreted in a workable fashion.

PUBLIC CONVENIENCE AND NECESSITY

Few things are necessities in life, and motor transportation service is not one of them. The Commission must decide to what degree the public will find the service offered to be of use, whether it duplicates existing service, and will merely draw off customers from firms already in operation. The Commission must inquire as to the quantity and quality of existing service.[6] The would-be carrier must prove this willingness and fitness to serve.

APPLICANT FITNESS TO SERVE

The applicant's fitness is a matter of great importance. Although, at first glance, the fact that the carrier is applying for a certificate might indicate a willingness to serve, the Commission must assure itself that the applicant is not merely attempting to forestall potential competition and has serious intentions of rendering service.

Fitness involves the carrier's equipment, facilities, business record, general reputation, and other matters which would reflect upon his ability to serve the public in a satisfactory manner.

PROTECTION OF EXISTING CARRIERS

An important element in Commission consideration is the factor of protecting the rights of existing carriers. Assuming that the extant carriers have conducted their affairs properly, they deserve and receive consideration from the Commission in considering new requests. The Commission is especially interested in protecting the status of common

---

[6] See Parkhill Extension—Oil Field Commodities. 46 M.C.C. 403, 410. Also Producers Transport, Inc., Extension, Benyol, 54 M.C.C. 621, 624.

carriers from the competition of applicants for contract service, since common carriage service is considered to be the backbone of the transportation system. Some degree of controversy has arisen over the issue of protecting existing carriers. Clearly, it is difficult to draw any line between protecting the legitimate rights of existing carriers from unwarranted competition and an arbitrary decision of refusal to allow an applicant to enter the field.[7]

Since the early 1950's, the problem of entry into the field has been increasingly difficult. The member of available routes which are economically sound has been greatly reduced as more carriers were authorized by the Commission, and considerable evidence exists that an excess number of carriers are in operation in many areas in relation to the number of shippers who require service.

In part, the problem is alleviated by the fact that certificates specify commodities to be carried, as well as the routes and geographic area served. Thus, as noted earlier, motor carriers are typically specialized carriers, and a large number can be accommodated in a given area.[8]

TERMS AND CONDITIONS OF CERTIFICATES
(I.C. Act, Sec. 208a)

In issuing a certificate, the Commission is empowered to impose various conditions upon its use. These items and conditions are characteristically very precise and detailed. As indicated above, such items as termini, routes, points served, intermediate points, and products carried are specified in detail. Each case must, of course, be dealt with upon its own merits.[9]

CONTRACT CARRIERS, DUAL OPERATIONS
(I.C. Act, Sec. 209a)

Another contrast between rail and motor carriers is the existence of contract carriers in large number. Generally speaking, the issuance

---

[7] Omaha & C.B. Ry. & Bridge Co., Common Carrier Application 49 M.C.C., 445, 465.

[8] For example, in 1960, there were 37 motor freight carriers serving Greenville, S. C., a city of 66,000 population. In contrast, Greenville was adequately served by four railroads. J. W. Bennett, Jr., Joseph L. Frye, Hugh S. Norton, and F. L. Hendrix, *op. cit.*

[9] Nudelman Common Carrier Application, 28 M.C.C., 91, 93, 95. Also Interstate Commerce Commission v. Southwest Freight Lines, Inc., 86 F. Supp. 587, 592, and Gay's Express, Inc., v. Haigis and Nichols, 43 M.C.C., 277, 280.

of permits is based upon criteria identical to that relating to issuance of certificate. That is, the applicant must be fit, willing and able to perform the service, and the issuance of the permit must be in the public interest. To a degree, the performance of contract carriage is akin to private carriage, since the service is available only to those who have specific contracts. Consequently, the element of public interest is not so crucial as is true of common carriage.

Unless the Commission decrees otherwise in response to a special set of circumstances, the operation jointly of common and contract carriage is not permitted.[10]

MERGERS AND TEMPORARY AUTHORITY
(I.C. Act, Secs. 212b and 5)

The purchase, sale, or transfer of a certificate must be approved by the Interstate Commerce Commission.[11] Since World War II, mergers and consolidations in the motor carrier industry have been numerous. As in the case of issuance of certificates, the criteria of approval center around the public interest. Frequently, when an existing carrier providing service to the public is apt to cease operations because of financial or other difficulties, the Commission will deem it to be in the public interest to preserve the service by allowing acquisition by another carrier. The Commission has been careful not to allow interlocking interests to arise through financial control.[12]

The term public interest is interpreted by the Commission to include the interest of competing carriers, and the Commission has failed to approve proposed transactions which would endanger the operations of existing carriers.[13]

The Commission's interest in mergers and transfers of rights extends into broad areas, viz., the financial arrangements of the transaction itself, the interests of employees and the general "climate" of the proposed transaction.

Mere speculation in rights, as opposed to the actual intent to operate such rights, is not permitted. The object of acquiring rights must be the provision of transportation service and not speculation per se. However, rights can be sold, as, for example, when a carrier goes out of business.

---

[10] Oilfields Trucking Co.—Purchase—Dunbar, 5 M.C.C., 137, 139.

[11] Section 5 lays down certain statutory regulations governing transfer. Subsection 10 of Section 5 exempts certain small operations where the public interest would be minimal. (Wooten-Purchase—Columbia, 49 M.C.C., 586, 591.)

[12] Peerless, Inc.-Control-Karst, 39 M.C.C., 683, 696.

[13] Chicago, B.&O. R.R. Co. Control 271 I C C 63, 157.

It frequently happens that the rights of one carrier complement those of another and that the two sets of rights can be combined into a stronger system, given Commission approval.

Intense competition in recent years has made strengthening of rights desirable, and the Commission has been generally liberal in allowing consolidation to take place. Some critical reaction has been directed toward the Commission on these grounds, although it does not seem to be sound in view of all the factors.[14]

The Commission has also been fairly generous in the granting of permission for lease and for temporary authority to operate. Temporary authority may be granted, and, in the interim period, the Commission may make a determination as to making the acquisition permanent.

Section 212a also covers the procedure relating to revocation and suspension of certificates for various causes. The Commission has used this power very sparingly. The section protects the carrier from arbitrary actions by the regulatory authorities, and the law provides that the certificate or permit cannot be revoked except for wilful failure to comply with Commission orders after a reasonable time. Except for those cases where certificates have been cancelled due to errors in issuance, the Commission has been more than generous in administering this power.[15]

RATES AND CHARGES (I.C. Act, Sec. 216a)

In discussing the application of rate regulation to the rail carriers above, it will be remembered that much of the regulatory material related to the competitive relationship between the various modes, especially rail and motor carriers.

Fundamentally, the regulation of motor carrier rates and charges is the same as that applying to rail carriers, viz., rates and charges must be reasonable and non-discriminatory in nature. Due to the unique nature of motor carriers, there is no long and short haul clause in Part II, nor are motor carriers required to respect shipper wishes

---

[14] *Trucking Mergers, Concentration, and Small Business: An Analysis of Interstate Commerce Commission Policy, 1950-56.* Report prepared for the Select Committee on Small Business, U. S. Senate, by Walter Adams and James B. Hendry (Washington).

[15] See Boulevard Transit Lines, Inc., v. United States, 77 F. Supp. 594, 595; joint Northeastern Motor Carrier Association, Inc., v. Rose and Welloff, 43 M.C.C., 487, 488; Lincoln Tunnel Apps. 44 M.C.C., 665, 671; On-time Transfer Co. v. Buckingham, 44 M.C.C., 389, 397; Riss and Co., Inc., v. United States, 100 F. Supp. 468, 474.

in regard to routing, although they do so in fact. Motor carriers may join with rail or water carriers in the establishment of through rates, although, except for "piggy-back" service, they seldom do; and they are not required to do so. No provision for reparations appears in Part II of the act.

Common carriers must file and publish rates which are to be open to public inspection. As is true of rail carriers, rebates are prohibited, and due notice of thirty days must be given for rate changes to become effective.

The rule of rate making is characteristically vague; in general, it duplicates Section 15a of Part I, except that mention is made of the Commission's duty to preserve the inherent advantages in deference to the national transportation policy. As in the case of railroads, the ultimate question is whether the rate falls within the zone of reasonableness.[16] Products of high value may be expected to return an amount in excess of the actual costs assignable to performance of the transportation.[17]

The fact that such a significant portion of motor carrier costs is variable has presented the Commission with the task of adopting a somewhat different view of costs, as related to rates, than was historically true of rail carriers. The complexities of adjusting costs and observing the provisions of the national transportation policy in rate regulation will be discussed in a later portion of the book.

The Commission is empowered to suspend and investigate rates upon complaint or upon its own initiative.

Motor carriers customarily engage in rate making through the device of rate bureaus. However, it is much more common for motor carriers to depart from the rates devised by the bureau than is true of rail service.

MISCELLANEOUS REGULATORY DUTIES IN REGARD TO MOTOR CARRIERS

The Commission has varied powers over motor carriers regarding schedules (Sec. 218a), over standards of service for passenger and freight carriers (Sec. 216b), insurance (Sec. 215), filing of reports and uniform accounts (Sec. 220), issuance of securities (Sec. 20a), and other matters such as the provision of auxiliary services, loading and supply of equipment. Some of these items, such as insurance, are

[16] Dairy & Packing House Products from Central Points, 44 M.C.C., 39, 43.
[17] Tobacco L.T.L., Wilson 61, M.C.C. 159, 162.

unique to the motor carrier industry, but, for the most part, these requirements parallel those relating to rail transportation.

In addition to the above items, the Interstate Commerce Commission is charged with the responsibility of administering safety regulations. The safety regulations (Sec. 204) apply to all motor vehicles operating in interstate commerce, including those that are exempt from economic regulation. Highly detailed regulations regarding the vehicle, the qualifications of the driver and necessary equipment are set forth.

STATE REGULATION OF MOTOR CARRIERS

The regulations discussed above are entirely on the federal level. Motor carriers, much more so than railroads, are influenced by state regulation.

Aside from property taxes and related matters, railroads are little affected by state legislation. Motor carriers, however, using the public highways and operating vehicles which, as personal property, are registered in a given state, are much influenced by these regulations.

These regulations fall generally into two classes: (1) taxation and (2) police powers, such as regulations on size and weight of vehicles, state safety requirements, and other matters.

Each of the forty-nine political jurisdictions in the continental United States has related, but often very heterogeneous, regulations regarding these matters. For many years, motor carriers have found these regulations, and especially the fact that many differences are present them, a major problem. Discussions of some of these problems will be found below.[18] Both state governments and motor carriers have strong arguments on their sides of these complex questions. States must finance and protect the highways.[19] Motor carriers must be able to operate without undue burden when passing from state to state. Although much progress has been made in making state regula-

---

[18] For some recent discussions of these matters, see Hugh S. Norton, *Highway Barriers in 20 States* (U. S. Department of Agriculture, March 1957). For a discussion of the effects of such regulations see Josephine Ayre, *Effects of State and Local Regulations in Interstate Movement of Agricultural Products by Highway, op. cit.* For earlier discussion and a comparison over time, see *Interstate Trade Barriers Affecting Motor-Vehicle Transportation,* Senate Doc. No. 81, 79th Congress, 1st session, 1945.

[19] Motor carriers often point out that in many states revenues derived from vehicle taxes are diverted into other channels; and the claim is often made that if these revenues were used only for highways, there would be no problem.

tions more practicable and also more uniform, much remains to be done.

BROKERAGE REGULATION

Transportation brokerage, as noted, is important in the motor carrier industry. The Interstate Commerce Commission has the power to regulate brokers but has not seen fit to do so, since the role of brokers is very limited and adequate regulation is undertaken by the states, e.g., Florida, where brokerage is important for "exempt" carriers.

GENERAL EVALUATION OF MOTOR CARRIER REGULATION

Unlike the area of railroad regulation, which has become well established over time, the body of motor regulation is more in a state of flux. Federal regulation of motor carriers has been in effect for slightly less than thirty years. These have been years of growth and change for the motor carrier industry, and regulation has been subjected to great stress as a result.

Also, the heterogeneous structure of the industry has been a problem from the beginning, and this situation has not greatly eased.

The motor carrier industry, especially the more informal branches, has not accepted regulation without some difficulty, and enforcement has been and will continue to be a serious problem.

Various policy issues relating to these points will be discussed in following chapters, but it can be seen here that motor carrier regulation is still in the formative stage.

Summary

The regulatory legislation regarding motor carriers is less extensive but more complex than that regarding railroads. Due largely to the structure of the industry, the motor carrier industry is much more difficult to regulate, although, to be sure, some weight must be given to the time which has elapsed in the case of rail regulation. Many areas of railroad regulation are complete (except for the intermodal rate problems), while the regulation of motor carriers is still very much an active matter.

CHAPTER XV

Regulation of Air Carriers

Air carriers became subject to comprehensive regulation in 1938 with the passage of the Civil Aeronautics Act of that year. This act, loosely patterned on the Interstate Commerce Act, represented the first really comprehensive federal legislation dealing with air transport.

Unlike other modes of transportation, it was clear from the earliest days of the industry that any effective regulation in aviation would have to be national in scope. Prior to 1925, such regulation as existed was entirely in the area of technical and safety regulation. Although several states adopted controlling legislation, the first federal legislation came soon after the Kelley Act of 1925,[1] providing for private operation of the air mail with the passage of the Air Commerce Act of 1926. The Act of 1926 established a Bureau of Aeronautics within the Department of Commerce, which began immediately to provide for extensions of the lighted airways and to license both aircraft and pilots. Thus, the commercial aviation industry (as opposed to the

---

[1] Before the Kelley Act was passed, regular air mail service had been provided in the United States since 1918, by the Army Air Corps at first largely as a training device. On August 12, 1918, the Post Office Department took over the service. The Department continued to operate the service (using federal equipment) until 1925, when the Kelley Act was passed providing for private contractors to operate the service. Except for the "cancellation period" in 1934, the contract arrangement has continued.

military flying services) began to operate on a stable basis. The Kelley Act of 1925 had provided for carriage of mail through competitive bidding by private operators. The Post Office Department was to administer the provisions of the act. More than any single factor, the promise of air mail contracts converted the industry from the "barnstorming" and flying circus activities, which had largely characterized it since World War I, into something approximating a sound industry. The prospect of air mail revenue made it possible for an operator to invest capital on a rational basis and to purchase equipment with long range plans in mind. The airline operators, thus, entered upon a lengthy period of dependence upon air mail payments as a source of revenue and, thus, in turn, their concern with the Post Office Department policies. Although in the strict sense the air mail and postal regulations were not part of the regulatory history of the airlines, the fact remains that in the early years of the industry (1925-1935) the air mail revenue represented the difference between success and failure. No airline could have existed on passenger revenues in those times, except in very special cases. Without any consideration of the justice or injustice of subsidy or the degree of subsidy incorporated in the air mail payments, it seems fair to say that the industry could not have progressed rapidly without them. Few early operators bothered even to install seats in early mail planes, and it was not until the experiments financed by the Guggenheim Foundation with Western Air Express in 1927 that any serious thought was given to the passenger traffic.[2]

The McNary-Watres Act of 1930, compensating operators on the basis of space provided for mail instead of weight of mail carried, was also instrumental in stimulating passenger experimentation.[3] The importance of air mail revenue continued for some time, as illustrated by Table 15-1.

---

[2] The Daniel Guggenheim Fund for the Promotion of Aeronautics was established in 1926. A sum of $2,500,000 was to be used to help the cause of civil aviation. Western Air Express (later Western Air Lines) was selected as a test case, since it had already begun to carry passengers. The loan made it possible for W.A.E. to purchase new equipment. So successful was the experiment that W.A.E. paid the loan through passenger earnings within two years. This experiment did much to demonstrate feasibility of passenger service to skeptical operators.

[3] H.R. 11704, *An Act to Amend the Air Mail Act of February 7, 1925*, as amended, 1930. The space × miles formula was intended to provide an incentive for operators to provide excess space, which then might be utilized for passenger carriage. The Boeing-40, an open cockpit mail plane used in the mid-1920's had a cabin for two passengers. The space, although not used for mail, was paid for, and operators were encouraged to make use of it for potential passengers, which they could with little addition to costs.

TABLE 15-1

AIRMAIL PAYMENTS, AS A PERCENTAGE OF TOTAL
AIR LINE OPERATING INCOME, SELECTED YEARS

Year	Percentage of Income
1931	82
1935	39
1940	26
1945	15
1958	5.4*
1960	5.3**

* Includes 1.8 per cent "public service revenue," 3.6 per cent payment for mail service
** 1.9 per cent "public service revenue," 3.4 per cent mail pay.
Source: Air Transport Association.

It can be seen that although the Post Office Department was never formally charged with regulating the air transportation industry, its policy of awarding contracts to "responsible" bidders and its leverage through the air mail pay provisions made it very influential as a stabilizing force in the industry until 1938 when the Civil Aeronautics Act was passed.[4] The act, coupled with the growing importance of passenger traffic, reduced the role of the department, although it is still important.[5]

Following the air mail "scandals" of 1934-35, the need for a new approach was clearly evident. The airlines, dependent as they were on federal policy, needed a clear guide line. A brief interlude followed the restoration of contracts and the stop gap Air Mail Act of 1934, during which regulatory authority was divided between the Post

---

[4] In his definitive study of the problem, Spencer says: "In effect (under the Watres Act), the Postmaster General was a one-man public utility commission having authority not only over rates of compensation, including compensation for losses incurred in passenger service, but also over such matters as route location, route consolidations, and extensions, contract bidding conditions, service standards, equipment and personnel, and systems of accounts." Francis A. Spencer, *Air Mail Pay and the Government* (Washington: The Brookings Institution, 1941), p. 43.

[5] The unfortunate consequences of the Post Office Department's policy, as encountered in Smith, *op. cit.*, pp. 214 ff., are well known. The activities of Postmasters General New and Brown, although laudable, seem to prove that regulation must be carried out by an agency charged with that duty, and not as a by-product of awarding contracts for the performance of service. Viewing the situation from the vantage point of some thirty years and with political detachment, the net effects of the New-Brown policy seem to be beneficial rather than otherwise, and Messrs. Farley and Roosevelt were no doubt carried away by the political aspects of the situation.

Office Department, the Interstate Commerce Commission and the Department of Commerce. The confusion which resulted from the overlapping authority was completely unsatisfactory. During the brief period between 1934 and 1938, a number of bills and proposals was introduced in an attempt to solve the air transport regulatory problems. The Act of 1938 was designed to provide a regulatory pattern similar to that of the Interstate Commerce Commission. The new act differed from the Interstate Commerce format in several important ways. It was decided after some conflict to establish a new regulatory agency apart from the Commission. President Roosevelt had been in favor of using the Commission for this purpose, but he was later convinced of the wisdom of a new approach. The second major difference was the fact that the Civil Aeronautics Act was not only regulatory but promotional in nature, i.e., the Civil Aeronautics Authority was directed to "encourage the development of an air transportation system properly adapted to the present and future needs of the foreign and domestic commerce of the United States, of the Postal Service, and of the national defense."[6] To a degree, this mandate was made applicable to the other carriers in the Transportation Act of 1940. However, it is stronger and has been more rigorously administered in the case of air carriers.

The Authority was composed of five members who, as in the case of the ICC, were appointed by the President with the advice and consent of the Senate and with due regard for political balance. The members were appointed for six year terms. The administrator was to be appointed under the same terms, but was to serve at the pleasure of the President. (C. A. Act, Secs. 201a and 201c.) This arrangement, though somewhat novel, worked well enough.

THE ACT OF 1938

Entry Control   (C.A. Act, Sec. 401e-1)

The Authority faced a problem somewhat similar to that which confronted the Bureau of Motor Carriers, except that it was on a much smaller scale. An airline (with some exceptions, to be noted later) must obtain a certificate of convenience and necessity. Since the area of possible profitable operation for an airline is relatively limited and since there were already airlines in operation at the time, the bulk of the present trunk lines was certified at the time the

---

[6] Sec. 2 (25 Stat. 980, U. S. C. 402).

act was passed through an appropriate grandfather clause, May 14, 1938, being the critical date. In the early years, there was still some conflict between the Authority and the Post Office, since an airline might be certified by the Authority and still be economically handicapped by not having a mail contract. As passenger traffic became more important, this problem eased somewhat. The qualifications necessary for a certificate involved the well-known factors of fitness, ability, willingness to serve, and other items similar to those in the Motor Carrier Act. Since the operation of an airline, unlike the early motor carriers, required substantial capital and technical ability, there were relatively few applicants.[7] In effect, those who had qualified for mail contracts could very likely also qualify for a certificate. While some problems of route allocations arose, on the whole, the certification procedure was accomplished with dispatch. No doubt, the extremely unsettled conditions, which had prevailed following the cancellation of the air mail contracts and the unsatisfactory act of 1934, had put the airlines in a ready frame of mind and the act was welcomed as a stabilizing force. Carriers not able to qualify under the grandfather clause were required to seek certificates in the usual way, i.e., proof of convenience and necessity.

Rates and Fares   (C.A., Act, Sec. 1002)

The familiar pattern of the Interstate Commerce Act was followed relative to control over rates and fares. Carriers were required to file a schedule of charges. Charges were to be reasonable and there was to be no discrimination.

The rule of rate making was somewhat more specific than for other modes, in that the Authority was directed to consider the inherent advantages of air transportation and, within limits, to encourage air transportation. Since the air carriers were at this time almost exclusively concerned with a rather specialized passenger traffic, little friction was caused with the other modes through the relationship of rates.[8] Other rate matters, suspension, division between carriers, and

---

[7] The Ford tri-motor transport, widely used in the late 1920's, cost about $50,000. The Curtis "Condor," last of the bi-plane transports, was more expensive; and, even the small Stinson, a popular plane for short hops, cost some $24,000. The Douglas DC-3, popular in the late 1930's, cost some $250,000.

[8] In the early years, air travel was, to all intents and purposes, separate and distinct from surface travel, and the markets were not really competitive.

through rates all were brought under regulation. The Authority was empowered to suspend rates and to specify rates when necessary.

Miscellaneous Powers and Duties

The carriers were required to submit reports of various types as determined by the Authority. Control over mergers, extensions, interlocking directorates and other financial operations was vested in the Authority.

An important aspect of air transport regulation was the problem of air safety. An Air Safety Board was created by the Act of 1938, which dealt with aircraft, pilot qualification, and operation of the airway system. The Board was independent of the Authority in order to assume unbiased investigation of accidents.

Administration of the Act

In 1940, only two years after the Act was passed, a substantial reorganization was undertaken to promote more efficient enforcement of the Act. The Civil Aeronautics Authority became the Civil Aeronautics Board. The Board was put into the Department of Commerce for administrative purposes. The Air Safety Board was abolished, and its functions were assumed by the Civil Aeronautics Board. The Board was put into the Department of Commerce for administrative purposes. The Air Safety Board was abolished, and its functions were assumed by the Civil Aeronautics Board. The Board became concerned with economic regulation while the Civil Aeronautics Administration devoted itself to operational matters, including pilot certification, enforcement of the safety program, and airway operation. Again, in 1958, substantial organizational changes were made by the Federal Aviation Act of 1958.[9]

The purpose of this Act was to clarify the relationship between the Civil Aeronautics Board and its economic regulatory functions and the non-economic activity of the Civil Aeronautics Authority. This was done by creating the Federal Aviation Agency under the direction of an administrator. The function of the Agency was to combine and administer the provisions relating to safety and airway operation. Not only had there been some overlapping of authority,

---

[9] Public Law 85-726; 72 Stat. 731.

but the control of air space had become such a serious problem that some positive approach was needed.[10]

Thus, under the existing law, the Civil Aeronautics Board continues to be responsible for economic regulation, including:

1. The regulation of fares and rates for the carriage of persons and property.

2. The fixing of subsidy and service mail rates.

3. The guarantee of loans to certain classes of carriers for the purchase of flight equipment.

4. The enforcement of the economic provisions of the law.

5. The approval or disapproval of mergers, control and interlocking relationships and of intercarrier agreements affecting air transportation.

6. The regulation of air carrier accounting practices and of air carrier reporting systems.

7. The maintenance of public records of traiffc, schedules, and other material required to be filed by air carriers.

8. The licensing of domestic air routes and, with the approval of the President, of international air routes operated by the United States and foreign air carriers.

9. Participation in the negotiation of air agreements between the United States and other governments covering the exchange of air rights, in cooperation with the State Department, and authorization of the navigation of foreign civil aircraft in the United States.

10. Assuring protection of the public by (a) requiring the performance of safe and adequate air carrier service and (b) eliminating rate discriminations and unfair competition or unfair and deceptive practices in air transportation.

11. Investigation and determination of probable causes of civil aircraft accidents.

12. Adjudication of appeals from safety enforcement decisions of the Administrator of the Federal Aviation Agency and participation when appropriate in safety rule making proceedings to the Administrator.

The Federal Aviation Agency is responsible for non-economic regulation. The Federal Aviation Agency must:

1. Regulate the use of navigable air space of the United States; acquire, establish, operate, and improve air navigation facilities;

---

[10] By 1958, air traffic had become very complicated with the tremendous increase in civil and military flying. The problem had become important to the public and congressional opinion was aroused. The operation of air traffic control is largely an F.A.A. responsibility, and much needs to be done before the technical problems are solved.

prescribe air traffic rules for all aircraft; and conduct related research and development activities.

2. Rule on the location of substantial alteration of any military or civilian airport, rocket or missile site involving the expenditure of federal funds. (This provision extends to military airports, the identical review of airport locations which had been practiced by the Civil Aeronautics Administration with reference to non-military airports since 1938.)

3. Make and apply all safety rules.

g airman, aircraft, and airline and rating air agencies and gthens the right of an airman non-renewal of a certificate

l Aviation Agency, especially ir space, are highly involved,) are involved. Thus, while s not been simple and will uture, the issues involved are blems faced by the Board. A e overtones is the administra-

cal to assume that, since the eration at a relatively early have managed to avoid many erce Commission had marked ase. As might be expected, almost in the first days of potential routes was limited, d the problem of awarding or of awarding them to a o maximize the number of in an economic sense hinges transportation firms produce things being equal, produce social gain. If, on the con- en competition and a number referable. No clear evidence although the cost of modern e operation would indicate s are extant and that larger Experience has been almost impossible to accumulate, since equipment changes have occurred with great rapidity. Political and public policy has generally been on the side of competition, and it seems likely that the Board has been forced to pursue a more liberal entry policy than would be indicated by the economic factors alone. It seems likely also that, for the trunk line carriers at least, the economies of scale and costs of operation are changing in character from what they were a decade or more ago.

In practice, the Board has generally allowed competition in cases where traffic or potential traffic would support two or more carriers. Where traffic is light, the general policy has been to rely on a single strong carrier. In the Colonial case, for example, the Board viewed the New York-Florida traffic as being heavy enough to permit competition at the termini, although intermediate low traffic points were protected.[11] Where traffic potential is great, for example, Washington, D. C., many carriers are permitted to participate.[12] Clearly, the Board has held on to the theory, usually justified, that additional traffic will support additional service. In general, since the end of World War II, the Board has followed a rather liberal route award policy. On occasion, this policy has produced more competition than the carriers could deal with in the short run.[13] Three of the trunk lines extant in 1950 had been merged into other trunk carriers by 1961. This is not to indicate that the Board's policy has been productive of excess competition, but does indicate that the Board has pushed the competitive situation and has not allowed traffic growth to proceed far without certifying additional service. Unfortunately, the route structure cannot be considered on a segmentized basis. Service on one or two routes might well be shared by several carriers while other routes served by the same carriers might be best served by one, or two at the most. The ramifications of traffic on one route will carry over to others. A policy of strengthening a carrier by awarding an attractive route may so dilute traffic as to put stronger carriers into a dangerous position. Air carriers have, even more so than other modes, relied strongly on costly non-price competitive factors to attract traffic. The Board, Congress, and the public would raise serious questions about

---

[11] Colonial Airlines, Inc. *et al.*, Atlantic Seaboard Operation, 4 C.A.B. 633 (1944).

[12] Eastern Airlines, Inc. *et al.*, Additional Washington Service, 4 C.A.B. 325, 350 (1943).

[13] In the Pennsylvania Central case, 6 C.A.B. 217. 245-246 (1944), P.C.A. was extended into New York in competition with T.W.A. on the Pittsburgh route. P.C.A. became Capital Airlines, which remained one of the weakest trunk carriers until it was absorbed by United Air Lines in 1961. Capital had several weak spots, but the route structure was generally considered to be the main problem. It seems clear that no matter how alert and efficient management might be, a poor route structure is almost impossible to overcome.

any rate policy which would endanger safe and efficient operation. The air carrier is, consequently, very sensitive to competition, and Board policy makers must be aware of this. Precise knowledge of how many firms to admit to assure the health of the industry and also the public welfare would be the epitome of regulatory performance and has not yet come into existence.

Since World War II, the Board has faced increasing pressure to allow entrance into the field. The Board's solution to the problem, not a very satisfactory one, was to allow limited entry in the guise of the "non-scheduled" carriers.[14] These carriers, many concentrating on cargo carriage, were allowed to operate on a non-scheduled basis similar to the "exempt" carriers in the area of motor transport. Experience in this attempt has not been entirely satisfactory. The "non-skeds" have not themselves prospered and have likely drained off some traffic from the scheduled carriers, both freight and passenger.[15] Much of the passenger traffic of these carriers consists of charter flights, including military personnel. Some serious questions have been raised as to their operation.

Another area which has been subject to question is the provision of feeder line service. As indicated in Chapter II, there are thirteen "feeder" or local service lines in operation. These lines connect smaller cities with the trunk lines and major metropolitan centers. To a considerable extent, the local service lines perform a service which is not attractive to the trunk carriers. In contrast to the trunk carriers which have been free of direct subsidy for some years, the feeder lines derive substantial revenue from subsidy.[16] Thus, the local carriers may be described as being approximately in the same position as the trunk carriers were in the mid-1930's as regards subsidy. Eventually, no doubt, this market will expand, although there seems to be a serious question as to how much traffic small cities can generate in relation to the capacity of the most efficient equipment which is available.[17]

The Board has provided for entry into the field of several types of air carriers, in addition to the trunk line carriers, viz., the "non-

---

[14] The Act of 1938 provided for various exemptions. including non-scheduled operations. Such carriers were of little importance in the industry before 1945.

[15] See No. 829, North American Airlines, Inc., et al., v. Civil Aeronautics Board (1957).

[16] In 1960, public service revenue accounted for $54 million out of $146.8 million of total revenue. Air Transport Association, *Facts and Figures, 1960.*

[17] Local service carriers have not standardized upon any plane. The DC-3, often used, carries 21 passengers which may be adequate, but the DC-3 is aging and costly to maintain. For heavier traffic, Convair is frequently used. Other standard piston aircraft are often too large, both in capacity and physical size, for efficient operation on short, low traffic routes and small airports.

scheduled carriers," the local service carriers, the all-cargo carriers and the helicopter lines. To some degree, these lines have overlapping functions. For example, the non-schedule carriers perform services which both the trunk carriers and the all-cargo lines would otherwise perform. The all-cargo lines and the trunk lines both transport cargo. Thus, Board policy has seemingly been to admit as many carriers into the field as possible by means of segmentizing the market. Unfortunately, the various segments of the market have been impossible to insulate completely. For example, the non-schedule carriers were for some time considered to be "coach" carriers, vis-a-vis, the "first class" service offered by the trunk carriers. In the normal course of events, the trunk carriers began to offer "coach" service, similar to first class service but shorn of some items such as meal service or the use of older and slower planes, with more unpopular hours of departure. Concurrently, the non-scheduled carriers began to upgrade their service with the result that the two services began to merge into each other. Although this policy of the Board, as regards entry, has not been highly successful, it is difficult to see how they could have acted otherwise and still satisfied the conflicting demands made upon them. In the North American case cited above, the service had become almost identical to that of scheduled carriers. In some cases the two classes are provided on the same aircraft having two compartments. In such instances, it is almost impossible to distinguish between them.

Perhaps the second most troublesome policy area is the fact that the Board has the legal obligation to encourage and promote air transportation as well as to regulate it. Clearly, these two obligations are not always compatible and may be in actual conflict. An illustration of the dilemma produced by such a dichotomy is found in the Board's treatment of the local service lines.

As noted above, the local service lines are still largely dependent upon subsidy (or "public service revenue" in the airline lexicon). Obviously, some of the lines could not survive in a free market economy. However, local pride and a somewhat liberal interpretation of the air transportation policy combine to keep them in operation. Some question may arise as to whether the Board is meeting its obligations as a regulatory agency or whether it can meet such obligations while acting in a promotional capacity.

A unique factor in the air transport area, which is not found in other modes, is the fact that overseas operations are of importance. U. S. carriers operating abroad must follow the same general procedure as domestic carriers in showing their fitness and ability to serve the proposed routes.

The United States is a charter member of the International Civil Air Organization. The I.A.C.O. has effected a number of bi-lateral agreements which provide for reciprocal landing and other rights. In the international area the views of the Department of State are considered along with other data in granting a certificate. Before World War II, Pan American Airways was the only major U. S. carrier on foreign routes. Since the war, carriers which had previously served the continential United States expanded into overseas markets. In general, the policy followed has been one of allowing several carriers to compete in certain areas, much as is true on the domestic scene. After much discussion, the U. S. decided against the common practice in foreign countries, viz., the "flag" carrier, i.e., a single carrier often governmentally owned or heavily subsidized. Competition on many of the overseas routes is very heavy, and, of course, foreign competition is largely outside the control of the Civil Aeronautics Board. For example, New York to Paris or New York to London are desirable routes and are served by many foreign lines, as well as several domestic carriers. Since most of the foreign lines are wholly or in part publicly owned and subsidized, competition is severe.

GENERAL EVALUATION OF AIR CARRIER REGULATION

The extent of air carrier regulation is substantial, even though it has a relatively brief history. It is clear that the framers of the Civil Aeronautics Act had the benefit of the previous legislation upon which to build. Unlike the motor carrier industry, the airlines are a homogeneous group and federal jurisdiction was a necessity from the very early days of the industry.

Except for the certification problems relating to the non-certified carriers, the regulation of air carriers has presented relatively few problems.

Summary

As this chapter has brought out, the regulation of air transportation is comprehensive in nature and of fairly recent origin. Many serious problems, both economic and technical, remain to be solved. The Civil Aeronautics Board operates in a fashion similar to that of the Interstate Commerce Commission, although with a broader mandate in the field of promotion. The technical aspects of regulation are more complex for air transportation than for other modes and are separately administered by the Federal Aviation Agency.

CHAPTER XVI

Regulation of Water Carriers, Pipelines and Indirect Carriers

WATER CARRIER REGULATION

Water carriers, although the oldest form of carriage, were not subject to any comprehensive economic regulation until quite recently. Many reasons account for this fact, but, as Locklin points out, the principal factor is the relatively competitive nature of the industry and the low level of fixed costs as compared with rail carriers.[1] With no obligation to provide or maintain a right of way, the water carrier avoids the major element of fixed costs which face rail carriers. However, the ease of entry and the low level of fixed costs may be of diminishing importance. At the present time, an inland water carrier hoping to compete with any degree of success must obtain modern tow boats and barges which involve substantial capital outlay.[2] Water transportation, both coastal and inland, has always had a high

---

[1] Locklin, *op. cit.*, pp. 738 5th Ed.

[2] A diesel tow boat of modern design producing 9,000 horse power and capable of moving 40,000 tons of cargo costs up to $1,700,000. Obviously, such a piece of equipment must be maintained largely dependent of its actual use and must be used intensively.

degree of governmental aid and control in a technical sense. As noted in an earlier chapter, waterway improvement, provision of aids such as markers and lighthouses, has been considered a public responsibility since colonial days. Water carriers have also been subject to rather detailed regulations concerning safety, qualifications of officers and related matters. However, since there seemed to be no pressing need for economic regulation, it was late in coming.

Early Regulations

Aside from regulations concerning ocean shipping, which is outside the scope of this book, the first federal regulation of waterways in the economic sense was enacted as Part I of the Interstate Commerce Act in 1887.

The Act of 1887 had jurisdiction over common carriers, which involved both rail and water transportation when under common control or management, or when the shipment was continuous. Further extension came with the Hepburn Act of 1906, which gave the Interstate Commerce Commission power over joint rates and division over rates as between rail and water carriers. In a related area, the Panama Canal Act of 1912 gave the Commission authority to force a rail carrier to make physical connection with a water carrier and prohibited railroad control or ownership of waterways connecting with railroads unless the Commission gave specific approval as being consistent with the public interest.

Legislation relating to coastal and Great Lakes shipping, as well as foreign shipping, was enacted as the Shipping Board Act of 1916. This Act was not comprehensive in any sense. The most important provisions related to prohibition of discriminatory practices and requirements for the publication of rates.

The Intercoastal Shipping Act of 1933 made further minor changes. It applied only to intercoastal shippers via the Panama Canal. Carriers were required to file and publish rates and give thirty days' notice of intent to change rates. Modest powers of suspension were granted to the Shipping Board in regard to rates. In 1938, an amendment to this Act extended its jurisdiction to coastwise and Great Lakes common carriers.

With the exception of the provisions under Part I of the Interstate Commerce Act, the matters referred to above were under the enforcement of the United States Shipping Board and its successor, the Maritime Commission. Thus, there was dual responsibility shared by the Interstate Commerce Commission and the Shipping Board—Maritime Commission for the legislation which existed. By the late 1930's, it was clear that the existing legislation was both incomplete and confused. No provisions for entry control were in existence which, in view of the competitive nature of water transportation, was a serious omission. There were substantial areas which were not subject to any regulation. It appeared that the degree of competition prevailing in the industry was the main factor making for instability and that some control over entry was called for.

In 1940, Part III of the Interstate Commerce Act was passed, which imposed a more comprehensive and also more unified system of regulation. However, due to the nature of the service, there were still substantial areas which were exempt from regulation. These exemptions bear some resemblance to the Motor Carrier Act of 1935.

Those water carriers which are made exempt from the provisions of the Act are numerous and important. One estimate is that only about 10 per cent of all tonnage shipped by water is subject to regulation.[3] An enumeration of the principal exemptions will indicate why so little water transportation comes under the Commission's control.

1. The transportation of commodities in bulk is exempt when the cargo space of the vessel in which such commodities are transported is being used for the carrying of not more than three such commodities. This exemption does not apply, however, to transportation which was subject to the Intercoastal Shipping Act of 1933. Since some transportation of commodities in bulk was subject to that Act, the exemption is not so broad as might at first appear. The Commission has held, furthermore, that the bulk exemption does not apply when commodities are transported in the same tow as bulk commodities.

2. Transportation of liquid cargoes in bulk in tank vessels is also exempt from regulation, a very significant exemption relating mostly to petroleum products.

3. Transportation by contract carriers is exempt when, "by reason of the inherent nature of the commodities transported, their requirement of special equipment, or their shipment in bulk," it is not actually and substantially competitive with transportation by any common carrier which is subject to Parts I, II, or III of the Act. Contract carriers claiming exemption under this provision must make application to the Commission for such exemption.

4. Private carriers are exempt, since the Act applies only to common and contract carriers, and there is a further exemption of

³ Interstate Commerce Commission, *Annual Report*, 1946, p. 36.

carriers transporting property of a person who owns all or sub-stantially all of the voting stock of such carrier.

5. There is an exemption provided for transportation which is incidental to transportation by railroad, motor carrier, or express com-pany and which is in the nature of transfer, collection or delivery services in terminal areas or has to do with the performance of floatage, car ferry, lighterage, or towage.

In addition to the above exemptions, there are certain other con-ditional exemptions. The conditional or qualified nature of these ex-emptions arises from the fact that the carriers are exempt except to the extent that the Commission shall find, and by order declare, that application of the Act "is necessary to carry out the national transpor-tation policy declared in this Act." The conditional or qualified exemp-tions are (1) transportation in interstate commerce by water solely within the limits of a single harbor or between places in contiguous harbors, when not a part of a through movement to or from places beyond; (2) transportation by small craft of not more than one hundred tons carrying capacity and certain other small craft; and (3) ferries and certain other special types of operations.

The exemption of bulk cargoes is based in part on the belief that such transportation is not competitive with railroads or motor carriers.

Common Carrier Regulation

Water common carriers require a certificate of convenience and necessity. As in the case of other carriers, the certificate is issued on grounds of the carrier's being fit, willing and able to perform the service and showing a need for the service.

The Commission requires rates to be reasonable and that rates be published and available for inspection. Upon complaint or on its own motion, the Commission may suspend a rate for purpose of investiga-tion.

Unjust and unreasonable charges are not permitted. The carrier must provide reasonable service and maintain reasonable facilities. Reasonable facilities for interchange of traffic within and with other modes are required.

Part III contains a rule of rate making similar to that in Part I, directing the Commission to give due consideration to the effect of rates upon the movement of traffic by other modes. Contract carriers are required to have a permit and are otherwise subject to the same regulations as those applicable to common carriers.

Implementation of the Act

As noted above, the great bulk of water carriage is not subject to regulation. It was pointed out in Chapter II that more than 80 per cent of the tonnage moving on the inland waterways was made up of seven commodities. Most of these commodities move in bulk, liquid or solid, and frequently by private carrier. Consequently, much of the cargo moving is exempt under two categories.

The requirements regarding entry have, no doubt, had stabilizing influence upon the industry; but, as noted above, this problem would, no doubt, have eased as costs of entry increased.

Although considerable effort has been expended to bring about more rail-water shipping, very little has actually been done. Both the Denison Act of 1928 and the Transportation Act of 1940 provided for joint through rates and interchange. For several reasons, joint rail barge traffic has not grown. In general, rail carriers have not encouraged such traffic in their rate structures. As Fair & Williams point out, the applications for "fourth section relief" have increased almost 300 per cent between 1945 and 1957, most of them due to water competition.[4] Costs of transfer are high, especially where river transfer points are concerned. Probably the greatest advantage in water transportation occurs where the origin and destination are both on water points. Costs of transfer and time involved for rail-water service undermine much of the advantage which would otherwise be present.

Thus, in part because of the extensive area of exempt carriage and the relative unimportance of rail-barge traffic, the regulation of water carriage has not had substantial effects upon the transportation industry.

Miscellaneous Regulations

The water transportation industry is much concerned with technical regulation imposed by the United States Coast Guard and by the Corps of Engineers, insofar as their operations are concerned. Also, rather stringent regulations concerning employee relations apply to seamen in a somewhat more rigorous fashion than is true for other carrier employees.

---

[4] Marvin L. Fair and Ernest W. Williams, Jr., *Economics of Transportation* (Rev. ed.; New York: Harper & Row, 1960), p. 479.

REGULATION OF PIPELINES

Demand for pipeline regulation came at a relatively early date in the history of the industry. Much the same criticisms which were directed against the railroads, especially discrimination in rates and practices, were also brought against the pipeline carriers.[5] However, one very substantial difference in the industry structure must be noted. Pipelines were almost always built and operated by oil producing or refining companies rather than by a transportation enterprise per se.

This distinction was of immediate importance in 1906 when the Hepburn Act was passed to regulate the lines. The Hepburn Act, which was incorporated into the Interstate Commerce Act, required pipeline operators to publish and file tariffs, and the Commission was given control over accounts. The pipeline operators immediately claimed that they were in the oil business and were engaged in transportation merely as an adjunct to that enterprise. There was ample evidence that the oil producers who owned pipelines were enjoying a substantial cost advantage over the small operator who was obliged to ship by rail. This element, in addition to the fact that pipelines were engaged in transportation in direct competition with railroads, brought about substantial public sentiment in favor of regulation. The Commission held that all pipelines were considered to be in common carriage transportation, a rather liberal interpretation of the situation which, although it did not pass unchallenged, was supported.[6]

These legal provisions were amended and made more specific in the Transportation Act of 1920, which defined a pipeline common carrier so as to include all pipeline carriers engaged in interstate commerce. The provisions of the Act were applicable to all pipeline carriers of oil or other commodities, except gas, and movements which are partly by pipeline and partly by rail.

The Commission has undertaken a valuation of pipeline properties. However, it has allowed considerably higher rates of return for pipelines than for other carriers due to the increased economic hazards of pipeline operation.[7]

---

[5] As was the case with railroads, various emotional factors were important. The dominance of Standard Oil in the production and marketing of oil was doubtless a factor of importance in the demand for regulation.

[6] The Pipeline cases, 234 U. S. 548 (1914).

[7] *Reduced Pipeline Rates and Gathering Charges,* 243 I.C.C., 115, 142 (1940).

Several major differences exist between regulation applying to pipelines and that applying to other modes: (1) The so-called "Commodities Clause" of the Interstate Commerce Act, which prohibits railroads from transporting commodities in interstate commerce which they have produced or in the production of which they are interested, does not apply to pipelines; (2) there is no control over the construction of new lines or of extensions to existing lines; (3) there is no control over abandonment of pipelines; (4) there is no control over the security issues of pipeline companies; and (5) there is no regulation of consolidations and acquisitions of control. None of these areas has presented problems which seemed to call for regulation.

In actual practice, the scope of regulation for pipelines has been rather limited. The Interstate Commerce Commission has found only limited need for implementation of its powers. Most of the complaints regarding pipeline operation have centered around the tender requirements, i.e., the amount of oil necessary for a shipper to tender before his shipment will be accepted. The basis of the tender requirement is clearly the amount of oil which can be economically handled by the technical facilities. Obviously, the amount can be set in arbitrary fashion and used so as to discharge competition from small producers.[8] In recent years (1956) a pipeline has been constructed by the Southern Pacific Company, and extensions have been made since that time.[9] It will be interesting to see how this common carrier facility operates as part of the pipeline industry in the traditional pattern. As Wolbert points out, one reason for oil producers undertaking the building and operation of a pipeline was the fact that integration was an economic necessity in the oil refining and marketing industry. It would seem equally logical for a pipeline to be integrated into another type of transport technology, such as, a railroad.

In summary, the regulation of pipeline transportation has presented few serious problems due largely to the high degree of integration in the industry and to the fact that the traffic is generally profitable in nature. In effect, control of the oil producing companies was tantamount to control of the pipelines.

---

[8] See Brundred Bros. v. Prairie Pipeline Co. *et al.*, 68 I C C 458 (1922). Also, for the technical aspects involved, see Wolbert, *op. cit.*, pp. 26 ff.

[9] *Southern Pacific Bulletin*, March 1959.

REGULATION OF FREIGHT FORWARDERS

Federal regulation of forwarders is embodied in Part IV of the Interstate Commerce Act, enacted in May 1942.

Regulation came rather late to the freight forwarders and seems to have been designed not so much to solve specific problems or abuses, but to clarify the status of these carriers. As noted earlier, the forwarders occupy a dual status, in that they are shippers in one sense and that they are legally carriers in another sense.

The Act defines a forwarder as one other than a carrier who holds himself out to the general public to provide transportation —assembles and consolidates, breaks up, and utilizes in whole or part the services of carriers subject to Parts I, II, or III.

Entry Control

The Act requires a forwarder to obtain a permit which is issued by the Commission upon the usual showing of fitness, willingness to serve, and that the service will be consistent with national transportation policy.

The Commission may attach such terms and conditions as are necessary and may suspend or revoke a permit if the holder wilfully fails to comply with the law or Commission orders. Although a permit may not be issued to a carrier subject to other parts of the Act, other carriers can and often do control forwarders.

Cooperative shippers associations, as defined by the Agricultural Marketing Act of 1929, are exempt and, as noted earlier, these operations are important in scope. An appropriate grandfather clause provided protection for those in the field.

Rates and Service

A forwarder subject to the Act must provide the service which it holds itself out for at reasonable and just rates. No undue preference or prejudice will be permitted. A rule of rate making similar to that in Parts I, II and III is included. Tariffs are to be on file and open to public inspection.

Miscellaneous Provisions

Although freight forwarders are not permitted to own or control carriers, carriers subject to Parts I, II and III are permitted to control forwarders. Forwarders must provide adequate insurance protection to those using their services. There are the usual provisions for reports and uniform accounts. One unique feature of the regulatory format is that forwarders are specifically defined by law as common carriers. No serious problems have been encountered in the implementation of the Act. Some modification was necessary in order to facilitate more efficient motor carrier–freight forwarder operations.[10]

GENERAL EVALUATION OF WATER CARRIER, PIPELINE AND INDIRECT CARRIER REGULATION

Largely because of their nature, these carriers have presented few serious regulatory problems. Pipelines, in paticular, have been brought under regulation with little stress and no special difficulties have been encountered.

Water carriers, because of their large areas of exemption, and freight forwarders, due to their dual status, have created some difficulties for the Commission.

The effectiveness of all these types of regulation has been greatly enhanced by the fact that all the modes concerned are made up of a small number of firms.

Summary

As this chapter has brought out, the regulation of these modes has proceeded on a piece-meal basis as the need arose. Strangely enough, water transportation, which is the oldest form of transport, is one of the most recent to bear regulation. Both water carriers and freight forwarders present fairly serious problems relative to their role in the transport complex vis-a-vis the other carriers.

---

[10] *Freight Forwarders, Motor Common Carriers, Agreements*, 272 I C C 413 (1948).

CHAPTER XVII

Fair Return on Fair Value and the Rate Level

The concept of fair return on fair value has had, as noted in Chapter XIII, a long and somewhat uncertain history. The social and economic justification for the concept is clear beyond all doubt. It would be neither justice nor wisdom to regulate rates in such a manner as to deprive the owners of the industries so regulated of a fair income on property so used. Aside from the basic injustice and illegality (violation of the due process clause) of this procedure, society would soon find that capital was not being attracted to those industries, and they would be operating at a disadvantage to the detriment of society.

It is not (or should not be) the purpose of regulation to make it impossible for sellers to render adequate service and secure a reasonable profit. Although under non-compensatory rates some temporary advantage will accrue to buyers, they will soon find that the service is not available or of lower quality than they wish. An enterprise must acquire sufficient income from the sale of its services, not only to remain in business but also to set aside or acquire funds for reserve and for capital formation. It must be able to invest in newer and more efficient equipment to meet competition and to render the highest standards of service. On the other hand, an industry subject to regulation would not be fulfilling its legal and moral obligations if it were to make unduly high profits due to its franchised status.

The word "value" is used here in a somewhat special sense. Value to the economist is exchange value or market value. In this case, such concepts of value are not relevant. Railroad or public utility property is not sold or exchanged on any recognized market. Value is used here in the sense of an engineering valuation of property. We must note carefully also that the *value* spoken of here does not relate to the earning ability of the business organization concerned. It would be circular reasoning to evaluate property for regulatory purposes on its earning capacity. Further, the valuation is in terms of the whole plant or the sum total of property used to produce the service. A building, a bridge or line of railroad is useless in isolation but very valuable as part of a railroad system or company. As we might well appreciate, it is one thing to discuss this problem in terms of theory and another to approach it in a legal fashion in such a manner as to apply it in specific situations. Although the earning ability of a property cannot be used to measure value for regulatory purposes, it is in our economic scheme of things of clear basic importance. A modern, well-constructed railroad built to connect two abandoned mining towns would have no earning power and hence no value from the standpoint of one who wished to operate the railroad for income purposes. Common stock would have no market and the plant would have no economic function. However, from the standpoint of the physical property, buildings, rolling stock and roadway, the enterprise would represent a considerable investment and, in this sense, value.

In such a case, we might have a plant costing $10,000,000 and having no earning power. Let us now turn the example the other way round and look at the opposite situation. Suppose that a railroad constructed in 1880 to serve two mining communities has been brought to life by the sudden rise of uranium mining in these towns, and traffic soars to high levels. We then have a plant fallen into decay and worth, let us say, $100,000 with tremendous earning capacity and thus very valuable from an investment viewpoint. Investors would be well aware that the physical plant was fit only for the junk yard; yet, while the uranium activity lasts, the earning capacity of the firm is most attractive.

Thus, value in the physical sense and value in the market or earning capacity sense are widely different concepts, indeed.

In the first case above, the owners of a fine property have no chance of realizing a return on its great physical *value*. In the second case, the owners of the firm have the opportunity to realize large earnings in a plant which has little physical *value*. These are, to be sure, matters of chance. In those areas of the economy not subject to regulation, situations of this type arise constantly, and no public policy questions are at issue.

If, for example, an entrepreneur builds a very expensive restaurant and invests $100,000, and for reasons of inept management or business risk the enterprise fails, there is no one to blame other than himself. On the other hand, his competitor may have a thriving business in a ramshackle building which, by business acumen or windfall, is extremely profitable. There are no moral, ethical or legal questions of public responsibility in such cases.

When, however, there is public regulation of rates and the property is for public "convenience and necessity," serious ethical and legal matters must be taken into consideration. Let us now turn to the legal aspects of the problem.

THE LEGISLATIVE AND JUDICIAL FACTORS

Although the legislative and judicial factors relating to this concept are interwoven with the economic factors, it seems wise to discuss them in separate fashion, keeping in mind the fact that these factors cannot be separated in practice.

Legal Status of the Rate Level Prior to 1920

Before 1920, the principal emphasis upon rate control was oriented toward specific rates as opposed to the rate level per se. This was a logical development stemming from the original act. Many individual rates (see Chapter XIX) were tested as to their reasonableness, and little attention was paid to the rate level. There seem to be several reasons for this.

Most rate questions before 1920 were concerned with discrimination and involved complaints of individuals. There was no such concept at this time, as the national economy and railroads were generally prosperous. In addition, the Interstate Commerce Commission had been fully occupied with the regulatory activities which it had at that time and would have been hard pressed to assume such sophisticated duties as those involved in this area.

The legal concept of preventing confiscatory rates and destruction of property rights was embodied in the case of *Stone vs. Farmers Loan & Trust Co.* In the Stone case, the court said,

> This power to regulate is not the power to destroy, and limitation is not the equivalent of confiscation . . . the state cannot require a railroad corporation to carry persons or property without reward.[1]

Judicial review was established in a later case.[2]

In its most simple concept, the Stone case erected a bulwark against rate regulation at so low a level as to destroy the value of the property. Later in the *Smyth vs. Ames* case, previously cited, this concept was enlarged to embrace the concept of a *reasonable* return, which would enable carriers to operate on a sound basis. In essence, this was a more liberal and generous interpretation of the basic philosophy embodied in the Stone case. There is clearly a wide gap between a rate level which *avoids destruction* of the property and one which provides for a *reasonable* return. For example, a carrier might be assured that the rate level would not be set at a point which would be confiscatory. If this were interpreted in a literal sense, this might mean that the carrier could continue to operate and maintain itself so as to avoid collapse. On the other hand, a reasonable return would or could be much more liberal, providing for capital improvements over and above mere existence.

A unique and interesting problem in relation to the use of rate of return is discussed by Averch and Johnson in their article, "Behavior of the Firm Under Regulatory Constraint." These authors feel that a misallocation of resources may result when rate of return is used as a pricing regulatory guide by the regulatory authorities. Especially in those industries where a large element of fixed costs exists, there is a danger that the firm may have an incentive to operate at a loss in some markets.[3]

There are, to be sure, few, if any, guide lines in this area. No standards exist as to how much capital should be put into a given plant in an industry in order to preserve or enhance the value of the property. It might be argued, for example, that the railroads fell far behind in the years 1930-1945 because there were relatively modest amounts invested in new or improved equipment. Capital expenditures never rose above $500,000,000, except for 1937 when they rose to $509,000,000, having fallen steadily since 1923, when they totaled slightly less than a billion dollars. However, during these years, improvements in equipment were not of a drastic nature and the

---

[1] Stone *et al.* vs. Farmers Loan and Trust Co., 116 U. S. 307, 331 (1886).

[2] Chicago, Milwaukee and St. Paul Co. vs. Minnesota, 134 U. S. 418, 458 (1890).

[3] Harvey Averch and Leland J. Johnson, "Behavior of the Firm Under Regulatory Constraint," 1962, pp. 1052 ff. *American Economic Review*, Vol. LII, No. 2, December.

penalties of operating with antiquated equipment were not apparent. However, from 1948 to 1954, expenditures were more than one billion for every year, as the railroads undertook to replace their motive power fleet and to make other plant improvements. (See Table 17-1.)

TABLE 17-1

TOTAL CAPITAL EXPENDURES, U. S. CLASS I RAILROADS,
SELECTED YEARS

Year	Total Capital Expenditures
1922	$ 429,273,000
1924	874,744,000
1926	885,086,000
1928	676,665,000
1930	872,608,000
1932	167,194,000
1934	212,712,000
1936	298,991,000
1938	226,937,000
1940	429,147,000
1942	534,897,000
1944	560,112,000
1946	561,957,000
1948	1,273,484,000
1950	1,065,842,000
1952	1,340,912,000
1954	820,246,000
1956	1,227,857,000
1958	738,036,000
1960	919,154,000

Source: Association of American Railroads, *Railroad Transportation, A Statistical Record, 1921-1959*, and *A Review of Railroad Operations in 1961* (Washington), p. 15.

Clearly, these improvements were necessary, and failure to make them before put the railroads under a handicap in terms of competition. On the other hand, the old equipment was capable of being operated, and, in the low income years of 1930-1940, capital expenditures might have been considered imprudent. It can be seen that "reasonable" or "unreasonable" levels of capital formation cannot be easily determined in any given case.

The formal relationship between the rate of return and specific rates was established by Section 15a in the Transportation Act of 1920, amended many times at later dates. The court did not, in the case of *Smyth vs. Ames,* establish a procedure for calculating the fair value of property and, in a later case, made it clear that this was a technical problem which could be left to the regulatory commission.[4]

The struggle to solve the valuation problem previously mentioned must be elaborated upon at this point. In *Smyth vs. Ames,* the court listed a large number of factors or elements which might be taken into account in a determination of value: (1) the original cost of construction and the amount expended in permanent improvements, (2) the present as compared with the original cost of construction, (3) the amount of stocks and bonds, (4) the value of stocks and bonds, and (5) the probable earning capacity of the property. In two cases, the Commission rejected the amount of stocks and bonds[5] and the probable earning capacity of the firm.[6]. Thus, the issue turns on the two factors of (1) original cost and (2) cost of reproduction of the plant. The area of disagreement is somewhat narrowed, but there is still great difficulty. Let us examine first, the original cost. In the first place, to determine original cost, it would be necessary to have adequate historical records which were not always available. In Chapter XIII, it was noted that many elements of rail property were constructed during the years from 1850 to the time of valuation. There are obviously many practical problems, but, more important, there were serious theoretical ones. The original cost might well have no relevance to the present situation because of the rise and fall of prices or other economic changes. Some elements of the plant, such as land, had an original cost of little or nothing and might, in 1920, have been very valuable. On the other hand, buildings and equipment acquired in 1870 might have had little value in 1920. In a period of rising prices, investors might be penalized if the value for rate making purposes was based on original cost calculated at low prices; while, on the other hand, a period of falling prices might put the investor in a better position.

In the mid-1920's, price levels were generally higher than they had been in the years before the turn of the century, when much rail plant was built. After 1929, when prices fell, there was a shift in relationships. We must also consider the role of "prudent" investment. If a carrier, through inept management, made large investments which

---

[4] Los Angeles Gas and Electric Co. vs. Railroad Commission of California, 289 U. S. 287 (1933).

[5] Institutional Investors vs. Chicago, Milwaukee, St. Paul & Pacific Railroad Co., 318 U. S. 523, 540 (1943).

[6] Knoxville vs. Knoxville Water Co., 212 U. S. 1, 11 (1909).

were unwise or unnecessary, the public should not be expected to pay for such investments through high rates.

Original cost may be computed by adding the cost of original property, plus additions and betterments made since that time. Thus, if the property included a bridge which had cost $70,000 in 1878 and was upgraded in 1918 at a cost of $40,000, the total original cost would be $110,000, less accumulated depreciation. A second method is to make a physical inventory of property and determine the original cost by the use of company records or through the use of other cost data. These two methods will produce the same result. For old properties, which were acquired when accounting procedures were crude or non-existent, it was frequently necessary to evaluate the property by the use of independent data rather than company records.

It can be seen that this concept is not simple to apply. Let us now turn our attention to the problem of reproduction value.

This concept may be thought of as assuming that the plant as it now stands was to be destroyed and replaced under existing circumstances. It can be seen that this presents certain problems. Some immediate problems come to mind.

First of all, it seems clear that, if, for example, the Southern Railway were to be built anew, it would be considerably different. Surely, the large and handsome stations built before the turn of the century in many cities and now used at perhaps 10 per cent of capacity would not be reproduced. Or, if they were to be reproduced, would it be possible to do so and at what cost? Even small town depots in various parts of the nation contain woodwork and stone or brick work which would be produced (if at all) at costs of $3 or $4 per hour as opposed to $1 or $2 per day in 1880. On the other hand, the Chinese laborers who built the Central Pacific worked with mule carts and hand tools. Modern earthmoving equipment could construct the line in a fraction of the time required for the original construction.

It would, of course, be possible to estimate the cost of reproducing all (except land) of the carrier property, although it can be seen from the examples cited above that far-reaching assumptions might be required in order to prevent a drastic over or under valuation. Some arbitrary decisions must be made as to which investments were prudent and which imprudent. The cathedral-like urban railway stations in many major cities doubtless were prudent when built and would be sheer folly in 1960.

Obviously, neither cost of reproduction nor original cost is a satisfactory yardstick for the purpose at hand. In either case, questions arise in regard to "going value," "good will" and other intangible values. Land is especially troublesome. For example, the land surrounding that occupied by Grand Central Station in Manhattan is of fabulous value. In fact, the New York Central derives substantial revenue from the "air" rights paid by builders who occupy space over the maze of underground tracks under the terminal area. The land surrounding the Santa Fe's Raton Pass in New Mexico is worth very little, but the pass per se is very valuable to a railroad seeking to cross the Continental Divide at that point. As noted in Chapter XIII, these problems were rendered, in large part, moot by the O'Fallon decision, previously cited.[7] The long and complicated effort of the Interstate Commerce Commission to evaluate the railroads was put to a legal test in the O'Fallon case when (as noted in Chapter XIII) the court refused to uphold the evaluation "formula" which the Commission had established.

In two later cases, *Federal Power Commission vs. Natural Gas Pipeline Company*[8] and the Hope case,[9] the court apparently embraced the credit standard as a measure of fair return and also served notice that, although the procedure of valuation was within the province of the regulatory commission, the courts would not hesitate to intervene in the situation if necessary, i.e., if there was lack of due process or danger of confiscation.

As Pegrum points out,

The clear conclusion to be drawn from the controversy over reasonable rates is that price fixing is an extremely complex problem involving difficult economic and constitutional issues.[10]

Let us now turn to the economic and administrative aspects of the problem, keeping in mind the previous warning that these issues are interrelated.

Economic and Administrative Aspects of the Doctrine

It is essential at this point to distinguish between the rate level and individual rates. The rate level determines the revenue which the carrier will earn by the sale of its services; thus, it is the aggregate

---

[7] A number of these technical problems are discussed in the definitive work, James C. Bonbright, *The Valuation of Property* (New York: McGraw-Hill Book Co., 1937).

[8] 315 U. S. 575 (1942).

[9] Federal Power Commission vs. Hope Natural Gas Co., 321 U. S. 591 (1944).

[10] Dudley F. Pegrum, *Public Regulation of Business* (Homewood, Ill.: Richard D. Irwin, Inc., 1959), p. 256.

of individual rates. The rate level should be high enough to compensate the carrier for its services and provide funds for other purposes, most importantly the formation or attraction of capital or credit. Historically, the railroad industry in its efforts to raise capital has been forced to rely heavily on sale of bonds rather than common stocks. Investors, fearing that earnings would not be high, were willing, however, to accept bonds which were secure or at least more secure than common stocks. The result of this situation has been (among other things) that the railroads increased their already high fixed costs by adding the need to pay interest on long term debt.

Before 1920, the concept of a rate level which could be adjusted by raising or lowering freight rates was realistic. At this time, virtually all intercity traffic moved by rail, and the demand for rail traffic was inelastic in the sense that there were no close substitutes for it. The railroad industry was generally in sound condition, and no serious problems were foreseen in the immediate future.

In the capitalistic economy, investors must provide funds for capital improvements, and they are attracted or discouraged by the prospect of earnings. In order to take advantage of new technology and increase plant efficiency, the carrier must have funds available; and, whether these funds come from earnings, the sale of securities or from borrowing directly from financial institutions, the earning prospects must be favorable or, in short, the credit of the firm must be adequate.

No specific time period is relevant. An industry may operate for many years without any need for capital beyond the normal replacement of plant and equipment. However, due to a technological breakthrough or a long period of low maintenance, capital requirements may be extraordinary at some other time. In the rail industry, for example, the "diesel revolution" from 1945-55 required vast amounts of capital. Both earnings and the need for capital are subject to wide variation.

Capital for expansion or technological change must come from two sources: (1) funds which are available from current earnings or which have been set aside in past periods by the organization and (2) borrowing from others by sale of securities or loans secured in some fashion by a claim upon the carrier property. In either case, the firm must compete for funds in the market with other firms and industries seeking capital.[11]

Publicly controlled enterprises must, like other industries, be able

---

[11] A third source not included here would be public funds, a means generally avoided by railroads, except in a period of great stress as in 1932-35.

to secure capital at reasonable or realistic rates. Although the publicly regulated industry has a measure of security to offer the investor, this is more nearly true of those industries which enjoy a franchise which makes them artificial monopolies, e.g., light and power companies.

The problem of capital attraction is especially serious in an industry such as the railroads where growth is not likely. The investor may be attracted to an investment where earnings are regulated, if security is high and if there are attractive prospects of growth. This is true, for example, of the light and power companies which have encountered little difficulty in attracting capital due chiefly to the rapidly increasing demand for the product which overcomes the investors' qualms about regulated earnings.

Moody's Manual indicates the cost of railroad capital in the mid-1950's, when a high level of capital formation was underway, was 4.08 per cent for railroads and 3.35 per cent for utilities in general.[12]

In the competitive situation which existed in the mid-1930's, the rate of return was subject to pressure from two directions, since the railroads found that not only was the motor carrier industry attracting much traffic, but, in order to meet this competition, it was often necessary to make capital expenditures. There were some competitive moves which could be made without capital expenditure, but many, if not most, of such actions required new capital. In short, capital was needed at the very time at which it was unavailable.

Under ideal circumstances, the carrier (a railroad) should be able to meet its regular expenses, wages, fuel, etc., pay interest or dividends on its securities, maintain the property in satisfactory condition and set aside emergency funds, all from earnings in transportation service.[13] If the carrier fails to meet these goals, various courses are open to it. It may reduce expenditures in some areas such as maintenance, although this is only a temporary expedient since this work must be done in the future (often at more expense than would have been the case originally). If the carrier cannot meet its obligations, the alternative may be to put the firm into receivership and later reorganize the company and scale down the debt obligations of the firm to the point where they can be paid out of earnings.

As noted earlier, the reorganization process is not, in the operat-

---

[12] *Moody's Manual of Investments* (New York: Moody's Investors Service, 1953).

[13] Many carriers have income from other sources, such as sale or lease of lands, holdings in other companies, and other investments. These earnings, although very important to the carrier, do not enter into this situation.

ing sense, of any consequence. The company is financially and legally reborn, but it continues to use its plant to produce transportation service as before. In actual fact, a company which has gone through reorganization may be better off in the long run than one which has managed to struggle along under adverse conditions just short of outright collapse. A railroad often emerges from a long period of receivership in a much stronger financial position than it had before. Although, as noted earlier, the junior securities holders may be "washed out," the ability of the firm to attract capital may be very little diminished. This is especially true of the credit necessary to buy equipment, since it will be remembered that the equipment title does not pass so long as the trust is in force, and lenders have little hesitation about lending funds for such a purpose. One of the most discouraging aspects of the failure to earn adequate revenue is that a vicious circle is created. If the firm cannot find funds to upgrade its plant and exploit new processes, the costs rise, service may deteriorate, and the prognosis becomes more discouraging than it was before.

It may be well at this point to make some observation about these matters. The railroad plant consists of many elements, such as roadway, line side facilities, buildings and rolling stock. The standards of maintenance and replacement of these items is subject to rather wide variation and depends, in large part, on the financial condition of the company. For example, the roadway and rolling stock might be kept in the best of condition by a policy of intensive maintenance, a clearly desirable goal. On the other hand, the maintenance work may be reduced in scope, and it may be some time before any adverse effect makes itself known in terms of inefficient operations. There is, thus, a strong temptation to reduce maintenance in times of financial stress. However, prolonged failure to perform this service will ultimately become obvious, and some work must be undertaken if the plant is to be used in the future.

The degree of flexibility in rail plant is very substantial and, in some ways, deceptive. During World War II, for example, the tremendous increase in traffic was accommodated with very little increase in plant. While this policy has some merit, the reactivation of retired equipment does not make for efficient operations. It seems very likely that the use of passenger equipment of antique vintage damaged the public image of rail travel and led to decline of traffic in the postwar years.

However, the most serious flaw is the fact that lack of technological progress obscures the need for capital improvements. The basic design of railroad rolling stock, freight cars in particular, did not change for many years. The railroads, thus, found it possible to operate by replacing worn-out equipment with new equipment or rebuilt cars of the same design. The net units in service declined during the 1930's, due in part to larger cars replacing smaller cars but also in response to the reduced demand of those years.[14]

Thus, at the end of World War II, the rail carriers found themselves with much obsolete equipment of antiquated design. Unfortunately, also, the railroad plant is so vast and the parts so interdependent that modest capital expenditures were of little significance, taken in themselves. That is to say, new locomotives were of little use if the more efficient line haul operations are nullified by delay in yards and terminals which had long since become inadequate.

THE RATE LEVEL, 1920-1940

It was pointed out in an earlier chapter that the Act of 1920 was almost entirely undermined by the economic changes taking place soon after its passage. From 1920 until the Emergency Act of 1933, the significance of the rate level as a regulatory tool was becoming highly questionable. In essence, the failure of the fair return concept was that it is oriented around need and not based on market conditions.

World War I, in which the railroads were under federal operation for some time, was followed by short but intensive financial problems for the railroads. In addition to the need to refurbish plant, labor relations were becoming serious and labor costs, as well as others, increased. Fortunately, these problems were eased by the general prosperity of the late 1920's. Although there was no general awareness of the fact, the rise of competition was near at hand and had become a factor by 1930.

The original Section 15a directed the Commission to:
initiate, modify, establish or adjust . . . rates so that carriers as a whole (or as a whole in each of such rate groups or territories as the Commission may from time to time designate) will, under honest, efficient and economical management and reasonable expenditures for maintenance of way, structures, and equipment,

---

[14] From the mid-1920's to 1960, average freight cars in use fell from 2.3 million to 1.6 million, while capacity rose from 45.9 tons to 55.5 tons. Passenger cars in use fell from 53,216 to 25,800 in the same years. Locomotives were reduced from 59,553 to 29,080 in these years, although average tractive effort increased from 49,000 pounds to 60,000 pounds. *Yearbook of Railroad Information, op. cit.,* pp. 10-15.

earn an aggregate annual net railway operating income equal, as nearly as may be, to a fair return upon the aggregate value of the railway property of such carriers held for and used in the service of transportation.

After the deterioration in economic conditions, the revised Section 15a was enacted in 1933. Under this new provision, the Commission was ordered to give consideration as to the reasonableness of the rate level to the following factors:

to the effect of rates on the movement of traffic; to the need, in the public interest, of adequate and efficient railway transportation service at the lowest cost consistent with the furnishing of such service; and to the need for revenues sufficient to enable the carriers, under honest, economical, and efficient management, to provide such service.

It is of interest to note that return on fair value is not mentioned in the revised version.

As Locklin points out, one of the reasons for this omission was the practical difficulty of calculating the fair value and fair return.[15] There are other reasons which seem to boil down to the simple and obvious fact that the carriers were caught up in the general economic crisis of those years, and revenue needs were only one element in their relationship with other segments of the economy. The serious technical problems in attempting to evaluate the property of rail carriers, combined with the O'Fallon case previously cited, made valuation largely a dead issue, insofar as its specific objective was concerned. As Fair and Williams point out, valuation did not succeed because it was not realistic in view of the circumstances prevailing.[16] The significant factor was the fact that, unlike certain public utilities, the railroads were not, after 1930, in a franchised monopoly position. Also, and this factor covers a broad area, the vast scope and complexity of the task was not apparent. Many of the proponents of the valuation act were apparently of the opinion that the process of evaluation was a simple task which would be rapidly completed. While the valuation process failed in the technical sense, the principle of fair return on fair value was and continues to be an important regulatory factor, and the concept of a rate level sufficiently high to provide for the carrier welfare was the foundation on which most rate procedures were based for many years. As wages and prices of materials rose following

---

[15] Locklin, *op. cit.*, p. 324.
[16] Fair and Williams, *op. cit.*, p. 570.

World War I, "across-the-board" increases in rates became common. These increases were designed to bolster the rate of return of the carriers as a group. It had long since been recognized that certain well managed or well located carriers would make a higher rate of return than others, which, because of adverse circumstances, could not reach the fair and reasonable rate at all. Thus, the well-off carriers profited more under across-the-board increases than their more unfortunate fellows.

PRESENT STATUS OF THE FAIR VALUE-FAIR RETURN CONCEPT

Figure 17-1 illustrates, in a general way, the various elements of the rate level. It can be seen that the rate level depends upon many factors, which are in turn related to other factors, many of which, if not most, are beyond the control of either carrier management or regulatory policy. For example, item 5, general economic outlook, is a macro-economic factor. If there is a general decline in the level of economic activity, all carriers would lose traffic, some more than others. In 1930-1932, motor carriers gained traffic due to the move toward small shipments. There is some question that such an effect would again take place.

In other cases, the terms have very little specific meaning and are almost impossible to define in any generalized fashion. For example, "sound management" is a very subjective term. It seems likely that evidence of fraud, conversion of funds, collusion to destroy the firm, and similar actions would be clearly classified as unsound management. However, an honest and hard-working management, dull and lacking in foresight, would probably be classed as sound in this context. Also, it was noted earlier that the route and points served may be so unproductive of traffic that even the most adroit management could not deal satisfactorily with them.

The rate of return for railroads after the depressed situation of the 1930's never rose above 6 per cent, except in 1942 and 1943, and this hard economic fact did grave damage to the concept. However, fair return on fair value is still very much alive as a rule of thumb. The fear that railroads would earn excessive profits has been replaced by a fear that the industry, as a whole, would not have adequate earnings due to loss of traffic and increased material and labor costs. The fact that in three years after 1930 the return fell to less than 1 per cent

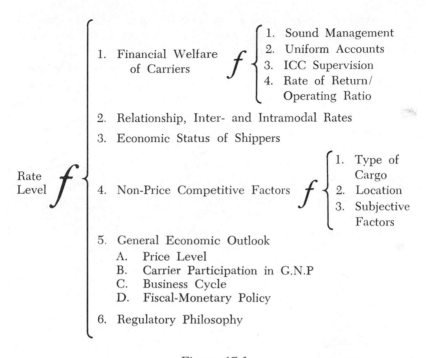

Figure 17-1

CARRIER RATE LEVEL, DETERMINING FACTORS

demonstrated the futility of merely allowing the carriers higher rates in order to maintain a sound system. Except for its policy of allowing rate increases to offset increasing costs, the Commission is powerless to change the situation, since the Commission has no power over the demand for rail service, except in the exercise of its power over entry of and rates changed by other carriers, motor carriers in particular. As traffic, both freight and passenger, has been drifting to other modes, rail traffic has declined at a rapid rate, and, although the Commission was fairly generous in allowing increases, rising costs and wages (other carriers were also increasing rates) drove net income down from the mid-1950's on until, in 1961, the figure reached $382 million. (It was $903 million in 1952. In 1961, the return had fallen to 1.97.)[17]

---

[17] Association of American Railroads, *A Review of Railroad Operations* (Washington: 1961).

A word of caution is in order at this point. The student must recall that the rail carriers were engaged in substantial capital formation during the immediate post World War II era. Much was done to modernize plant and equipment; and, as a consequence, the efficiency of the plant was greatly increased, despite the fact that a considerable reduction was made in holdings of real property and obsolete rolling stock. The net effect was to increase total investment in plant from roughly $29 billion in 1945 to approximately $36 billion in 1960.[18]

Other matters would indicate that the rail carriers may be in less stringent circumstances than the return would indicate viewed in isolation. It must be kept in mind that rate of return may be low in any given case because of more expensive and efficient equipment. Perhaps a simple example would make this clear. Suppose an individual purchases a truck for commercial hauling, and the truck cost $10,000. If he depreciates the truck at the rate of $1,000 per year, the vehicle would be worth $5,000 at the end of the fifth year of operation. If he makes $5,000 in the first year, his return on investment is 50 per cent. Even if his business should decline and in the fifth year he makes only $3,000, the truck now being worth $5,000, his rate of return is higher and will be higher still when the tenth year has passed. If after the tenth year he should buy a new vehicle for $10,000 to replace the original, the rate of return (assuming no increase in business) would fall to a new low, although the new vehicle might be much more efficient and enable him to attract more business.

It seems clear that the purchase of new and upgraded equipment is bound to have an adverse effect upon the rate of return per se in the immediate future. It is equally clear that the firm makes these expenditures in order to enhance its future earnings position and, in a sense, is taking a calculated risk that its market position will improve or at least remain stable. If these conditions do not materialize for one reason or another, the firm is in serious trouble. From 1945 to 1955, the railroads made large capital expenditures for upgrading the plant. Diesel locomotives, new yard facilities, and other improvements were undertaken, and, so long as traffic levels remained high, the railroads were in satisfactory condition. After 1957, when traffic declined, the situation deteriorated. However, it seems more than likely that the improvements in plant were instrumental in preventing an even more serious decline in the face of rising costs and falling traffic.

---

[18] *Yearbook of Railroad Information,* 1961 ed., *op. cit.,* p. 23.

RAILROAD FINANCE AND THE RATE LEVEL

The income of a railroad (excluding non-operating income) comes from two main sources: (1) passenger traffic and (2) freight traffic (including mail, express, etc.); of these two sources, the latter is far more important. With very few exceptions, revenue from freight transportation amounts to more than three-fourths of the total. As passenger service declines, the total traffic consists more and more of freight revenues, and, in recent years, freight revenue has accounted for an increasing portion of the total. See Table 17-2.

TABLE 17-2

RAIL FREIGHT AND PASSENGER REVENUES, SELECTED YEARS
(CLASS I RAILROADS)

Year	Freight Revenue	Passenger Revenue
1921	$3,924,120,000	$1,153,792,000
1931	3,254,668,000	551,047,000
1941	4,447,568,000	514,687,000
1951	8,634,101,000	900,310,000
1959	8,312,181,000	651,168,000
1960	8,025,422,955	640,268,065
1961	7,739,044,138	624,688,484
1962	7,990,790,612	619,057,156

Source: Association of American Railroads, *Railroad Transportation, A Statistical Record* (Washington: 1960); and Association of Southeastern Railroads, *Railroad Information* (1963).

In 1930, the revenue per ton mile amounted to 1.10 cents, declined to .75 cents in 1940, rose during the war years and reached a peak in 1955 at about 1.49 cents, falling to 1.37 cents in 1961.[19] Rail traffic reached a post war peak in 1956 and has declined since that time. As was pointed out earlier, the rail industry has not been able to increase its share of traffic relative to the growth of the gross national product. Unfortunately, also, much of the traffic lost to other modes was the most lucrative.

Thus, the income of the industry has been subject to rather wide

---

[19] *A Review of Railroad Operations, op. cit.,* p. 14.

variations, especially after 1930 when available traffic was reduced both in absolute amount and relative quantities under the influence of the depression and the rise of competition.

The major expenditures of rail carriers are shown in Table 17-3. As the table indicates, wages represent roughly half of the total outlay, followed by materials and supplies. The third highest category, taxes, represents some 10 per cent of the total. The level of all these items has increased greatly since World War II.

TABLE 17-3

MAJOR OPERATING EXPENDITURES, U. S. CLASS I RAILROADS
SELECTED YEARS (CENTS PER DOLLAR OF GROSS REVENUE)

Year	Total Operating Revenues	Labor (Salaries and Wages)	Fuel and Power Locomotives	Other Material and Supplies and Miscellaneous	Total Expenses and Taxes	Net Railway Operating Income
1922	100.0	44.4	9.5	20.3	86.3	13.7
1924	100.0	44.3	7.5	18.7	83.6	16.4
1926	100.0	42.6	6.5	18.5	81.0	19.0
1928	100.0	43.0	6.0	17.6	80.8	19.2
1930	100.0	44.8	5.5	17.3	83.5	16.5
1932	100.0	45.9	5.7	15.9	89.6	10.4
1934	100.0	44.1	6.1	15.5	85.9	14.1
1936	100.0	42.9	6.2	16.2	83.5	16.5
1938	100.0	46.5	6.7	15.9	89.5	10.5
1940	100.0	43.2	6.1	16.3	84.1	15.9
1942	100.0	37.1	5.4	13.3	80.1	19.9
1944	100.0	38.7	6.0	14.6	88.3	11.7
1946	100.0	52.1	7.1	16.8	91.9	8.1
1948	100.0	46.9	7.9	15.6	89.6	10.4
1950	100.0	46.2	5.9	15.2	89.0	11.0
1952	100.0	47.9	4.9	16.1	89.8	10.2
1954	100.0	49.4	4.5	16.4	90.7	9.3
1956	100.0	47.9	4.2	16.0	89.9	10.1
1958	100.0	49.3	3.8	15.4	92.0	8.0

Source: Association of American Railroads, *Railroad Transportation, A Statistical Record, 1921-1959,* and *A Review of Railroad Operations in 1961* (Washington), p. 15.

Using 1947-1949 as a base, the Association of American Railroads estimates that total material prices have risen 145 per cent up to

1962. To offset these effects, the railroads have proceeded on several fronts. Non-essential expenditures have been reduced; new labor-saving devices have enabled the carriers to reduce total employment. However, increases in wages and rigid enforcement of work rules have prevented any significant reduction in total wage costs. From 1950 to 1960, employees decreased from 1.2 million to 780,000. During this same period, total payroll actually rose slightly from 4.6 million to 4.8 million. Railroads also made valiant efforts to reduce costs through various improvements in equipment and in these efforts have met with some success, although not as much as was hoped for. In this instance, we again encounter a two-edged effect. New equipment, for example, a diesel locomotive, must be intensively utilized in order to bear the costs. A steam locomotive, built new in 1948 and providing 3,000 horsepower, would have cost roughly $270,000; and, while this represented a large price increase over 1936-1941 prices (112 per cent), equal horsepower in diesel locomotive form would have cost almost $400,000.[20] Also, one must recall that many steam locomotives, if not most, were fully "written off" in the accounting sense, and no strong incentive existed to maximize their utilization. Few diesels were fully paid for, and intensive utilization was thus a major item. Rail management had few qualms about putting steam locomotives in storage, but it was unthinkable to follow such a practice with diesels. The same analysis relates, in somewhat lesser degree, to the other equipment.

As Table 17-4 indicates, the various standard indicators of efficient operation have improved consistently since 1952. Also, although these efforts are still young, the railroads have become more aggressive in seeking traffic and in analyzing the market for their services. It cannot be denied that the railroads have used a high degree of initiative in attempting to raise the rate level. These efforts may bear fruit in the freight traffic area, but a realistic appraisal of the passenger situation is not encouraging. While many railroads pay lip service to passenger service, it seems likely that few of them really are seriously interested in such traffic. Unfortunately, the elimination of passenger trains has an adverse cumulative effect in that connections must be made for long distance travel.

In addition to these internal efforts, they have had recourse to both general and selective rate increases, and the Commission has been reasonably generous in permitting such increases, totaling 107.7 per cent for the nation as a whole between 1946 and 1958. Two major

---

[20] All data from ICC Statement No. 5025, *op. cit.*

TABLE 17-4

INDICATORS OF RAIL OPERATING EFFICIENCY, 1952-1961

Year	Net Ton-Miles Per Loaded Car-Mile	Car-Miles Per Freight Train-Mile	Freight-Train Miles Per Train-Hour	Gross Ton-Miles Per Freight Train-Hour
1952	32.5	61.6	17.6	49,113
1953	32.1	63.2	18.2	51,750
1954	31.4	65.0	18.7	53,897
1955	32.1	66.2	18.6	55,770
1956	33.0	67.2	18.6	57,071
1957	33.4	69.3	18.8	59,218
1958	33.0	70.7	19.2	60,807
1959	33.3	69.6	19.5	61,924
1960	34.0	70.2	19.5	63,096
1961	34.7	71.0	19.9	65,621

Source: Association of American Railroads, *A Review of Railroad Operation in 1961* (Washington), p. 28.

items have prevented these actions from having the desired effect. In the first place, a grant of a rate increase by the regulatory authority does not mean that revenue will automatically increase. It is true, of course, that the other modes were also increasing rates so that traffic did not flee from the rails solely because of rate increases. The second factor was the fact that the rate changing process was very slow. From 1945 to 1960, the prices of rail supplies and costs of labor rose rapidly. Railroads found that the time elapsed between a rate request and the permission to publish such rates often was very long, sometimes a full year. Meanwhile, prices were still rising.

It seems clear from the above that the rail carriers were caught in a four-way squeeze. (1) Despite their efforts, increasing costs and wages largely nullified their hopes to hold the line of expenses. (2) Competing air and motor carriers were active in their quest for traffic. (3) The slow and time-consuming process of Commission procedure had the effect of forcing the railroads to file a series of requests in order to remain at parity. (4) Although less significant than the other three, the carriers were unable to eliminate or reduce marginal service. Many branch lines were not even earning "out-of-pocket" costs and would have been eliminated by prudent management, if it had been legally possible to do so. Neither the Commission nor the railroads were able to cope with this problem, since the decision was often in the hands of state regulatory bodies. There was no economic reason for these continued operations, but social and political factors often made abandonment impossible in some cases.

Measuring the economic welfare of the railroads is a most complex problem. It must be noted at the outset that there are differences of great magnitude within the industry. In general, eastern railroads are less prosperous than western roads.[21] Many reasons, such as length of haul, industrial shifts, and other factors, have contributed to this situation. On the other hand, there are individual railroads in all sections of the country which are far above the average in earnings. In many cases this is due to some specific factor such as location or traffic carried, or it may, in many instances, be due to extraordinary management.

In addition to those discussed above, several factors appear to be clearly visible as major contributors to the financial problems. (1) Serious overcapacity. In the East, in particular, there is every likelihood that the railroad network is too dense and that there is overcapacity in almost every element of the plant. Real property is held in great excess of the need, and the situation is aggravated by taxes imposed on these vast holdings. (2) Rigid and antiquated work rules and customs. These rules have led to "featherbedding" on the part of workers and to a lack of imagination on the part of management. (3) Vigorous and growing competition from other carriers and a failure to meet or even recognize this competition until it had reached major proportions.

Thus, there is a paradox of an industry with tremendous physical plant and providing the major share of intercity transportation faced with, in general, an inadequate and declining level of revenue.

In the years immediately following World War II, traffic levels were high enough to provide all the modes with a satisfactory level of traffic. Also, in this period of general inflation, rate increases were both necessary and practicable. All carriers were making rate increases, generally led by the railroads. This situation prevailed from the end of World War II through the Korean War and up until approximately 1956-57, at which time competition became more intense.

Thus, further increase in rates in order to increase revenue became impracticable and served only to divert rail traffic to other modes. Although the other modes had increased rates also, they had been careful to maintain the existing differentials, and much traffic began

---

[21] *Eastern Railroad Problems*, Eastern Railroad Presidents' Conference, Jersey City, 1961.

to move by private carriage, a fact which was alarming to all the for-hire modes.

It then became clear and was stressed by the Commission that the general rate level was no longer useful as a criterion for increasing revenues and that an effort must be made to increase revenue by selective and carefully chosen rate adjustments and improvements in service.

We must wait and see if traffic moving by rail will increase. Thus, it would appear that railroads, as a whole, hope that by these cost reducing innovations they can move the present volume of traffic at profitable rates.

FAIR RETURN ON FAIR VALUE IN REGARD TO OTHER CARRIERS

Fortunately, the concept of fair return on fair value has had little relationship to other carriers, except indirectly. The reason for this becomes clear when it is recalled that other carriers have had, until recent years, little investment in plant aside from vehicles.

A "fair" return on the value of motor carrier property, for example, might mean a return which was totally inadequate for meeting the general standards mentioned above. On the other hand, a motor carrier, having modest capital investment, may have great earning power, and the rate of return may be extremely large. This is especially true of specialized carriers. For example, a small firm, operating half a dozen vehicles valued at $70,000, may, due to the nature of its operation, have no investment in terminals or other real property. If such a carrier enjoyed an income of only $7,000 per year, the return on investment would be 10 per cent.

The Interstate Commerce Commission has not attempted to apply the principle of fair return on fair value to the general level of rates for motor carriers, using in its place, the operating ratio.[22] In addition to the low investment, the competitive nature of the motor carriers would preclude the use of the fair value–fair return standard.

Much the same problem has been faced by the Civil Aeronautics Board in its dealings with airline rates. The Board has broken away from the traditional fair return on fair value approach, because of the elements of competition and risk, but no clear course of action is yet visible.[23]

---

[22] See Middle West General Increases, 48 M.C.C. 541, 552-53 (1948).

[23] See *General Passenger Fare Investigation*, Civil Aeronautics Board, Docket No. 8008, Order No. E-10279, May 10, 1956.

OPERATING RATIO AS A MEASURE OF ECONOMIC WELFARE

A frequently encountered financial rule of thumb is the operating ratio, i.e., the ratio of income to operating expenses. If, for example, the carrier expends 75 per cent of its operating income on operating costs, the operating ratio would be 75 per cent. Both motor and air carriers urge reliance upon operating ratios as a measure of their economic welfare.

The operating ratio must be interpreted with care, since it may be deceptive. Generally, a low operating ratio means that the carrier is operating in an efficient manner and is an indication of sound management. Rail operating ratios generally fall in the area of 75 to 85 per cent (see Table 17-5). Motor carrier operating ratios are higher, frequently above 90 per cent.

TABLE 17-5

RAILROAD OPERATING RATIOS, SELECTED YEARS, 1921-1959

Year	Total	Year	Total
1921	82.71	1941	68.53
1923	77.83	1943	62.48
1925	74.10	1945	79.21
1927	74.54	1947	78.27
1929	71.76	1949	80.32
1931	76.97	1951	77.39
1933	72.66	1953	76.29
1935	75.11	1955	75.66
1937	74.87	1957	78.42
1939	73.05	1959	78.42

Source: *Yearbook of Railroad Information, op. cit.*

It will be noted in Table 17-5 that operating ratios have remained steady during the decade 1950-60. This reflects the fact that, although costs have risen during the decade, rates have also increased. It also indicates that major operating economies have been achieved by the railroads but does not indicate the wisdom of future soundness of these policies.

In order to properly understand the operating ratios, several factors must be taken into account. A low ratio may mean that

TABLE 17-6

CLASS I MOTOR CARRIERS,
OPERATING RATIOS, SELECTED YEARS

Year	Total
1946	96.4
1950	93.0
1953	96.1
1956	96.5
1959	95.8

Source: National Transportation Policy, *op. cit.*, p. 77.

operations have been carried on without proper provision for the future; or, in other words, the management may have created problems for themselves or for their successors by reduced maintenance.

It is always a major problem for carrier management (or any other management) to draw the line between necessary services and those which are superfluous. There is or may be a time lag between the reduction in expenditures and the consequences of those policies. Thus, management may follow a policy which is, on the surface, prudent and economical, only to bring about a serious crisis at some future date, knowing that this will be a problem to someone else.

For motor carriers, the operating ratio is almost completely undependable as a measure of financial status. In particular, a small carrier may have owner-officers of the company who draw large salaries which are, of course, operating expenses. It thus appears to the casual observer that the "firm" is in financial straits, which, in a technical sense, is true. However, the officers and owners of the firm are well compensated.

One sometimes encounters operating ratios in the motor carrier industry which exceed 100 per cent. This means, clearly, that the operating revenues have failed to cover the expenses. In the motor carrier and in the other modes, valuation has never been attempted, and reliance is placed upon the national transportation policy with results as discussed in Chapter XX.

Summary

As this chapter has brought out, the concept of "fair return on fair value" has been substantially eliminated as a working concept in the regulatory framework. The complexity of the procedure and the drastic change in the competitive situation after 1930 were the causes of this fact. However, the broad concept of fair return on fair value is still very much alive and stands as a bulwark against confiscatory rates.

Also, it should be clear that the financial welfare and policies of the carriers cannot be measured by any single or simple standard. The rate of return, the operating ratio, the ability of the firm to attract capital are all of importance, and no one standard can be used in isolation. In a competitive world, prudent management cannot become overly concerned with any one indicator but must consider the overall welfare of the industry, taking the longest possible view, and, insofar as possible, must forecast future events.

CHAPTER XVIII

Discrimination and Its Control

It was pointed out in Chapter X that a major factor in the public demand for rail regulation was the widespread practice of various forms of discrimination in pricing or in the standards of service provided. It must be made clear at the outset that discrimination per se is not in any way reprehensible and is indeed a frequently encountered practice in our daily affairs. Our economic folkways have long accepted the fact that prices of goods and services vary among groups or places, and few questions arise.

However, in the public utility regulatory framework, such practices are not looked upon with favor. In general, the basic question revolves around what can be referred to as unjustified discrimination, or discrimination which does not have a firm foundation based on the cost of providing the service to the user in question.

Discrimination may occur in various forms: Personal discrimination, unequal treatment of persons or firms, commodity discrimination which consists of unjustified discrimination between or among various commodities, and discrimination of a geographic nature. Here, again, one must, at the outset, stress the fact that the basis of legal control must rest on "unjustified" discrimination.

Clearly, the incentive for such practices was based on the desire to exploit any market advantages which existed and to protect the carrier from competition from others at points where service over-lapped.

THE THEORY OF PRICE DISCRIMINATION

The possibility of price discrimination exists because of imper-fections in the market. As Joan Robinson puts it,

> . . . under conditions of perfect competition price discrimination could not exist even if the market could be easily divided into separate parts. In each section of the market, the demand would be perfectly elastic and every seller would prefer to sell his whole output in that section of the market in which he could obtain the highest price. The attempt to do so would, of course, drive the price down to the competitive level, and there would be only one price throughout the whole market.[1]

Since the conditions described by Robinson do not exist, i.e., the market for transportation services is not perfect, there is ample opportunity and incentive for price discrimination.

The buyer of transportation service is often in a position where his alternatives are few or entirely absent. The producer of wheat in Kansas cannot ship coal if he finds that coal is less expensive to trans-port, nor can the traveler destined to Boston fly to Chicago because the rate is lower. The buyer does, however, have some degree of choice, insofar as he can alter the form or choose between various market areas for his product.

The seller of the service, to the extent that he can recognize and exploit the differences in demand elasticities, will undertake to do so, insofar as the politico-economic framework will allow.

A further factor which will influence the seller in his ability and desire to engage in price discrimination will be the costs involved. If a commodity or service can be produced at a given cost and sold in different markets at differing prices, then there is a clear advantage in so doing.

A textbook, for example, might be produced at a cost of $6 per unit and sold in college bookstores at $7.50 and in commercial book-stores at $8.25. The seller would naturally wish to sell as many copies in the commercial store as possible. These two markets are

---

[1] Joan Robinson, *The Economics of Imperfect Competition* (London: The Macmillan Co., 1948), p. 179 and Chapter XVI for a discussion of the moral aspects and social implications of discrimination.

insulated from one another to a degree; and, if a group of students began to buy books and sell them to commercial store customers at a price of $7.75, the publisher's commercial market would break down. In other cases where the markets are entirely separated, arbitrage is not possible, e.g., the sale of medical services or electric power to householders.

There are probably few cases where there is perfect separation or where the costs of the items and ability to serve two markets are identical. However, a degree of price discrimination is possible in many markets. It may be feasible for a manufacturer, for example, to produce two lines of a product—for example, an appliance for household use. The same basic item may be sold, and the "brand name model" may differ from the standard or "economy model" by the addition of minor innovations, which cost very little. Here, again, the seller will "push" the brand name and attempt to maximize the price differential, even though the costs are almost the same.

Figure 18-1 illustrates a common situation where discrimination can arise through a kink in the demand curve. The demand curve D is bent or kinked in such a way as to give two distinct market situa-

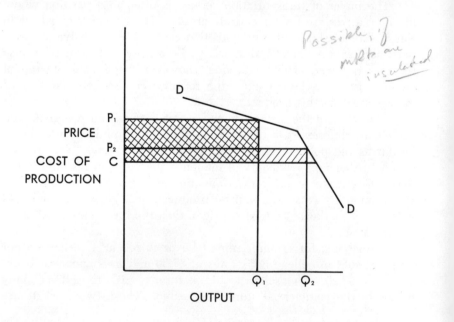

Price Cost of Production Output

Fig. 18-1

tions, although the cost of producing all units is equal. Two prices, P_1 and a lower price P_2, exist. So long as the markets remain insulated from each other, the two prices can be maintained.

If price P_1 were the sole price, amount Q_1 would be sold at that price; but, when by the shape of the demand curve price P_2 is charged, an additional amount can be produced and sold, thus increasing the profitable area shown by the lightly shaded portion.

The major cause of most types of discrimination is competition between sellers or, in the case at hand, competition between transportation firms. Further, the competition is concentrated on particular types of traffic which the carrier wishes to attract, and he is thus willing to make extraordinary concessions.

These concessions may take an infinite variety of forms such as favorable rates, rebates, false damage claims, free services or more complete service than is rendered to other non-favored shippers, and other price or non-price advantages. In short, the carrier is willing to enhance its bargaining power by granting unique advantages to a desirable customer.

The original approach may be made by the carrier or by the shipper who recognizes the fact that he is in a position of power and seeks to take advantage of the fact. The shipper may have some leverage because of the volume of his potential cargo or by virtue of the high rates applying to his produce; and, by a threat of diverting his traffic to other carriers or other modes, he forces cooperation from the carrier. A serious shortcoming is that the logical outcome of this practice is that the carriers put themselves in a worse position than they were in before.

In the first place, it is almost impossible to keep such arrangements secret; and, secondly, other carriers are in as good a position to make concessions as the one who made the first move. Thus, in short order, all shippers who can wield power will be anxious to climb on the gravy train, and the carriers will be outbidding each other for the traffic, to the point where each of them is extending favors beyond their original intent and financial capacity.

The various forms of discrimination commonly encountered in the transportation industry can be examined as follows:

PLACE OR GEOGRAPHIC DISCRIMINATION

This form of discrimination involved unjustified price differentials between cities or regions. Perhaps the most common form was that intended to deal with water competition. In Figure 18-2, the rate from A to B is much lower than the rate from A to C, even though the distance is only slightly greater. The objective here is clearly for the railroad to compete with water carriers, since A and B are both located on the river, whereas C is located at an inland point. In Figure 18-3 another form of the same type is seen. In this case, rail-

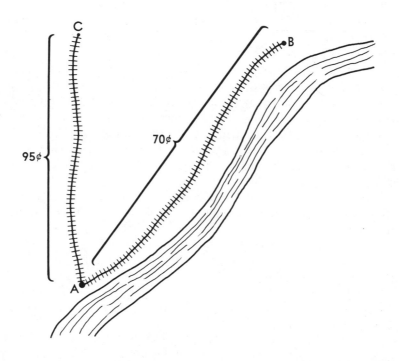

Fig. 18-2

Geographic Discrimination Due to Water Competition

roads X and Y compete for traffic to and from A and B. However, railroad X has a monopoly on traffic to and from C and may reduce rates between A and B at the expense of C.

Not all instances of place or geographic discrimination were instituted by the carriers. In many cases shipper pressure was a factor. Thus, if in the example a group of shippers were facing serious threats from competing shippers in C (for traffic to B), they might bring pressure to bear upon the carriers in order to put C at a disadvantage.[2]

------

[2] Carriers encounter a great deal of pressure from Chambers of Commerce and regional shipper groups who feel that they are at a disadvantage in attempting

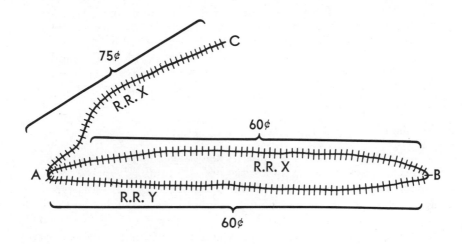

Fig. 18-3

Geographic Discrimination Due to Monopoly Position

Geographic discrimination is often very complex and subject to great controversy, involving political and regional interests. One of the most pressing questions which arises is the limit of carrier responsibility. If a given point is poorly located by reason of geography, the carrier cannot be expected to redress these disadvantages by leaning in the opposite direction.

Nor can a carrier undertake to resolve discrimination over which it has no control. It would not be either just or practicable to deprive a location of its natural advantages in order to overcome a naturally poor location of another community. Carriers are often anxious or are under pressure to establish rates which will have the effect of "equalizing" or neutralizing the advantages of one point, thus giving a break to the less fortunate areas.

In one famous case, the carrier attempted to encourage traffic in some points and thus kept rates on lumber from Eau Claire, Wisconsin (a city which had some inherent advantages) somewhat higher than

to establish a new form of economic activity at that point or to retain an advantage which is being threatened by growth in another area.

the rates from other points. This action was rejected by the Commission's saying, in part:

> That rates should be fixed in inverse proportion to the natural advantages of competing towns, with the view of equalizing 'commercial conditions,' as they are sometimes described, is a proposition unsupported by law and quite at variance with every consideration of justice. Each community is entitled to the benefits arising from its location and natural conditions, and any exaction of charges unreasonable in themselves or relatively unjust, by which those benefits are neutralized or impaired, contravenes alike the provisions and the policy of the statute.[3]

In other cases, the Commission made clear its position in refusing to adjust rates in order to overcome a natural advantage and has reinforced this attitude on other occasions.[4] Cases of this type are awkward, since every community is anxious to maximize any advantage it can possibly put forth as regards its economic well being. Especially in the years since World War II, when industrial expansion and dispersion have moved rapidly, many communities have been able to challenge the traditional leaders in an industry.

Serious question arises also as to what constitutes a natural advantage after various conditions have changed. Before World War II, Pittsburgh and the Chicago-Gary area might have been said to have a natural advantage which extended even to the West Coast steel markets. The rise of steel producing facilities in Utah and California makes this advantage somewhat questionable. An area which has had in the past an advantage and sees this advantage being eroded by various factors will be most anxious to avoid further loss due to freight rate discrimination, or what it chooses to view as discrimination.

There are frequent cases where a rail carrier is involved in a situation which is discriminatory, but cannot by itself remedy the situation. In Figure 18-4 this situation is illustrated. In Figure 18-4, railroads M and N both serve points A and B, but points D and C are served by N and M, respectively. Thus, if D and C are serving market area A, also served by B, the carriers can, by their own actions, control the relationship between A and B. However, C and D are out-

---

[3] Eau Claire Board of Trade v. Chicago, Milwaukee & St. Paul R. R. Co., 4 ICC 65, 77 (1892).

[4] Port Arthur Board of Trade v. Abilene & Southern Ry. Co., 27 ICC 388, 402 (1913); Sheridan Chamber of Commerce v. Chicago, Burlington & Quincy R. R. Co., 28 ICC 250, 262 (1913); Florida Pulp & Paper Co. v. Alabama Great Southern R. Co., 266 ICC 331, 334 (1946).

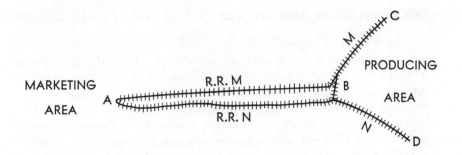

Fig. 18-4
Geographic Discrimination, Unilateral Control

side the control of one of the carriers acting alone. Under the so-called "Ashland Rule," the carrier is held responsible only for situations within its control. In this case, the Supreme Court said:

> The test of the discrimination is the ability of one of the carriers
> participating in two through routes from the two points of origin
> to the same point of destination to put an end to the discrimination
> by its own act.[5]

The types of geographic discrimination referred to above relate to Section 3 of the Interstate Commerce Act. In order for a Section 3 complaint to be valid, it must, in general, meet three conditions, viz.: (1) The localities involved in the alleged discrimination are in a competitive relationship, (2) actual injury has occurred as a result of the rate relationship complained of, and (3) the discriminatory relationship is inexplicable on grounds of differing conditions of transportation. Discrimination may be present, even if rates to two points are the same, since there may be differences which would dictate a lower rate for one point.

It can be seen that this is an involved matter. The determination as to the degree of competitive relationship existing between two points may be a formidable exercise. Also, the proof of injury may be very difficult to show. In some cases, the Commission has allowed consideration for potential injury, but, in most cases, proof is required. Another type of geographic discrimination occurs by violation of the Long and Short Haul Clause, Section 4. These cases are discussed below.

---

[5] Ashland Fire Brick Co. v. Southern Railway Co., 22 ICC 115, 120 (1911).

DISCRIMINATION AND THE LONG AND SHORT HAUL CLAUSE

As noted in Chapter X, the long and short haul problem was of early importance in the regulatory framework. The original enforcement of this clause was more cumbersome than was true of other provisions, with the possible exception of the rate provisions. The frequent violation of what appeared to be common sense economic principles, such as charging more for shipments to Spokane than to Seattle from Chicago although the distance is some three hundred miles less, was viewed with strong distaste. It will be remembered that the original act made it unlawful for railroads to:

> receive any greater compensation in the aggregate for the transportation of passengers or of like kind of property, *under substantially similar circumstances and conditions,* for a shorter than for a longer distance over the same line, in the same direction, the shorter being included within the longer distance.

In trying to provide some degree of flexibility by including the words in italics, the Congress opened the door to widespread legal evasion of the intent of the clause. A wide range of actions could be excused on grounds that the conditions prevailing were not similar. An obvious escape hatch was the element of competition, especially with non-regulated carriers and, in particular, water carriers. Since the Commission had no jurisdiction over these carriers, it was hardly in a position to force the rail carriers to ignore this competition. In the South, in particular, where such conditions were widespread, there were thousands of such rates which might be justified on competitive grounds.

This view was upheld by the courts (overruling the Commission) in the Alabama Midland Case in 1897, a development which, in the Commission's view, rendered the 4th section of no value.[6] The court held that competition from carriers subject to the Commission, as well as those not subject, was sufficient to justify carriers' departure from the clause without Commission approval. However, the Congress acted with uncommon speed and, in 1910, in the Mann-Elkins Act struck out the words "under substantially similar circumstances and conditions."

Although they now held the whip, the Commission proceeded slowly in order not to upset the rate structure, and many years passed before all the requests for relief could be judged.

Further amendment came in 1920 and in the Act of 1940. In 1920, the power of the Commission to grant relief was made subject

---

[6] Interstate Commerce Commission v. Alabama Midland Railway Co., 168 U. S. 144 (1897).

to these conditions: (1) that the reduced through rates covered by fourth section relief were reasonably compensatory, (2) that relief would not be granted to meet merely potential rather than actual water competition, and (3) that, when relief was granted to a circuitous route, higher charges would not be allowed at intermediate points on the circuitous line where distances are not greater than the through distance via the direct line.[7]

The third condition was not realistic, since many conditions might justify differentials, and it was repealed in 1940. The Act of 1940, bringing the water carriers under Commission regulation, made for a substantially different situation than had previously prevailed. Since water carriers were now under control, the Commission was somewhat more stringent about granting relief, although, as pointed out in an earlier chapter, water competition is still the major factor in the 4th section relief.

As is true of other forms of discrimination, the rise of competitive modes has somewhat reduced the importance of long and short haul problems.

PERSONAL DISCRIMINATION

This type of discrimination took several forms involving individuals and companies. As an example, the rather common practice of allowing lower rates or arranging for rebates (refunding part of the rate paid) for a large shipper as opposed to a small shipper under similar circumstances.

Again, in this case, the incentive often came from the shipper who was able to withhold significant amounts of traffic unless the carrier complied. Numerous and well known examples of this practice, e.g., the famous Standard Oil activities in the late nineteenth century,[8] have occurred in the past. Personal discrimination was bitterly resented by shippers for obvious reasons, particularly because it was difficult to detect and emphasized the existing advantage of the large and powerful firm.

For obvious reasons, both carrier and shipper wished to keep these arrangements secret. This intensified the dilemma of the unfavored shippers, since they had no way of knowing what, if any, agreements had been made between the other two parties. Once these

---

[7] 41 Stat. 480 c. 91, sec. 406 (1920).

[8] See the classic, Ida M. Tarbell, *The History of the Standard Oil Company* (New York: The Macmillan Co., 1933).

arrangements became common knowledge, the obvious result was pressure to be included in the group which carriers might or might not be willing to comply with.

It is not an easy task to draw a line between justifiable and unjustified discrimination in many cases. Thus, it is widely recognized that a difference between carload or truckload traffic and less than car or truckload traffic is permissible. The reader can quickly see that it would be a short and logical step to making a distinction between large producers shipping 100 carloads per week and a shipper originating only 10 carloads per week.[9]

There are also some complex moral judgments involved here, such as whether these arrangements are secret or open and well known. It seems likely that much of the early resentment was directed as much at the means of procedure as at the practice per se.

The number of opportunities for personal discrimination is almost without limit, since virtually every facet of the carrier-shipper relationship might be subject to some form of preferential treatment: Payment of rebates, false claims, undue allowance for use of shipper-owned facilities such as private cars, or terminal facilities.

The carrier might render superior service or inferior service in such a way as to be almost impossible to detect or correct. He may inform the shipper in advance of certain contemplated changes; and, prior to regulation, the "midnight" or "flying" tariff was a common form of discrimination. In these cases, the shipper in favor was given personal notice of contemplated changes in rates, or changes were made and withdrawn as soon as the shipper had taken advantage of them.

Large shippers were not the only ones to be given special treatment. Prudent rail management found it advisable to distribute free passes with a liberal hand among legislators, judges, newspaper men and others whose influence was deemed to be substantial.[10]

---

[9] In many countries, including Canada, "agreed charges," i.e., rates based on large quantities, are legal. Under this system, a shipper agrees to ship a minimum amount of material which is assured to the carrier. As a *quid pro quo*, the carrier agrees upon a special rate. These agreements run for indefinite periods of time. The major advantage to the carrier is the fact that the traffic in question is assured to it so long as the agreement is in force.

[10] A common form of this type of practice was the loan of private cars or interline handling of private cars belonging to highly placed industrial shippers. As Lucius Beebe points out in his entertaining book, *Mansions on Rails* (Oakland: Howell-North Press, 1960), p. 201, Palm Beach, Newport, and other popular watering places were crowded with these cars in season until the Commission began to impose stringent regulations. Following the downturn in 1929 and the more rigid ICC requirements, the private railroad car (as distinguished from the official business car) began to wane, and, in the early 1960's, only one was in operation.

False billing, overweight or misdescribed commodities, improper classification and other types of personal discrimination were widespread, and it seems likely that no enforcement system could eliminate all of these problems at all times.

Although the consequences of personal discrimination were not so widespread as those involving cities or regions as in the case of geographic discrimination, the public reaction was probably more marked than in cases of place discrimination. The analysis of the effects of place discrimination was complex and required the talents of the rate specialist and economic geographer, but the average man could see the practice and results of personal discrimination.

COMMODITY DISCRIMINATION

In this case, the focus was upon the commodity carried. Here, again, the line of just and unjust practice is hard to draw. In early years, railroads often carried products from their own lands or products in which they had an interest (for example, coal at very low or at no charge) and were thus able to drive other producers to the wall, since they did not operate their own transportation facilities.[11] However, in the usual meaning of the situation, the products of producers or manufacturers are discriminated against.

To be sure, the whole classification system is an exercise in discrimination. If two products were similar in nature, weight, volume, durability, value, etc., and yet were assigned substantially different rates, it is likely that unjust discrimination would exist. The student will recall that the balancing of the various factors was a delicate operation indeed; consequently, a rather high differential might well fall within the legal limits. As in the case of place discrimination, there are many competitive relationships which must be taken into account. Various products serve various purposes and are sold in competing markets. For example, it might be justified for a carrier to charge a higher rate on a more highly finished commodity than one only partly finished. Clay used for roofing tile might, with approval, be assigned a lower rate than clay to be used for fine pottery. Frequently, a change in rate structure among commodities will have serious and far-reaching effects in the industrial organization in force

---

[11] The commodities clause made this practice illegal. In cases where a railroad is wholly owned by another company, e.g., a mining company, the railroad charges the legal rate and bills the parent company. In these cases, the end result is the transfer of money from one pocket to another, but the legal formalities are observed.

at any given time. If a processing industry has grown up in a given area and rates should change so that the finished product might be shipped further than had previously been the case, then some painful dislocation might take place.

In one rather well known case, limestone being widely used in the District of Columbia in the federal building program in the early 1930's was sent from Indiana in rough form and was cut to order in the Washington, D. C. area. The same rate on uncut stone as on cut stone made possible to do the cutting at either origin or destination. Naturally, those who had an economic interest in doing the finishing in Washington protested this situation. Several elements of this case are worth consideration here, since it relates to the example of transportation of copper and copper ore cited in an earlier chapter. In this case, for example, it could be argued that the waste which would be left behind in cutting should not be transported to the terminal point, since this would be a needless expense. This factor would dictate processing in Indiana. On the other hand, it could be argued that the element of damage is greater if the finished stones are to be transported some six hundred or seven hundred miles to be used, and, thus, they should be finished in Washington. At any rate, the Commission did not agree that the disadvantage of the Washington processors should be removed by a rate adjustment.

> . . . it is our duty to remove that undue disadvantage and undue prejudice to complainants which is occasioned by freight rates, but we may not equalize any other advantages or disadvantages enjoyed or suffered by the parties. In order to remove the undue prejudice caused by the rate adjustment, and that adjustment only, the spread established between the rates on rough and dressed stone must be based upon their differences in transportation characteristics. Interveners are therefore correct in their contention that the relationship of the rates involved should not be based upon the amount of waste in dressing stone.[12]

In this case, then, such discrimination as existed against the Washington cutters was not considered to be undue or unjust.

The discrimination which is complained of must be real and specific, and the commodities must be truly competitive in nature. For example, meat to be used for dog food would not be considered as being competitive with meat to be used for human consumption, and there is no necessary relationship between the rates of the two products. In one often cited case, a differential on silica sand and

---

[12] O'Meara v. Baltimore & Ohio R. R. Co., 183 ICC 3, 15 (1932).

common sand was not disturbed, since they are not used for the same purpose.[13]

However, market considerations do not stand alone. Differences in costs of service or differences in value of the products may also justify a differential, as may the extent of carrier competition.[14]

These competitive relationships are of such complexity that they must be decided on an *ad hoc* basis. For example, aluminum, copper, and stainless steel may be highly competitive in some cases and not in any way competitive in others. Two products may be similar in physical characteristics but not in purpose, such as gasoline and home heating oil; or two commodities such as coal and heating oil may serve the same purpose but be entirely different in nature.

In this case, as in others, there must be actual damage in order to prove discrimination.

EFFECTS OF DISCRIMINATION

The economic effects of unjustified discrimination can be far reaching. A community or an entire region might be made to flourish or decay because of such practices. To the extent that advantageous rates might cause an economic function to be carried on in a place which was not suitable otherwise, and thus make the activity more expensive, society would lose. However, it does not seem that such a situation is too likely to occur in the modern economy.

Freight rates are only one of many factors which determine industrial location. A favorable freight rate alone would not be, in most cases at least, enough to determine location. However, combined with other factors, they may be very significant.

For example, an industry may have grown up in a given area in years past because of various factors—labor, natural resources, etc. The carriers might be able to enhance these advantages and through discrimination make it more difficult for another area to move into the industry, even though it may have many factors in its favor. Such practices are much more unlikely now than they were in years past when there was less intermodal competition.

For example, flour milling is carried on in many parts of the

---

[13] Illinois Sand Traffic Bureau v. Atchison, Topeka and Santa Fe Railway Co., 152 ICC 749, 753 (1929).

[14] California Growers' and Shippers' Protective League v. Southern Pacific Co., 100 ICC 79, 105 (1925); also Atlas Cereal Co. v. Atchison, Topeka & Santa Fe Railway Co., 89 ICC 212, 218 (1924).

United States. Grain and grain products are carried by rail, truck and barge. With this rapidly developing intermodal competition and with the pressure brought by regional interest, it is not likely that one area could be put at a disadvantage for long.[15]

So many historical accidents and interrelated factors come into this situation that any evaluation of the effects is most tenuous. There may be no pressing economic reason for an industry to center around a given area rather than many other areas which one could name. However, once these factors become effective, so many external economies are developed that favorable freight rates would have little effect. The complexities of the situation would require that both raw materials inbound and finished products outbound must be considered. Low rates on shipping finished goods would be meaningless, if rates on raw materials used to manufacture the product were high.

The opportunities for commodity discrimination have been very much reduced by competition between the modes. There are relatively few shippers who do not have recourse to different modes or to private carriage, and the ability of the carriers to extract a high rate is very limited.

There are, however, frequent instances, often arising from proposed rate reductions, which raise the threat of discrimination and at least provide an opportunity to claim that such a threat exists. The difficulty with most of these situations is that there is usually no solution which will be satisfactory to all parties. If shoe manufacturers in St. Louis are injured by a rate change which makes shoes manufactured in New Jersey more attractive price-wise, a return to the old rate will help the St. Louis manufacturers but will bring cries of discrimination from the eastern shoe manufacturers; the shoe will be on the other foot, so to speak.

These interests become especially hard to balance as industrial growth and dispersion take place. Many products, which were produced in the northeastern United States in 1920, are now produced in the West and South. Under these circumstances, it becomes impossible to avoid injury to someone's interest.

On the other hand, there has been an increasing tendency to centralize the production of some products which were at one time locally produced, as noted in Chapter IX. In 1910, it was a small town, indeed, which did not have its own bakery and brewery. In 1960,

---

[15] There is an almost infinite number of conflicting interests at work in these matters. For example, not only shippers, competing carriers, and others are parties at interest, but federal agencies are often concerned, e.g., U. S. Department of Agriculture, Tennessee Valley Authority, and others.

both of these products, especially beer, was produced for the national market, and the local brands were relatively few.

CONTROL OF DISCRIMINATION

It will be remembered that one of the major factors in the passage of the Interstate Commerce Act was the deep-seated fear and resentment against the practice of various forms of discrimination. Sections 2, 3, 4, and 6 all related to this problem.

Section 2 made it unlawful for a carrier to charge one person more than another for rendering similar services under substantially similar situations. A shipper who feels that he has a valid claim in such instances may proceed to have the rate set aside, if, after examining the data and evaluating the situation, the regulatory body concludes that the rate is indeed unjustly discriminatory and that injury has been done.

Section 3 prohibited, in a broad sense, any undue preference or prejudice. Section 4, the Long and Short Haul Clause, was designed to eliminate geographical discrimination, and its history has been recounted at some length.

Section 6 is related to the problem by requiring the publication of rates and schedules and providing for their inspection by the public, in order to avoid the secret rate or the "midnight" tariff so frequently encountered before regulation was adopted.

As was true with other sections of the Act, these outwardly simple provisions were not easy to implement. One of the complicating factors, as noted earlier, was the fact that shippers were able to bring pressure upon carriers of such a degree that carriers were forced to break the law. The Elkins Act of 1903 helped to solve this problem by making both parties guilty.

However, as we have seen, a loophole existed in the phrase, "substantially similar conditions." It was easy to argue that conditions were sufficiently different to require and justify a rate differential. Such arguments were particularly effective where geographical or commodity questions were concerned until the law was amended. Personal discrimination was more easily dealt with, since it was often more clear cut in nature and involved fewer persons.

The present framework of control designed to deal with these problems is as follows:

1. Carriers, as noted, are required to publish rates and to adhere to these rates and to collect charges in a reasonable time.

2. Advance notice of rate changes must be given.
3. Published rates must be open to public inspection.
4. Rebates are unlawful, and both parties are liable.
5. All claims for damage must be investigated and justified.
6. Any services provided (transit, storage, etc.) must be provided to all shippers who are in similar circumstances.
7. Car supply, construction of sidings, and other services must be non-discriminatory.

It can be seen that, if these regulations are observed, there would be little opportunity for discrimination. In evaluating charges of discrimination, the regulatory bodies must take into account the competitive situation which exists. It was pointed out earlier that many instances of rail relief from the long-short haul clause (Section 4) are based upon the presence of water competition.

It is likely that discrimination would be short lived in any case, since political and regional interests will interest themselves in this situation. Many instances are on record in which a given area or industry made and often sustained charges of rate discrimination.[16]

It must be noted that there is potential danger here, in that the various geographic locations will naturally fight very hard for any concessions they may be able to secure. It would be highly questionable to distort the natural economic relationships or to cancel out some real economic advantage by equalizing rates because of pressure from selfish interests.

The rise of the motor carrier industry with the large number of firms and the competitive structure of that industry is much closer to the competitive end of the scale than were rail carriers, and discrimination was less likely. The possibility of private carriage makes the danger of serious damage to even the small shipper rather remote, and there has never been need for a long and short haul clause in Part II of the Act.

No one would argue the fact that the carriers should be prevented from engaging in discrimination due to a monopoly position, and all would agree that no industry or firm should be treated unfairly as to transport costs. On the other hand, there is a serious possibility that in eliminating the unjustified discrimination, some perfectly justified and sound economic relationship may be distorted. For example,

---

[16] Southern Class Rate Investigation, 100 ICC 513 (1925); Consolidated Southwestern Cases 123, ICC 203 (1927). There are many examples of this type of litigation.

regional interests may be so active in protecting themselves that some factors may be overlooked. The undue extension of "blanket rates" is an example of such abuse. If a locality can make a case for itself and is able to raise the question of discrimination, it may then be "blanketed in" and enjoy an artificial advantage.

It seems likely that serious discrimination is not frequently encountered in the modern transport system. The large number of carriers of all types, in addition to the dynamic changes in population and economic activity, makes discrimination, except in isolated cases, rather rare. When there are many alternatives open to the buyer, the problem of discrimination becomes much less serious and, in fact, has little, if any, public significance. In a monopoly situation, the buyer must either accept the fact that discrimination may exist or do without the service, but, where alternatives are present, he has some choice. To be sure, this is a two-edged sword. When a high degree of competition exists, the carriers may resort to various discriminatory practices in order to assure a share of the traffic, especially from large shippers. Many students of the field seem to hold the opinion that carriers might do well to engage in more price discrimination than they now can or wish to do.[17]

Naturally, a rather significant degree of discrimination does exist in various forms and is generally accepted, in that the "victim" is often free to pursue alternatives. For example, a common carrier cannot refuse to accept shipments which are within his capability. The carrier can, however, make it clear through rate minima, circuitous routing, arduous packing requirements, etc., that such traffic is not welcome. The shipper soon realizes that his best interests would be served by patronizing another mode or providing his own transportation.[18] The fact that these alternatives exist makes him less prone to make an issue of the matter, since he is not seriously injured by the situation. To be sure, it is impossible to eliminate all discriminatory situations which might exist, since some are beyond the reach of regulation. The regulatory body cannot make the small shipper big nor can it alter the geography of the nation, nor change the physical character of the product.

---

[17] For example, see Robert A. Nelson, "Administered Rates and Competition," *Official Proceedings of the New York Railroad Club*, New York, 1958.

[18] In one case, a motor carrier will accept small shipments bound for a nearby point. These shipments are then backhauled some distance away from the destination in order to be processed through the home terminal. The result is a full day's delay. Shippers soon find other means, which is the goal of the carrier.

Summary

This chapter has examined the policy problems brought about by the discrimination issue. Discrimination was very significant in bringing to a head the movement for regulation. The Interstate Commerce Commission has probably had more success in controlling this problem than any other major problem area, and, indeed, discrimination has largely been eliminated. It must be remembered, however, that it is not simple to draw the line between reasonable and unreasonable discrimination. It is possible that, in its efforts to prevent unreasonable discrimination, the Commission has prevented some exercise of reasonable and economically sound price discrimination. Fortunately, both the carriers and the Commission itself recognize this problem and improvements are likely.

CHAPTER XIX

Control Over Rates

In a previous chapter, the regulatory problems incident to the over-all level of rates were considered. Let us now turn our attention to the problem of control over specific rates.

Recalling the material in Chapter VII relative to pricing of transportation service, the student will remember that many factors were taken into consideration by the carrier in its efforts to price the service in the most remunerative fashion.

The shipper views the rate paid for transportation as an element in the cost of production, and he is thus interested in keeping this rate as low as practicable within the limits of satisfactory service. The shipper may, depending upon the economic factors involved, take a very broad view of the rate and the whole rate level, or he may concern himself entirely with the rate or rates which apply to the material or products in which he deals. Let us examine this further, moving from the narrow interpretation to the broad.

In the narrowest sense, the shipper might be interested only in the specific rate applying to his commodity. If, for example, a producer of a given product knows that he can sell his product in a given market at a specific price and that a rate increase or decrease will influence his sales for good or ill, he will either support or oppose rate actions relative to his specific situation. In some cases where the relative rates paid by various producers do not change, the individual producer may have little interest in the rate unless and until the demand for his product begins to be influenced. In short, unless the relative competitive position of the producer is altered, he may be indifferent to rate changes. This would be especially likely, if the producer sells F.O.B. (at the factory price) and the transportation is paid by the buyer. However, this indifference will vanish if a source near to the market should develop.

The key phrase is clearly "the relative competitive position" of the shipper. An importer of expensive automobiles may, for example, sell at the F.O.B. price in New York and, since his is an exclusive or sole import, add whatever shipping costs are incurred to the point of delivery. On the other hand, a sophisticated shipper may be forced to interest himself in a whole galaxy of rates or in the aggregate rate level. For example, the Aluminum Company of America produces various aluminum products in finished or semi-finished condition at various plants throughout the nation. The traffic department at ALCOA would be interested in aluminum rates on various products from many points to many points, and, also, they would be just as interested in rates on steel, copper, bronze, and other metals which may be as competitive in the aluminum markets as those products of Reynolds Metals and other specific aluminum producers. To carry this analysis a step further, an industrial trade association some years ago made a study of passenger fares in order to determine the degree (if any) to which rates on the product concerned contributed to costs of other services, especially passenger carriage. Obviously then, the interest of the shipper may range from modest concern with the specific rate for a single product to a highly analytical and sophisticated concern with rates of many products and, in some cases, the rate level per se. In a substantial number of cases the producers make mutual agreements designed to eliminate freight rate differences and give equal opportunity to the remote producers to compete in major marketing areas. Such agreements are commonly found in highly concentrated industries dominated by a few firms. Often such agreements founder when competition begins to increase. A major shortcoming of such policy is the fact that the producers may operate for many years taking transportation costs as a non-competitive item, thus ignoring cost reducing innovations.

Since rates are published and apply to all without discrimination, there is no room for negotiation in the usual sense between the shipper and the carrier in any specific transaction. However, shippers or shipper associations may and do undertake to change the rate in light of changing circumstances. Thus, a published rate might be changed, and, in this sense, rates can be negotiated between the parties involved.

Commodity rates are an example of this situation, and, in fact, commodity rates are of more importance than class rates in the total movement of goods.

In view of the fact that most carriers are in a competitive position, they are disposed to consider reasonable suggestions from shippers in the rate making procedure.

The carrier is interested in both the overall rate level and in the level of specific rates. One might assume that, if all the individual rates were at their proper level, the overall rate level would be satisfactory. However, the reverse is not true; i.e., the rate level might be satisfactory to the carriers and the individual rates might be badly out of adjustment. The carriers and the shippers both realize that every specific rate cannot be properly adjusted at every point in time, no matter how desirable this may be. The process of transport pricing is, as in most industries, more of an art than a science. The allocation of common costs and the estimation of demand for service are largely empirical in nature. Carriers have been somewhat inclined to overlook the desirable elements in close analysis of rates and have only in recent years undertaken any serious market research. Until a given rate has become seriously out of adjustment, there may be no way of knowing what is taking place. The rate which prevails at any one time for a specific product is the best estimate of the carrier's view of the situation. No doubt, rates in a given case could be increased, and the carrier would be able to make more profit. In other cases, a reduction would reap more profit. These cases come about through miscalculation of the elasticity of demand or through failure to recognize changing circumstances.

The carrier faces a problem of so adjusting rates that the maximum benefit is realized, or, in other words, the carrier must attempt to set in each case the rate which brings the most profitable traffic onto the lines of the carrier and maximizes the total revenue. Since these factors differ among modes due to the technological and other factors involved, it seems instructive to discuss these factors on a modal basis.

The rail plant is, as previously pointed out, built to large scale. Thus, up to the point of diminishing returns, additional traffic will be desirable. These relationships are frequently illustrated by the long-run cost curve in Figure 19-1. In this case, the plant of the rail firm is assumed to be subject to long-run expansion in three stages—Plant 1, Plant 2, and Plant 3—each providing a lower average cost

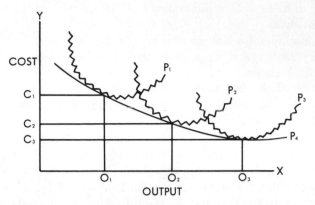

P₁, P₂, P₃, INTERMEDIATE CURVES
P₄, LONG RUN COST CURVE

Fig. 19-1

per unit. These curves are commonly shown as smooth curves, but it seems more appropriate to illustrate them here as saw-tooth, since additions to and improvements in plant do not follow a smooth course but come in irregular increments.[1] In each case, the curve begins to climb after the optimum point has been reached, indicating that the optimum capacity of the plant has been exceeded. This requires plant additions or upgrading or a reduction of output. As noted in Part II, the interrelationships between the various elements of the rail plant are not linear and are difficult to control. If a railroad has free capacity, any additional traffic might be welcome, although care must be taken to see that it does not incur out-of-pocket costs (the costs directly related to its carriage) which are in excess of the revenue derived from carrying it. To put this another way, the marginal revenue must exceed the marginal cost, or the carrier will lose money with each unit moved.

It must be remembered here that the carrier may have some excess capacity in one part of the plant but none in another. For example, an airline may have excess planes or seats which could be filled but, because of airport limitations, have no space to load or

---

[1] Some disagreement exists among economists about the efficacy of illustrating the intermediate cost curves in this fashion. However, it seems deceptive to portray the intermediate curves as smooth, although the long-run cost curve or envelope curve might be so illustrated, in view of the fact that these increments to plant are apt to be merged into one another and smoothed out as time passes.

unload passengers, handle baggage or other matters, thus cancelling out the capacity. Some of these added costs may be impossible to allocate (e.g., executive time) but are, nonetheless, real and must be taken into account in some arbitrary fashion.

In Figure 19-2, this basic principle is illustrated. If the output (ton-miles or other appropriate measure) exceeds O-T, the marginal

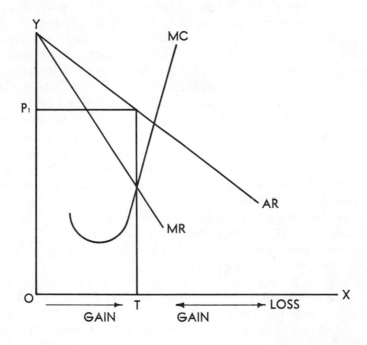

Fig. 19-2

cost is greater than the marginal revenue. If, however, the marginal revenue exceeds the marginal cost, additional units of traffic can be moved with profit. Movements along the X axis toward point T from O result in a gain per unit of traffic. Movements beyond T result in a loss per unit since MC is greater than MR. Thus, point T is a point of equilibrium so long as the plant characteristics remain the same as assumed in the diagram. The output OT can be sold at price P_1 (determined by the demand curve AR). It will be recalled from the material in Chapter V that the determination of the cost of transporting a commodity is not a precise exercise. However, insofar as it may be available, such knowledge may be used by the carrier in its pricing policy. It is highly desirable for each and every commodity to make contribution to the overall cost or fully allocated costs, although this may not in every case be done, especially with rail traffic. It might at times be necessary to carry traffic which does not do so in the hope that the return may be greater in the near future.

Motor carriers having less physical plant and more variable costs are in a somewhat different situation from rail carriers. However, the basic principles of rate-cost relationships apply to motor and other carriers. Motor carrier plant is more easily adjusted than is true of rail plant; changes can be made more quickly, and innovations, at least in recent years, have been rapid. However, a large motor carrier may have problems somewhat similar to those of the railroad as its physical plant grows in size and complexity. Thus, a terminal may be replaced and increase capacity to the point where further changes are necessary in order to maximize the efficiency of the new facility.

No plant, especially one so large and involved as that of a transportation enterprise, is new or modern at any given time in all respects. Always some portions are more advanced in design or more productive than others, and the successful integration of these varied elements is a major managerial problem.

Carriers must pay close attention to the physical factors relating to the service. The student will recall that the costs of service for various products differ greatly and that they must, to a large extent, be allocated on an arbitrary basis.

Although the carrier might be more than willing to carry a commodity at a rate lower than the fully distributed cost, it will seldom be willing or be permitted to carry it at a rate which does not cover the "out-of-pocket costs," those directly related to the service, or those which would be avoided if the service was not performed.

These costs differ, not only as between carriers due to the varying technologies involved, but also depending upon traffic flow, density and volume, equipment utilization and other factors, all of which are subject to rapid change. If, for example, a carrier can devise a more efficient process or design more efficient equipment, this may give rise to an opportunity to reduce rates on desirable traffic. If, on the other hand, costs increase, a rate increase may be essential.

Rising costs from 1945 to 1955 were experienced by all carriers, and little opposition came from the shippers whose markets were not sensitive to increasing prices. During these years, the common practice was to increase rates by a fixed figure "across the board." These tactics could be justified to a degree by the fact that costs were rising rapidly and the demand for service was relatively inelastic. In the late 1950's, this method became somewhat dangerous as shippers encountered resistance to price increases. The general rate increases began to include more "hold downs" or exceptions and rate increases became more selective. Also, greater efforts were made to analyze the market, and all carriers, especially rail, began to make selective reductions. Such reductions, especially when coupled with service improvements, were effective, and this matter is considered in a following chapter devoted to intermodal competition.

THE DEMAND FOR THE SERVICE

The individual shipper is concerned with the production and sale of a given product or a line of products. He wishes to sell these products over the largest market area possible and to obtain the maximum profit. The cost of transportation is for him one of many elements in the cost of production. The relative importance of this cost will depend on the character of the product and on its total value, as was pointed out in earlier chapters.

Since common carrier rates are published and open for public inspection, any shipper will be aware of what his competitors are paying, and relative rates are taken into account in product pricing.[2]

From the shipper viewpoint this fact eliminates any question as to rates being an element in competition. For example, if two coal producers are located in West Virginia and shipping to Norfolk for export, each knows the other's freight rate, and economies leading to a price reduction will arise from other sources. In this case, the rate is not a competitive factor. In other cases where rate regulation is absent, the competitive aspects of the rate are very important. In the exempt agricultural transportation area, for example, the sale price of a load of produce sold at auction in Boston will probably not vary much from any other load of comparable quality. However, if the grower has managed to secure a reduction of $100 by skillful bargaining with the trucker, he is in an obviously better position than his competitor.[3]

---

[2] However, it will be recalled that rates of contract carriers and, of course, costs of private trucking are not available to those outside the firm.

[3] It is interesting to note that shippers strongly support the National Agricultural Transportation League, an organization which *interalia* attempts to stabilize rates by working through the broker network. Historical evidence indicates that shippers' desire for rate stability was a major factor in regulatory legislation in 1887 and in 1935. It seems likely that rate stability is more desirable in the view of the shipper than the random chance of gain or loss arising from freely fluctuating rates.

CHARACTER OF THE PRODUCT

The physical nature of the product is clearly of basic importance. A fragile high value product presents serious transportation problems, in that great care and often special equipment are necessary to handle it successfully. The shipper of such a product is aware of these problems and does not expect to pay the low rates such as those paid by a shipper of sand and gravel. In any event, the rate cannot exceed the value added by transportation, since at that point the commodity will not move. If the physical character of a given commodity is so distinct that it can move only by one mode, then the shipper has no choice, and he will be entirely dependent upon the rate charged by that carrier. On the other hand, if the product can move by various modes, the shipper can exercise some judgment and take advantage of the competitive situation which exists.

The way in which the commodity can be loaded or packed will influence the rate. The reader will recall that the factor which is perhaps equal to or greater than the others is the market value or money value of the commodity.

In its deliberations regarding the reasonableness of a rate, the regulatory bodies must weigh all of these factors.

THE THEORY OF RATE CONTROL

It is obvious that the need for rate control arises from the fact that the consumer is limited in his choice of service outlets, since a monopoly or a monopolistic situation exists or is assumed to exist.

Secondly, a clear implication is made that the commodity or service in question is vital or at least very important to the buyer. Both of these conditions existed in the years when the regulatory framework of the Interstate Commerce Act was erected. Under these circumstances, the regulatory body takes the place of the market mechanism in the price setting process. As the reader now knows, the ultimate objective of the regulator is to arrive at a "fair or reasonable" price. Many elements enter into this situation, since the shipper wants not only a reasonable rate, but one which is reasonable in the context of service and other factors. As noted elsewhere, rate regulation was originally thought of as being a matter of prevention of high rates established by a powerful monopolistic organization. Later with the rise of competition, this attitude changed and other problems arose, as will be recounted in the following chapter.

SPECIFIC RATES

Let us consider the procedure by which a specific rate is established and control is applied by the regulatory commissions. Suppose that a railroad or motor carrier (either individually or through the rate bureau) establishes a rate of 30 cents per hundred pounds on commodity X between points A and B. This rate would have been established after careful study of the situation. First, consideration would have been given to the physical character of the commodity in question. Is X a valuable commodity, is it durable or fragile, or is it likely to damage other freight? Is it easy to load; does it require special equipment or technical know-how?

Secondly, the competitive aspects of the matter would be examined. By what means is the commodity now moving; are other modes seeking to obtain this traffic?

Thirdly, some forecast would need to be made as to the likely future results of the rate. Would it encourage traffic in the area concerned; would it disturb existing relationships unduly?

These factors are, as we know, highly interdependent. A given commodity may be such that it is likely to move only by one mode. However, the market for the product, its use or intrinsic value may be such that the monopolistic advantage of the mode may be of little value in exploiting the profit possibilities.

In other cases, the goods may be so highly thought of as traffic that the carriers will vie with one another to obtain it. Certainly, the seller will not make large concessions to capture a buyer who is already using his service and who has little opportunity to use alternatives. However, even here an intelligent seller will attempt to maximize sales and profits.[4]

Some estimate will have to be made as to the economic status of the industry producing the product. Even if the product is "rail bound" or "truck bound," if the producers are not in a profitable position, high rates will have the effect only of depressing them still further and reducing traffic potential.

PROCEDURAL MATTERS

Suppose the rate on commodity X is in question and, if after these factors have been examined and weighed, the rate of 30 cents

---

[4] A local power company with a franchise monopoly may still stimulate power sales by a scale of rates designed to attract the volume buyer and to induce the small user to increase consumption.

is published. Notification at least thirty days in advance of the effective date has been given, and the rate is to become effective. This represents the carrier's best judgment of the situation. That is to say, though the rate proposed may not be the most advantageous rate possible, the carrier using such information as is available to it has made the best possible attempt to make it so. Naturally, the analysis leading to an optimum rate (maximum profit for the carrier) may require information not available to the carrier authorities. For obvious reasons, the shipper will not be anxious to disclose such information.

The responsibilities of the Commission become more complex when, as in the years after World War II, rate increases take the form of across-the-board increases rather than specific changes. Perhaps, also, we must remind ourselves that we are talking now about two-party relationships between buyer and seller and not about the three-party relationships which will be encountered in Chapter XX.

At an early date, limitations were placed upon the Commission as to the promotion of shipper welfare. It was thought in the early years that rates might be so regulated as to increase welfare of certain groups. In the case of *Northern Pacific Railway vs. North Dakota,* it was pointed out that the full cost of the service must be recovered.[5]

In a similar vein, the Commission has refused to reduce rates because certain products were used for laudable purposes, e.g., education or public welfare in general.[6] There is little question that the Commission is on sound ground in this area. It would seem logical to raise rates on the "socially undesirable" products (if anyone is so brave as to draw up a list). Clearly, there are no criteria which would be acceptable, nor is there reason to require carriers to subsidize "socially desirable" products any more than to require steel or oil producers to do likewise. The next move (if any) is up to the shippers or other carriers or interested groups. It may well be that the rate is accepted without question by all parties.[7]

If, however, a complaint arises, the regulatory commission must investigate the situation and, if it appears to be valid complaint, will suspend the rate and undertake an investigation. Also, the regulatory body can undertake such a proceeding on its own initiative without

---

[5] 236 U. S. 585, 597.

[6] *Rate Structure Investigation,* Part 5, Furniture, 177, ICC 5, 62 (1931).

[7] This might not mean that all was well, since, unless shippers had no choice, they might merely shift to another mode without any recourse to the regulatory machinery. Thus, the carrier might find itself with traffic drifting away because of its ill-informed action in the pricing area.

outside complaints. The complaints may take various forms; for example, shippers may feel that the rate is too high and other carriers may feel it is too low. If the rate is an important one and there are many parties at interest, the proceedings may extend over a long period. Hearings are held at which data in the form of briefs, cost statements, forecasts of traffic and related matters are presented. The task of the regulatory body at this point is to weigh these factors against the national interest and within the framework of the law. It will be remembered that the Commission has great range in these matters. It can declare the rate to be unreasonable without suggesting another rate, or it may substitute a specific rate.

Whereas the consideration of the *rate level* involves macro-economic factors of the broadest nature, a specific rate question is an exercise in micro-economics. The regulatory body can probably be more precise in its calculations in this type of case.

The Commission must take great care in these cases to avoid merely allowing its judgment to supersede the judgment of the carrier management. That is, unless the rate of 30 cents would be discriminatory or injurious, the Commission would probably allow it to become effective, even though in its judgment a rate of 25 cents might be more effective in attracting traffic.

Because of the large number of factors involved and the fact that these factors are subject to substantial change, the criteria of reasonableness are not universal. Each instance must be considered *ad hoc*, and a rate change held to be reasonable under one set of circumstances may not be so under other circumstances.

Certainly, most of the doubt centers around the question as to whether the rate is compensatory. However, the proof of the compensatory nature of the rate is not of interest enough to make it reasonable. Further analysis, taking into account the entire range of factors, must be undertaken. Since these matters take time, it may happen that the time limit for suspension (seven months) may expire. At the end of this period, the carrier may then put the proposed rate into effect, although legal action may block this move. The ultimate decision may be in the hands of the courts, if, as often happens, the Commission decision is not satisfactory to one of the parties. The time element is a serious one, and much thought has been given to some means of reducing the time involved.

In periods of rising prices or of dynamic competition, the substantial amounts of time consumed can be serious indeed and constitutes one of the most pressing regulatory problems.

Summary

Early in this chapter, it was noted that a fundamental assumption in rate control was the lack of an alternative outlet for the shipper. This assumption has largely been undermined by developments since 1940, viz., the wider range of intercarrier competition and the rise of private carriage. The number of shippers who are "tied to" one mode is rapidly diminishing. As a result of these factors, the importance of specific rates has been somewhat reduced, insofar as it relates to protection of the shipper, and, on the other hand, is enhanced as it is related to the protection of the carrier. In short, the real battleground has shifted into the area of intermodal competition.[8] While specific rate control is still important to the shipper, its significance as a national policy matter is less important than formerly. However, the importance to the specific shipper is great, especially in the sense that the choice of carrier and the ability to serve various markets may hinge on these rate relationships. The intermodal rate problems will be considered in the following chapter.

---

[8] Although, of course, the rates of individual shippers, particularly for certain commodities, are the crux of this battle. See, for example, *Manufactured Tobacco from Kentucky, North Carolina, and Virginia to the South*, 292, ICC 427 (1954).

CHAPTER XX

Control Over Intermodal and Intramodal Competition

Perhaps no Commission function has changed in its basic philosophy in recent years as much as the policy of control over this area. As was pointed out in an earlier chapter, the Interstate Commerce Act did not provide for or anticipate the need for control of competition between modes but only competition of an intramodal nature. Indeed, the intense competition between and among rail carriers, which often became destructive, was one of the major problems which control over rates was designed to eliminate.

Long before the Commission was established, the carriers themselves recognized this problem and attempted to control competition by their own efforts. Before discussing the legal limits within which intermodal competition may be conducted, let us glance briefly at the measures taken by the industry to deal with these problems.

CONTROLS ESTABLISHED BY THE INDUSTRY

By 1900, many railroad managements had become aware of the serious consequences of intense or "cutthroat" competition and had made numerous attempts to control competition by informal agreements. In addition to rate matters, these agreements related to division of territory, pooling and other matters of mutual interest.

As might be expected, these agreements, having no legal status, were often broken. It will be recalled that, due to the cost structure of railroads, there was great pressure to attract traffic; and, while an agreement might hold together for a while, it almost always came apart under the pressure of declining traffic. There were always some marginal carriers or some maverick managements who were prone to cut rates, either through ignorance or irresponsibility. When the first move was made, the other parties had little choice but to follow in order to protect their own standing. Perhaps the strongest force in favor of control of competition was the financial community. One of the major activities of J. P. Morgan in his role of railroad reorganizer was to force rail management to restrain themselves from entering each other's spheres of influence.[1] Even so powerful a figure as Morgan did not always succeed, as his troubles with the Reading would indicate.[2] Also, there were men who, like Harriman, were outside Morgan's circle and had no interest in his objectives and were independent of him in a financial sense. Morgan often placed one of his associates, usually Coster or Spencer, on the board of railroads he had organized. When the Richmond Terminal was made into the Southern Railway, Spencer became president.

However, by 1910, the era of railroad building had come to an end, and the construction of the Western Pacific by George Gould in 1909 represents the last of the major attempts to extend into hostile territory.[3] Of all the competitive practices, the entry into preempted territory probably was considered to be the most serious and brought severe measures against the interloper. Indeed, it was the most serious, in the economic sense, because of the permanent nature of the problem. Rate cuts could be restored and the relative positions of the carriers would be the same. Actual construction of a line presented a much more serious problem. Unless the new line was to be abandoned entirely after it was built, it would have to be operated and would upset the distribution of traffic in the area; in either case the waste

---

[1] While there are many accounts of these activities, one of the most readable is found in Frederick Lewis Allen, *The Great Pierpont Morgan* (Harper & Row). Less objective is the account written by his son-in-law; Herbert L. Satterlee, *J. Pierpont Morgan, An Intimate Portrait* (New York: The Macmillan Co., 1939).

[2] Morgan had trouble with both the Reading and the New Haven Railroads in preventing undue expansion by overly ambitious management.

[3] George Gould lacked his father's touch and was unsuccessful in his venture to complete a transcontinental system and, in fact, brought serious trouble to his whole system by this act.

was clearly undesirable. Frequently, the threat of undertaking construction was enough to bring about the desired results.[4] Sometimes,
as in the case of the Western Pacific mentioned above, the passage
of time and industrial development justified these ventures, but more
often the excess capacity remained to harass the future management.
Even when the move paid off, the period of time (30 years in the
Western Pacific case) was too great to be of immediate benefit. While
the financier was able to influence building by withholding funds,
his influence in the rate area was more limited. Control over rates
was only, in part, undertaken by the carriers. At an early date, rate
bureaus were established, although in this area, as well as others,
voluntary cooperation was likely to be unstable.

Carriers competed for traffic, both by rate reductions and by
agreements relating to routing. Consequently, control of connecting
carriers became important. Harriman, for example, controlled the
Union Pacific-Southern Pacific-Illinois Central group which gave a
single line from Chicago to the Pacific Coast. Naturally, traffic originating on the Southern Pacific was interchanged to the East with the
Union Pacific. The Missouri-Pacific-Denver & Rio Grande Western-
Western Pacific group was, in turn, under the Gould domination. To
the North, Hill held sway with the Great Northern and the Northern
Pacific. Thus, these three men had influence over a substantial part
of western mileage.

The result was, thus, a tendency to compete on a system or group
basis rather than on an individual railroad basis. This development
was very helpful in the control of competition on a self-imposed basis;
since, for example, Harriman and Hill together or Gould and Harriman
in tandem controlled a substantial part of the western mileage, a two-
party agreement had a much greater chance of success than a multi-
party agreement. While such pacts were not ironclad, there is no
doubt that the "cutthroat" type of competition prevailing in the 1870's
was greatly reduced. On the other hand, this situation brought on
rather destructive personal struggles for control as that between Hill
and Harriman in 1907.[5]

The rate bureau or conference established by all types of carriers

---

[4] There are many such cases. The South Pennsylvania, for example, was
undertaken to chastise the Pennsylvania Railroad. It was never completed, and
the roadbed, which had been graded, became a part of the Pennsylvania Turnpike.

[5] Morgan, who was supporting Hill, was in Europe at this time, and he
would, no doubt, have prevented any such action if he had been in New York.
This was probably the last of the great railroad wars, which had been frequent
in earlier years. These activities infuriated Morgan, who had in all his business
dealings been opposed to excessive and uncontrolled competition.

has, in addition to other objectives, the object of reducing predatory rate cuts and of making information available to all parties.

Generally speaking, motor carriers did not have the rather elaborate structure which railroads had in order to reduce competitive stress but relied at an early date upon legislative control.

The very heterogenous structure of the motor carrier industry was, of course, a serious barrier (and largely remains so) to any effective control of intramodal competition. Effective control must rest upon common objectives and, even then, has small chance of success; as we saw in the case of the railroads where no common ground is available, the chances of success are greatly reduced. The trucking industry was one of the parties participating in the NRA code in the early 1930's, and the present American Trucking Associations, Inc. grew largely from that effort. However, this group influenced, and still influences, only a small portion of the vast industry. Consequently, much of the motor carrier industry was not amenable to industry-imposed controls, and self-imposed control has never been very effective. As we have seen, for industry, in general, self-imposed control on the intramodal level, although necessary, was never successful. Let us, thus, turn our attention to outside regulatory aspects of this area.

COMMISSION CONTROL OF INTRAMODAL COMPETITION

The Interstate Commerce Commission controls intramodal relationships in several ways: (1) through rate control, (2) control over entry and financial activities, (3) control over mergers and consolidations, and (4) control over divisions of revenues from joint hauls and shipper control of routing.

By 1920, the Interstate Commerce Commission had all of these matters well in hand. It is probable that the Commission provided the outside authority which was needed and which could not be exercised by the carriers themselves, even though they recognized the need for such action. Rate controls, although not perfect, were at least adequate for the time. Entry was no real problem after 1910, and the Commission had gained a high degree of control over financial affairs and was empowered to supervise division of rates. The shipper was in control of routing. Except for the rate level, which was discussed in a preceding chapter, the Commission had adequate power to deal effectively with these problems. Intramodal competition had, in short, been brought under control.

The natural outcome of this situation was twofold: (1) an emphasis upon non-price competition and (2) a continuation of the process of bringing various lines under common control. Competition became benign. Underlying this situation was the basic fact that from 1910 to 1930 economic development and growth was producing enough traffic for all, and, indeed, the traffic might be said to have caught up with the overbuilding of past years.

It might well be argued that the moderate competition based on non-price factors during the years 1910-1930 was unfortunate, in that it was apt to make railroad management feel that competition was a thing of the past. Indeed, there seems to be ample evidence that rail management in the early 1930's could not grasp the fact that motor carriage was really a serious threat. The relatively low level of competition was also a result of the high degree of cooperation existing in the industry, especially rail. It was not likely that, in an industry where equipment was standardized and interchanged among the firms, much was to be gained by innovation in plant, nor was it possible for one firm to take much of an independent line. Rates, transit times and other service factors were gradually brought into almost complete uniformity within the modes. Under these circumstances, intramodal competition became more and more unimportant.

With minor variations, this situation prevailed until 1935. To be sure, a degree of intermodal competition existed between rail and water carriers, but this was a minor problem compared to what was to come after 1930.

COMMISSION CONTROL OF INTERMODAL COMPETITION

The rise of intermodal competition on a large scale provided by the motor carriers seriously undermined the Commission's framework of control.[6] To put the matter briefly, the Commission had built up its procedure on the assumption that the problem was one of intramodal competition. After 1935, the most pressing question was one of intermodal competition, and the Commission had to formulate a new regulatory philosophy to deal with this problem. Actually, the forces of change had been building up for some time, certainly since 1920 when a clear change in direction took place. The fear of monopoly

---

[6] Various alternative courses of action were open to Congress, in addition to the one followed. See George W. Hilton, "Barriers to Competitive Rate Making," *Interstate Commerce Practitioners' Journal*, Vol. XXIX, No. 9, June 1962, pp. 1084 ff.

and personal discrimination had largely begun to wane by 1910. During World War I and immediately thereafter, other problems were more pressing.

It seems likely that the carriers were themselves largely unaware of the magnitude of competition which was to develop. There was, thus, a tendency for the rail carriers to underestimate the seriousness of the situation until it had become too extensive to ignore. The motor truck was viewed as a short range vehicle, useful in local drayage but in no way a serious threat to intercity traffic.[7] By 1932, this view was obviously unrealistic and a change in policy was necessary.

THE CONFLICTING PATTERNS OF THE 1930'S

The problem would have been serious in any case, but it was further complicated by the fact that the economic downturn after 1929 made the competitive situation extremely sensitive, as was pointed out in Chapter XII. It seems obvious that much of the thought given to the problem from 1930 until 1940 centered around the immediate problems incident to the depression and were not thought of as being basic problems of intermodel relationships. Declining traffic and reduced rail earnings had resulted in the passage of the Emergency Act of 1933.

The Transportation Act of 1940 fell far short of being a beacon to guide the Commission through the shoals of this competitive relationship. The so-called transportation policy embodied in the Act proved to be a collection of well-written platitudes of little value as an operating document. The Congressional mandate to "preserve the inherent advantages" of the various modes clearly could not be interpreted to universal satisfaction. The Commission found itself in somewhat of a stalemate, since Commission approval of any aggressive rate policy by one mode was bound to have serious repercussions on other modes.

Also, at this time, federal economic policy, as reflected in the National Recovery Act and other legislation, was oriented toward price stability and the prevention of aggressive actions, which would lead to aggressive price policies and increased unemployment. This policy did not change fundamentally until World War II began.

---

[7] For example, a 1913 issue of *Railway Age* pointed out that the motor vehicle was useful as a means of transport in and around the city to a radius of three miles. The author also pointed out that in the immediate downtown area the horse was without a peer.

One of the major barriers to Commission effectiveness in this task was the fact that, aside from control over entry which was very difficult to implement, there was no control over output; and this fact, coupled with the great overcapacity of those years, put tremendous pressure on the props which the Commission had used to shore up the sagging minimum rate structure. In some other areas, notably in farm price control, the controlling agency was given power to restrict output, and in the NRA output was at least discouraged. The Commission never had such power.[8]

Fortunately, from 1940 to 1955, traffic levels were high enough that competition did not become acute. Although truck participation rose during these years from 10 per cent to 17 per cent of the aggregate ton-mile service performed while the rail share fell from 61.3 per cent to 49 per cent, total rail ton-miles rose in absolute terms.[9]

Thus, in the unstable times of the 1930's, the Commission was forced to embark upon the task of regulating the relationship of rates of one mode to those of another. Since the cost patterns of the rail and motor carrier industries were entirely different, this proved to be a considerable task indeed and is far from complete. In the earliest days, 1930-1935, the motor carriers, operating on a highly informal basis, had almost no fixed costs, since they frequently leased space for terminals, had no office staff, and in other ways were "shoe string" operators. Further, they were often unaware of their true costs and were prone to underestimate them. As the industry grew, more formal arrangements were necessary, at least for common carriers; and management became more realistic and sophisticated, but not until the rate structure was seriously undermined.

The pioneer motor carriers had proceeded to set rates on the basis of existing rail rates, often adapting rail classifications to their use. Since the carrying capacity and operating range of the motor vehicle were quite limited in the early years, the motor carriers concentrated on short hauls of high value traffic; and, although the amount of traffic taken from the railroads was not great in the aggregate, it was serious in the revenue sense.

For the most part, the Commission operated on the theory that motor carrier service was superior to rail service in quality and a higher rate for most commodities would be appropriate.[10] On the

---

[8] The performance of both the NRA and the farm price-support policies would indicate that chance of success was very little in any case.

[9] Interstate Commerce Commission, Bureau of Transport Economics and Statistics.

[10] There are many such cases. Typical of this principle are Office Supplies from Gloucester, Mass. to Chicago, 245 ICC 669, 671 (1941), and Candy from Reading, Pa. to Baltimore, Md., 237 ICC 89, 95 (1940).

other hand, the railroads were denied a reduction in rates on aluminum products which they had made in order to regain traffic moving by barge. The Commission held that barge service was so inferior to rail that a large differential was needed, in this case 47 cents.[11] In a general sense, the Commission's view was valid, although each shipper was naturally forced to make this evaluation for himself. For the most part, transit times by truck were less than rail; and truck service was door to door, whereas rail service had not, in the past, included pick-up and delivery service. Other factors of importance were that the shippers in the depression years were often forced to purchase in small lots (and trucks were well suited to this need) and the motor carriers were often more willing to make various concessions such as driver loading, all somewhat minor but significant in the depression years.

MOTOR-RAIL RATE RELATIONSHIPS, COMMISSION POLICY

The primary problem faced by the Commission was in the area of rail-motor rates. It is not easy to determine a pattern in this area, since there are so many factors to consider and these factors are very fluid in character.[12]

It was noted above that the motor carrier frequently was in possession of advantages of a service nature. In a situation where a clear-cut service advantage existed, a policy of rate parity would most often be expected to drive traffic off the rails. In many instances of this type, it has been Commission policy to permit rails to reduce rates in order to remain competitive. Thus, rate relationships per se were largely meaningless unless service factors were included in the analysis.

Naturally, service factors are very much different for one shipper as opposed to another. A shipper, who by the nature of his product needs little service, is obviously attracted by low rates. Conversely, a shipper, who needs high standards of service, speed, refrigeration or careful handling, is not in a position to gain from rate reduction if service deteriorates.

Given the economic character of motor carriers (especially before 1940), viz., low fixed costs and highly adjustable plant, they were often able to undercut rail rates on desirable traffic. It must also be

---

[11] Aluminum Articles from Texas to Illinois and Iowa, 293 ICC 467.

[12] For the student who wishes to pursue this matter in greater detail, an excellent source is Ernest W. Williams, Jr., *The Regulation of Rail-Motor Rate Competition* (New York: Harper and Row, 1958), esp. Ch. 2 and 3.

remembered that motor carriers have a narrower responsibility as common carriers, and before 1935 they had no obligations at all. On the other hand, rail carriers were more apt to have some "rail-bound traffic" which could sustain them in the event of a competitive price cutting situation, although this may be a somewhat lesser advantage than has often been thought.

A study was made, based on 1955 data, showing the ratio of carload freight revenue to fully distributed costs.[13] Some 48 items (ICC commodity classes) have a ratio of less than 100 to fully distributed costs or, in other words, produce revenue less than the fully distributed costs of transporting them on a carload basis. The ratio ranges from 99 to 70. Among these items are the following, which by their nature are largely rail-bound: products of mines, products of forests, coal, coke, common brick, lead and zinc ore, tile, and sewer pipe. Many of the most competitive products (liquor, tobacco products, electrical equipment, drugs and toilet preparations) produce revenues ranging from a low of 143 to a high of 206 per cent of fully distributed costs. It might be noted in passing that many of the high ratio items move by private carrier. The desirability of some of the rail-bound traffic is highly questionable. While some traffic moves from one mode to another in response to rate or service advantages, there are frequently institutional factors which may inhibit traffic shifts. Once a management has become acclimated to dealing with a given mode and in some cases constructed facilities of a specific nature, it may be reluctant to change, except in the face of very strong inducements.

From 1935 when the Motor Carrier Act was passed until 1940 when the National Transportation Policy was enacted, the Commission was largely feeling its way. Section 15a (7), stemming from the national policy, placed the burden of proof upon the petitioning carrier in the event of proposals to reduce rates in order to compete for competitive traffic. As a rule of thumb, the carrier was required to show that the proposed rate was intended to meet specific competitive situations and that the proposed rate was compensatory.

Now let us examine these factors in more detail. The requirement that a rate reduction must be undertaken to meet specific competitive situations was intended to prevent carriers from making changes in order to secure more traffic when there was no real competitive threat.[14] Generally speaking, the Commission was opposed

---

[13] *Problems of the Railroads, op. cit.,* p. 1220.

[14] This policy had to be revised when private motor carriage became a factor. In this case, traffic lost seldom returned, since the shipper had made an investment in carrier equipment, and he was reluctant to change back to for-hire carriage.

to rate changes which would merely divert traffic from one mode to another unless some real advantage was present.[15] It seems clear that a basic premise of this policy is an assumption that there is little or no overcapacity in the industry. At various times, especially after 1935, serious overcapacity existed. Under such circumstances, carriers were naturally anxious to attempt to divert any traffic which they could possibly find. Furthermore, it would be a dull management, indeed, which could not cite some advantage in order to justify the move. The Commission was also reluctant to permit a rate reduction unless the carrier making the proposal was faced with a clearly recognized service disadvantage.

The evaluation of these factors is highly complex, and their fluid character is illustrated by the following example. In a series of cases involving the transportation of new automobiles, the Commission allowed railroads to quote rates considerably lower than motor rates.[16] Motor carriers argued with some justice that rail carriers could achieve many of the advantages attributed to motor carriers, if they made an effort to do so. Interestingly enough, the railroads, in the late 1950's, did regain much automobile traffic through a combination of rate reductions and service improvements. One of the complexities of this relationship is the fact that most service advantages add to the cost of production. Furthermore, as was indicated earlier, the reaction of shippers to service advantages vis-a-vis rate advantage is very difficult to predict.

The Commission has generally remained firm in its conviction that rates must be compensatory.[17] Although at first glance it may appear that carriers should be permitted to lose money if they desire, the Commission has followed the theory that non-compensatory rates will mean that other shippers will be paying rates in excess of what they should be or the standards of service will decline. A further objection to non-compensatory rates is that they may be used as a temporary expedient to drive out competition, whereupon the rates would be increased.

It is almost always necessary for the carrier proposing rate reductions to present data bearing upon the alleged compensatory nature

---

[15] However, the Commission has, as in the cigarette cases cited in Chapter XIX, seemed to follow a policy of splitting the traffic in order to give both rail and motor carriers "an even break" in participation.

[16] Automobiles from Memphis to Arkansas and Louisiana, 245 ICC 334 (1941); Automobiles from the East to Louisiana and Arkansas, 245 ICC 785 (1941).

[17] See, for example, Magazines in Official Territory, 246 ICC 325, 330 (1941); also, Paper and Paper Articles Between Western Truck Line Points, 186 ICC 536, 546 (1932).

of the new rate. Likewise, competing carriers and adversely affected shippers may attack these data in an effort to prove that the proposals are non-compensatory. In addition to the data presented by carriers in their requests for rate changes, the regulatory commissions have collected much data through their own efforts. Unfortunately, these data may be of little use in any specific situation but are useful as a general guide.

In any particular case the variables are not only large in number but may be unique in nature. For example, a carrier may claim that new equipment of superior design will enable it to reduce rates and that the new rates will be compensatory, even if they are not now. The presence or absence of back haul traffic will have an influence upon the cost situation. To complicate the situation further, forecasting is required. It may be that a rate claimed to be non-compensatory and which is, in fact, below the out-of-pocket costs may become compensatory as traffic increases and would, thus, be in the public interest at some future date. The pitfalls involved in this type of analysis are obvious.

One writer exploring recent rate cases puts forth the view that congressional intent as expressed in the Act of 1958 is not clear and as a result the normal competitive price competition among carriers might be interpreted as being destructive.[18]

There is much to support this viewpoint, and a high degree of uncertainty exists to say the least.

"OUT-OF-POCKET COSTS," THEORY AND PRACTICE

In theory, out-of-pocket costs should be a minimum below which rates should not be allowed to go, since these costs represent the actual costs directly related to performing the service in question. Even if the service is performed at this level, the overhead costs related to the shipment must be regained from other classes of traffic.[19] This is true in the long run, although for some time these losses may be regained from reduced expenditures in cost areas which are postponable, such as maintenance, and in reduced earnings to stockholders. Obviously, if, in the long run, the plant is to be kept up to standard and capital is to be attracted, then the costs of doing business will

---

[18] Robert A. Nelson, "Rate Making in Transportation—Congressional Intent," *Duke Law Journal*, Vol. 1960, No. 2, p. 221.

[19] See comments of Commissioner Alldredge in Petroleum from Robinson, Illinois to Indiana, 255 ICC 85, 92, 93.

have to be paid. However, the degree to which other shippers may bear these costs is difficult to determine in any given case. To illustrate, if the car-mile out-of-pocket costs of hauling commodity X between two points amount to 32 cents and the total fully allocated costs, including all overhead expenses, amount to 16 cents, then the total cost would be 48 cents. If the rate is set at 32 cents, then the other 16 cents must be recovered elsewhere, or the carrier will be forced to render inferior service unless some technological innovation can be found. If, in the above example, the rate should be set at a level below 32 cents, then each unit moved fails to cover the direct cost attributed to it, and the transporter is losing on each movement made. If this situation is sustained for any length of time, the only course of action is to eliminate such operations. It will be remembered that the economic character of the various carriers will determine the length of time for which such policies can be carried on. On the other hand, if the rate was set, say, at 40 cents, the "out-of-pocket" costs would be recovered, and some contribution would be made to the overhead costs as well. If the rate was set at 48 cents, then all costs of doing business (including the economic normal profit) would be recovered. Thus, there is a range of 16 cents between "out-of-pocket" costs and fully distributed costs where a rate might be set with full approval of the Commission.

There is increasing evidence that the Commission is likely to approve rate reductions if it can be assured that the new rates are sufficiently remunerative to cover the costs of the carrier proposing the rate. Further, the Commission seems more inclined than in past years to permit some experimentation in the rate structure. These experiments, although inclined to be somewhat upsetting to the carriers are likely to be a source of progress. Certain it is that progress in understanding these relationships will not come via a policy of rigid adherence to the status quo.

The key to the question is the regulatory body and its view of the term "reasonably compensatory." That is to say, the regulatory body allows some flexibility in the situation by adopting the view that rates should be reasonably compensatory and deciding on an *ad hoc* basis whether the rates in question meet this test. In order to reach a conclusion, the Commission examines cost data and compares the proposed rate with rates already in existence. Cost data relate to ton-mile or car-mile earnings to be anticipated by the new rate. There is apparent here a twofold assumption: (1) the cost data are known and (2) the data presented are accurate and true. These assumptions, in turn, require certain arbitrary procedures. It was pointed out earlier that the distinction between fixed and variable costs is often difficult to draw. Also, in projecting traffic levels, the carrier must make some rather vague estimates. These facts mean that such figures are most difficult to defend from attack; and, thus, the cost data, and especially the estimates of future traffic, provide a frequent battleground in rate hearings. Every effort is made to convince the regulatory authorities that the cost data are scientific and complete or, on the other hand, that they are incorrect and fail to take into account many important elements of cost. These high level sophisticated presentations make it difficult for the layman (and often the commissioners) to evaluate the situation clearly.

REASONABLE RATES IN INTERMODAL COMPETITION

The decision as to the reasonableness of a given rate depends upon many factors. It has been previously pointed out that a rate must fall between cost of service and value of service, and, as noted above, the cost of service is frequently a matter of debate in a rate hearing.

In all, there are four major items which relate to the reasonableness of a rate in the legal sense:

1. The potential car-mile, or ton-mile earnings which can be anticipated by the proposed rate.
2. The anticipated costs which are related to the service.
3. Potential effects upon the shipper and competing modes of transportation.
4. Possible creation of undue preference or prejudice against shippers or against a geographic area.

Of these items, numbers 1 and 2 are essentially statistical in nature. Although these data and the procedure relating to their calculation are often called into question, they do at least serve as a fairly reasonable bench-mark. Item number 1 is an exercise in market research and is subject to all the disadvantages of that inexact science.[20]

Items 3 and 4, on the contrary, are almost entirely subjective in nature. It would be hard to conceive of a rate change which could not have some effect upon a group of shippers at some point or upon carriers in competition. In practice, a rate hearing may be attended

---

[20] For an interesting treatment of the fundamentals of this problem, see Robert Ferber and P. J. Verdoom, *Research Methods in Economics and Business* (New York: The Macmillan Co., 1962).

by representatives of dozens of groups whose interest in the matter is tenuous indeed.

The Commission must hold hearings at which arguments pro and con are presented along with exhibits and data of all kinds. In this manner the Commission must weigh the evidence and reach some conclusion. These matters are of great concern to many groups other than the carriers. Chambers of Commerce, trade associations and others will be interested parties. Clearly, the Commission cannot please everyone and frequency pleases no one!

These proceedings illustrate the fact that relative rates, rather than absolute rates, are at issue. That is, if an area or an industry has a relative advantage, they may be little concerned with rate increases if the differential is preserved.

This is true to an even greater extent of the modes, and, as was noted, they often support each other in pressing for an increase. However, a proposal for reduction which may eliminate the differential is met with dismay.

If, as during the years 1945-55, costs were creeping upward, rate increases were common to all carriers. However, when (after costs have become firm) the carrier finds his rival seeking reduction, he may be caught between rising costs in his industry and a threat of reduction by the competitors which is very alarming. A serious element in trying to gauge the effects of a change is that the various modes and carriers concerned have "cried wolf" so often in the past that their lamentations are thought of as being a matter of course.

Motor carriers, in particular, have often made the claim that they would be eliminated if competition were allowed to rule unmitigated. Does this seem to be a likely development in our modern economy? As noted above, the motor carriers have accounted for increasing amounts of traffic through the years since 1930, rising to more than 22 per cent of the total intercity freight in 1960. The trucking industry has estimated that population shifts due to the rise of new industrial plants located off of rail lines and other factors are apt to increase motor carrier traffic to a greater extent in the future.[21] The motor transportation industry operates vehicles which have a substantial advantage in many ways. The industry has already reached a position of performing almost one-fourth of the aggregate ton-mile service in the economy. Social and economic changes point in encouraging directions. Does it, thus, seem likely that this industry can be destroyed by market competition? It seems more likely that motor transportation is in greater danger from private carriage and illegal or quasi-

---

[21] American Trucking Associations, Inc., *Changing Patterns in Transportation* (Washington, D. C.: 1960).

legal operations of non-regulated motor carriers than from rail competition.

Further, the motor carrier industry is not without other safeguards. The antitrust laws are still in force. The motor transport
industry is not without spokesmen before Congress.[22] One can hardly
visualize this industry passing from the scene. To be sure, since the
industry is highly segmentized, certain areas are vulnerable to competition. As noted above, auto transporters have received a blow.
However, the *industry* is intact. Several brands of automobiles have
dropped out of the market since 1945, but the automobile *industry*
is hardly in danger of collapse. The normal rise and fall of firms and
industrial change due to the workings of the market cannot and
should not be prevented. Neither the Interstate Commerce Commission nor any other group can act to prevent this economic development, painful though it may be to certain segments of the economy.

"THE PUBLIC INTEREST"

The ultimate test of Commission policy in this area, as in others,
is the preservation or promotion of the public interest. No one would
argue that the interests of any carrier or mode should take precedence
over the interest of the public. The public interest embraces a wide
area and is not always easily determined. There are many instances
where public interest does not square with individual interest. Also
there are frequent cases in which the public interest may be served
by following a policy opposite to that followed under other circumstances.

The first and very complex decision to be made is that of allowing
or refusing to allow entry into the industry. The consequences of
excessive competition are very well known; at the same time, allowing
too few carriers is equally bad. If error is to be made, it is probably
more desirable to allow too many carriers than to allow too few, the
advantage being that some leeway is allowed for more consumer
choice and for maximum play of competitive forces. It seems likely
that the regulatory commissions have generally allowed more carriers
than were actually necessary, knowing that some of the more inefficient would fall by the wayside. There is no guarantee that a carrier,
when admitted to the industry, will then be allowed to remain under
any and all conditions which might prevail. A permit or certificate is

---

[22] This suggests the possible relevance of J. K. Galbraith's theory of countervailing power as a form of control. See *American Capitalism* (Boston: Houghton
Mifflin Co., 1952).

not a franchise, but merely a "hunting license" which allows the carrier to enter the market and compete for available traffic. In some quarters there appears to be the attitude that the regulatory agencies, by allowing entry, assume responsibility for the carrier and must not allow the firm to suffer the consequences of competition. This is not (or should not be) the case. Even here, some exception must be noted. The ideal situation, which seldom prevails, is to have the exact number of firms necessary to serve the public with efficiency and at reasonable rates.

The commissions also face the problem of attempting to control the quality as well as the quantity, i.e., to prohibit, insofar as possible, carriers lacking adequate equipment or those who operate dishonestly from gaining entry into the field. These latter qualifications are relatively simple. Unfortunately, the other points are in serious question. Naturally, a would-be carrier, seeking entry, is seriously disturbed if entry is denied him, even though the possibility of his success is remote.

The regulatory bodies must gauge the effect which entry of a new firm will have and measure the qualifications of the firm to the best of their ability. Aside from the fact that mistakes can easily be made, the conditions change rapidly. From 1940 to 1945, the national interest was to have all the means of transport available. From 1955 to 1960, any further entry would be merely contributing to an already crowded situation.

An example of the multiple goals in this area is the Commission's policy in regard to common carriers vis-a-vis contract carriers. The Commission feels that it is in the public interest to maintain a healthy system of common carriage. However, those who find private carriage or contract carriage to be in their interest cannot be ignored. The national interest also may require that very uneconomic practices be followed. National defense considerations, for example, may dictate highly wasteful activities. The regulatory groups are constantly involved with these allocative matters, which are broad policy issues, and will be considered further in a later chapter.

THE TRANSPORTATION ACT OF 1958 AND INTERMODAL COMPETITION

The Transportation Act of 1958 was enacted to provide a guide line for the Commission in making its way through the morass of inter-carrier relationships. It is unfortunate that, having once begun this necessary task, the Congress either in error or by design failed to carry it to completion. The new section 15a (3) reads as follows:

> In a proceeding involving competition between carriers of different modes of transportation subject to this act, the Commission, in determining whether a rate is lower than a reasonable minimum rate, shall consider the facts and circumstances attending the movement of the traffic by the carrier or carriers to which the rate is applicable. Rates of a carrier shall not be held up to particular level to protect the traffic of any other mode of transportation, given due consideration to the objectives of the national transportation policy declared in this act.

The significance of the above statement is found in the last portion of the final sentence, "giving due consideration to the objectives of the national transportation policy. . ." If the Commission was, indeed, seeking guidance, this must have been a blow! After having stated that a carrier was now free to propose and the Commission was free to approve rates which might influence the traffic of another carrier, the Congress, to a large extent, nullified the whole thing by inserting the reference to the national policy.

From 1944, when in the Eastern-Central Motor Carriers Case[23] the Supreme Court, in reversing a Commission ruling, had chided the Commission for not taking the policy into consideration, the Commission had been slowly working its way out of the policy strait jacket. For a time after 1944, the Commission was dutiful in its strict observance of the national policy, although, in more recent years, it had become more inclined not to treat the policy as an ironclad directive. The railroads characterized the former policy as "umbrella rate making" and, as can be imagined, were most unhappy to be held in check. The Act of 1958 was, at first glance, a confirmation of the de facto policy enunciated in the New Automobile case previously cited. The admonition of the Congress to remain faithful to the national policy preserved and, in deed, gave new life to the ambiguity of the pre-1958 era. One student of the problem, after careful study, has concluded that no visable change has taken place in Commission policy since the Act of 1958 was passed, saying:

> We are now in a position to suggest an answer to the purpose for which this paper is addressed, namely, how, if at all, has the 1958 amendment to section 15a affected the ICC's policies with respect to the regulation of interagency competitive ratemaking? On the basis of a detailed examination of fifty-nine cases on the rail I. and S. docket decided over a period of thirty-four months, the writer's answer to the foregoing question is simply that he

---

[23] U. S. 321, U. S. 194 (1944).

is unable to detect any significant change in the Commission's policies as compared with those which Professor Williams found to prevail during the period preceding the 1958 law.[24]

The outcome of this situation is yet to be seen and will be discussed further as a policy matter in a later chapter.

Summary

This chapter has examined the serious policy issue of intramodel and intermodel competition, a problem which has likely consumed more time and effort than any other issue. Since this problem was relatively insignificant before 1935 when the Commission became responsible for motor carrier regulation, it was not contemplated in the original act.

Except for the largely inadequate guidance provided by the national policy, the Commission has largely been forced to proceed on a trial and error basis, complicated by the fluid character of the problems encountered and by the lack of control in many areas. This problem is far from finished and will, no doubt, continue to be of major importance. Further consideration will be given to these matters in Chapter XXIII.

---

[24] Robert W. Harbeson, "The Regulation of Interagency Rate Competition Under the Transportation Act of 1958," *ICC Practitioners' Journal*, Vol. XXX, December, 1962, Sec. 1, No. 3, p. 303.

CHAPTER XXI

Transport Consolidation and Integration

In the United States, the various modes of transport have generally been separately owned and operated. No real evidence exists as to the reasons for this development, and apparently it was entirely a matter of historical accident. Since before regulation, there were no legal barriers which would have prevented the integration of a new technology into an existing mode. In other industries the new technological techniques are either developed or captured by the existing related industries and may come to dominate the parent activity, e.g., bicycle makers turning to automobiles and radio manufacturers turning to television. In one sense, this is rather remarkable because of the fact that carriers much more than other business firms have carried on their business with a high degree of cooperation.

Cooperation among the firms in a given mode has been very important, and, while not so extensive, intermodal cooperation has always been widespread. It seems wise at this point to distinguish between the various terms. Cooperation is merely informal joint use of the modes, as in the case where a shipper might use rail to a given point and then complete the movement by truck. Consolidation generally refers to the formal joining together of firms within the same mode. Integration, on the other hand, is most often used to describe common ownership of differing modes.

364

INTRAMODAL CONSOLIDATION

Almost all of our major rail systems, many large truck lines and airlines are the result of mergers and consolidations which have taken place over the years.[1] It was typical in the early development of a carrier that it should be conceived as a local project to serve local needs, and, under these assumptions, the building of extensive carriers would have been impossible with local capital alone. A natural development was the joining together of these small segments, in order to have a more efficient and far-reaching system.

This process was limited only by the capital requirements, the managerial problems which exist and, at a later date, various legal barriers.

Throughout the industry, there are various degrees of control on an intramodal level which must be defined: (1) outright ownership and operation as a result of merger, (2) control and operation (often by lease)[2] of a firm which remains independent in ownership, and (3) financial domination with no control over operations or management policy. In all modes, especially in the rail industry, all three of these situations exist.

There are clearly varied purposes and implications involved in these policies. A carrier may wish to control another, in order to be assured that traffic will be interchanged in its favor or to provide a unified operation. On the other hand, the goal may be entirely the desire to enjoy the financial benefits which may be available.

The desire to control the traffic and to obtain a more direct route is, without doubt, the most important goal of intramodal consolidation. There are many instances where intense rivalry has existed between carriers to control a strategic route or interchange connection.

---

[1] The Northern Pacific and the Western Pacific are the only major railroads now essentially the same as they were when originally built. Even the Western Pacific has an addition, constructed in the early 1930's. Neither of these roads acquired others.

[2] In most cases, these leases are for periods of 99 years or 999 years; in such cases one might venture to say that they are permanent. Also, the lessee firm operates in most cases as a completely indistinguishable part of the lessor firm. Thus, the Texas and New Orleans operates as part of the Southern Pacific and, in the operating sense, is completely integrated into the Southern Pacific system. On the other hand, the Cotton Belt operates as an independent carrier but is controlled by the Southern Pacific. The third case is illustrated by the Norfolk and Western, in which the Pennsylvania holds a major interest. The N & W is a completely independent road, and the Pennsylvania is interested only in the income from its investment.

In the rail industry, this has often resulted in joint ownership of a strategic route, as in the case of the Richmond, Fredericksburg and Potomac. This road owns the shortest route between Washington, D. C., and Richmond, Virginia, is owned by several roads and is operated as an independent company.

The Legal Limitations

Before carrying this discussion further, let us review briefly the legal requirements relating to the problem. It will be remembered that the Interstate Commerce Act provided for control over mergers, consolidations, financial arrangements, and other matters relative to the control problem. However, all these controls are such that the regulatory agency has a degree of flexibility and may use its judgment. In the Panama Canal Act, the Congress prohibited rail control of water carriers but, even in this case, made it possible for the Commission to permit such control "in the public interest." No mention of control of rail by truck lines or airlines is made, since at the time the legislation was passed it was not contemplated that any such occasion would arise.

In short, the regulatory bodies have a substantial area of control over the carriers in this area. The Sherman Act and related legislation in the anti-trust field apply to carriers (except rate bureaus), and these provisions would be implemented by the Justice Department, if it was felt that restraint of trade was a significant factor. Historically, most of the action in this area has centered around intramodal competition. In the broadest terms, the Commission and the Civil Aeronautics Board have followed a policy of preventing the creation of any undue advantage or substantial elimination of competition.

It has been pointed out earlier that the fear of monopoly dominated regulatory policy before 1920. In this climate, the obvious reaction was to oppose strongly any serious attempts at consolidation.

HISTORICAL ASPECTS OF CONSOLIDATION IN THE RAILROAD INDUSTRY

Following 1920, the attitude changed, and the Commission, far from looking askance at consolidation, attempted to encourage and promote it, at least on paper; and, in the Act of 1920, further consolidation was made the national policy. In adopting this attitude, the Commission and the Congress recognized the fact that there had been overbuilding in earlier years and that there were many railroads which had no real chance of success as independent companies.[3] Certain restrictions or conditions were attached to this policy, as follows:

The Act directed the Interstate Commerce Commission to prepare and adopt a plan for the consolidation of the railway properties of the United States into a limited number of systems. In drawing up this plan, the Commission was required to observe certain general principles. These were (1) that competition should be preserved "as fully as possible," (2) that, wherever practicable, the existing routes and channels of trade and commerce were to be maintained and (3) that, subject to the foregoing requirements, the systems should be of approximately equal earning power under a uniform level of rates.

The task given to the Interstate Commerce Commission to prepare a consolidation plan was not an easy one, and the Commission recognized this fact. It was noted in Chapter XX that the railroad leaders of the late nineteenth and early twentieth centuries had attempted, by various means, to control intramodal competition by the establishment of communities of interest. These matters also related to consolidation. The Goulds, Harriman, Hill, Huntington, and later the Van Sweringen brothers all entertained ideas of further consolidation and the establishment of a transcontinental system. Of course, each of these men was forced to proceed on a more or less unilateral basis, and no "master plan" for consolidation existed. There was fear, which was later justified, that any "master plan" was likely to arouse conflicting interests.

The first tentative plan issued by the Commission was prepared by Professor William Z. Ripley of Harvard, at that time a well-known railroad authority.[4]

The fears of the Commission were justified, since no one seemed willing to endorse the plan, and the Commission asked to be relieved of its responsibility. The Congress refused to release the Commission, however, and it was forced to continue its efforts.

During the 1920's, railroads were active in the purchase of securities and in other ways seeking to expand their influence over other rail properties, none of which resulted in any solid consolidation.

Failing in its request to be released from its assignment, the Commission decided in 1928 to proceed with its mission. The result of these efforts was released in December 1929 and was like other

---

[3] For years, the question of consolidation and of federal ownership of railroads was a perennial topic of academic debate teams and, in the early 1920's, was a lively item of public discussion.

[4] *In the Matter of Consolidation of Railway Properties*, 63 ICC 455.

efforts of this sort, engulfed by the market crash and subsequent economic collapse. The plan itself was not satisfactory and was, in any case, doomed to failure in view of the prevailing conditions.[5]

This plan was modified in 1932 into a four party plan by the consolidation conferences to provide four eastern systems, a plan accepted by the Commission in June 1932.[6] The economic situation made it impossible to put the plan into effect.

Further efforts were made shortly in the form of the Coolidge Committee, a group under the chairmanship of the former President and actually performed by the staff of the Brookings Institution.[7] Barriger calls this report the finest and most logical report ever written on the subject.[8] It was not acceptable, however, to many parties and was never adopted.

Many others interested themselves in the problem during these desperate years, but the next formal plan was the Prince Plan of 1933. This, the last of the formal "plans," was instigated by Mr. Roosevelt when President-elect and paid for by a public-spirited Boston financier, F. H. Prince. The actual author was the consolidation expert and rail authority, J. W. Barriger, later President of the Pittsburgh and Lake Erie Railroad. The merit of the Prince plan was that it attacked the problem of duplication of rail facilities and attempted to preserve competition at principal industrial centers.[9]

Of course, all of these plans were permissive, in that no requirement to merge was embodied and the positive action was up to the railroads. Aside from much discussion, the plans were largely ignored.

The basic objective of the various plans was to strengthen the total system by proceeding on a regional basis to merge the small and weak roads into a unified system with the hope that several strong systems would then prevail in each area of the country.

The weakness in this analysis soon became clear. The strong roads did not wish to ally themselves with those which had been poorly planned or poorly managed. In other words, where the planners hoped that a strong and weak road combination would produce a strong road, the carriers feared that the result would be a weak road. To cite an example, in the southeastern United States, any of the railroads serving that area would have been desirous of merging

---

[5] *In the Matter of Consolidation of the Railway Properties,* 159 ICC 522.

[6] *In the Matter of Consolidation of the Railway Properties,* 185 ICC 403.

[7] See Moulton and Associates, *American Transportation Problem, op. cit.*

[8] John W. Barriger, "Why Consolidation," in *Revolution in Transportation,* ed. Karl M. Ruppenthal (Stanford: Graduate School of Business, Stanford University, 1960), p. 25.

[9] See *Poor's Manual of Railroads,* 1935, pp. 39-48.

with the Norfolk and Western, a very strong and prosperous road. On the other hand, none wanted the Norfolk Southern, a road in chronic difficulty.

It was ironic, indeed, that at this time (1930-1940) the benefits of soundly conceived consolidations would have been of far-reaching consequence. Rail carriers were suffering from overcapacity due both to the decline in traffic and the competition from motor and air transportation. Consolidations would have made it possible to dispose of surplus equipment and plant and to adjust the scale of operations to the traffic conditions which existed.

Unfortunately, as we know, this was not feasible. Capital necessary to undertake major consolidations was not available. Many major railroads were themselves in serious financial straits and were in no position to enter into a protracted transaction requiring a large amount of money, when the money market was demoralized. Indeed, the railroads were themselves far from embarking upon such adventures, seeking funds chiefly from public sources. Speaking of the Reconstruction Finance Corporation, Schumpeter says:

> Primarily intended as a support to banks and cognate institutions, and as an agency to carry part of the burden of loans that were noneligible in the sense of the reserve bank legislation [i.e., unable to secure adequate credit from member institutions], its scope naturally included the only type of big business that was seriously threatened, railroads.[10]

At the end of the 1930's, prospects for consolidation had improved somewhat, although certainly not very much. However, the Commission again addressed itself to this problem.

The Act of 1940 considered the problem and made certain changes in the policy as follows:

First, the requirement that railroad consolidations or unifications should conform to a Commission-made plan of consolidation, drawn up in advance, was eliminated.

Included in the law relating to consolidations was the enumeration of certain factors which should be taken into consideration in the determination of whether a proposed consolidation or unification was in the public interest. These factors are:

> (1) the effect of the proposed transaction upon adequate transportation service to the public; (2) the effect upon the public interest of the inclusion, or failure to include, other railroads in the territory involved in the proposed transaction; (3) the total fixed

---

[10] Joseph A. Schumpeter, *Business Cycles,* Vol. II (New York: McGraw-Hill Book Co., 1939), pp. 940, 941.

charges resulting from the proposed transaction; and (4) the interest of the carrier employees affected.

The new element in the consolidation provisions of the law was the addition of provisions designed to protect railroad labor affected by consolidations. The Commission was directed to require, as a condition of its approval of a consolidation or unification, that there be a "fair and equitable arrangement" to protect the interests of railroad employees affected. The Act further required that the Commission should include terms and conditions in its order of approval, which would provide that for four years the affected employees should not be placed in a worse position with respect to their employment as a result of the consolidation or unification. The Commission may require that labor be protected for a period longer than four years, and unions may make demands on their own behalf which are more stringent than the legal provisions.

It can be seen that the addition of the provisions of the Act of 1940 made the prospect of consolidation somewhat remote. If the Commission and the carriers were required to observe all these conditions in a literal sense, the scope of the task would be gigantic. In part because of these restrictions and for other reasons, interest in consolidation lagged, and there were few moves between 1940 and the end of World War II.[11]

After 1945, a revival of interest took place. Between 1945 and 1960, six combinations were completed, and, in the early 1960's, much greater interest has been shown.[12] It would appear that almost all groups are now generally in favor of rail mergers, with the exception of labor. The reasons for this renewal of interest are not hard to find. The serious plight of the rail carriers is well known, and merger seems to be at least one solution to their problems. The importance of eliminating duplicate and indirect mileage has increased greatly as the competition from other carriers has become acute, and pressures for consolidation are greater, as Barriger says:

> The pressure to consolidate is now largely generated by traffic losses to other forms of transportation. I say 'largely' because there are other factors as well, including inflationary trends of wages and prices, obsolete working-rules with employees, over-

---

[11] The Gulf, Mobile and Ohio was a result of the merger between the Mobile and Ohio and the Gulf, Mobile and Northern in 1940 and was probably the most important.

[12] Some of these, e.g, the Pere Marquette-Chesapeake and Ohio, merely formalized a long-standing relationship. In other cases and in most contemplated mergers, the parties have, in the past, been completely independent of each other and, in some cases, serious competitors.

regulation and mounting taxation. While it is hoped that pressures from these sources will be relieved, their effects will be mitigated by consolidation. The most disturbing new factor is loss of volume to competing forms of transportation. Whether this loss is cause or effect is immaterial at this point. The fact is that railroads, especially in the East, are losing volume, some absolutely and others relatively.[13]

Unless the management of these duplicating systems have common ground, the chance of success seems remote.

Advantages of Rail Consolidation

The financial savings resulting from consolidation would, without doubt, be of major proportions.[14] These savings would accrue, for the most part, from elimination of duplicate facilities, elimination of redundant workers, and the use of the most efficient facilities in each case.

Sizable savings would also result from standardized procedures in maintenance, purchasing of supplies, and related activities. However, a major source of savings would be the intensive utilization of the most efficient route for line haul operations, which is often impossible under independent ownership.

An example is seen in Figure 21-1. Suppose railroad M and railroad N are competing for traffic from A to C, both important points. Railroad N serves point B, a point of less importance, and has a circuitous route to point C, while railroad M has a direct route. So long as the two roads are under separate ownership, railroad N will compete for through traffic on its lines. If, however, the two roads are under single ownership, the through traffic from A to C would be routed over M, and N would be used only for traffic to B.

Sizable savings would accrue from the more intensive utilization of equipment and the reduced need for returning empty cars to the home road and the likelihood of increased utilization, which would

---

[13] John W. Barriger, "Why Consolidation," *op. cit.*, p. 15.

[14] Any reliable estimates of total savings are, of course, very much subject to question. One writer estimates the total as $1 billion per year (Gilbert Burck, "A Plan to Save the Railroads," *Fortune*, August 1958). Under any circumstances, the savings would not be realized for some years, in view of the legal protection due to various groups and the fact that a rearrangement of the physical plant would take a long time to complete. Any significant reduction in the labor force would also take some time. A common approach to this problem is to avoid any outright layoffs by failing to replace workers as they die or retire, a very humanitarian practice but also a very slow procedure.

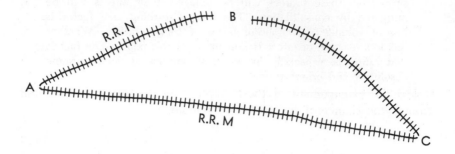

Fig. 21-1

reduce the total number of units necessary to perform a given level of service.

Further savings would be found in reduced time spent in yards and terminals (much transit time is used up by delays in yards and switching), solid blocking of cars and less need for transferring cars from one road to another. There would also be greater opportunities for standardization of equipment, which would again reduce the total car fleet and improve its efficiency.

Under the present system, those railroads which have adequate numbers of new cars complain with justice that the daily fees paid by roads using these cars are not adequate and that this factor eliminates any incentive for the roads with few cars to make further investments.

Barriers to Consolidation

While much discussion has taken place in recent years and many prospective mergers are in the wind, few actual mergers have taken place due to both internal and external factors.

Internal factors: It was noted above that labor almost always formally opposes a proposal to merge. Economists would be quick to point out that rail consolidations would probably preserve more jobs than any program of arbitrary make-work policy. It is, however, very difficult to convince workers and unions who are immediately concerned of the wisdom of long range restraint. It seems more than likely that workers will continue to be fearful of merger policies, despite the fact that attrition would probably solve the workers' problems. One important factor is that attrition does not aid the union. It is likely, however, that others who pay lip service to merger plans do not, in the final analysis, look upon them with favor. Not surprisingly, the carrying out of a major consolidation is a staggering effort in itself. The stockholders must agree to a plan; the regulatory agencies must agree (after long study). In any given case, opposition will come, not only from labor but from competing carriers of all modes, from communities and other groups. Even under the most favorable circumstances, the completion of the procedure is extremely time consuming. A consolidation may upset long-standing relationships, and the results may be difficult to forecast. Not the least of these matters will be the fact that carrier executives will be concerned with their future status. Elimination of surplus workers does not refer only to wage earners. The resulting system cannot have two presidents, and some shifting on the "totem pole" will be necessary. Having spent a number of years as an employee of a given company often competing with the other road in the merger, the officer may have a serious problem in adjusting.[15] These problems are most serious when the merger concerns two railroads of equal size and power. If a small road is purchased by a large road, the situation is not so likely to arise.

A frequently mentioned disadvantage of consolidation and also integration is the problem of management. There is no question that management would constitute a major problem, but there is no reason to believe that the problems would be insurmountable.

In 1960, the New England States, along with New York State, had almost 16,000 miles of railroad. If all these miles were consolidated into a single system, the mileage would be somewhat greater than the 13,073 miles operated by the Santa Fe over a much larger geographic area.

However, the immediate result of the merger would be the elimination of much surplus mileage. The New Haven and the Boston & Maine serve many duplicate points in southern New England, and these routes could be eliminated. In almost all areas of the nation, except for the far West, there is a high degree of duplication. These facts do not eliminate the management problem, but they do make it a great deal less formidable than would appear at first glance.

---

[15] Leonard, an authority of mergers, cites this as a major stumbling block. See W. N. Leonard, *Railway Consolidation Under the Transportation Act of 1920* (New York: Columbia University Press, 1946).

CONSOLIDATION IN THE OTHER MODES

Motor

Since World War II, motor carrier growth and consolidation have been moving at a rapid pace. There seem to be several reasons for this development.

1. The death or retirement of many of the original founders of the successful motor carrier firms.
2. The natural desire on the part of the motor carrier management to explore the possibilities of economies arising from large-scale operation.
3. Legislative and administrative policies such as the extremely narrow definition of rights, restrictions on "tacking," the growth of the "agricultural" exemption, and of private carriage.
4. Growing marketing areas served by motor carriers, necessitating consolidated operations.
5. Increasingly severe competition in the years following World War II.

Such consolidations will be likely to result in a situation of regional oligopoly in place of the atomistic competition which has characterized the motor transportation industry. There is no indication that such a situation would be detrimental to the shipping public; it might, in fact, result in increased service through stronger, well-integrated companies, and, in fact, this seems to have been the case in many instances.

The advantage of consolidation in this area is essentially the same as those in the rail system, although the degree of potential savings is probably much less, due obviously to the fact that motor carriers have no right of way and much less plant facilities than the railroads.

While some writers see a serious danger in this movement, it does not seem likely that any problems will develop.[16]

There is considerable opinion that the degree of competition in most areas of the trucking industry is too intense for the continued welfare of the industry. This relates especially to item 3 above. The

---

[16] Walter Adams and James B. Hendry, *Trucking Mergers, Concentration, and Small Business: An Analysis of Interstate Commerce Commission Policy, 1950-56,* Report prepared for the Select Committee on Small Business, U. S. Senate (Washington, D.C.: Government Printing Office, 1957).

Commission has often granted such narrow operating rights that virtually the only solution is the joining together of several carriers in order to secure reasonable commodity or geographic authority.

The relatively simple structure of motor carriers and the fact that the stockholders are often so few make for much less difficulty in carrying a merger to completion.

There is often a chain reaction set off by a major motor carrier merger. This can be illustrated in Figure 21-2.

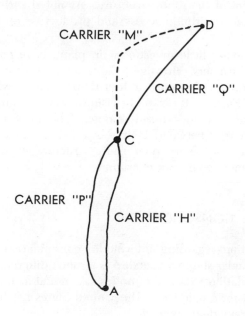

Fig. 21-2

Suppose that carrier "H" and "P" have authority from A to C and at C interchange with "Q" freight destined to D, an important point. Now let us assume that carrier "H" acquires carrier "Q" and has a single line movement from A to D. Carrier "P" is now at a disadvantage and will be highly opposed to interchanging traffic with its rival. Carrier "P" will thus attempt to ally itself with another carrier in order to serve D in a direct fashion, such as carrier "M". The reader will recall that direct one line service is very important to motor carriers.

In a recent case in the Southeast, the acquisition of a Midwest carrier by one operating, for the most part, along the eastern seaboard upset several carriers who had relied on interchange from carrier X for cargoes in the Midwest. This set off a round of mergers in an effort to make up for loss of tonnage formerly interchanged.

Air Carriers

In terms of numbers, the merger movement is small but none-theless significant. The major advantage in airline mergers is clearly the improvement of the route structure. As noted earlier, good route structure is vital to airline success and productive routes are few in number.

Airlines, having little investment in plant, have no strong incentive such as rail carriers. However, the time seems to be drawing near when the operation of planes at less than capacity will be a major disadvantage. Further, the rapidly rising costs of equipment put the small carrier at a serious disadvantage. The most recent case (in 1960) of the merger between United Air Lines and Capital Airlines was a clear case of a very poor route structure imposing a burden which management could not overcome.

INTERMODAL CONSOLIDATION

The situation regarding intermodal consolidation or integration of the modes under single ownership is a much different problem from that of consolidation within the modes. As noted at the outset of this chapter, the historic practice in the United States has held in favor of separate and individual ownership.

In theory, this makes no real sense. In essence, the various modes are merely different processes or methods of producing the same service, viz., transportation, in the same manner as the Bell System's using various technological means, e.g., voice phone or teletype to provide communication service.

POLICY BACKGROUND

As noted, the regulatory bodies have wide latitude in this area, being empowered to approve mergers, consolidations and other actions, if, in the judgment of the regulatory body, the action is in the public interest. While the modes are, in great part, operated independently of each other, there are instances of common ownership which have existed for some years. Railroad ownership and operation of motor carrier service are fairly widespread. Many railroads began to operate motor carrier service in some fashion before 1935 and, as a consequence, obtained grandfather rights. In some cases such as the Southern Pacific, the motor carrier operation (Pacific Motor Transport) is a wholly owned subsidiary of the parent company and operates with considerable autonomy. In other cases, the motor operations are used only to supplement the rail service, feeding traffic into the rail system for further transportation. In general, the Interstate Commerce Commission has been, over the years, reluctant to approve rail-owned motor carriage which does not opeate chiefly as supplementary service. There are, however, some signs that this policy is changing, as will be noted later.

Before World War II, railroads engaged in rather extensive motor bus operations. Water carrier operations, except for those directly related such as lighterage, ferry transfer, etc., are almost unknown; and, in a recent case, the Commission denied an application by the Southern Pacific and Illinois Central to take control of the John I. Hay Barge Line, a common carrier operating on the Mississippi River.[17] Other cases are pending, and there is no reason to feel that the Hay case will be a matter of precedent. There are no instances in the United States in which an air carrier is operated by rail or vice versa.[18] Neither are there instances where a motor carrier owns and operates a rail carrier, although there are cases where a rail carrier has become dominated by motor operations.[19]

Recent developments, such as the renewed interest in "piggybacking" and movement of trailers by coastal vessels, act to promote integration at least, if the participants can overcome their ingrained suspicion long enough to operate effectively.

In theory at least, the regulatory agencies could approve any combination of merger or consolidation, either inter- or intramodal, if the proposal was in the public interest.

There seems to be revival of interest in the consolidation of various modes of transport, both within and outside of the industry. It remains to be seen if there is developed a true transportation company which would operate a truly integrated service.

---

[17] In Finance Docket No. 20940, March 8, 1962.

[18] There are cases where rail and air have operated joint services. In the early 1930's, transcontinental service was offered by an air carrier using rail service to cross the dangerous mountain areas.

[19] The East Tennessee & Western North Carolina operates motor carriage much more extensive than its rail operation.

The major objection to integration is voiced by the motor carriers who fear that the objective of the rail carriers would be to acquire and then eliminate motor carrier service. Before 1940, this fear may have been justified; however, in recent years, evidence would indicate that rail carriers have, at long last, recognized the function of motor carrier service and wish to operate in that field. Section 5 (2) (b) of the Interstate Commerce Commission requires that the use of motor service by a railroad must be to the public advantage.[20]

Over the years, the Commission's policy has been to impose certain restrictions in the form of conditions which must exist in order for motor operations to be in the public interest.

Condition I limits the service to be performed by truck to the transportation of the rail traffic of the railroad. The service must, in general, be of an auxiliary and supplemental nature. For example, in Figure 21-3, the railroad operating from A to B with a branch line to C would probably be allowed to operate motor carriage to C from point D as an auxiliary and supplemental service. It would probably not be allowed to operate direct motor service from A to B, or from B to F where no rail service exists.

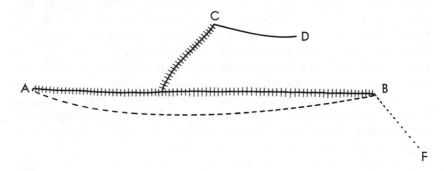

Fig. 21-3

The second condition limits service to points which are rail stations. Condition 3 limits the service by prohibiting the service between certain named "key points," A and B in Figure 21-3. Determination of key points is not easy, and some controversy has existed.[21]

Condition 4 requires that all contractual arrangements between the rail and motor parties be reported to the Commission and be

---

[20] U. S. C. Section 5 (2)(b).

[21] Kansas City S. Transport Co., Inc., Common Carrier Application, 28 MCC, 5, 11.

subject to such revision as necessary to be fair and equitable to all parties.

The fifth condition reserves to the Commission the right to make future changes as may be necessary to adhere to the auxiliary and supplemental nature of the service.

Some more liberal interpretation of these requirements has been evident in recent years, but, as the Commission has pointed out, any substantial change must come from the Congress.[22]

The revival of interest in piggyback operations has brought the whole scope of rail-motor operations up for further consideration.

Much remains to be seen as to how these operations will influence the situation.[23] An important factor is the growing use of piggyback operations by freight forwarders. These activities are, by nature, intermodal and promise an enhanced degree of integration.

POLICY ISSUES AND PROSPECTS

In its struggle with the issues of consolidation and integration, the Commission has, as usual, been faced with the ambiguities of the national transportation policy.

Clearly, the question at issue is whether the various inherent advantages would be preserved by further consolidation and integration.

It is not easy to see how the national interest would be possibly impaired by further consolidation, and, indeed, the interests of the transportation industry would clearly be served by such a policy.

There seems to be general agreement that the transportation industry, as it is now constituted, has substantial over capacity. This over capacity is both inter- and intramodal, and, so long as separate ownership exists, there is incentive to utilize this over capacity.

It does not seem likely that any one of the modes would be allowed to pass out of existence by common owners, since all of them provide a specific service. It will become increasingly difficult for the Commission to find sound ground as trends toward piggybacking and other quasi-integrated operations become more important. The concept of separate and distinct ownership as a sacred creed makes no sense, especially in face of the growing trend toward diversification throughout industry. It is to be hoped that the artificial legal barriers will soon be removed.

---

[22] Baltimore and A. R. Co. Purchase—Bison Lines, Inc., 60 MCC 509, 518.
[23] Movement of Highway Trailers by Rail, 293 ICC, 93, 96.

Summary

As this chapter has brought out, the concept of consolidation has been basic to the industry for many years and is indeed now proceeding at a rapid pace. The combination of carriers on an intermodal or integrated basis is less common and, from the policy standpoint, more difficult to accomplish. However, the barriers are legal and not economic. It is to be hoped that continued progress toward integration will be made.

PART V

Problems and Prospects

"Societies, like individuals, have their moral crises and their spiritual revolutions. The student can observe the results which these cataclysms produce, but he can hardly without presumption attempt to appraise them, for it is at the fire which they have kindled that his own small taper has been lit."

R. H. TAWNEY

Religion and the Rise of Capitalism

CHAPTER XXII

Carrier Management Problems

The management of a carrier in the strict sense presents problems identical to those which arise in any firm, viz., the operation of the enterprise in order to secure a profit with a minimum expenditure of resources. "In essence, management is simply the process of decision making and control over the actions of human beings for the express purpose of attaining predetermined goals."[1] As expressed by a classic work on the subject, "Management is the unseen force which drives all that is physical within a factory. It synchronizes human relationships and is by far the most vitalizing factor in our present industrial age."[2] Although the fundamentals of management, as expressed by the above definitions, are applicable to any business enterprise, the transportation firm clearly presents certain unique problems.

Perhaps most important of these is the fact that the transportation enterprise is, by its nature, physically extensive, i.e., the plant of a transportation firm is apt to be located at a number of geographically separated points. For example, the Consolidated Freightways System (a motor carrier) carries on operations in thirty-one states, including Hawaii and Alaska. The Santa Fe Railroad operates and manages

---

[1] Stanley Vauce, *Industrial Administration* (New York: McGraw-Hill Book Co., 1959), p. 1.

[2] Richard H. Landsburgh and William R. Spriegel, *Industrial Management,* (3d ed. New York: John Wiley & Sons, Inc., 1940).

real property and rolling stock in eleven states from Chicago to the
West Coast. Thus, the span of control is, of necessity, very long with
regional officials having, in general, a substantial degree of authority.
In the railroad field, the generally time honored procedure has been
to rely upon the geographical division of the property with an executive officer (usually a division superintendent) assigned to each
division in whom a high degree of authority is vested. Especially in
the years before the development of modern communications, the
division officer was largely dependent upon his own judgment in making decisions and had great authority, as well as absolute responsibility
for results. Staff officers at headquarters were not, for the most part,
in the chain of command and the division officer reported directly to
the general manager, who, in turn, was responsible to the vice president for operations or a comparable executive officer.

Each division had a complement of line and staff officers in
charge of maintenance, supply, and other areas, which enabled the
division superintendent to perform his task with all supporting activities under his control. The reader will note that this organization
plan has strong military overtones and, indeed, was probably adopted
from the military organization.[3] This type of organization naturally
put much emphasis upon experience and strong individual compe-
tence as opposed to reliance upon a staff. Over the years, the emphasis
upon local authority has made it necessary to rigidify the operating
procedure, and a premium has been put on "operating by the book."

For various reasons, rail management developed a strong and
rigid tradition of advancement through the ranks, with little chance
of rapid upward movement even for the able candidate, except in rare
cases.

A further consequence was the emphasis placed on operating
officers as opposed to staff officers, insofar as advancement was concerned. Operating experience was generally considered to be a
fundamental qualification for higher management, and exceptions were
few. However, a frequent exception at the very top is found in the
case of those skilled in finance. In the years before 1910 when one

---

[3] In addition to the similarity of problems faced, a number of early railroad
builders and administrators were drawn from military circles. These men undoubtedly had a strong influence upon the organization of the railroads in their
formative years. Generals Dodge, McClellan, Sherman, and other prominent
Civil War figures were associated with railroad building and management during
their lives. An excellent philosophical discussion of the background of railroad
management techniques is found in Thomas C. Cochran, *Railroad Leaders, 1845-
1890,* Studies in Entrepreneurial History (Cambridge: Harvard University Press,
1953).

man control was more common, those in control were, in their own eyes at least, managers in the highest sense. For example, Jay Gould, who was considered by his contemporaries to be a speculator pure and simple, was in one sense at least a manager. His stewardship of the Missouri Pacific was in contrast to his actions in the Erie, a model of highly personal management.[4]

Collis P. Huntington of the Southern Pacific "Big Four" is reported to have said that Gould was a speculator whom he would not attempt to beat in Wall Street but that, on the other hand, he (Huntington) was a railroad manager whom Gould could not beat.[5] Perhaps the most efficient one-man management figure was Hill of the Great Northern. Hill was unique among early builders, in that he saw the value of building to high standards for the long-run operating efficiency of the carrier. He also saw the value of well-laid-out feeder lines. Hill, unlike some early builders, spent his early years in the transportation business, and he was not building as a speculative venture in the sense that the Central Pacific was built. Harriman was Hill's only peer in the building and operation of railroads, and he had no superiors. Following 1910, the era of one man control came to an end, except for the very small railroad, and the "professional" manager came into his own.

Railroad management faced other problems peculiar to their industry, in that an unusually high degree of interindustry cooperation soon came to be necessary. The operation of the railroads as a "system" means that each company must take into account the fact that other firms will be directly influenced by what is done. A serious consequence of this integration of the system is the limits placed upon innovation. No major rail carrier can proceed to undertake major modifications in equipment or in operating technique without gauging the effect upon the other firms. Closely related to this factor is the necessity for merging public and private interests. Cochran points out how the railroad leaders of the 1880's recognized with great reluctance the necessity of dealing with public authorities. In general, the task was undertaken with considerable distaste, although it was recognized as necessary in order to carry on the work of "building the country." Little credit was given to the politician and, at best, he was considered to be misguided.

---

[4] Julius Grodinsky, *Jay Gould, His Business Career, 1867-1892* (Philadelphia: University of Pennsylvania Press, 1957), pp. 577 ff.

[5] Richard O'Connor, *Gould's Millions* (New York: Doubleday Co., 1962). However, Lewis, *op. cit.*, points out that Huntington's contemporaries did not consider him to be much of a railroad manager, although he was a promoter and manipulator without a peer.

In the same vein, C. P. Huntington, in the famous Colton letters, shows a most pragmatic approach to his legislative dealings.[6]

Railroads have been closely regulated for many years, and management must pursue a policy which recognizes these facts. Especially in the competitive situation which the railroads have faced since 1930, public policy considerations complicate management problems greatly. In light of the above factors, the ideal railroad executive would be a man who can operate a division involving complex details, combining day to day routine with emergencies and later in his career accept the broad responsibilities of quasi-public enterprise, interlaced with competition.

In recent years, more emphasis has been put upon staff functions, with some railroads reducing the authority of the division officer and lodging more authority in general officers. This is especially true of very small or very large railroads. On the largest railroads the divisions are sometimes organized into regions or other areas. On small railroads general officers can exercise a greater span of authority and often supervise the entire system from headquarters. As is true of most organizations, the imposition of more layers of authority complicates the flow of communication throughout the organization and makes decision making more difficult and cumbersome.

Railroads have historically carried on many functions which were only indirectly related to transportation, such as sale of land and industrial and agricultural development which have required highly specialized staff talents.

A major factor in railroad management is the lasting influence which is imposed by past managerial decisions. Once a rail route has been chosen and the road constructed, there is a limit as to what even the best management can do. The line can be upgraded and substantially rebuilt and re-equipped as was done with the Union Pacific under the Harriman influence early in the century. However, unless the potential is present in terms of traffic, such measures are of no avail. Early decisions or historical accidents, such as the Baltimore and Ohio's exclusion from direct entry into Manhattan, may hamper management for years into the future. Probably more than in any other industry, such decisions are beyond recall for many years.

On the other hand, a strong and forward looking management can often transform an indifferent physical plant into a profitable and efficient road by judicious management and some exercise of imagination.[7] Some railroads, e.g., the Pennsylvania and the Santa Fe,

---

[6] See Cochran, op. cit., pp. 197 ff., and Lewis, op. cit., pp. 316 ff.

[7] James H. Lemley, The Gulf, Mobile & Ohio (Chicago: Richard D. Irwin Company, 1953).

apparently enjoyed the advantages of sound original decisions along with efficient management throughout the years. In other cases, notably the Southern Pacific, monopolistic advantages and area economic development would have overcome all but the worst management.[8] Since the life of a railroad is very long, it is possible for sound management and regional development to overcome many problems given a sufficient period of time. For example, the Western Pacific, from its building in 1909 until World War II, was almost constantly in financial difficulty. It had been built without immediate traffic potential and, although soundly engineered, did not come into its own until the area was more fully developed, despite the existence of better than average management.[9] The examples cited above would lead one to speculate that the role of management is of little consequence compared to historical factors and outside factors such as regional development. To a degree, this is true, although, to be sure, the management must be able to appreciate and grasp these opportunities. Rail management has often been cited as lacking in foresight and imagination, and there can be little doubt that many years of "following the book," which characterizes most rail executives, has a stultifying effect. Because of the restrictive framework within which he operates, a rail executive on the way up seldom has opportunity to exercise a talent for innovation. Until recently, railroads have not been active in recruitment of young men with college training except within the engineering field.

Upward movement is extremely slow and, in recent years, has been inhibited by the fact that the industry itself was not growing. The railroads, thus, face a somewhat unfortunate problem of being in need of high caliber management personnel to solve problems which make the attraction of such men extremely difficult.

The lack of foresight is especially serious in the area of pricing. Every industry must pay close attention to price policies, and the railroads ignored these problems for many years. Market research

[8] George H. Burgess and Miles C. Kennedy, *Centennial History of the Pennsylvania Railroad* (Philadelphia: The Pennsylvania Railroad, 1946); John D. Galloway, *The First Transcontinental Railroad* (New York: Simmons-Boardman Co., 1950); L. L. Watters, *Steel Trails to Santa Fe* (Lawrence: University of Kansas Press, 1950).

[9] From the engineering standpoint, the Western Pacific was vastly superior to the competing Southern Pacific at the time of construction. It seems likely that the Southern Pacific, at least until 1900, was in a monopolistic position of such strength that it could hardly have avoided making money. The Western Pacific, built by George Gould, illustrates the classic management error in the railroad field of building in advance of the available traffic. The Southern Pacific illustrates the other error often made by management in the early days, viz., rapid and haphazard construction in order to reap benefits without delay, with subsequent upgrading becoming necessary in short order.

was almost unknown in the industry, a fact which made the competitive blows from motor and air carriers more serious. Only recently have railroads become aware of the need for basic market research.

Equally serious has been the reluctance of the railroads to revise their equipment policies. From 1900 until the "diesel revolution" in 1945-55, motive power was almost unchanged except for increases in size. This policy, although somewhat advantageous in the short run, was to have serious repercussions upon the competitive position of the carrier.[10] Likewise, freight and passenger equipment was allowed to become unduly obsolete before it was replaced. The effects of this policy, especially on the level of passenger traffic, are difficult to evaluate. Clearly, the equipment policies need to be re-examined in the light of modern needs.[11]

It has been pointed out that the problem of railroad management is, to a degree, unique, in that the freight and passenger operations are, in effect, two completely different enterprises. Freight service involves essentially a large scale wholesale effort, while the passenger business is essentially a retail operation, catering to people on a personal basis. Railroads are strongly oriented around production. Their forte is mass production of transportation service. The plant is geared for mass production of uniform transport service.

Some railroads, mostly those in the West, made serious efforts to retain and enhance passenger services. These efforts, even when they have the full support of management, have not been outstandingly successful. As stated by one railroad official:

> Southern Pacific spent over $34 million in the postwar period for new equipment for its premier passenger runs "to hold and if possible enhance our position." A new Shasta Daylight actually stimulated business at first, and in its early years averaged about 400 passengers per day the year around. In 1957, the average had fallen to less than 300 per day, and in the winter months under 200. There have been similar declines in loadings of all premier trains. In an effort to counter this decline Southern Pacific has advertised extensively by TV, radio, magazine, newspaper and billboard, established family and other special fares, will call and mail services, new nonwait ticket offices, inexpensive meal services and a host of other refinements.[12]

---

[10] Hugh S. Norton, "An Economic Analysis of the Diesel Locomotive in the Railroad Industry of the United States" (doctoral dissertation, George Washington University, 1956).

[11] George Terborgh, *Dynamic Equipment Policy* (New York: McGraw-Hill Book Co., 1949).

[12] *Modern Railroads*, "Wanted, A Crash Program to Save the Railroad Business," March 1958, p. 95.

An eastern railroad president, strongly committed to passenger service improvement, recited the following experience in trying to resuscitate the faltering passenger side of the business.

When the new management of the New York Central took office in the summer of 1954, one of our first actions was to see how railroad passenger travel could be stimulated by better service and through improvements in operating technology. Previous managements have also spent considerable time and thought in this field. Lightweight, streamlined equipment, air-conditioned coaches and sleepers, and diesel engines which eliminated smoke and cinders had all made their appearance since 1934. And since World War II, the Central spent a quarter of a billion dollars for improved passenger service facilities and new passenger cars and $14 million in advertising the service.

We contracted with Pullman-Standard to build a lightweight, low center-of-gravity train. On our first run of the Aerotrain between Chicago and Detroit, we were able to transport 250 passengers with an expenditure for fuel less than would have been used by two Cadillacs. Then what happened? About this time a tremendous spiral of wage inflation and within 14 months the nationally negotiated wages increases for railroad labor added $62 million a year to the payroll of the New York Central Railroad. During that same period our taxes were substantially increased. For example, the taxes on our passenger bridge over the Harlem River were multiplied 700 per cent from $70,000 to $490,000 per year and the franchise tax on the tunnel entering Grand Central Terminal jumped over $1,050,000 per year to $2,500,000 per year. As a result, we found that the gross revenues of these trains did not now meet the out-of-pocket costs.

In 1956 we backed up our passenger service with the largest expenditures for advertising and promotion the system ever spent, and still our losses for that year went to $48 million. At least, as large a deficit was incurred in 1957.[13]

In the decade 1946-1957, the railroads expended $1.13 billion for passenger service equipment, acquiring 6,403 new cars and 2,132 diesel locomotives, replacing about 15 per cent of the cars on hand as of 1947. These steps did not, unfortunately, bring the hoped-for results, as noted in the above testimony and by the financial status of passenger service.[14] It is not surprising that many rail officials

---

[13] Alfred E. Perlman, President, New York Central Railroad, Testimony before the Senate Surface Transportation Subcommittee, *Problems of the Railroads, op. cit.*, Vol. 1, p. 229.

[14] Interstate Commerce Commission, "Report on Railroad Passenger Train Deficit," Doc. 31954, May 1959.

seem to have reached the conclusion that passenger service is not worth making efforts to regain. The effects of these experiences are especially serious, since many railroad managements were at best no more than tolerant of passenger service and often hostile, regarding it as a waste of time and effort.[15]

A readable and interesting comment on the inherent difficulties of rail passenger management is found in a lay magazine devoted to rail interests.

> . . . psychologically and organizationally the industry is not prepared to wage the passenger train's war of survival.
>
> In essence, railroading is a wholesale or industrial function. It is a factory producing mass transportation in trainload lots for the consumption of a relatively few buyers, i.e., shippers. This end of the business accounts for 85 percent of what's in the till. It follows that the executives and directors of railroads are overwhelmingly men selected for their proven ability to sell freight transportation or—and more likely—produce it. Baltimore & Ohio's Howard E. Simpson is the solitary president of a major carrier who came up through the passenger department.
>
> Freight and passenger mix like Scotch and ginger ale. The care and handling of passengers is a retail or consumer service. How many American corporations have successfully blended wholesale and retail? One student of the subject declares that "it's like expecting the foreman of a U.S. Steel sheet rolling mill to be able to manage an A & P supermarket . . ."
>
> How not to run passenger trains:
>
> The typical American railroad has a passenger department—which is and isn't. It is usually held responsible to a traffic vice president (who in turn is preoccupied with freight business), and its mission is to sell passenger travel and such allied accounts as baggage, mail, and express. On a few roads the passenger traffic manager, by sheer force of personality, holds considerable sway in the official family and his opinions are respected. But he is still a salesman rather than a true executive. On three roads— Central, Pennsy, and Southern Pacific—the passenger department rates a vice presidency and this officer may be charged with the financial responsibility for passenger traffic profit and loss. In no instance is the passenger man granted both responsibility and authority.
>
> In other words, the P.T.M. is supposed to conduct his business out of facilities designed by the engineering department,

---

[15] See comments, *National Transportation Policy, op. cit.,* pp. 330, 331. On many roads, management has frankly made no effort to retain passenger service or at best allowed the passenger traffic department to experiment on a very limited budget.

aboard equipment provided by the mechanical department, on schedules established by the operating department, and with a budget made up by the finance department. All of these gentlemen who design and produce the passenger product, however well intentioned, are by instinct wholesalers of transportation.

What takes place is apt to be this:

Typical gondola design objectives might be, "How cheap can we get it?" or "How long will it last?" For passenger equipment the emphasis should shift to utilization potential, ease of maintenance, and manpower economies. But it seldom does. . . . Example: Passenger cars, unlike buses, and aircraft, are notable for their lack of pullout or package-type components, thus a minor repair on brake rigging or an air-conditioning unit is apt to tie up the car in the shops.

In the Middle West recently a huge old barn of a depot was razed because it stood in the path of a new expressway. Presented with the chance to make a fresh start, the passenger department designed a contemporary station, cheap to erect and maintain, geared to the space requirements of present-day traffic, pleasing to the eye. Then the engineering department located it near the outskirts on an inaccessible and unattractive site by a roundhouse! True, the building was erected on rail real estate adjacent to other company facilities. But it broke all the rules of marketing by obliging patrons to place themselves at the railroad's convenience instead of vice versa.[16]

While the need for market surveys and studies is frequently cited, the fact remains that many such studies have been made in past years. Likewise, railroads are often cited for their lack of efforts, yet, when these efforts are made, little positive advantage seems to result. It seems more than likely that the private automobile and the aircraft have, in combination, damaged the rail passenger potential beyond recall, except perhaps by some extraordinary circumstance.

MANAGEMENT AND THE MOTOR CARRIER

Motor carriers, as noted in Chapter II, are organized on a much more informal basis than is true of railroads. However, the same basic problems exist, viz., the need to control widely scattered operations and to supervise employees at distant points. Motor carriers are generally smaller than rail carriers, and, although they have operations at many points, the physical property is considerably less.

---

[16] *Trains, The Magazine of Railroading,* April 1959 (Milwaukee: Kalmbach Publishing Co.)

The motor carrier counterpart of the division is the terminal. The terminal manager is the key man in the organization, being generally responsible for operations in and out of the terminal, as well as those in the terminal per se.

Some larger carriers employ a regional or area manager who supervises terminals, although, more commonly, the terminal managers report directly to the operations or general manager at the general office. In the motor carrier industry, even more than in the rail industry, emphasis has been on operations. Staff functions have been generally subsidiary to operations, and the ranks of top management have been recruited largely from operating personnel. Unlike the railroads, many motor carrier firms are operated as partnerships, proprietorships, or small closely held corporations. As a consequence, management and ownership have often been vested in the same person or group.

The founder-sole owner is still a familiar figure in the motor carrier industry. Although the small motor carrier, in particular, has tended to ignore staff functions, large carriers have been forced to recognize the value of staff efforts, especially in such areas as dealing with regulatory authorities, training of personnel, and like matters. The trend toward staff management can be expected to continue as more founder-owners pass from the scene and as firms grow in size and complexity.

Whereas railroad management structures tend to be relatively uniform, motor carriers are widely divergent, ranging from the four or five truck firm with a single owner-manager to the largest firms operating several thousand vehicles and employing an elaborate staff organization.

One of the particular problem areas facing motor carrier management has been the need for continuous dealing with the public authorities. The use of highways and payment of fees related to highway use has, as noted elsewhere, been a serious problem for many years. Likewise, the use of public highways has created problems in the carrier relationships with the public who must also use the highways. This dual public relations problem has consumed many hours of executive time and effort. As a young industry, the motor carriers have avoided, thus far, many of the problems of the railroads in the management area. In the years following World War II, the motor carrier began an active program of seeking management talent from college trained ranks, and this program has continued.

It seems likely that the major problems of the motor carriers in the management area center around the transition from small scale to large scale industry now in progress. That is to say, the rapid growth of the industry has brought several serious managerial problems, especially in the areas of finance and state taxation. In the early years of the industry, financial problems were mainly limited to the provision of capital for short term needs. Equipment and other property was generally acquired on a piecemeal basis as the business grew, and there was virtually no long term debt in the entire industry. Commensurate with industry growth, capital needs, especially those for equipment, have increased greatly. Vendor credit, personal loans on short term notes satisfactory for modest purchases made by small carriers, are not adequate for present needs. Likewise, terminals and other property needs have increased since the early days of the industry. Some more adequate means must be found of dealing with these problems. Carrier growth has brought similar problems in the area of taxes. As noted in Chapter II, the concept of highway finance is changing rapidly, and carrier management must adjust to these new concepts.

Motor carriers have never developed the degree of interindustry cooperation which has characterized the railroads. The degree of heterogeneity in the industry has prevented such a development, although the various segments of the industry do cooperate in many areas of common interest. As a conseqeunce, the industry has split into a number of groups, each pursuing its own interests, often to the detriment of the group as a whole. Carrier management must devise some means of consolidating these various interests.

While the small firm still dominates the industry, evidence is growing that the large firm will be the key to the future. As yet, the economics of size in the motor carrier industry are largely untried.[17] Only a handful of firms operate more than a few hundred vehicles, and most carriers confine their operations to a few states.

Death and retirement of the founders of the industry bring more and more pressure to merge and consolidate. Mergers and consolidations, in turn, give a new fund of experience as to the practicable size of the motor carrier firm. One factor seems to be clear beyond all doubt, viz., the fact that managerial problems increase rapidly as operations become more geographically widespread. The rough

---

[17] Few authors have considered the problem of economies of scale, and most are not optimistic, e.g., Merril J. Roberts, "Transport Regulation and the Railroad Problem," *Southern Economic Journal,* January 1957. It seems likely that some of these writers overlook managerial economies and concentrate on the technology. Empirical observation and judgment indicate that economies are possible.

and ready, cut and try, methods of the pioneer motor carrier operations would be sadly out of place in the modern and complex industry. The "second generation" of motor carrier managers is now coming into positions of authority. These men, facing different problems and having substantially different training than the "first generation," have yet to prove themselves.

Another major problem has faced the motor carrier in recent years in the rapid increase in private carriage. In part, this is a policy and regulatory problem, and those aspects will be treated in Chapter XXIII. It is in large measure, however, a management problem. Private carriage may have many cost advantages, although these are largely unexplored and likely to be overrated.[18] Nonetheless, a firm moving into transportation (aside from empty threats to bring about rate reduction) seems to indicate that some dissatisfaction is present. A firm deciding to make its own steel or operate its own cafeteria or making any other self-supply decision must have decided that it can do the job better than those selling such services. It is, thus, incumbent upon the seller to convince his customer by performance that his product or service is superior. Legislative action will help this problem by stamping out the outright illegal and quasi-legal (gray area) operations. However, legal procedures short of an outright ban on private carriage, which is not conceivable, will not solve the basic problem. The fore-hire carriers must convince the shipper by their own service that private carriage would be foolish except in those few cases where special conditions prevail. In those cases where a clear-cut advantage in favor of private carriage exists, the common carrier must, in all likelihood, recognize the fact that this traffic is not subject to competition. Unfortunately, when traffic is undertaken by private carriage, it may never return to for-hire forms, since an investment has been made and must be amortized.

MANAGEMENT PROBLEMS IN THE AIR TRANSPORTATION INDUSTRY

The air transport industry has faced many of the same problems as those prevailing in the motor carrier field and stemming from the same source, viz., rapid growth and changes in ownership. Just before

---

[18] Empirical evidence indicates that few firms embarking upon private carriage have adequate knowledge of the costs and managerial know-how required for success. A study of these factors might counsel moderation. See Kenneth U. Flood, "Questions in Company-Operated Transport," *Harvard Business Review,* January-February 1961.

World War II, the airlines were largely owned by small groups and frequently controlled by one individual. The rapid postwar growth made owner-management largely impossible and the airlines, like the motor carriers, were forced to expand the scope of their activities. As noted earlier, airlines, like motor carriers, have begun to face serious financial problems, especially in purchase of equipment. Airlines are also apparently entering a period in which mergers and consolidation will play a large part. As in railroads, the management of an air carrier may be largely at the mercy of the route structure. It seems likely that even the most efficient management would be unable to successfully manage a carrier without desirable routes. Larger and more costly equipment has intensified this problem and drawn a sharper line between large and small airlines.

Airlines, by their nature, have even more widespread physical operations than other carriers, being world wide in some cases. Like other carriers also, the operating department plays a large part in airline management. However, airlines have traditionally been more market oriented and have given substantial time and attention to customer relations. As is true of motor carriers, airlines own little real property and have carried on few activities not closely related to airline operation per se. Airline management has been drawn in general from sources within the industry. A unique problem in the airlines exists in the form of the relationship of the pilots to the middle management group. As pointed out in Chapter IV on Transportation Labor, the pilots occupy a strong position by virtue of their training and play a key role in the industry. Frequently, the senior pilots enjoy earnings superior to those of middle management groups. In many cases, pilots move into management positions, and, in other cases, such jobs are filled by those rising from the ranks of agents, clerks, and other non-pilot personnel. Airlines have not attracted college-trained people, since entrance salaries, aside from the pilots, have not been high.

As airlines continue to grow and develop, especially in movement of freight, the breadth of management problems will increase, and airlines will be forced to develop more sophisticated management techniques.

Although air and motor routes are not physically fixed, as is true of rail lines, the advantage of well laid out and lucrative route structures is obvious. Eastern Air Lines, for example, for many years enjoyed the advantage of sound management and the heavy traffic potential of the New York to Florida route. Since air and motor route structures are subject to administrative fiat, management must spend a great deal of time and effort seeking new route authorities or fending off would-be entrants.

MANAGEMENT PROBLEMS IN OTHER MODES

The operations of water carriers are undoubtedly the most specialized of the various carrier enterprises. Water carrier operations, both inland and coastal, are unique.

The indirect carrier problems are essentially those of the line-haul carriers, and no particular problems exist, other than the fact that for forwarders the margin between costs and rates is paper thin.

Perhaps the major problem facing all modes is the necessity for cooperation and broad-gauge understanding of the inter-modal problems. The various carrier-management groups have mastered the technical details of their own modes. The problem now pressing is to recognize the inter-model problems and the virtues of inter-modal cooperation.

CARRIERS AND MODERN MANAGEMENT

All carriers have shown interest in, and have much to gain from, the techniques of modern management. Various operations—research techniques, especially linear programming—have many applications to transportation management.[19] The development of these techniques, along with necessary computing equipment, promises to provide a fertile field for management, although the surface has hardly been scratched at present.[20] Before maximum use can be made of these procedures, much more must be done in the area of training personnel and educating management to the potential advantage of such management tools.[21]

---

[19] A recent compilation of such problems shows examples such as the following: "Operations Research in Aircraft Maintenance," *Operations Research*, American Management Association Special Report No. 13, 1956; *The Allocation of Switching Work in a System of Classification Yards* (Rand Corp., 1953); William W. Cooper and Abraham Charnes, "Transportation Scheduling by Linear Programming," *Proceedings of the Conference on Operations Research in Marketing*, January 29-31, 1953 (Cleveland: Case Institute of Technology), pp. 62-71.

[20] One important use is in academic training. At the University of Tennessee, Professor Ronald Boling and others have developed a "management game" adapted to a transportation firm. The student teams feed decision data into the computer which will yield the results of this decision based on certain assumptions which have been "programmed" into the computer.

[21] The drastic changes in market and distribution now in progress will force carriers to deal with such concepts. See "The Short Order Economy," *Fortune*, August 1962.

It would appear that all carriers must put less emphasis on operations as a source of executive personnel and stress broad background as opposed to long experience in the organization. The railroad industry, in particular, has shown great reluctance to acquire top management from outside the industry. Technical training has also been overemphasized in the sense that competent persons trained in general management, liberal arts, and humanities have found promotion and, indeed, even a beginning on the management ladder difficult to attain. Due notice must be taken that operating problems, although important, are becoming less significant relative to policy problems facing management. All carriers, and railroads in particular, must reduce the current stress placed on seniority in choosing executives. Much more emphasis must be placed upon research of all types, especially market research, if the industry is to obtain its proper share of economic growth.

For some reason, carriers seem to fall into the serious error of stressing operating convenience at the expense of customer convenience. Perhaps because the operating departments are as a matter of necessity given ultimate authority in many matters, they often seem to dominate the entire organization. Railroads have long been noted for their lack of public relations sense, and many airlines seem to be in danger of following the same path. No one would argue that marketing considerations should overrule the judgment of operations personnel where safety or feasibility are concerned, but a close balance must be kept. This is perhaps the greatest challenge to transportation management in general.

Another characteristic of transportation management appears to be a failure to recognize the merit of competition in the form of technological progress. In the 1830's, the canal operators refused to recognize the potential of the railroad and failed to (as they could have done) capture it. Likewise, the railroads were unable to see the virtues of the motor truck until legislative barriers were raised.[22]

No clear reasons for this lack of foresight present themselves. Other regulated industries, such as the telephone system, have been in the vanguard of technological development and have been highly successful in integrating new techniques into their operations.[23]

---

[22] Only a handful of railroads, e.g., the Southern Pacific, was aware of the role to be played by trucks and thus secured "grandfather" rights. Until 1935, the railroads could have operated trucks without restriction. After that date, serious legal problems had to be overcome.

[23] One factor of importance is the fact that carriers as a group have done little or no research, whereas the Bell Telephone System has been famous for years as a research pioneer. To what extent research would have helped is problematical.

One possible explanation of this factor is again the emphasis on operations in high level management, although this hardly accounts for the almost irrational hostility toward other carriers, of which there are many illustrations in railroad history. Whatever the reasons, this factor has had and will continue to have a profound influence upon the transportation industry.

Carrier Management Areas in Need of Study and Improvement

Certain management practices in almost all modes need further study and improvement. While some modes or some firms are more adequate in these matters than others, some effort is clearly called for. None of these areas is definitive, and there are no textbook solutions, but they are grave and need the best management talent available.

Recruitment, Training and Development of Management Personnel

Until relatively recent times, few carriers have put serious effort into training of personnel or providing for systematic selection and promotion of promising staff members. In all modes, seniority is a strong factor in advancement of employees, and, within general limits, this presents few problems. Strong emphasis upon seniority and slow advancement through the ranks may, however, repel many outstanding young people who rightly or wrongly feel that advancement should be more open to superior talent. The rank and file of carrier employees, as was pointed out in Chapter IV, are quite well off as compared to their fellow employees in other industrial pursuits. Basic salaries, retirement and other fringe benefits are quite satisfactory. In the higher ranks of management, however, these advantages are less marked, and high level carrier executives are less well compensated on the average than their counterparts in industry generally. In past years, formal training has been less stressed than on-the-job experience as a way up the management ladder, but there are increasing signs that this feeling is giving way. In the trucking industry especially, where growth has been rapid in recent years, opportunities have been good, and carriers have recruited widely from collegiate ranks. Railroads have, until very recent years, continued to rely upon the "up from the ranks" method. One major barrier to rail recruiting seems to be the image, which appears in many younger persons, that the railroads and, indeed, the transportation industry, in general, is not a growth industry. The industry must make great efforts to paint an attractive picture to the younger individual.[24]

All carriers have, as noted, tended to put inadequate stress on the marketing-price functions of the business. Traffic executives in all modes have most often been brought through the ranks and thus frequently have a rather narrow outlook. The increased amount of rate research now being done will not be useful unless these executives can follow through successfully. Shortly after World War II, an organization was formed which should do much to remedy this situation in the future. The American Society of Traffic and Transportation, founded in 1946, is a certification organization, which operates an educational training program for all carrier personnel, but of special interest to carrier traffic and industrial traffic employees intent on advancement.

> The American Society of Traffic and Transportation, Inc. is devoted to the welfare of the individual in traffic and transportation and to the improvement of the transportation industry. As the Society grows in stature and as persons in the field increase their understanding of its value as a professional society, an appreciation of the meaning of its certificates of membership will develop, not merely in persons concerned with transportation, but among leaders in American industry generally.

> The formation of the Society was the climax of more than twenty years of earnest thought and effort. In those years, there had been frequent discussions of the need for setting up standards of education, experience, and ethics among men in traffic and transportation. Each national business organization in the field had expressed itself on the desirability of the establishment of a society to set up and guard such standards. . . .

> At the present time, more than two thousand leading traffic and transportation men and women in the country are banded together to finance and carry out the stated objectives of the Society, as set forth in its Constitution:

>> "To establish standards of knowledge, technical training, experience, conduct and ethics, and to encourage the attainment of high standards of education and technical training requisite to the proper performance of the various functions of transportation."[25]

---

[24] Somewhat of a paradox exists in the railroad field where, due to a long period of low rates of hiring, the average age of executives is very high. Thus, many opportunities exist for young executives, even at present industry growth levels.

[25] *Announcement, 1963-65*, Chicago, 1963, American Society of Traffic and Transportation, Inc.

The work of the Society is still young, but empirical evidence indicates that it is effective. Much remains to be done in these areas, but progress is being made.

Various educational institutions offer executive training programs, as well as the standard academic training leading to management positions.

Financial Management

All carriers, for various reasons, have encountered problems in financing, especially that related to new equipment which is vital to operating efficiency. Various new developments in the field, conditional sales, lease, and other instruments have been widely used to supplement the traditional equipment trust and vendor credit. Since motor and air equipment is subject to rapid change in design and efficiency, and railroad equipment is becoming more so, means must be available to finance this equipment in such a fashion as to obtain the maximum benefits from its acquisition. It has often been felt that the standard rail financing instruments were not suitable for motor carriers. However, an authority has stated the problem thus:

> Most of the basic types of equipment and long-term financing developed in the railroad field can be used in truck financing, with certain variations such as much shorter terms, i.e., in accord with economic life for the equipment. An increasing amount of new funds going into common carrier truckers is for the relocation and construction of new and more efficient terminals. Because so much of the trucking business is LTL, handling costs at terminals are high and more efficient terminal operations are, along with more modern equipment, a major area in which to cut costs.
>
> Increasing requirements for long term funds on the part of common carrier trucking companies are expected to continue, to the benefit of the companies, the shipping public and investors.[26]

Speaking of railroads, the same source says:

> In railroad equipment financing all the tools are now available for such financing by almost any railroad. For the profitable railroads which can afford Philadelphia Plan financing with its 20 percent down payments and 15-year repayment, there is no longer any problem of sufficient cash flow to cover full cost of equipment. For the less fortunate roads with poorer earnings there are available conditional sale financing and the purchase

<hr>

[26] *Holding, op. cit.*, p. 27.

lease, with 14-year depreciation protecting the roads' cash flow. Even for most of the marginal roads it is probable that a purchase-lease agreement can be worked out on a basis satisfactory to all parties.[27]

While equipment financing is of crucial importance, terminals and other real property facilities must also be considered. Sources of capital in these areas are more conventional, but motor carriers, in particular, have had considerable success with sale and lease-back methods of terminal financing. Long-run capital requirements for railroads depend, to be sure, on the importance of rail transport in the national transportation framework. Under any logical and realistic assumption, however, railroads will require substantial capital, even to maintain their present status. While capital formation has been brisk since 1947, with capital expenditures averaging about $1 billion per year, the net investment has increased only slightly due to the reduced need for capital equipment. It seems logical to assume that freight traffic will maintain present levels for some years into the future, although the future outlook for passenger service is bleak. Several estimates have been made of rail capital needs, based on varying assumptions. These estimates range from a high of $20 billion by J. W. Barriger[28] to a low of $14 billion by the Brookings Institution.[29]

Barriger's estimate seems unduly high and unrealistic; although the program he envisions would be highly desirable, it is not likely to materialize. The Brookings' estimate (under assumption of no significant change in demand for rail service or national transportation policy) seems most likely.

Nelson[30] estimates that about 43.6 per cent of rail capital expenditures came from external sources in the years 1946-1955, while, in the same period, 56.4 per cent came from internal sources. Most of the external funds came from equipment obligations as opposed to equity sources. In an earlier chapter, it was pointed out that rail earnings have not been high. The highest rate of return since 1946 was 4.31 per cent in 1948. More importantly, it has been below 4 per cent in every year since 1955, falling to 1.97 in 1962 and rising slightly to 2.67 in 1963.[31] During the years of Nelson's estimates, rates of return were higher, and it does not appear that railroads can hope to finance

[27] *Ibid.*
[28] Barriger, *Super Railroads, op. cit.*
[29] *National Transportation Policy, op. cit.*
[30] J. C. Nelson, *op. cit.*, p. 219.
[31] *A Review of Railroad Operations in 1962*, Washington, D. C., 1963, Association of American Railroads.

capital requirements or any substantial part of them from internal sources in the near future.

Likewise, external sources other than equipment financing do not appear to be likely. Management faces serious problems in this area.

Motor carrier financial problems are less serious, because of more modest needs and because of the growth situation. However, much depends upon the issues of highway finance and user charges, which were discussed in an earlier chapter. Airlines face somewhat similar problems; and the financing of modern aircraft is a particular type of problem. However, aircraft financing is in such a state of flux and the long-run effects of the large jet aircraft are so uncertain that little can be said in this area.

Public and Interindustry Relations

In other parts of this book it has been noted that carriers spend a substantial amount of time and effort, as well as money, attempting to get an advantage over each other in the public arena. This arises, of course, because of the strong element of public control. It is difficult to think of any other industry in which this situation exists to such a degree. All modes are either subject of detailed regulation, use the public facilities or both. It thus is necessary and will become more necessary in the future to develop a sound philosophy of dealing with these problems. It was noted earlier in this chapter that carriers, with the exception of air carriers, have never shown great talent for public relations. Management must take steps to remedy this situation. Carriers must be more willing to accept the advice of the marketing and advertising specialist, even if it sometimes conflicts with the advice of the operations department. Carriers using the public facilities have especially acute public relations problems, and they must be constantly aware of their importance.

Accounting and Control

In this area great progress has been made, chiefly via the recent developments in data processing and the recognition on the part of management that prompt evaluation of data is essential to adequate management control. It is especially vital for the carrier firm and, in particular, for the common carrier, with its fixed operating requirements, to be aware at all times of the trends in operating data, costs, loadings pick-up and delivery, tonnage at various terminals, etc. It has become customary for large motor carriers, for example, to hold daily early morning meetings of the executive staff to evaluate the data of the previous day's operations. This information has been processed during the night and is tabulated and ready for use the following day. Most all transport firms now make widespread use of data processing, both for their own management use and for reporting to regulatory agencies. Rational decisions cannot be made without data, and management should continue to develop these techniques, especially as an aid in developing cost data.

Obsolescence of Equipment

All carriers face major problems in making equipment decisions. The most basic advantage which any carrier may have is modern well-designed equipment which is economical to operate. For railroads, perhaps equipment is somewhat overshadowed by the roadway in importance, but, for other carriers, the role of equipment is supreme. Under ideal circumstances, the equipment should be the best available but well within the financial resources of the carrier. Replacement policy should not be too conservative so that technological advance runs too far ahead, nor too liberal so that finances are always under stress. As a rule of thumb, the actual service life of equipment runs much longer than its economic life. That is to say, it would be mechanically possible to operate 1930 trucks, 1920 locomotives or 1929 aircraft. It would, however, be imprudent to do so. The technology of vehicles is constantly changing. Some of these changes are superficial and some are major or in some cases (diesel locomotives and jet aircraft) represent a completely new departure. Railroads have often taken what might be called the "master mechanic's viewpoint," viz., so long as the equipment was serviceable, it should be used. This view was strengthened by the excessively long accounting periods used to calculate depreciation and the vast amount of equipment of ancient vintage which was on hand. Air carriers, on the other hand, have been forced to keep up a fast pace in technological change in order to avail themselves of the latest advantages. Obiously, carrier management must keep these policies constantly under view and replace equipment when necessary, but not excessively. A major problem here is that the rate of change cannot be forecast, and carriers may find themselves forced to make a move which they would rather defer until a later date. Motor carriers often replace equipment on an arbitrary basis, e.g., 2 years or a given number of miles, or on a second engine overhaul. Some motor carriers attempt to standardize the fleet, while others use various makes of equipment. There seems to be general agreement that railroads have been too slow in replacement and airlines have forced the pace. High level staff talent should be given the responsibility of continuous review of equipment policy.

Many carrier management problems, especially those relating to route, climate and, to some degree, public policy are outside the scope of management ability. However, many of those discussed above are controlable by management and should be given more systematic attention.

Summary

A unique aspect of carrier management is the high degree of public policy involved. Carrier executives cannot make major decisions without taking public policies into consideration, and the legal framework of regulation cannot be overlooked. For this reason and others, the carriers tend to become somewhat rigid in management practices. In past years, the management has tended to overlook some practices of modern management, but there are encouraging signs that these matters are being given more consideration.

Selected References for Further Study

The various texts relating to general business management are numerous, and some have been referred to in the text. Cochrane, *op. cit.*, is an interesting study in the philosophy of early railroad management. Periodical literature is a repository of discussions of modern management techniques. Two very adequate case books of recent issue are Baker, George P., and Germaine, Gayton E., *Case Problems in Transportation Management* (New York: McGraw-Hill Book Co., 1957), and Germaine, Gayton E., Glaskowsky, Nicholas A., Jr., and Heskett, J. L., *Highway Transportation Management* (New York: McGraw-Hill Book Co., 1963).

Trade journals mentioned elsewhere in the text are excellent for discussion of specific management problems of a current nature.

CHAPTER XXIII

Regulation in the Modern Economy, Problems and Policy Issues

In this and the next chapter, the student must contemplate what has been said in the immediately preceding chapter as to the practical and theoretical problems raised by the implementation of regulation as it influences the functioning of the transport system.

Our transport regulatory program began more than three quarters of a century ago. The Interstate Commerce Act and the Civil Aeronautics Act, the two major statements of regulatory policy and procedure, have been amended hundreds of times over the years in an effort to meet specific problems and issues. As we have seen, many of these legislative efforts have often fallen on evil days as a result of unforeseen changes in social and economic conditions, as in the Transportation Acts of 1920 and 1940.

In other cases, an item or regulation, which at one time appeared to be logical and just, has been distorted either through ignorance or illegal intent and has been allowed to go far beyond the apparent original intent of Congress, as in the case of the agricultural exemption. One of the major dangers of this problem is that after some time has elapsed it is almost impossible to return to the original goal without causing a major structural change. Transportation policy, like agricultural policy, has many obvious shortcomings; the remedies are not so visible.

Let us refresh our memories by recalling briefly the original goals and objectives of regulation. These goals were highly pragmatic in nature. In the view of the Grangers and their supporters, there were various specific problems which were in need of solution.

One observer has put the problem thus:

> Out of this dilemma arose the experiment of the mandatory and permanent commission agency as a great experiment in government structure to exercise the new controls over railroads and grain elevators and later over other public utility industries. The state legislatures and the Congress sought an effective creature to carry out desired controls. Beginning in 1871, ten states had set up mandatory commissions by the time Congress created the Interstate Commerce Commission in 1887. . . .
>
> The regulatory process constitutes a sharp departure from the **laissez faire** philosophy with which this country had long been imbued. Regulation of business actions in regard to prices, finances and acquisition of other firms represents a basic change in the property concept. Legal arrangements between government and business enterprise are modified. Control over combination and certification substantially affect the structures of industry. It is not surprising that our regulatory experience has been characterized, by frequent caution or chariness on the part of the Congress in granting clearly stated powers to regulatory bodies, by severe criticism of regulated industries and jealousy of the three conventional departments of government of the vast powers exercised. The American decision to regulate presented a peculiar problem of government structure because of the separation of powers in our government. Furthermore, to this date, we have not emulated England and some other countries in providing continuity in administrative policy by the use of a permanent ministry in the executive departments.[1]

As we have seen, the framers of the Act of 1887 had little concept of the Pandora's box which they were so eager to open. They underestimated both the complexity of the problems and the ability of the industry to find loopholes in the legislation. By 1910, the barriers had come clearly into focus, and the amendments necessary to implement the original act had largely been enacted. Passing through the interwar years with the emphasis on price stability and anti-depression policies, we have seen the shift in emphasis to the problems following World War II.[2] Let us then focus our attention

---

[1] Marvin L. Fair, "Some Observations on the Theory and Performance of the Independent Regulatory Agencies in Regulating the Public Utility Industries," *ICC Practitioners' Journal,* Vol. XXVII, No. 9, June 1960, p. 957.

[2] It seems logical to consider the legislation of the 1930's as essentially emergency in nature and subsidiary to the mainstream of legislative philosophy.

on the goals and purposes of regulation at the mid-point of the twentieth century. The economic status of many, if not most, of the carriers in all modes is precarious, to say the least. In some measure this unfortunate situation has developed from serious managerial shortcomings, but a great deal of it must be laid at the door of the regulatory bodies or of the Congress.

The major regulatory problems can be classified as follows:

1. Lack of a comprehensive regulatory philosophy with the consequent fragmented and conflicting goals and, related to this, the lack of a single and central regulatory body which results in empire building in many government agencies with even the most tenuous interest in transportation and in the proliferation of overlapping and conflicting authority.
2. The significant areas of exemption which results in very unequal treatment of carriers which are almost identical in other respects.
3. The frustrating attempts to use the national transportation policy as a working guide to regulation.
4. The failure to maintain the activities of the regulatory bodies at such standards as to be capable of performing its expanding and increasingly complex duties.
5. Inequality in public aids and treatment of the modes in related matters such as taxation and labor relations.

Let us examine these matters in more detail.

LACK OF A COMPREHENSIVE PHILOSOPHY OF REGULATION

The lack of a comprehensive regulatory philosophy means that there is frequent overlap and conflict as to the purposes of regulation on an intermodal basis. For example, the Civil Aernonautics Act directs the Board to, among other things, promote and encourage air transportation. No such provision exists in the Interstate Commerce Act. Thus, the Civil Aeronautics Board may carry out a number of programs which would not be possible in the Commission.

Also, under the existing circumstances, the various regulatory bodies tend to become advocates of the industry with which they are concerned, especially in the case of the CAB, since active promotion is part of the legal responsibility of the agency.

In view of the fact that the various modes are in competition with each other to varying degrees, a serious problem arises when differing standards of regulatory policy exist. However, it is obvious that, to a degree, standards need to differ. The regulated industries were, as we know, in different stages of development at the time of legislative control. In the case of railroads, the industry was largely mature and regulation was thought of as being a control mechanism to protect the public. In the case of airlines, regulation was thought of as being not only regulatory, but also a tool to aid in orderly development of an industry of national interest. In the motor area, it seems likely that regulation was, in large part, brought about to square with the fact that rail transport was regulated and to eliminate confusion. Recognizing these needs for diversity does not, to be sure, give us any guide as to how much diversity is desirable.

It would seem possible to make room for this diversity and at the same time eliminate outright conflict. It was noted in Chapter XII that the administrative agencies tend to become advocates of and take a paternalistic attitude towards the modes under their jurisdiction. No doubt, a certain amount of this is unavoidable and, to a degree at least, desirable.

The regulatory programs and the way in which they are administered by the commissions must be under constant observation.

An example of the complexities in this may be in order. From time to time in past years, the Interstate Commerce Commission has directed the railroads to take certain steps, insofar as safety is concerned. Orders have been issued to revise signal systems and to make changes in equipment and similar areas. These changes were made at railroad expense. In later years, problems of air traffic control have been treated as a public responsibility. It could be argued that this dual standard of responsibility is unfair and that air carriers should be forced to bear the burden themselves. However, the immediate counter claim could be made that not only are these burdens beyond the airlines' financial capability, but that they are also legitimate matters of public responsibility. The airlines would argue that, since civil and military aviation use the airways and airports, the issue transcends the interest of the airlines. This argument has merit, but it could be applied also to the separation of rail and highway crossings which has, in the past, been considered a rail responsibility in most cases. It seems clear beyond all doubt that there is no clean-cut way in which policy could, at this date, be made uniform.

However, it can be made more uniform. Airlines have, in large part, reached the stage where aid and assistance need to be re-evaluated.

The age-old problem of failure to meet changing circumstances remains.

As we have seen, numerous proposals have been made to establish a single regulatory body, most frequently as an executive department with cabinet status. The precise form of this agency would be of little consequence. The major question is one not of procedure but of philosophy. If the modes require variant regulatory policies, then it may be wise to continue the present system with minor modifications. If, on the other hand, the need is for a unified regulatory approach, there is clear need for a single regulatory agency. Let us assume that the first condition prevails and that only minor modification need be made. It was pointed out in Chapter XII that there are many federal bodies involved in formulating transport policy. Without regard for the need of a cabinet level department, the existing situation is clearly unnecessary and intolerable. Many of these groups have only the most tenuous interest in transportation and must often reach far to justify their activities. In so doing, they enter into areas far removed from their basic function and make for duplication and narrowly specialized programs.[3] To what extent consolidating these groups would eliminate the problems of duplication is problematical. The "unification" of the defense activities has not made a significant difference in the operation of that agency in the eyes of most observers. There is abundant evidence of duplication, even within some of the smaller federal agencies doing work in the same functional areas.

LACK OF UNIFORM POLICY AND THE EXEMPTIONS

Perhaps the most serious problem arising from the lack of uniform policy is that relating to the heterogeneous regulation which prevails in the industry.

We can recall that the water carriers, to a high degree, and the motor carriers, to a somewhat lesser degree, are exempt from certain economic regulation. To be sure, there were, and in some cases still

---

[3] For example, in recent years, the Interstate Commerce Commission, the House Committee on Interstate and Foreign Commerce, the U. S. Department of Agriculture, the Bureau of Public Roads, and various private research agencies have all issued reports on highway tax and legislative barriers to truck traffic. Unavoidably, these reports were largely duplicative, and it hardly seems necessary to have all these groups working in the same area, although each does have a somewhat different interest. One of the tasks of the Bureau of the Budget is to try to eliminate as much of this duplication as possible, but, when these functions have been underway for many years, relatively little can be done.

are, sound reasons for these areas of omission. It is true that the owner-operators in the "exempt" areas of motor transport would be most difficult to regulate. Likewise, much of the bulk shipments moving by barge are of little interest to carriers of other types. However, where competitive cargoes are involved, the situation becomes most unfortunate. Coal, grain, chemicals and certain other products are rail-barge competitive, and lack of regulation brings about serious consequences. Although much of the traffic moving by exempt motor carriage is not attractive to railroads, the trip lease and other operations arising largely through the lack of uniform regulation undermine the rate structure seriously.

Further, the lack of information in the hands of the Commission, due to the fact that regulation is not in force, makes it difficult to evaluate and enforce existing regulation. For example, the Commission knows relatively little about the method of operation, composition and numbers of carriers operating in the exempt field, but such information is necessary in order to evaluate the impact of these carriers on the other elements of the transportation industry. In early years, the element of exempt carriage was relatively unimportant, but this is no longer the case. Private intercity carriage, which was only 21 per cent of the gross ton miles in 1946 increased to 33 per cent by 1959. Unregulated motor carriage increased an estimated 350 per cent from 1949 to 1956 and surpassed the total of unregulated water carriage which had previously been the largest of the unregulated areas.[4]

Naturally, those who enjoy the benefits of this situation are anxious to prevent any change in the status quo, but these pressures must be overcome if any satisfactory solution to these matters is to be found.

A prime example of this type of problem is found in cases where a regulated carrier seeks, via rate reduction, to regain traffic and must seek Commission approval to do so. Meanwhile, the exempt carriers can proceed to do as they wish, since their rates are entirely a matter of agreement between the two parties concerned.

It is hard to believe that such circumstances as these were in the minds of the Congress when the exemptions were enacted. The fact that a program of regulation would present difficult problems is not sufficient ground for allowing the area to go unregulated. Nor is it sound, as we have seen so frequently, to assume that necessary regulation can be put into effect later. Once the program becomes established and those who enjoy exemption become accustomed to

---

[4] *National Transportation Policy, op. cit.,* p. 49.

their favorable status, any attempt to alter these circumstances will be resisted with vigor. The exemption program should be subject to constant observation and review. Those who enjoy an exemption should be frequently called upon to demonstrate the need for and justice of such status in the public interest.

A weakness of the present system is the fact that the benefits of exemption extend to those who were not originally intended and who, in many cases, have little or no need for such benefits. For example, the agricultural exemption may benefit farmers in the true sense, but it also is a boon, perhaps to a greater degree, to processors and dealers in food products. Likewise, the water carrier exemptions are of great value to oil and chemical producers who can hardly be said to be in need of preferential treatment. One notes, with interest, that any attempts to repeal or reduce the scope of the exemptions are met with routine opposition by the various pressure groups operating on the Washington scene.

Lack of uniform policy has a serious effect in the provision of facilities. There is no coordination among the various regulatory agencies in the provision of federal aid and assistance. In addition to the technical problems thus created which will be treated later in this chapter, a common result is oversupply of certain facilities and under-supply of others.

The most obvious example of this situation is the provision of waterway facilities. The determination of waterway facilities is made by the Corps of Engineers. The Corps does an efficient job, but, unfortunately, they must perforce consider the situation in isolation. No attempt is made to evaluate the need for a given facility in co-operation with the whole transport system. The results of this are obvious. The user of other services is forced to pay via taxes for the water service which he does not use. There is every probability of acquiring excess facilities which are uncoordinated with the other modes. As Moulton points out, the oversupply of transport services is almost inevitable when the Government provides a right of way.[5]

Much the same situation prevails in the provision of feeder air-line services to small communities. In many cases, local traffic is insufficient to justify these operations, and they must depend upon public funds. Again, in this instance, no attempt is made to put these services into proper focus in the aggregate transportation system. Naturally, those who have an economic interest in these enterprises are happy to avail themselves of the opportunity to enter a business

---

[5] H. G. Moulton, *Controlling Factors in Economic Development* (Washington: The Brookings Institution, 1949), p. 186.

and to avoid the hazards of an inadequate market. Likewise, the regulatory-promotional agency has some interest in enhancing its own status and cannot realistically be expected to bar the door to these marginal activities. Unfortunately, even if the regulatory agency does block questionable operation, there is always a real danger of political pressure from other sources.[6]

Naturally, there must be sufficient attention given to the technological differences in the modes. However, these are principally matters of engineering and technical problems. A regulatory agency cannot restrain and regulate and encourage and nurture at the same time.

DEPENDENCE ON THE NATIONAL POLICY

On several occasions in this book, we have had occasion to refer to the weaknesses of the national policy, and this must be counted as a major policy shortcoming. It is very difficult to conceive that the Commission would, except in the very broadest sense, rely upon the policy statement as a guide for concrete action. The policy is a well written statement, but it cannot in any sense be used as a working document. It can perhaps be compared to a college catalogue in which students are exhorted to be ladies and gentlemen, but the formal rules of student conduct are long and detailed. It is not expected that any formal compliance with the "policy" is to be enforced. The overall objectives and goals of the national policy are, by any standards, desirable to all. Their implementation is, however, another matter.

There seems to be a clear course of action in this case which would solve the problem. Make it clear to all interested parties that the national policy is a highly generalized statement of intent and that the regulatory bodies must have adequate scope in which to operate. Each and every administrative policy or action of the Commission need not square with the statement of policy, although the policy could be useful as a overall long range (very long range) goal.

By raising questions of interpretation of such meaningless concepts as "inherent advantages," "adequate economical and efficient service" and other semantic generalities, the carrier can block any

---

[6] As noted in an earlier chapter, there has been remarkably little conflict of interest or political chicanery in the transport regulatory agencies, given the number of opportunities which arise.

conceivable action of the Commission. It is clearly impossible to
operate on the basis of a literal interpretation of the policy statement, as it would be impossible to literally conform each and every
governmental policy to the Constitution.

PLANS TO REORGANIZE THE COMMISSION

It was pointed out in an earlier chapter that the Commission
plan has often been changed in order to enhance its effectiveness
as a regulatory body. Since the early years of the twentieth century,
a large number of plans has been considered and, in some cases,
adopted to bring about modifications in the way in which the Commission does its work.[7] Assuming that the basic outline of regulatory
policy will remain as is, these plans have as their objective the
"streamlining" of the Commission procedure, elimination of duplication of activities and other such matters, all highly commendable.
Unfortunately, as we know, governmental agencies are not easily
reorganized; and, while these plans have helped, it cannot be said
that any major improvements have been made. It is likely that the
basic problems of the Commission, lack of funds and lukewarm
public and legislative support, quickly overcome any gains resulting
from internal organization. This should not, of course, mean that
plans to improve the Commission are futile and should not be entertained. While results are not usually as much as might be hoped
for, there is always opportunity for gain.

Many of the administrative problems of the regulatory bodies
were noted in Chapter XII. It would appear that most of these
difficulties center around the fact that the regulatory agencies are
bound by the complexity of their tasks, and constant review of their
procedures is imperative. In a recent and widely known *cause
célèbre*, a resigning member of the Civil Aeronautics Board made
what seems to be a concise statement of the situation relative to the
Civil Aeronautics Board.

> The C.A.B. is a creature imprisoned by its own structure and pro-
> cedures . . . it is unable to form a clear policy . . . to make sound

---

[7] For example, *Investigation of Executive Agencies of the Government*,
Senate Report No. 1275, 75th Cong., 2d sess. (1937); *Transportation and National Policy*, House Document No. 833, 77th Cong., 2d sess. (1942); *Practices
and Procedures of Government Control*, House Document No. 678, 78th Cong.,
2d sess. (1944); and, more recently, The Booze, Allen and Hamilton Study,
Organization and Procedures, Survey of the Interstate Commerce Commission,
November 1960.

and comprehensive plans. It is unable to administer its affairs with vigor and dispatch.[8]

This is a strong, but just, indictment. The need for more adequate personnel, more money, status and other factors are, as noted in Chapter XII, inseparable. These groups cannot solve their problems by any number of reorganization plans until the basic problems are solved. Inadequate or short term personnel cannot operate a plan of procedure with any degree of success. The problem here is that judgment is necessary. The commissions are not, except for some of their functions, able to operate on a routine "by-the-book" fashion. Each policy problem is unique, and no reference to the organization manual will solve those problems. In the routine areas, those relating to minor rate changes, issuance of routine documents and other matters, the form of organization can be very important. In these areas, however, the need seems to be clear for more personnel and more money.

No amount of regulation will solve the basic problem of providing the Commission with the proper regulatory philosophy and outlook. As we noted in an earlier chapter, the Commission operates under various pressures, and the members of the Commission are not always as expert as they might be. One thoughtful analysis of policy problems comes to this conclusion:

> However, it must be recognized that most of the failure and mistakes of commission regulation are to be laid at the door of the agencies themselves.
>
> Frequently it is evident that a commission or board has departed from a truly judicial handling of a problem because of yielding to the pressures of private interests which it is supposed to regulate. These pressures take various forms. They include the propaganda of the carrier industries regulated, threats to oppose reappointment, and a constant stream of letters and speeches condemning the action or proposed action of the commission. [Recent] sessions of Congress both developed substantial evidence that certain members of federal commissions had violated the ethics and responsibility of their office not only in de novo actions taken but also in reversing decisions. The complexity of the problems with which a regulatory commission deals is such that cooperation between the agency and the industries regulated is required. The matters at issue are often so technical and involved that extensive contact with representatives of the regulated industries is desirable and, in fact, necessary. It is a matter of how

---

[8] Louis J. Hector, Letter of transmittal of Memorandum to the President on *Problems of the C.A.B. and Independent Regulatory Commission*, September 10, 1959.

circumspect the commissioners and employees are in industry
. associations. It is the obligation of a commissioner to preserve
these contacts in terms of time and manner so as not to jeopardize
his judicial detachment. Some critics may overlook the fact that
organized carriers and shippers often help a commission to
counter local and individual pressures and to serve the broader
national interest. A court may aspire to operate in a more or less
legal vacuum, but this is not possible in effective commission
regulation because of the constant changes in the industries
regulated and in concepts of public interest.[9]

Reorganization can help to more effectively process the routine
work load, but it cannot solve the deeply-rooted philosophical problems of the regulatory group.

The Commission has, for years, been seriously understaffed in
both the Washington office and the field offices. Many of the routine functions, such as safety regulation, cannot be performed under
the present system, and the Congress must seriously consider the
wisdom of continuing to expect that these functions will be performed in a satisfactory manner until adequate manpower is available. If, in making this decision, question arises as to the ultimate
worth of some Commission policies in view of the cost, then these
questions must be determined in the legislative branch.

INEQUALITY OF PUBLIC AIDS

For many years in the United States, our public policy has been
well disposed toward public aid toward transportation. All of the
modes, with the exception of pipelines and the indirect carriers, have
benefited greatly from various forms of public aid, and some of the
modes are at the present time enjoying a degree of public aid, although
the extent is subject to controversy, as we have seen. Public aid has
taken many forms and extended to the four major carriers over a
period of many years.

Since waterways, airways and highways are available to the
general public use, expenditures in these areas are not for the use
of any one mode, although the modes using those facilities are, of
course, benefited by those expenditures.

The most serious pitfall in the analysis of aids is the lack of adequate analytical tools with which to evaluate the situation. This
shortcoming was well expressed in a recent government study of
national transportation policy.

------

[9] Marvin L. Fair, op. cit., p. 964.

Unfortunately, adequate tools and methods of analysis and evaluation are not presently available. The use of economic analysis in public investment decision-making in recent years has received increasing attention, but the only specific tool that has had significant application is the benefit-cost ratio. And the primary use of this device has been in the analysis of projects and programs in the water-resources field. In the transport field, benefit-cost ratios have been used in the evaluation of inland waterway projects and to a limited extent in connection with highway investment. There has been almost no use of analytical procedures for airways and airports. In the case of waterway projects, benefit-cost ratios are used primarily for justification, but in the highway field their primary use is in the ranking of projects. There is a need for analytical procedures for both justification and ranking. Only justified projects and programs should be undertaken at all and the best projects should be undertaken first.

Although critics have pointed out several weaknesses in the benefit-cost ratio as a decision-making device, it seems to be the best tool of analysis that has been widely used. It should receive wider use in the highway field and should be applied in airways and airport investment decisions. But it needs to be studied and improved.[10]

Complexity is a serious barrier to the study of any subject, but it does not mean that the study should not be undertaken. Especially in this area, where ignorance serves the partisan advantage of the competing modes, it cannot be tolerated. Every mode is fond of hiding behind the statement that it "pays its fair share." This has long been a safe hiding place, since the "fair share" is not known. Some progress is being made along these lines, but not nearly enough.

The complexity of the aid problem can be discussed more adequately on a modal basis. Let us consider this problem in chronological order, using the various modes as a framework.

Aid to Waterways

From colonial times, aid to waterway development and maintenance have been considered to be a function of the federal government and, to some extent, of the states. Most waterways are multipurpose, as noted in Chapter III, in that they serve not only for navigation, but for flood control, power generation and recreation.

---

[10] Rationale of Federal Transportation Policy, op. cit., p. 42.

This means, of course, that the benefits of aid are widely diffused, although it still seems fair to say that the major benefit accrues to those who live near or on waterway developments.

By 1962, federal expenditures for waterway aid (exclusive of the Great Lakes and coastal harbors) was estimated at $3.1 billion.[11]

Certain of these costs, those relating to locks and navigation aids, for example, are attributable to navigation per se. However, the great bulk of the waterway costs are non-assignable, since they are common to the whole project. From the transportation standpoint, the waterways carriers, public and private, benefit greatly from the provision of a right of way at public expense. It has been historic policy that the waterways should be free of user charges. Although this principle has been questioned in recent years, it seems likely that no fundamental change will take place.[12]

Needless to say, railroads and other groups support user charges, although waterway operators still oppose the principle. This is a unique situation. Other transport agencies using public facilities agree in principle to user charges, although they disagree as to the level of such charges.

No doubt, the competitive stance of the waterway operators would be damaged by even a small user charge. However, equity among not only transport agencies, but also shippers would indicate that a user charge would be just in this situation.

Aid to Railroads

Rail aid has taken various forms over the years—land grants, tax exemptions, loans and cash grants. Except for the land grants discussed in Chapter II, most of these aids have come from state and local governments. Like airlines in recent years, communities were anxious to secure rail service, and grants of land, tax freedom and other concessions were frequently given. However, the great bulk of rail construction was undertaken by private enterprise. Aid to

---

[11] *Annual Reports,* Chief of Engineers, U. S. Army. Also, U. S. Bureau of the Budget, *Annual Budgets.*

[12] In his transportation program, President Kennedy, in 1962, recommended a user charge in the form of a tax on fuel used on waterways. See *Message from the President of the United States Relative to the Transportation System of Our Nation,* House Document No. 384, 87th Cong., 2d sess.

The history of the free waterway idea is interesting, going back to the early colonial period. See *National Transportation Policy,* Committee on Interstate and Foreign Commerce, *op. cit.,* p. 197. Other presidents and many study groups have recommended user charges.

railroads (except for loans in emergency periods) came to an end by about 1900. Land grants by the federal government came to an end in 1871, and, even in the West and far West, the public view had begun to change from encouragement to hostility. A widely accepted estimate of the value of lands granted is that made by the Board of Investigation and Research in 1944, placing the value at somewhat over $440 million.[13] As noted in Chapter II, the railroads, although paying no user charges, did transport federal property at reduced rates for many years. By 1943, the total benefit to the government from this service was estimated at $580 million.[14] Land grant reductions came to an end in 1946. Since 1900, no direct aid has been tendered to railroads. During the 1930's, the Reconstruction Finance Corporation made rail loans, as indicated earlier, and, in 1958, provisions were made for emergency loans, although this latter provision has not been widely used.

Aid to Airways

Airway aid has taken two principal forms—aid via air mail payments and aid in the building and maintenance of airway and airport facilities. As noted in Chapter III, air mail pay was of fundamental importance in airway operation before World War II. Although, in the earlier years, the amount of subsidy was high, the subsidy element was reduced and the payment for service factor increased. By 1960, domestic trunk airlines had become free of subsidy. Airport facilities have, for the most part, been provided by local governments. Local interests have been anxious to obtain airline service, and the municipal airport has become a standard method of procedure.

Air traffic control and navigation facilities have been generally the responsibility of the federal government with the lighted airways in 1923. Total federal aid to airways is estimated at $2.4 billion.[15] Federal, state and local aid to airports, up to 1960, is estimated at $2.78 billion, including certain administrative costs.[16]

---

[13] Board of Investigation and Research, *Land Grants to Railroads and Related Rates* (Washington, D. C.: 1944), p. 25 (mimeographed).

[14] *Ibid.,* p. 42.

[15] *Annual Reports* of the Postmaster General and *Annual Budgets* of the U. S.

[16] *The National Airport Program,* S. Doc. 95, 83d Cong., 2d sess., p. 34; Hearings before the Subcommittee of the Committee on Interstate and Foreign Commerce on bills to amend the Federal Airport Act, U. S. Senate, April 14-17, 1958, p. 6; *Amendments to Federal Airport Act,* Report No. 93, U. S. House of Representatives, 86th Cong., 1st sess., p. 6; Budgets of the U. S. Government; and *The Airport and Its Neighbors,* President's Airport Commission, May 16, 1952, p. 95.

road, the facts must be taken into account that these vehicles are heavier, larger and run more miles than the average private vehicle. The argument as to the "fair share" of motor carrier taxation is an old one, with many emotional aspects. Suffice it to say at this point, that the issue is by no means closed. The weight-distance tax and others are still in the experimental stage, and highway users are doubtless facing a new evaluation of their financial obligations as concepts change.

The historical evaluation of transport aids is long and complex. It was pointed out earlier that the decisions made in 1860 or 1930 are beyond recall for good or ill. Current aid policies are, however, capable of being modified and should be subject to constant observation and frequent reevaluation. Sectional or regional advantage has no place in the national transportation program, and adequate thought must be given to the competitive realities of the situation. Aid given to one mode does more than aid that mode. It may have far-reaching repercussions in the competitive relationship between the modes. In the past, insufficient attention has been paid to these factors. We must cease to consider these issues in isolation and view the aggregate problem. Subsidiary facets of the policy such as public works, defense and related public policy matters cannot be eliminated from the analysis, but they must be recognized and not accorded major importance.

Further, these factors change over time. In 1915, there was opposition to aid for highways, since only those few wealthy automobile owners benefited. In 1960, with almost 75 million private cars on the roads, the direct benefits of highway aids are widely diffused far beyond the motor carrier industry. In an earlier chapter, it was pointed out that these decisions represented an *ex post* allocation of resources and must be accepted as valid expressions of public policy. There are, however, certain current inequities of treatment in this area which need to be examined. The first of these areas relates to taxation. Railroads, since they own such expensive real property, bear a heavy burden of taxation, especially in the local and state level. In rural areas, in particular, rail property taxation often forms the base of township or county finance and has for many years. Motor, air and water carriers own relatively little real property, although they pay user charges for use of facilities. These user charges, though substantial, are greatly exceeded by the rail tax payments, and railroads claim, with some justice, that they are at a disadvantage in this situation.

Another area of substantial lack of uniformity occurs in the area of labor relations. Rail and air employees are (as noted in Chapter

IV) under the jurisdiction of the Railway Labor Act of 1926. Motor carrier employees are covered by the Labor Management Relations Act of 1947. Also, railroad employees are under a federally sponsored retirement act requiring an employer contribution of 6.25 per cent. Rail employees also enjoy, as noted in an earlier chapter, considerable security in the event of rail consolidation and, in general, have substantial benefits aside from those which they might be able to gain from collective bargaining. Other carrier employees enjoy benefits due to collective bargaining activities. It seems likely that railroads are forced to deal somewhat more generously with their employees than other carriers as a matter of law, although, to be sure, other transportation modes face strong union demands. There is a substantial difference between union demands and legislative control over union-management relations, which, as is the case here, oriented around avoidance of major disputes. No matter how relevant this policy was in 1926, it needs to be reevaluated in the mid-1960's.

HOW FAR SHOULD RELAXATION OF REGULATION GO?

The ultimate question is clearly that of the degree to which, if any, regulation should be relaxed. Few would hold that no relaxation should take place, but much controversy centers around the extent of relaxation. One can view this problem in two ways. If the primary goal is to make regulation more uniform, then the remedy might be to extend regulation to those areas now only partially regulated and thus increase the sum total of regulation. A second way would be to eliminate some regulation and bring the presently regulated carriers into line with those less regulated.

The optimum course hinges upon two questions. Do we need more or less regulation, and can we effectively administer the regulation now extant or to be put into effect? An elaborate regulatory system on paper without adequate enforcement procedure is clearly undesirable, and we must also consider here the cost of the enforcement procedure relative to the social and economic benefits received.

CAN THE MARKET MECHANISM DO THE JOB?

Fortunately, there is a way out of this dilemma, viz., greater dependence upon the market mechanism. Let us recognize that we no longer have large areas of monopoly in the transportation field. An increasing range of goods can be carried by either rail, truck or other modes. The Interstate Commerce Commission does not have any way, nor does it need a way to recognize the inherent advantages present in a mode of transport. Every mode has some advantages for a shipper, depending upon his location, his product, his market. No one mode can be everything to every shipper. The Rolls-Royce and the Volkswagen both have inherent advantages and shortcomings. A prospective purchaser must weigh his needs against the price he is able or willing to pay in order to make a choice. It would be foolish for each manufacturer to make obviously false claims. The Rolls-Royce is not an "economy" car, but it has other obvious advantages. Likewise, the railroad is not used to advantage in making small package shipments within a radius of one hundred miles; there is no reason it should be. However, it has the great advantage of low cost mass goods movement, clearly demonstrated by the flow of goods.

Carriers are apt to claim every advantage as a means of attracting shippers, but this advertising "puff" need not be accepted as a basis of resource allocation. If railroads can transport new automobiles at rates and with sufficient speed and care as to cause shippers to tender such traffic, much of which was formerly moved by truck, who is to deny that this is a clear manifestation of the market mechanism demonstrating an inherent advantage? In the years 1930-1950, traffic trends were in the opposite direction, and this was rightly hailed as the working of competitive forces. Perhaps by 1965, technological change or rate adjustments will bring about a third change in the flow of traffic. No regulatory group, no matter how wise and nobly motivated, can predict changes of this type, given our present analytical and forecasting apparatus, nor indeed do they need to. One cannot expect rate regulation to eliminate every case of inequity or economic hardship which may arise.

Nor can one expect regulation to "preserve" the inherent advantages of an industry. If it has any function along this line, it might be to prevent "predatory" actions in competition, assuming that such actions can be identified and separated from the normal competitive policies. Placing a limit upon the degree of rate competition which can be carried on, on either an intermodal or an intramodal basis, may have some merit; however, great care must be exercised to see that a carrier is not prevented from a reasonable exploitation of the market advantages which may be present. This would seem to be the true measure of the preservation of the inherent advantages. In our present transportation complex, each mode has various degrees of price and non-price advantage vis-a-vis the others. When one examines the economic function of transport, the opportunity for non-price competition seems to be very much limited. Shippers expect a standard of service; and, if this standard, based upon experience in the market, is achieved, the shipper will be relatively indifferent to further extensions on the service level. Unlike manufacturers of consumer goods, the transporter, as part of the service industries, has only limited range in the area of differentiating his product or service outlet. Consequently, the transporter must rely heavily (on an intermodal basis) upon price competition. Historically, the carriers have emphasized non-price competition on an intramodal basis as a result of their preregulation experiences with the destructive competition which arose out of drastic rate reductions. Cooperative rate making by the bureau method thus became the accepted procedure, and experience would indicate that price competition on an intramodal level would not be practicable.

However, on an intermodal basis, where non-price factors have more vitality, price competition on a more rigorous basis seems desirable. Shippers would then be able to weigh the advantage of relative rates against the scale of non-price factors which are relevant to any given situation. To be sure, there are some shippers who, by reason of location or product character, cannot take advantage of intermodal competition; but, fortunately, the number of such shippers is diminishing as transport technology improves.

Carriers, on the other hand, would be able to exploit those areas where non-price factors are strong or, to use a much-maligned phrase, charge "what the traffic will bear." Charging what the traffic will bear is not reprehensible except where, as in the case of a franchised industry, the buyer has no alternative source. Assuming that alternatives are available and there is no collusion and that the buyer is reasonably well informed, no serious problems exist. There is no reason to feel that the buyer of transportation service is not as rational in his buying decisions as the buyer of other products and services. The antitrust laws are designed to prevent undue restraint of trade, market collusion, price fixing, and other market practices deemed reprehensible by society. Although there may be doubts as to the efficiency and efficacy of such legislation, the Sherman Act and related statutes represent the public's current best judgment as to how to deal with the situation. While it is easy to point to the complexity of such policies and to ascribe the inefficiency of the workings of the antitrust laws to the growth of business and the corporate form of organization, as Pegrum wisely points out, this does not justify an attack on *laissez faire* per se.[20] The limits of economic policy are also vividly described

---

[20] Dudley F. Pegrum, *op. cit.*, pp. 690 ff.

by Robbins in his classic work on the nature and significance of economic science.

> The irrational element in the economist's universe of discourse lies behind the individual valuation as we have seen already, there is no means available for determining the probable movement of the relative scales of valuation.[21]

We must accept the fact that public regulation of business can only be successful on the broadest basis. Detailed regulation of market relationships and other micro-economic factors seems bound to founder on the shoals of technical inefficiency and the lack of adequate tools for determining and forecasting economic change.

The market mechanism, although by no means perfect, is an efficient allocating device in aggregate terms. Unless regulation can improve on the allocative process and, at the same time, provide for the welfare of the industry, as well as the public interest, regulation has little to recommend it. This is especially true of highly detailed regulation of a micro-economic character which consumes so much time and energy in our present system.

There may be substantial areas of rate regulation, especially on an intermodal basis where regulation can be and should be relaxed. Some relaxation seems desirable also in the provisions relative to entry of firms into the industry. In this area and in the detailed commodity-points served regulation of the motor carriers, the Commission faces its major problems. Referring here to the previously mentioned problem of administration, the Commission has an almost impossible task of enforcement. The infamous "gray area" of motor transportation illustrates the scope of this task.[22] It is hard to conceive of a practicable enforcement procedure which would be adequate in this complex case. The thousands of private and agricultural product carriers provide an almost limitless opportunity for wilful and inadvertent violation of the Act.

By increasing the enforcement staff many fold and devising highly burdensome and complex procedures, the Commission could, no doubt, solve this problem. Serious question arises as to the social and economic worth of this procedure vis-a-vis the cost. As the recent Senate study points out, the problem may be not in overregulation per se, but in the fact that we have a false interpretation as to what constitutes desirable competition in so heterogeneous an industry as transporta-

---

[21] Lionel Robbins, *An Essay on the Nature and Significance of Economic Science* (London: The Macmillan Co., 1948) pp. 126-127.

[22] *Gray Area of Transportation Operations,* Interstate Commerce Commission, Statement No. 6010, July 1960.

tion.[23] In the public utilities field, where close regulation but no competition is found (due to their franchised status), firms are in an extremely satisfactory condition and encounter no trouble in attracting capital and earning an adequate income.

No clear answer can be given at this point as to the desirable level of regulation. What must be done is to eliminate, insofar as possible, the shortcomings of the present system. If and when this has been done, the framework of the system must itself be studied to see what basic changes need to be made. In the following chapter, these problems will be further examined and recommendations made.

---

[23] *National Transportation Policy, op. cit.*, p. 30.

CHAPTER XXIV

Review and Policy Considerations

In the preceding chapter, the policy shortcomings of regulation in the modern economy were examined. Let us now review what we have said about the transportation industry and perhaps propose certain recommendations.

As we have seen, the transportation industry is an industry which, although consisting of separate modes, is, nonetheless, highly integrated and, to a large extent, operates as a unit. The transportation industry, although performing a vital economic and social function, has, in recent years, faced serious economic problems. In large measure these problems have arisen from technological changes and shifts in consumer tastes or income. An example of this type of change is the change in intercity passenger transportation since 1930. Changes of this type are to be expected and are highly desirable in a dynamic economy. Naturally, these changes bring about dislocation and economic distress, as do all such actions. The unique element in the transportation industry is the role of public policy stemming from regulation.

In a regulated and quasi-public industry, as we have seen, these shifts are more difficult to bring about smoothly than is the case in the non-regulated industry. So many institutional factors, out-of-date legal requirements and other matters must be accounted for that the process of adjusting to changing circumstances becomes highly complex. Further, serious issues arise as to the degree of aid and assistance which should be granted by the public authorities. The economic and social alterations which have been taking place in the industry since 1930 demand maximum flexibility in order to be accommodated with minimum dislocation. It can be argued that a major function of regulation is to ease the impact of these developments. We must, however, exercise great care that this function is not carried so far that the beneficial and, to a great extent, irresistible effects will be prevented from running their course. The national policy with regard to agriculture has, for example, been so intent on shielding those concerned from the impact of change that the normal course of events has been interrupted. A recent study states the problem thus:

> Rapid technological advances, and increasing capital investment, have made it possible for fewer and fewer American farmers to supply the food and fiber needs of larger and larger numbers of people. American farmers have shown great initiative and competence in responding to the opportunity thus created. They have taken up the latest production methods with a speed that amazes the administrators of agriculture in planned economies.
>
> Net migration out of agriculture has been going on for 40 years, and at a rapid rate. Nevertheless, the movement of people from agriculture has not been fast enough to take full advantage of the opportunity that improving farm technology and increasing capital create for raising the living standards of the American people, including, of course, farmers. Costs of movement, lack of knowledge of nonfarm job opportunities, lack of training for nonfarm work, in some periods inadequate rate of movement out of agriculture. National agricultural policy has not focussed on removing these obstacles, but has tended itself to deter the out-movement by concealing the necessity for it.[1]

Nor must we err in the opposite direction by forcing technological changes prematurely, thus putting an undue burden upon those in competition with the developing industry. There seems to be ample evidence that both these shortcomings have been found in our recent transportation policy. The orderly development of transportation (i.e., in accord with the economic needs) has frequently been thwarted or artificially stimulated by public policy. Let us recall that the major modes, rail, air and motor, were all at one time, or at the present time, given substantial aid which enabled

---

[1] *An Adaptive Program for Agriculture* (New York: Committee for Economic Development, 1962), pp. 7 ff.

them to develop faster than they normally would have done. These policies were justified on grounds of desirable economic development, national security and various other desirable grounds. It was noted earlier that these matters are now done and can be relegated to the realm of history. Our task at this point is to look into the future, not the past.

THE TRANSPORTATION SYSTEM AT MID-CENTURY

At the mid-point of the twentieth century, we have in the United States a complex and, by all measures, an adequate transportation system. While it is easy to focus our attention on the dramatic shifts which have taken place in the past three decades, there are certain fundamental facts which must be noted. Railroads still perform the bulk of inter-city freight ton-mile service, and our present economy is dependent upon them. The motor carriers perform a smaller though vital share of ton-mile service, and our modern transportation system would be impossible in their absence. Likewise, pipelines and water carriers perform essential services. In the passenger field the private automobile performs the major share of intercity and urban passenger service, and an increasing share of our resources is being devoted to its accommodation. Air carriers are increasingly important and dominate the common carrier segment of passenger transportation, while bus and especially rail lose ground in this sector. While these changing patterns are significant, the single most important fact which is clear is that each of these modes plays a vital part in the whole system. Each mode is needed, although it seems very likely that each is not needed in its present capacity. Let us compare this situation to the automobile industry. The auto industry produces a wide variety of cars, ranging from the custom built sports car of special design and the Cadillac town car to the Jeep and the lowest price business coupe. Total output varies but may reach, in one year, six million. There is wide variation within the models; perhaps only a few thousand town cars are produced while several million four door sedans might be turned out. Likewise, several million of the total cars produced might be Fords or Chevrolets, and only a relative handful of Chrysler Imperials might be marketed. The automobile industry thus produces in accord with the total market, which is highly segmented according to consumer demand. No producer (or division of a large company) can hope to serve the whole market, although they can try to do so in

theory. There is thus a market for automobiles, but this is meaningless to the market forecasters in the Cadillac Division of General
Motors, since the relevant frame of reference for them is the "luxury"
car market. In the transportation industry much the same situation
prevails. There is a transportation market, but, due to shipper custom,
technological needs and other factors, this market is segmented
among the modes. The economy needs and can use all the modes,
but not all their present capacity. There appears to be a rather
substantial degree of excess capacity in the industry; and, although
to an extent this is inherent, much of it arises because of error and
must be allowed to pass out of existence.

To be sure, overcapacity is a relative matter. It may be argued
that overcapacity exists because of inadequate growth in the economy.
To what extent the present transportation system would be faced
with overcapacity if the rate of economic growth were to be greatly
increased is a matter of debate. There are those who claim that
the rate of economic growth is insufficient and that the economy
could operate on a higher level. These matters of economic policy
are beyond the scope of this book. It seems clear, however, that,
except in wartime or at other times of peak demand, much of our
passenger-carrying capacity (for hire) is redundant. Also, as was
noted earlier, much of the existing capacity is made up of obsolete
facilities which, except for periods of unusual stress, would be better
left unused. The private automobile has long been the mainstay of
intercity passenger carriage, and the motor truck is being used to
such an extent as to endanger the future growth of common carriage
in the freight area.[2] Under these circumstances, the appropriate
capacity for the national welfare becomes somewhat difficult to
measure. As some authorities point out, the common carrier may
become a "residual" carrier.[3] In his message on transportation submitted to the Congress in late 1962, the President noted this problem,
saying:

> . . . Investment or capacity should be neither substantially
> above nor substantially below these requirements—for chronic
> excess capacity involves misuse of resources, and lack of adequate
> capacity jeopardizes progress. The resources devoted to provision
> of transportation service should be used in the most effective and
> efficient manner possible, and this, in turn, means that users of
> transport facilities should be provided with incentives to use

[2] See *Decline of Common Carriage*, Hearings before the Surface Transportation Subcommittee, Committee on Interstate and Foreign Commerce, U. S.
Senate, 1961, pp. 222 ff.

[3] See Leon N. Moses, *Traffic World*, November 10, 1962, p. 37.

whatever form of transportation which provides them with the service they desire at the lowest total cost, both public and private.

This basic objective can and must be achieved primarily by continued reliance on unsubsidized privately-owned facilities, operating under the incentives of private profit and the checks of competition to the maximum extent practicable. The role of public policy should be to provide a consistent and comprehensive framework and equal competitive opportunity that will achieve this objective at the lowest economic and social cost to the Nation.

This means a more coordinated Federal policy and a less segmented approach. It means equality of opportunity for all forms of transportation and their users and undue preference to none. It means greater reliance on the forces of competition and less reliance on the restraints of regulation. And it means that, to the extent possible, the users of transportation services should bear the full costs of the services they use, whether those services are provided privately or publicly.[4]

Undoubtedly, much of this overcapacity exists because of a refusal on the part of management and the regulators to recognize the limitations of the mode.

An example of this is the determination of railroads for some time to continue the use of train service in the traditional manner on branch lines and the similar determination of truckers to attempt long hauls in cases where they cannot compete. Naturally, there is an incentive for carriers to push into all markets possible, but, when they are repelled by market forces, they must accept this (until circumstances change) and not depend upon public policy to solve these problems.

The relationship between the problems of the carriers at mid-century and the state of regulation is a classic hen-egg problem. There can be little doubt that many of the shortcomings of management are due to over regulation. We have seen in this study that there are countless areas where the prerogatives of management have been taken over with the best of intentions and sometimes unavoidably by the regulatory authorities. This fact tends to blunt the edge of competitive actions and diminishes the role of aggressive innovation. Especially where such conditions have prevailed over many years, as is true in the railroad field, management tends to concentrate on routine operational matters at the expense of policy issues. There is also an unfortunate influence on the regulatory authority, in that

---

[4] House Document No. 384, 87th Congress, 2d. sess., *Message from the President of the United States, Relative to the Transportation System of Our Nation.*

they may put themselves *in loco parentis* and assume that their role is to guide the management onto the paths of virtue. Unfortunately, as we have seen, the regulatory bodies are ill-equipped to perform this task, even if, indeed, they are supposed to do so.

As is evident, these areas are not clearly black or white. Only the rash would advocate a wholesale repeal of regulation across the board, and we must approach this problem, not with a meat cleaver but a scalpel.

It seems necessary, at the outset, to note certain areas of managerial and regulatory ignorance where more information is needed before an intelligent program can be formulated. It has been said often that transportation has been over-studied, and, indeed, there has been a plethora of studies in recent years. Yet, it may not be true that there has been an excess of studies. Is there any complex industry about which too much can be known? The dynamic inter-relationships involved in transportation are highly complex, and pro-ceeding without clear knowledge of the reactions would be the worst folly.[5]

A recent statement regarding this problem expresses it as follows:

> Unfortunately, rational action cannot at present be assumed. It requires, among other things, a reasonable knowledge of the costs of performing service and of their behavior with changes in volume of traffic. It requires also a knowledge of the market con-ditions and of the capabilities of competitors. None of this wide range of essential knowledge is today available in applicable and usable form. Hence, only some progress can be made at present toward a greater freedom from control and larger reliance upon the competitive processes. Yet such progress as is possible ought to be undertaken and the conditions created which, in the longer run, will permit a transition to the minimum of regulation and of Government participation. In consequence, great emphasis should be placed upon perfecting cost-finding techniques and providing adequate market information so that the industries may be equipped to behave responsibly under a less comprehensive regulatory structure. This will necessitate the assumption of con-siderable leadership by Government and will necessarily take considerable time. An orderly transition over some rather lengthy period is, moreover, indicated. For important interests exist which were founded upon the expectation that Government policy would continue in present channels. Such interests are entitled to notice and to a reasonable period of time for adjustment to new policies.[6]

---

[5] The Hoch-Smith resolution previously mentioned was probably the worst example of this policy; however, runner-up candidates are not hard to find.

[6] Rationale of Federal Transportation Policy, *op. cit.,* p. 8.

AREAS IN NEED OF FURTHER STUDY

1. The relationship between fore-hire, agriculturally exempt, and private motor carriers, including leases, back-haul traffic and the so-called "gray area."

It is impossible to react in an intelligent fashion to the unknown. Neither carrier management nor the regulatory authorities are aware of the extent and scope of the operations of the exempt carriers and especially of their impact upon the market. Unless these data are forthcoming, any attempts to integrate these operations into the common carrier framework are based upon ignorance and cannot succeed. The long awaited census of transportation may throw some light on this situation, although what is needed, as indicated in point 2 below, is a thorough study of the market structure of the industry.

2. Commodity movements, business and economic characteristics of the unregulated motor carriers, especially their impact upon regulated motor carrier markets.

3. The impact of user charges of various levels upon the economic status of water carriers.

As we saw in an earlier chapter, this is a problem which has given rise to substantial controversy. Although water carrier operators have stoutly maintained that the industry could not bear any user charge and still maintain its competitive position, this remains to be seen in fact. The effects of various user charges of varied levels need to be explored and measured. If, indeed, it proves to be impossible for such charges to be borne, then serious questions arise as to the economic feasibility of water transportation. Here, again, the question is one of relationship. Water transportation in isolation is no doubt beneficial to the economy, but we must remember that water transport competes with other forms of commercial transportation in the market.

4. Financial and administrative burden upon motor carriers, relative to highway use by interstate carriers.

This problem is similar to that above; however, the motor carriers accept the principle of user charges, although doubt exists as to the proper level. Many studies have been conducted in this area, and, while progress is very slow, there seems to be some evidence that it is being made. Motor carrier fees and taxes are still largely arbitrary and have been developed over a period of years for no good reason, but there is an increasing tendency to construct fees on a scientific basis.

5. Responsibility of air carriers for safety and traffic control expenditures.

6. Role of local service air carriers in the aggregate transportation system relative to cost.

The appropriate role of the local service air carriers as a part of the whole transport system needs to be thought through. The economic contribution of some of these carriers is doubtful. It is likely that the economies of scale in the industry are such that there is a need for feeder service from smaller points. However, it is equally likely that many of the points served by the local service lines have little need for air service, except to bolster civic pride. An alternate policy, which the CAB has apparently used from time to time, is to require the trunk lines to serve small cities as a *quid pro quo* for serving the major traffic points. The local service lines like waterway projects need to be viewed, not in isolation but in the whole transport complex.

7. Role of specific waterway projects in the aggregate transportation system.

8. Further study needs to be given to the present necessity for continuing in effect the commodities clause. The commodities clause, although no doubt soundly conceived at the time it was passed, is of questionable value under present circumstances.

9. Proposals have been made for repeal of parts of the 4th Section (long and short haul clause). It is contended that such action would simplify the rate structure and the impact would not be serious, insofar as competition is concerned. Something is to be said for this, but further study is necessary.

10. Further study needs to be given to the frequently made proposal to create a federal department of transportation on a cabinet level. This proposal would be highly appealing if it could be assumed that its virtues would actually come to pass, viz., that the present system of multi-transportation functions spread throughout the government would be eliminated through consolidation. As was noted in an earlier chapter, past experience in attempting to consolidate governmental functions does not give much ground for optimism.

All these matters were discussed at various points in preceding chapters, and it will be remembered that there was no determinate solution. There is something to be said on both sides of these questions, and, so far, they have generated more heat than light.

The fact that our knowledge is incomplete does not mean, of course, that it need remain so. A competent and unbiased study group could gather and analyze much useful information in all these areas. In other areas it seems clear that some recommendations can be made, at least of a tentative nature. It will be seen that some of these recommendations involve areas discussed above, where more information is needed. Despite this fact, some tentative steps might be taken with little danger of serious error.

    1. Extend the agricultural exemption to other carriers.

    To what extent the agricultural exemption would be used by other carriers is doubtful, since much of this traffic is not considered as desirable; nor in many cases are non-motor carriers really suitable for such traffic. However, to the extent that such traffic is competitive, all modes should be on equal footing. An alternative would be to repeal the exemption completely, but this seems politically impossible, and extension of the exemption would at least restore the modes to a condition of parity.

    The recommendation to extend the exemption is made on the assumption that it would not be practicable to eliminate that now existing. If such action were politically feasible, it would seem to be highly desirable as an alternative. An extension would raise serious problems and might adversely affect the public interest. The comments of the Doyle report in this area are worth noting:

> It is almost axiomatic, as the Interstate Commerce Commission has frequently pointed out, that regulation of transportation is rendered ineffective by substantial exemption therefrom. If, as a national policy, we expect to retain the status of transportation as regulated competition, intermediate between regulated monopoly and general industry unregulated except by antitrust laws, then in all logic we must not emasculate our policy of regulated competition.
>
> Equality of treatment of the several modes is a sound objective of our national transportation policy to which this entire study has been dedicated. We have, however, also established the position that the national interest must take precedence over any other, more limited interest. If regulation is rendered ineffective by large-scale exemption therefrom, and if regulation is essential, then any extension of exemption, even in the interests of equity, is contrary to the public interest.
>
> In view of an unofficial railroad estimate that extension of agricultural and bulk exemption to the railroads would deregulate approximately 70 percent of their carload tonnage, we conclude that any such action would make regulation of transportation so generally ineffective that it would be, of necessity, abandoned.

These facilities are used by non-commercial fliers and, to some extent, by military aviation. The airway control system is greatly increased in complexity because of the military flying needs, and, thus, these facilities are, to some extent, multi-purpose.

Airlines pay certain user charges in the form of rentals and other airport charges and in the form of fuel taxes. There is no question but what these payments are far less than the total costs and will become less adequate as the costs of modern traffic control systems become fully known.

Aid to Motor Carriers

Highway building and maintenance have, as pointed out in Chapter II, been considered a public responsibility for many years. Federal aid began in 1916 and has increased through the years to the 90-10 ratio of the Interstate System. State expenditures have also grown with the number of vehicles, and local-state highway expenditures are a major element of state finance. In recent years, highway expenditures have been second only to education as a state function. From 1927-1957, state highway expenditures rose from $1.8 billion to $7.7 billion.[17] In the latter year, these expenditures amounted to roughly 20 per cent of total state expenditures, being second to education ($14.5 billion) and exceeding public welfare, the third category, by a wide margin. Total state and federal highway expenditures are estimated at $149.3 billion.[18]

These expenditures are, of course, of benefit to all highway users, of which the commercial motor carriers form only a small part. The organized trucking industry estimates that commercial motor trucks paid $2.796 billion in user charges of all types in 1957.[19]

It was pointed out in Chapter II that much disagreement exists as to the amount of tax liability on the part of motor carriers. While for-hire trucks constitute some 16 per cent of the total vehicles on the

---

[17] Troy J. Cauley, *Public Finance and the General Welfare* (Columbus: Charles E. Merrill Books, Inc., 1960), p. 45.

[18] U. S. Department of Commerce, Bureau of Public Roads, *Highway Statistics Summary to 1955*, Tables HF-201 and 202 for years through 1947; *Highway Finance 1948-57*, April 1958, Tables HF-1 and HF-2 for year 1948; and Bureau of Public Roads releases, February 1960, Tables HF-1 and HF-2 for years 1949-1960.

[19] *American Trucking Trends*, 1960, American Trucking Associations, Inc., pp. 12-13. These payments were distributed as follows: Out of each tax dollar—motor fuel, 49.2 cents; registration, 34.8 cents; bridge-tunnel, road fees, 7.7 cents; special county and city fees, 2.6 cents; and motor carrier taxes, 5.7 cents.

As stated in the preceding sections of this chapter, we recommend that exemption from regulation, with certain exceptions, be gradually eliminated in the national public interest.[7]

2.   Repeal Section 22 of the Interstate Commerce Act. This section provides that federal government shipments may be moved at rates arrived at by negotiation. There is no valid reason under present circumstances for this provision and it would be removed, at least on an experimental basis.

In a third category are some recommendations which can be made at this time without much serious doubt as to their effect:

1.   Clarify the status of the national transportation policy and emphasize the fact that it is a general statement of overall intent and not in any way a working directive.

2.   Review the intermodal rate regulatory policy and remove any intent that the version of Section 15-A, as expressed in the Transportation Act of 1958, is the correct policy.

That is to say, reduce the emphasis put upon the level of competing rates in situations where rate reductions are under consideration. It was noted in Chapter XX that recent cases (since 1958) have followed this general trend and should be continued.

3.   Set up and use an advisory group for the ICC and the CAB, similar to the advisory groups now extant in other federal agencies such as the Department of Commerce.

The quasi-judicial nature of the Interstate Commerce Commission and the Civil Aeronautics Board has inhibited the use of these groups in the past. However, the research and administrative activities of these bodies could benefit greatly from an informal infusion of outside opinion and thinking on various issues.

4.   More closely define the relationship between the Undersecretary of Commerce for Transportation and the Interstate Commerce Commission and the Civil Aeronautics Board and, specifically, transfer the promotional activities of the CAB and the Corps of Engineers to the Office of the Undersecretary.

5.   Broaden the currently narrow controls over motor carrier point to point and commodity authority in order to give greater flexibility.

The fragmentation of motor carrier operating rights has long since passed the point where it served the public interest. The original intent was, of course, to prevent the motor carriers from expanding irrationally in every direction. With the increasing number of firms entering the field and the need to control competition, the situation

---

[7] National Transportation Policy, *op. cit.*, p. 533.

has become detrimental to the welfare of the shipping public.[8] In addressing itself to this problem, the Senate Committee Report concludes:

> It seems beyond question that a reorientation of regulatory thinking in respect to motor common carrier authorizations is long overdue. The public interest not only demands that new authorizations emphasize efficiency in our system of highway transport, but that restrictions which result in avoidable economic cost or which prevent a common carrier from realizing his full service potential be removed from existing authorizations. We recognize that rationalization of the presently fragmented and confused situation will be a long, expensive, and often painful undertaking. We believe it necessary in our national interest and that it will repay a hundredfold the effort and investment required.[9]

This problem is somewhat similar to that existing in the certification of routes in the airline industry and has a similar remedy. As the study notes, the solution to this problem is a difficult and painful one, but necessary to rational regulation in the motor carrier industry.

Under the present system, the narrow definition of rights is burdensome, especially where cast against the background of the commodity restrictions. There seems to be little question that these factors have increased the attraction of private carriage and have in other ways been a problem for both carriers and shippers.

6.   Remove artificial barriers to consolidation and integration (except for the antitrust acts) and encourage the formation of true "transportation" companies. Allow carriers to integrate and to acquire interests in both transportation and non-transportation enterprises.

7.   Continue to study the problems of the Commission and to upgrade personnel throughout. Add staff in order to carry out the present responsibilities of the Commission such as safety, review of routine requests and other matters. Enlarge the research functions of the Commission and the Board, especially with regard to rates and costs, and follow the policy of the Federal Reserve Board and other such bodies by bringing in outside authorities for special studies and internships.

8.   One recommendation almost universally accepted is the need for more rigid enforcement of motor carrier safety regulations. These regulations are necessary and are meaningless unless vigorously

---

[8] See as an example the comments of Commissioner Goff in *Application of Alterman Transport Lines,* (MC-107107, SUB 122). Other examples occur in Adams and Hendry, *op. cit.*

[9] National Transportation Policy, *op. cit.,* p. 550.

enforced. Various checks by the Interstate Commerce Commission
have revealed a woeful lack of enforcement, and there is much
evidence that the carriers fail to take these regulations seriously.
This is a problem which requires close and continuous cooperation
with state officials, since these officers frequently have closer contact
with the motor carriers through their own duties. More Commission
personnel and larger appropriations are the key to this problem.

Because of the scope of the motor carrier industry and, especially,
the informal operations of many of its segments, it may be that these
effective enforcements cannot be achieved by the methods now in
use. If this is so, some change may be needed, but, until some further
effort is made, no conclusion can be reached.

As would be expected, these proposals, most of them appearing
from time to time, have elicited substantial opinion both pro and con.

In the first group (those needing further study), there is partisan
support for certain of these proposals. Railroad interests, for example,
have generally supported the proposal for a Department of Transportation. Both rail and motor carriers favor study of the "gray area,"
and rail carriers have supported the transportation census, although
some motor carriers, notably the private carriers, have been either
moderately interested or opposed. Rail carriers favor repeal or modification of the 4th Section, motor carriers are indifferent, and water
carriers strongly oppose it.

In most cases, unfortunately, recommendations for further study
are viewed as delaying tactics. It seems highly likely, for example,
that various proposals regarding user charges could be and have been
"studied" for years without any significant agreement as to their
proper level. It costs nothing for a carrier to agree that it should pay
its "fair share" and then fail to agree as to what constitutes the fair
share.

In the second and third groups, tentative and firm recommendations, there is, to a surprising extent, agreement but with strong
pockets of resistance. All of these proposals have been advocated by
various groups. The areas of agreement are especially surprising in
view of the large number of groups interested in transportation problems. All of the groups listed below have, in recent years, put forth
a more or less comprehensive transportation program.

Federal and Other Public Sources
    The Executive Office of the President
    The Congress
    The Department of Commerce
    The Interstate Commerce Commission

Foundations and Non-Transportation Associations
    American Enterprise Association
    The National Grange
    The U. S. Chamber of Commerce
    National Coal Association
    National Association of Railway & Public Utilities Commissioners

Non-Partisan Transportation Groups
    American Society of Traffic and Transportation
    Transportation Association of America

Partisan Transportation Groups
    American Trucking Associations
    Association of American Railroads
    Air Transport Association of America
    American Waterways Operators Association

In addition to these groups, splinter proposals have been forthcoming from other related bodies which have a fragmentary interest in some matter. There are also countless proposals by individual writers appearing in the professional and learned journals.

Contrary to what one would think, there is a surprising degree of agreement as to the elements of a broad program. Many of the proposals recommended above are endorsed by two or more of the studies mentioned. One must note, however, that agreement in principle does not always mean agreement in specific fact, and theory does not translate itself into practice.

User charges (in theory) are endorsed by all groups except waterway operators. All agree on the need for further improvement in Commission and Board organization and procedure. Widespread agreement exists as to the need for more rate making study, although specific proposals such as those relating to Section 15a bring about substantial disagreement.

Certain of these recommendations are of considerable scope and cannot in all likelihood be enacted except by stages. There is here, as elsewhere, a substantial degree of ignorance and prejudice. For example, there are those who oppose some proposal because they have been told by their trade association representatives that they should be against it; others see dangers of monopoly where it no longer exists. As was noted earlier, the number of vested interests is very large. Also, there is wide diversity of opinion. For example, almost all authorities feel that rail mergers are both advantageous to the ailing railroads and relatively harmless to the competitive structure of the industry; yet, in a recent session of Congress, a bill was introduced which would remove the authority of the Commission in this area. In the same Congress, at least eleven bills were introduced which would substantially alter major areas of national policy toward transportation.

THE RAILROADS, A SPECIAL PROBLEM

In the chapter on management, some of the railroad problems were pointed out; and in the preceding chapter it was noted that at mid-century, none of the modes was financially as strong as desirable to meet the needs of the modern economy. This presents a real challenge for both management and policy makers. While railroads carried approximately 45 percent of the intercity ton-miles in recent years, the Association of American Railroads has commented on these figures as follows:

> Moreover, the comparison here does not give a true expression of the relative importance of railroads and motor carriers, because the revenue derived by motor carriers per ton-mile is much greater than that obtained by the railroads. Statistics are not available for the revenues derived by unregulated for-hire carriers and for the worth of services performed by private carriers. We do have them for regulated motor carriers. Class 1, 2, and 3 intercity motor carriers reporting to the Interstate Commerce Commission carried 32.3 percent of the ton-miles carried by all motor carriers in the year 1957, or approximately 6.23 percent of total intercity ton-miles of all forms of transportation in that year. For that transportation, such regulated motor carriers derived $6,165,190,000, which contrasts with $9,200 million of freight service revenue obtained by the railroads for transporting 46.31 percent of the total intercity ton-miles transported in that year. It is safe to estimate that the total value of transportation service rendered by motor carriers in intercity traffic very substantially exceeded the revenues derived by the railroads. Thus, measured by dollars, the railroads are today a minority factor in freight transportation in the United States, and their share continues to decline. In this respect, the following paragraphs from the 72d Annual Report of the Interstate Commerce Commission, 1958, page 9, are significant.
>
> "Ton-miles of all carriers in 1957 were 1,352,131 million, a slight decline from the all-time record of 1,360,142 million in 1956. Figures for both years exclude coastwise and intercoastal water traffic and nonrevenue ton-miles of railroads. With the exception of the railroads, the levels for 1957 were above those

for 1956. Waterway traffic in 1957 was well above the level of the previous year, and pipeline and highway traffic showed slight increases. The air ton-miles again showed a sizable percentage increase (6.7 per cent), but remained less than half of a per cent of the total.

"While the railroad share of the total declined, the shares of other means of transport increased. The ton-miles by water, pipeline (oil), and air were the highest yet recorded. Revision of the preliminary highway figure may prove it to be a new record."[10]

These figures indicate with unmistakable clarity the impact of competing modes, especially the "exempt" carriers, on the "bread and butter" traffic of the railroads. This has implications for rail management who must closely examine the cost-service relationships which prevail in rail vis-a-vis other carrier service. Technological changes have greatly altered these relationships even in recent years. It has equally pressing implications for the regulators who must consider the role of the exempt carrier.

This matter has been clearly stated by a recent Congressional study:

> History is undoubtedly one of the severest problems of rail management in 1960—there is so much of it. Most of this history is that of a complete monopoly serving the public under detailed State and Federal regulation. The railroads did enjoy an unbroken monopoly from their maturity just prior to the Civil War until after the First World War. They were under Federal regulation for over 30 years of this period and the Interstate Commerce Commission matured as an organization with a single regulatory responsibility and with a vital and self-supporting industry to regulate. A long and comprehensive tradition of monopolistic self-determination and self-sufficiency grew up through these years on the part of both railroad management and the State and Federal regulators. The self-sufficiency seemed less sure in certain periods, i.e., 1913-16, 1921, and 1930-39, but it continued a reality and at present the railroads have enjoyed the greatest volume of profits, and for a longer period, since the late 1920's. Capital structures are in better condition and receiverships are at an all-time low.
>
> The aim of the regulators and the companies during the great period of effective monopoly was to provide a very complete service, and a very large volume of service, at generally reasonable

---

[10] Association of American Railroads, "Transport Diversification," report from, to the transportation study group of the Senate Committee on Interstate and Foreign Commerce (S. Res. 29 and 244), dated January 1960, pp. 4, 5.

prices. These prices were individually set to achieve many ends in marketing; the widest possible geographic distribution of raw materials; the beneficial provision of transportation service to as many citizens, farmers, and small businessmen as possible; and a distribution of finished products which, though expensive, was generally nondiscriminatory. The joint managers of this system, the commissions and the railroad officers, counted on traffic volume and the profit incentive to control the costs of doing business, while at the same time providing virtually omnipresent service. The package of rates and fares which supported this service did not need to be related to costs, nor to recover any specific cost. The sum total had only to attain an average sufficiency high to keep a majority of the companies solvent and profitable enough to attract capital.

The only really effective controls on costs were intraindustry competition, which featured the railroad scene until the depression of the 1930's, and the efforts of State and Federal regulators. Specific accounting and cost controls in the modern sense were neither needed nor used. Rates were changed in response to shipper pressures, to railroad competition, or in response to general increases in the cost of doing business. One of the situations produced by these broad methods was the extravagant application of taxes on railroad property by State and local governments. The railroads and the then captive shippers and passengers were regarded by these authorities as a prime and unlimited source of revenue.[11]

As we have seen in Chapter XXII, railroad management has made strong efforts to meet this challenge and in the freight area at least they have met with some success. In passenger traffic their goal has been more difficult to attain. There is an obvious need for more basic information on costs of service and on markets. More freedom and also more desire to use that freedom, to merge and consolidate. Increasing needs and desire to travel, defense needs and other factors point to an increasing market for rail service. Speaking of rail passenger service, the Doyle Report concludes:

> The railroad passenger business is not a mean national asset even at this time. Its present book investment is $3 to $5 billion of private capital. It still produces total annual revenues of over $1,200 million. It can still move 300 people in comfort and at a very high degree of safety at 80 miles an hour with only 3 or 4 men and only 1,500 horsepower. If this service goes to the museum with the stagecoach, it will not be for the same reasons. If a program to rationalize and revitalize rail passenger service cannot be carried out by existing managements because they

---

[11] National Transportation Policy, *op. cit.*, p. 290 ff.

cannot overcome the problems of equipment interchange, trackage rights, financial realinements, managerial realinements, and eliciting the reasonably unified cooperation of over 80 companies, a national railroad passenger service corporation should be considered.

Before we write this big business off, and it is big even by American standards, a very thorough economic and market analysis should be made with sufficient financing and a sufficient length of time to produce new empirical data from the car repair shop and the ticket counter on up. Operations analysis techniques should be employed in regard to scheduling, optimum consist, meshing with other railroad operations, etc. If the results of such a study indicate profitable operations based on conservative traffic and financial forecasts, a national passenger service corporation should be formed which would have complete control of marketing and producing the service. Such a corporation could move immediately to eliminate duplication, pool equipment and services, avoid circuitous routings planned to operate solely on owned tracks, centralize maintenance and install modern cost accounting and traffic reporting systems.[12]

The freight operations are not in such a serious position but many of the problems there at present are within the control of the policy makers. By every standard, the rail problem is illustrative of the challenge to policy formulation. The special aspects of this problem lie in the ironic fact that rail service needed by and any standard, and generally considered to be a basic element in our transportation system, has been in serious difficulty for some time. This is the face of general industrial prosperity. Clearly some policy revision is necessary in this case.

WHAT ARE THE GOALS OF POLICY?

Clearly, the overall goal for public policy in transportation, as in any other economic function, should be to promote the public interest. All too often our present policy seems to be designed chiefly to protect the various carriers and only to incidentally protect the public.

The function of regulation is to compensate for deficiencies in competition, not to act as a shelter from competition or to supplement the managerial talent of the carriers. Where normal competition does not work in the transportation industry as it does in other fields, regulation should be used to remedy this situation. It should never be

---

[12] *Ibid.*, p. 326.

used, as it often is, as a competitive weapon in the hands of the carriers. Regulation should be positive, not negative; constructive, not destructive.

Much of our regulation seems to be designed (or has become so due to other forces) to protect the carriers from each other rather than to protect the public. To be sure, minimum rate policy, for example, may protect the public in that it prevents deterioration of service, unsettled conditions due to failure of firms and other problems arising from financial instability. However, with the wide consumer choice now available, it seems questionable just how much protection the consumer needs in relation to what it costs him. Rate policy is often used as a weapon between shippers; certainly, this was not and should not be the goal of economic regulation. A succinct but sound statement of regulatory principles is found in the recommendations of the Transportation Association of America.[13]

1. There should be no legislative restriction against private carriers (the user performing transportation of his own goods for his own account) except for safety purposes.
2. Fair competition, both within regions and throughout the country as a whole, should be preserved in our transportation system subject only to such regulation as may be required in the public interest.
3. No regulation shall be imposed upon or continued in force with respect to any means of transportation unless such regulation is specifically required in the public interest.
4. No regulation shall be imposed upon any means of transportation merely because the public interest requires that it be imposed upon one or more other means of transportation.

PRESERVATION OF THE PUBLIC INTEREST

The most important goal, which must never be overlooked and which seems to have been lost sight of in our past efforts, is to direct policy toward the public interest and away from the narrow and partisan carrier interests. A succinct and strong statement of this goal appears in a recent analysis of transportation policy.[14]

It is necessary that transport regulation be directed more toward public rather than carrier interest. All modes have been

---

[13] *Sound Transportation for the National Welfare,* Chicago Transportation Association of America, 1953.

[14] John H. Frederick, *Improving National Transportation Policy* (Washington, D.C., American Enterprise Association, 1959), pp. 46-47.

brought under national government jurisdiction but as one reviews the development of regulation, it is clear that while the theoretical aspects of public interest have been considered, the importance of not taking any action, either in a business or legislative way, without first considering the carrier aspects of the problem has outweighed other factors. In other words, while the theoretical public interest—"the greatest good for the greatest number"—has undoubtedly been discussed many times, the fact remains that most of the definite action taken with respect to all forms of transportation by legislative bodies, regulatory commissions, or the courts, has been primarily the result of a compromise between the conflicts of the various opposing interests—carriers, shippers, labor and investors.

The public interest is the product of a complex equation. The framers of early transport regulation tended to treat the interest of shippers as identical with the general public interest. The interest of the shipper is, of course, a factor in the determination of the public interest, but it is not the only factor. Public interest includes, too, the interest of the carriers and the thousands of investors, but it does not necessarily follow that whatever measure is in the best interest of a particular mode of transport is in the public interest.

In a previous chapter, it was noted that the public claim was often lost in the cries of the professional lobby groups who spend their time attempting to influence policy. We must exercise great care that this effect is kept at a minimum. The public interest is hard to define and measure in this context, as in others, yet it is basic to the functions of our public policy institutions. It has often been noted that the strong role played by pressure groups in the modern government's economic activities leaves the public without an effective voice. In theory, of course, the commission is itself a representative of the public interest, but, in practice, it seems more than likely that the commission would tend to think of many issues as being a contest between the modes. The student of economic affairs encounters the phrase "in the public interest" frequently, but he will search fruitlessly for a definition of the term. Of course, the term has no meaning out of a specific context. A rate increase, in order to enable a carrier to improve its physical plant and render a higher quality of service, would perhaps be in the public interest. Allowing the entry of a firm or a number of firms, which would have the effect of bringing instability into the industry, would not be in the public interest, although it may seem so at first glance. What might be in the public interest in the short run might prove to be contrary to the public interest in the long run. Honest differences of opinions are mixed in with utter disregard of any but the narrow private interest of one mode or one firm. Determination and preservation of the public interest is not always possible, but it must be constantly in the minds and hearts of those who make and implement our policies.

Progress in these matters is slow and rightly so. Since the Coordinator of Transportation made his studies and reports in 1933, thirty years have passed. The Committee of Three (1938), National Resources Planning Board Study (1940), The President's Air Policy Commission (1947), Board of Investigation and Research (1944), and others have ploughed this ground, along with the more recent studies noted earlier in this chapter.[15] A surprising number of these recommendations is still valid. No one would argue that these matters should be undertaken without comprehensive study, but we must press for realistic and reasonable attitudes. Though admittedly slow, progress is made. The long recommended census of transportation is now a reality, and, certainly, this will be a basic analytical tool. Some signs are evident of a more flexible attitude toward intermodal rate relationships and toward consolidation and integration. The potential of a sound system is enormous and the penalties of failure are grave indeed. A recent statement puts the problem thus:

> The Nation requires policies which will encourage maximum efficiency in the performance of the transportation function. The transportation service is not, for the most part, an item of direct consumption. It is a facilitating service required in connection with virtually all production throughout the economy. A part of the cost of nearly all goods and services purchased by the public represents payment for transportation of one kind or another. Hence, a reduction in the cost of transport enhances the national product and enlarges the opportunities of all for the consumption of direct goods and services. Moreover, reduction of the cost of transport in relation to other things increases flexibility in the location of industry, in the exploitation of natural resources, and in the achievement of industrial efficiency. There is, in fact, a multiplier effect—for the quantity of improvement in the transport function is multiplied by the time goods reach the ultimate consumer.
>
> There is general and growing realization that less improvement has been made in distribution than in production of goods and that much of the remaining margin for the improvement of the Nation's economic efficiency lies in the area of distribution. Transportation is the largest single element within that area. And the rate of our economic progress is quite as capable of being slowed

---

[15] A complete list of these proposals is found in Dearing and Owen, *op. cit.*, pp. 440 ff. It is also interesting to note that many of the "critical defects" in policy listed in this book (1949) are still present in our system.

by an increase in the cost of transportation relative to other goods and services as it is by a shortage of transportation capacity or a shortfall in the quality of service.[16]

There is widespread recognition of the fact that our goals of regulation are not being realized, or, if so, it is at the expense of the economic well being of our transportation system. It is worthwhile here to quote the concluding paragraphs of the President's Message on Transportation delivered in April 1962.

> The troubles in our transportation system are deep; and no just and comprehensive set of goals—which meets all the needs of each mode of transportation as well as shippers, consumers, taxpayers and the general public—can be quickly or easily reached. But few areas of public concern are more basic to our progress as a nation. The Congress and all citizens, as well as all Federal agencies, have an increasing interest in and an increasing responsibility to be aware of the shortcomings of existing transportation policies; and the proposals contained in this message are intended to be a constructive basis for the exercise of that responsibility.
>
> The difficulty and the complexity of these basic troubles will not correct themselves with the mere passage of time. On the contrary, we cannot afford to delay further. Facing up to the realities of the situation, we must begin to make the painful decisions necessary to providing the transportation system required by the United States of today and tomorrow.[17]

It is a paradox that these words come at a time when economic growth would seem to indicate further development in transportation services to meet the needs of a growing economy.[18] It is also an unfortunate situation that, while we have the most technologically advanced physical plant in the world, we in the United States are beset by recurrent economic crises in the transportation system. Management policy and efficiency cannot be obtained by legislation; advances in technology cannot be obtained by legislation, but modernization of policy can be so achieved. We must move in that direction immediately.

The transportation system is a great and vital economic force. We must construct and administer a regulatory system which will help the industry to perform its function in the most efficient manner possible. No less goal is acceptable.

---

[16] *Rationale of Federal Transportation Policy* (Washington, D. C.; U. S. Department of Commerce, 1960), pp. 3-4.

[17] Message from the President, *op. cit.*, p. 17.

[18] See Sidney Sonnenblum and Joel Darmstadter, "Transportation in America's Economic Future," *Transportation Journal* (Chicago: American Society of Traffic and Transportation, Inc.), Winter, 1962.

INDEX

Index